DAVID HARDMAN

JUDGMENT AND DECISION MAKING

PSYCHOLOGICAL PERSPECTIVES

BPS TEXTBOOKS IN PSYCHOLOGY

BPS Blackwell

Judgment and
Decision Making

BPS Textbooks in Psychology

BPS Blackwell presents a comprehensive and authoritative series covering everything a student needs in order to complete an undergraduate degree in psychology. Refreshingly written to consider more than North American research, this series is the first to give a truly international perspective. Written by the very best names in the field, the series offers an extensive range of titles from introductory level through to final year optional modules, and every text fully complies with the BPS syllabus in that topic. No other series bears the BPS seal of approval!

Each book is supported by a companion website, featuring additional resource materials for both instructors and students, designed to encourage critical thinking, and providing for all your course lecturing and testing needs.

Published

Psychology edited by Miles Hewstone, Frank Fincham and Jonathan Foster

Personality and Individual Differences Tomas Chamorro-Premuzic

Introduction to Social Psychology, 4th edition edited by Miles Hewstone, Wolfgang Stroebe and Klaus Jonas

Psychopathology Graham Davey

Judgment and Decision Making David Hardman

Forthcoming

An Introduction to Reading Development and Reading Difficulties Kate Cain

Memory Chris Moulin and Martin Conway

Cognition John Groeger and Benjamin Clegg

Group Processes and Intergroup Relations Rhiannon Turner and Richard Crisp

An Introduction to Developmental Psychology, 2nd edition edited by Alan Slater and Gavin Bremner

Community Psychology Carolyn Kagan, Mark Burton, Paul Duckett, Rebecca Lawthom and Asiya Siddiquee

Psychobiology Chris Chandler

Evolutionary Psychology Uren Swami

David Hardman

Judgment and Decision Making
Psychological Perspectives

BPS TEXTBOOKS  IN PSYCHOLOGY

The British Psychological Society

BPS Blackwell

This edition first published 2009 by the British Psychological Society and Blackwell Publishing Ltd
© 2009 by David Hardman

BPS Blackwell is an imprint of Blackwell Publishing, which was acquired by John Wiley & Sons
in February 2007. Blackwell's publishing program has been merged with Wiley's global Scientific,
Technical, and Medical business to form Wiley-Blackwell.

Registered Office
John Wiley & Sons Ltd, The Atrium, Southern Gate, Chichester, West Sussex, PO19 8SQ, UK

Editorial Offices
350 Main Street, Malden, MA 02148-5020, USA
9600 Garsington Road, Oxford, OX4 2DQ, UK
The Atrium, Southern Gate, Chichester, West Sussex, PO19 8SQ, UK

For details of our global editorial offices, for customer services, and for information about how
to apply for permission to reuse the copyright material in this book please see our website at
www.wiley.com/wiley-blackwell.

The right of David Hardman to be identified as the author of this work has been asserted in accordance
with the Copyright, Designs and Patents Act 1988.

Library of Congress Cataloging-in-Publication Data

Hardman, David (David K.)
  Judgment and decision making: Psychological perspectives / David Hardman.
      p. cm. — (BPS textbooks in psychology)
  Includes bibliographical references and index.
  ISBN 978-1-4051-2398-3 (pbk. : alk. paper)   1. Judgment—textbooks.   2. Decision making—
Textbooks.   I. Title.
  BF447.H365 2009
  153.4′6—dc22   2008028048

A catalogue record for this book is available from the British Library.

Set in 9.5/11.5pt Dante by Graphicraft Limited, Hong Kong
Printed in Singapore by Fabulous Printers Pte Ltd

The British Psychological Society's free Research Digest e-mail service rounds up the latest research and
relates it to your syllabus in a user-friendly way. To subscribe go to www.researchdigest.org.uk or send
a blank e-mail to subscribe-rd@lists.bps.org.uk.

Reprinted October 2009, December 2009 and December 2010

Commissioning Editor: Andrew McAleer
Development Editors: Elizabeth Johnston and Louise Butler
Marketing Managers: Katherine Ward and Kathryn Atkinson
Production Editor: Hannah Rolls
Project Manager/Copyeditor: Janet Moth

This book is dedicated to my parents, Ken and Carol

....

Contents

Preface and Acknowledgements

My aim in this textbook is to provide accessible and up-to-date coverage of theory and research across a range of topics in judgment and decision making (JDM). In my own teaching, I have found that both my students and myself have been frustrated by textbooks that do not go into enough depth about certain topics. Certainly, there is much greater enthusiasm when we discuss the details of specific research studies, based on original papers. In this book, therefore, I have tried to go into more detail about JDM research, while covering both classic topics and emerging areas of interest.

For example, I have included chapters on dynamic decision making and everyday decision making (including the naturalistic decision making approach). There is also extensive coverage of research on social dilemmas (such as the ultimatum game) and a final chapter looking at intuitive versus reflective thinking. Several chapters, mostly those devoted to aspects of decision making, also include some material from the rapidly developing field of neuroscience.

A few comments are in order regarding my general approach to writing this book. Firstly, I have tried to minimise the use of technical notation and equations, although there are one or two places where I felt that a proper explanation benefited from their use. Secondly, I had to decide whether the final part of each chapter should simply summarise the main points or whether it should provide some sort of evaluative conclusion. After surveying other textbooks I decided that I preferred the former approach. For topics that are currently being keenly debated it would not be possible to give an evaluation without at least some academic readers concluding that I am biased. Also, for some chapters at least, the breadth of material covered did not allow for a straightforward evaluative conclusion. Therefore, my preference has been to summarise the main points and allow readers to draw their own conclusions.

Thirdly, at the end of each chapter following the introduction I have included some recommended readings. Many of these fall into the category of good popular science writings; original research papers and more technical writings can be found in the reference sections at the end of each chapter. For the benefit of students I have also included some end-of-chapter questions to aid in the revision and understanding of the material covered. There is a dedicated website for the book, including Powerpoint slides, at www.blackwellpublishing.com/judgment. There is also a blog site, with research updates, at http://judgmentanddecisionmaking.blogspot.com.

In short, I have tried to write the kind of JDM book that I would like to read. I very much hope that it is one that you will find worth reading. Feedback is welcome and you can contact me at d.hardman@londonmet.ac.uk.

Thanks are due to Clare Harries for steering me in the direction of Blackwell Publishing. I am very grateful to the patience and support of everyone at Blackwell, past and present, including Will Maddox, Elizabeth Johnston, Sarah Bird, Annie Rose, Peter Jones, Andrew McAleer, Janet Moth, and Hannah Rolls. I would also like to thank Donald Laming, Clare Harries, Matt Twyman, and one anonymous reviewer for their comments variously on an earlier draft of this book or on specific sections.

D.H.

1 Introduction and Overview: Judgments, Decisions, and Rationality

CHAPTER OUTLINE

INTRODUCTION

Everyone complains of his memory, and no one complains of his judgment. (La Rochefoucauld, 1678)

You've gotta make decisions. You've gotta keep making decisions, even if they're wrong decisions. You know . . . if you don't make decisions, you're stuffed. (Joe Simpson explaining his epic escape from a mountaineering accident, in the documentary movie Touching the Void*)*

Our waking lives are largely devoted to making judgments and decisions of one sort or another, whether judging if it is safe to cross the road, deciding to quit your job and live the dream, or choosing what colour to paint your apartment. Although we often conflate the terms 'judgment' and 'decision' in everyday language, judgments are essentially evaluations or estimates whereas decisions indicate an intention to pursue a particular course of action. The decisions we make are, of course, informed by our judgment.

There are so many types of judgments and decisions that it might seem hard to believe that there could be any common processes involved in the ways we think about them. However, consider the following occurrences (perhaps you will even recognise these situations):

- You have set your iPod to random shuffle, yet it seems to be playing certain artists more than others. Is there something wrong with your iPod's randomising device? In fact, occasional 'streaks' in outcomes are exactly what should be expected in random sequences.

- You are having a lively discussion with someone who has a very strongly held belief on the subject. It seems to you that there is no amount of evidence that will change his mind.

- There are a few purchases you have been thinking of making, but have held off from doing so on the grounds of expense. However, today you have just made a much larger expensive purchase, and shortly afterwards also made the smaller purchases you had been thinking about. Somehow, the large purchase seems to have made it easier to make the smaller purchases.

- You are in a meeting at work. As time goes by you realise that a number of people are tending to dominate the conversation. Decisions are reached where some people hardly speak or don't speak at all. Do the decisions really represent the majority view? Why did the chair not try to ensure that all voices were heard?

The fact that such situations are common reflects something important about our basic psychology. Determining the nature of that psychology is the subject of much research and the subject of this book.

The examples above give a small flavour of this book's content, which includes assessments of uncertainty and probability, argumentation and the assessment of evidence, the role of value in decision making, and group decision making. Along the way I shall also look at other phenomena and processes, such as being wise after the event, judgments of causation and association, judgments about what might have been, decisions under risk and uncertainty, judgments and decisions over time, risk perception and risk taking, and factors influencing cooperation and coordination.

WHAT IS RATIONALITY?

One of the topics occasionally discussed by JDM researchers is the extent to which people can be considered 'rational'. Rationality is normally taken to mean adherence to some normative model, such as probability theory or decision theory. As the subsequent chapters will present many instances where people do not behave in accordance with normative models, I want to take a moment in this first chapter to ponder the nature of rationality.

Classical economists have tended to assume rationality as a given, hence the phrase *rational economic man* (or to use more contemporary non-sexist parlance, the *rational actor*). Although research conducted by psychologists has noted many discrepancies from rational theory, economists often respond by noting differences between the laboratory situation and the real world. In particular, the psychologists' participants tend to be naive about the situation and are asked to make one-off decisions, sometimes without incentives for accurate responses. Economists have argued that as people gain experience of a particular domain they learn accordingly and so behave in a more rational way. There is some evidence to this effect, but also there is considerable evidence of economically irrational behaviour even among those who are experienced in a particular domain (e.g. Haigh & List, 2005).

However, violations of rational norms by species with longer evolutionary histories than the human race (e.g. Shafir, 1994) are not generally taken to indicate that animals are somehow *irrational*. Rather, it is assumed that the mechanisms that contribute to evolutionary fitness may nonetheless not predict behaviour in certain specific instances.

An analogy is occasionally drawn with visual perception. Figure 1.1 shows the Müller–Lyer illusion. Compare the horizontal line in (a) with that in (b). Virtually everyone agrees that (b) looks longer than (a). In fact, both lines are exactly the same length, as you can easily verify by placing a ruler against each. The research literature on visual perception is full of such illusions. Although the Müller–Lyer illusion may seem somewhat artificial, illusions

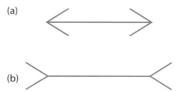

Figure 1.1. *The Müller–Lyer illusion*

can occur even when we perceive the natural environment. For example, an illusion that most people are not aware of until it is drawn to their attention is the *moon illusion*. Compare the size of the full moon when it is just above the horizon to when it is high in the sky. The full moon just above the horizon appears much larger.

Despite the existence of such visual 'errors', there is no concern among vision researchers that there needs to be a mass correction of our visual systems in order to prevent such illusions. Clearly, our visual systems have evolved in such a way as to help us successfully navigate our environments. Likewise, the occasional error in making judgments and decisions may be a small price to pay for a cognitive system that is otherwise well adapted to facilitating our survival and reproduction. In fact, individuals who score higher on measures of intelligence are *more* susceptible to visual illusions (Jensen, 1998).

Such observations have led some researchers to question attributions of irrationality to humans. As Ayton (2000, p.667) put it (in the style of Irving Berlin): 'Birds do it, bees do it, even educated Ph.D.s do it; why not violate normative rules of rationality?' Nonetheless, the nature of the contemporary environment is very different from that within which our ancestors evolved, such that both the visual and the intellectual environment can pose problems where any errors can be costly. In Britain, and no doubt some other countries too, the exit roads from motorways often have a series of stripes painted across them. This is because people adapt to the speed that they travel at on the motorway and sometimes fail to slow to an appropriate speed when they leave the motorway. To motorway drivers exiting on a slip road, the stripes seem to whizz by really quickly, which alerts them to the speed at which they are travelling, thus prompting them to slow down (Laming, 2004).

However, the kind of contemporary environments within which people make high-level decisions tend not to present such blatant wake-up calls. For instance, people who play lotteries, or other games of chance, often tend to behave as though sequential outcomes are causally connected. In the natural world, of course, people are quite well attuned to identifying the many real causal connections that exist between events. However, in a fair lottery there is no connection between events, so the likelihood of a particular number appearing in the next draw does not increase if that number has not appeared for a long time (see Chapter 3). In the realm of financial investment, the success of mutual funds is as hard to predict as the outcome of lotteries. Yet when choosing a fund people are probably more impressed to learn of that fund's success *last year* (which does *not* actually predict future performance) than they are to read about the humdrum fact that share prices can go down as well as up.

People also frequently lose out due to a tendency to focus on immediate concerns rather than distant ones. This means that many people fail to save sufficiently for their retirement (the phenomenon of future discounting is covered in Chapter 10).

These kinds of findings muddy the meaning of what it is to be rational. It seems that people often don't behave in their own best interests, so it is tempting to think of them as irrational. On the other hand, the success of the species as a whole suggests otherwise. Furthermore, rational thinking has come to be identified with highly analytical thinking that considers multiple options, yet in some environments there is evidence that simpler strategies can be more successful (see e.g. Chapters 2, 9 and 11). Indeed, by changing the decision environment we can sometimes change behaviour. For example, employees can be induced to invest more in their pension plans by the simple expedient of getting them to make an advance commitment. This commitment involves allowing one's company to deduct increasingly large amounts for one's pension in future years. Although people may back out of future increases when the time arrives, few people actually do.

Some authors have suggested that we should not use the term 'rationality' at all. For example, Gintis (2006) has referred to the *beliefs, preferences, and constraints* model of decision making whereby people use their beliefs to try and satisfy their preferences within certain constraints.

BOUNDED RATIONALITY

In the 1950s psychologists began to report examples of people's limitations in the domain of judgment and decision making. Herbert Simon (e.g. 1955, 1956) criticised rational models of decision making for ignoring situational and personal constraints such as time pressure and limited cognitive capacity. By way of illustration, consider the following quote from the former investment banker David Freud about his experience of decision making in the City of London:

> The currency was not cash but chaos. Transactions invariably took place at the edge of feasibility conducted under a competitive background under great time pressure. I found few committees of experts considering all the available evidence in wise conclave. Much more typical were decisions taken on the fly, by whoever happened to be available, based on a fraction of the full information. (Freud, 2006, pp.355–356)

Simon's own analyses of organisational decision making led him to propose that the mind had evolved short-cut strategies that delivered reasonable solutions to real-world problems (Simon, 1956), an idea that is known as *bounded rationality*.

Such mental short cuts, or *heuristics*, have formed the basis of two intense programmes of research. The first programme was summarised in the book *Judgment Under Uncertainty: Heuristics and Biases* (Kahneman *et al.*, 1982). Much of this research focused on the systematic errors (*biases*) that could occur through the use of heuristics, although the primary aim of this research was to elucidate the nature of the heuristics themselves, not to portray people as hopelessly irrational.

A second programme of research has emphasised the positive outcomes that can result from the use of heuristics, as summarised in the book *Simple Heuristics that Make Us Smart* (Gigerenzer *et al.*, 1999; see Chapters 2 and 9). This approach has placed special emphasis on the relationship between the human mind and the nature of the environment within which it evolved. In other words, the use of heuristics often leads to positive outcomes precisely because the heuristics themselves are the product of environmental contingencies. Computer simulations of heuristics have shown that they can indeed lead to accurate judgments, although – at the time of writing – the empirical evidence is somewhat more contentious.

A similar, though independent, approach has looked at the strategies for making choices that people adopt depending on their circumstances. The *adaptive decision maker* approach argues that people have a variety of possible strategies available to them when choosing between options, varying from fairly simplistic strategies to highly analytical ones (Payne *et al.*, 1993; see Chapter 8). The final choice of strategy depends on a trade-off between the effort required to implement the strategy and the importance of achieving high accuracy. In many circumstances, a reasonable level of accuracy can actually be achieved by using a less analytical strategy.

In Simon's (1955) paper on the limitations of human decision making, he wrote that 'we cannot, of course, rule out the possibility that the unconscious is a better decision-maker than the conscious' (p.104). In fact, there is now some evidence that the unconscious mind might well be better suited to making more complex decisions, with the conscious mind better at making simpler decisions (Dijksterhuis, 2004; Dijksterhuis & Nordgren, 2006). On the other hand, conscious thought does seem to be better at abstracting logical structure from the content and context within which it is embedded (Stanovich & West, 2000). As we shall see in Chapter 15, many researchers now propose a dual system theory of thinking involving fast unconscious processes, on the one hand, and slower conscious processes on the other.

AN OVERVIEW OF THE SUBSEQUENT CHAPTERS

Although I have ordered the following chapters in a way which made sense to me, in many cases it will be possible to read a given chapter without having read what has gone before.

Chapter 2 introduces a conceptual framework for thinking about predictive or diagnostic judgments. This framework is known as the *lens model*, and distinguishes between objective relations between, on the one hand, predictive cues and outcomes, and, on the other, the actual (subjective) way in which people use those cues. In other words, the objective relationship between cues and outcomes is based on how much importance *should* be attached to certain items of information when making a prediction or diagnosis; typically, though, people's subjective assessment of the importance of information does not correspond to the objective relationships. Social judgment theory uses the lens model framework to create statistical models that can be used for socially important predictions. One type of statistical model is based on the objective relationships between cues and outcome; another type of model is based on the subjective judgments of a person over a long series of cases. Although this approach is concerned with the importance (or weighting) attached to information, it does not specify the underlying cognitive processes. In the final part of the chapter, I describe the theory of probabilistic mental models, which describes certain short cuts (heuristics) that people might use when making a judgment.

Chapter 3 picks up where Chapter 2 leaves off, by describing two important heuristics that were proposed in the early 1970s: representativeness and availability. In addition I look at support theory, which draws attention to the way in which probability judgments are influenced by how specifically possibilities are described. I also look at the MINERVA-DM theory, which tries to place representativeness and availability within the framework of a wider theory of memory. Finally, I look at the topic of conditional probability and the debate over how best to improve people's ability to update their beliefs in the light of new evidence.

Chapter 4 explores the anchoring-and-adjustment heuristic and hindsight bias. Anchoring and adjustment is a cognitive process that people often use when making some kind of numerical estimate in the absence of certain knowledge. It assumes that an initial numerical value is used as an anchor point from which people make some (typically insufficient) adjustment. Hindsight bias is the tendency for people to overestimate – in retrospect – the predictability of outcomes that are now known to have occurred or not occurred. For both anchoring and adjustment and hindsight bias I shall further investigate the nature of the underlying processes.

Many judgments occur after a process of reasoning and argumentation, in which people assess theories and evidence. Chapter 5 introduces the notion of an argument as a formal structure. It then examines some common limitations in people's ability to process arguments, such as failing to properly distinguish between theory and data, allowing one's beliefs to override evidence. This chapter also looks at factors affecting the persuasiveness of communications.

Chapter 6 concerns judgments of association, causation, and counterfactual thinking. It looks at people's ability to assess the correct relationship between items of information, especially their ability to determine whether one variable has caused another. In particular, the chapter investigates the way in which people incorporate both evidence and their ideas about causal mechanisms in order to arrive at judgments. Counterfactual thinking is thinking about how things might have been different, and has also been linked to judgments of causation. People may engage in counterfactual thinking both in order to prepare for the future and to regulate their affective feelings.

Chapter 7 introduces the topic of decision making under risk and uncertainty. It shows how the theory regarded by many as normative – expected utility theory – fails to capture some aspects of decision making. The chapter reviews prospect theory as an account of decisions under risk and examines the neuroscience of valuation. It also explores how prospect theory has been developed to explain decision making under uncertainty. An alternative approach to this latter topic is described, based on optimal foraging theory. Another approach to decision making is based on the idea that people frequently switch their attention between different aspects of a decision. One such model – the priority heuristic – is described in further detail.

Chapter 8 looks at the psychology of preference and choice. It shows how people have been shown to violate certain axioms of rational choice and goes on to explore the notion of mental accounting. This refers to the cognitive operations involved in thinking about money, though these may extend to non-monetary choices too. As with other aspects of human thought, heuristic thinking may lead to a range of biases. Finally, I look at people's desire for choice, but the problems that ensue once they get it.

Chapter 9 concerns the topic of confidence and optimism in judgment and decision making. Specifically, there is considerable evidence that people are overconfident in a variety of domains. I review some of this evidence and examine the relationship between overconfidence and skill, perceptions of control, expertise, and gender.

Chapter 10 examines people's judgments and decisions where a time perspective is involved. This includes people's ability, or lack of it, to accurately forecast whether they can meet a deadline and their preference for imminent rewards rather than delayed rewards. This chapter also looks at the topic of affective forecasting, this being the ability to accurately predict one's own future feelings.

Chapter 11 examines dynamic decision making and everyday decision making. Dynamic decision research is largely laboratory-based, but concerns complex decisions in which later decisions are affected by earlier decisions, where the task environment itself may be complex, and where feedback may be delayed. This leads in to discussing everyday decision making which typically involves research conducted in real-life settings (and which is often also dynamic). I also look at the role of cognitive ability in relation to both types of decision making.

Chapter 12 looks at the topic of risk, involving people's perceptions of and responses to potential hazards, including activities they themselves may willingly engage in. This chapter shows how risks tend to be perceived along two dimensions ('dread' and 'unknown') and how our feelings may affect our judgments of risk. I also look at individual differences based on personality, sex, race, and expertise. I look, too, at the problems that 'risk compensation' poses for attempts to reduce risk, as well as the social amplification of risk and attempts to accurately communicate risk information.

Chapter 13 concerns decision making in groups and teams, and discusses the difficulties posed by social conformity, group polarisation, and other difficulties. The chapter also takes a critical look at the well-known 'groupthink' phenomenon, as well as the measures which have been proposed to guard against this. Chapter 13 also critically examines some of the techniques that have been proposed for making better-informed and more representative decisions. The chapter closes with a look at leadership and advice-taking.

Chapter 14 is about cooperation and coordination in human behaviour. These are often in tension with a motivation to behave in a self-interested fashion. Having introduced the concepts of game theory and behavioural game theory, I go on to explore the evolution of cooperation, and a range of factors that affect whether or not individuals behave in a self-interested way; for example, consideration of others; fear, greed, and punishment; trust; culture.

Chapter 15 takes a broad-brush approach to human thought. Specifically, it discusses the circumstances under which people engage in intuitive versus reflective thinking. After an initial review of individual differences in intelligence and reflectiveness, I go on to explore the idea that the intuitive and the reflective depend on two distinct systems for thinking and the implications for moral judgment. I also look at evidence suggesting that people lack insight into their underlying cognitions and that explanations of their own behaviour are post hoc rationalisations. Finally, I take a neuroscience perspective on intuition and rationality; in particular, I examine the role of emotion in decision making.

2 | The Nature and Analysis of Judgment

INTRODUCTION

In the first part of this chapter I shall introduce social judgment theory. This approach to judgment tries to identify the kind of information that people use when making a particular type of judgment, and how much weight they attach to different kinds of information. This kind of analysis typically focuses on individuals, in the sense that different people may use information differently. Furthermore, this approach can be used to try and improve judgment. In particular, the implementing of a judge's 'policy' in a statistical model almost invariably outperforms the judge on any future task in the same domain.

Although social judgment theory is interested in the importance that people attach to different kinds of information its approach is purely statistical; it does not describe the cognitive processes by which people reach a judgment. The theory of probabilistic mental models, described in the second half of the chapter, does provide a theory of judgment. In essence, it proposes that people seek one good reason to make a decision and stop searching for further information once such a reason has been found.

SOCIAL JUDGMENT THEORY

There are often numerous factors, or cues, that could contribute to the occurrence of some event. The challenge is to identify the cues that are relevant to diagnosing a cause or predicting an outcome, and to determine how much impact each factor should have. This is where social judgment theory (SJT) comes in.

SJT applies to judgments – particularly in professional settings – that are made repeatedly (e.g., psychiatric diagnoses, assessments of creditworthiness, parole board assessments, assessments of job candidates, and so on). By applying statistical analysis to a series of such judgments it is possible to describe the impact that different cues have on a particular type of judgment. Additionally, SJT is concerned with the creation of statistical models – often referred to as actuarial models – that can be used to predict future cases. These actuarial models are simply linear equations, or rules, for specifying how the relevant cues should be combined in making a judgment. As we shall see, a great deal of psychological research has shown that actuarial models outperform human judges.

Linear models

An example of a rule being used to specify how different cues should be combined was provided by Goldberg (1965). By analysing psychiatric patients' discharge diagnoses and their scores on 11 scales of the Minnesota Multiphasic Personality Inventory (MMPI), he was able to derive a simple rule for distinguishing between psychosis and neurosis. The rule, now known as the *Goldberg Rule*, involves adding scores from three scales and then subtracting scores from two other scales. If the resulting score is less than 45 then a diagnosis of neurosis is made; if the score is 45 or more then psychosis is diagnosed. Goldberg then went on to compare performance of the Goldberg Rule with that of 13 PhD clinical psychologists who had extensive MMPI experience and 16 advanced graduates in clinical psychology. On a new sample of 861 cases the Goldberg Rule predicted 70 per cent of the discharge diagnoses. The human judges, however, varied from just over 50 per cent to 67 per cent accuracy. In other words, not even the best human judge outperformed the actuarial model.

Let us consider the nature of such a decision rule a little further. When the outcomes are known in a series of cases, and where information about the cues is available, then a statistical procedure known as multiple linear regression analysis can be used to determine exactly how much impact each cue had. The general form of the resulting equation is shown in Equation 2.1. The term 'Y_E' is the criterion in the environment about which a judgment must be made and $x_1 - x_k$ are the cues that are used to predict the outcome. The value of each cue is multiplied by some weighting factor b_e that represents the impact of the cue in the overall series of outcomes (Note: b_{0e} is simply a constant in the equation, which is why it does not weight a cue). Finally, the term 'e' at the end of the equation represents error; it is any variation in outcome that was not predicted by the main part of the equation. It is this main part of the equation that forms the predictive model.

$$(2.1) \quad Y_E = \underbrace{b_{0e} + b_{1e}.x_1 + b_{2e}.x_2 + b_{3e}.x_3. \ldots b_{ke}.x_k}_{\text{Predictive model}} + e$$

For readers who have an aversion to equations of this sort, the main thing to remember is this: Equation 2.1 is a description of how cues relate to some known outcome, and the portion of the equation referred to as the 'predictive model' is what we should use in making future judgments of this sort.

It is also possible to use regression analysis to determine how much impact the various cues have on the judgments made by people. This does not even require knowledge of the actual outcome (for example in the Goldberg example, whether people are actually neurotic or psychotic). All that is needed are people's assessments of the cues and their final judgment in each case. In Equation 2.2 the subscript 's' indicates that the equation represents subjective judgments, as opposed to 'e' for environment in Equation 2.1. However, in all respects this is the same basic equation, except that the weightings b_s may be different, depending on how much importance the judge attached to the various cues.

$$(2.2) \quad Y_S = \underbrace{b_{0s} + b_{1s}.x_1 + b_{2s}.x_2 + b_{3s}.x_3. \ldots b_{ks}.x_k}_{\text{Bootstrap model}} + e$$

Again, the error term 'e' in Equation 2.2 represents the degree of variation in the judge's responses that cannot be captured by the main part of the equation. The equation minus the error term is known as a *bootstrap model*. When information is lacking about the true state of affairs, the bootstrap model can be used to implement the judge's own policy in a consistent fashion. This consistency means that bootstrap models are normally more accurate than the judge from which the model was derived. For example, Goldberg (1970) constructed bootstrap models of his 29 judges and looked to see which was most accurate on the cases where judge and model disagreed. The bootstrap models outperformed the judges.

The way of looking at judgment that has just been described is often represented visually, as shown in Figure 2.1. The left side indicates the criterion in the environment that is to be judged (Y_E) and the relationship of the various cues ($x_1 - x_k$) to that criterion. The predictive value of a cue (for example how frequently a symptom is associated with a particular illness) is known as its ecological validity. The right-hand side of the diagram represents the judge's consideration of those cues in arriving at a judgment (Y_S). If we also know the true status of the criterion in each case (e.g. disease present/not present), then we can also assess the overall accuracy of that person's judgments (r_A). This framework derives from Brunswik's work in visual perception (e.g. 1955) and is known as the *lens model*, because it assumes that we do not perceive the world directly but rather through a 'lens' consisting of various items of information (cues). Hammond (1955) is generally credited with the application of the lens model to higher-level judgments.

Before moving on, it is worth briefly noting that Brunswik promoted a research methodology known as *representative design*, which is a feature of research conducted within the lens model

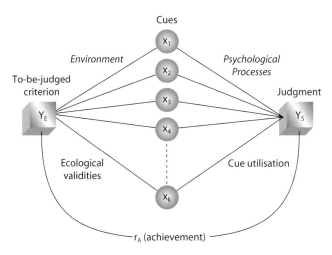

Figure 2.1. *The lens model*

framework. Rather than adopting the typical experimental technique of systematically manipulating a stimulus or stimuli of interest in order to see how people respond, a researcher using representative design randomly samples stimuli from the environment or creates stimuli in which environmental properties are preserved. Brunswik believed that the results of representatively designed studies were more generalisable to the real world than were the results of standard experimental studies. For more on representative design see Dhami *et al.* (2004).

Clinical versus actuarial prediction

Unaided human judgment is often referred to as clinical prediction. Several reviews have compared clinical and actuarial prediction, each concluding that actuarial models are superior (e.g. Grove *et al.*, 2000; Meehl, 1954, 1965; Sawyer, 1966). These reviews included studies that investigated experts engaged in tasks that were either representative of their normal occupational judgments or just *were* their normal occupational judgments. For example, Einhorn (1972) investigated the ability of three pathologists – one an international expert – to predict survival time following a diagnosis of Hodgkin's disease which, at the time of the research, was invariably fatal. The pathologists' judgments of severity did not predict survival time, whereas a statistical model based on their ratings of the patients' biopsies did show a small but statistically significant relationship with survival time.

The superiority of actuarial models is not restricted to the domains of mental or physical health. For example, Libby (1976) found that incorporating the financial ratios of companies into a statistical model led to better predictions of failure within the next three years than did the judgments of bank officers using the same information. Libby originally found that a bootstrap model of the judges was *not* superior to the judges themselves, but a reanalysis of his data showed this conclusion to be mistaken (Goldberg, 1976).

Other studies have found that people are still outperformed by actuarial models, even when they have access to additional information, such as might be obtained in an interview (e.g.

Sawyer, 1966; Wiggins, 1981). In fact, research in this area indicates that interviews are poor predictors of future performance (Figure 2.2). In one study, De Vaul *et al.* (1987) investigated student admissions to the medical school at the University of Texas. In 1979, out of 2200 potential students 800 were invited for interview. The interviews were conducted by two people, who then provided written assessments to a central committee. The committee members rated each candidate, and these ratings were combined to produce rankings for each candidate. The top 350 candidates were then matched to the applicants' own rankings of the schools to which they had applied, and eventually 150 students were selected for admission. However, at this point the medical school was required to increase its intake to 200 students. The only available applicants were those ranked between 700 and 800, 43 per cent of whom had not been offered a place at any medical school. When the additional 50 students were compared with the original 150 in terms of their later performance, no difference was found on any measure. De Vaul concluded that the interview procedure had been a waste of time.

Why do actuarial models outperform clinical judgment?

The general conclusion that people are less accurate than actuarial models should not be taken to imply that people are unimportant in the judgment process. Even when an actuarial model is used, people are necessary in order to choose the variables that are used in that model. People are also needed to code the variables in such a way that they have clear directional relationships. Dawes (1979) noted that linear models work well precisely when the predictor variables are good and where variables can be scaled in such a way that higher values on each predict higher values on the criterion.

However, people are less successful than actuarial methods in applying the right cues in the appropriate manner. In subsequent chapters, particularly Chapters 3–6, we shall look at some of the ways in which people actually make judgments that lead them to fall short of the optimum outcome. For now, it is enough to note the following:

- As I have already noted, people can be inconsistent whereas actuarial models never are.
- People sometimes rely on a piece of information that they think is relevant, but actually has little or no bearing on the thing they are trying to assess.
- People may consider relevant information, but weight it in the wrong way when making a judgment.
- When in receipt of additional information, people are prone to identifying individual cases as exceptions to the rule.
- Individuals working in particular domains may also be exposed to a skewed sample of events. Dawes *et al.* (1989) gave the example of a clinician who repeatedly examines juvenile delinquents for abnormalities in electroencephalogram (EEG) readings. If about half of these individuals do possess EEG abnormalities then the clinician may conclude that there is a link with

Figure 2.2. *Interviews tend to be a rather poor way of finding out about people*

delinquency. However, the clinician rarely gets to examine non-delinquent children, among whom EEG abnormalities are, in fact, quite common.

- Impressions gained during interviews are subject to the *fundamental attribution error*, whereby people underestimate the influence of situational factors on other people's behaviour.

- A lack of prompt, accurate feedback may prevent or impair the ability to learn the correct relationships between cues and criterion.

- People may be unduly influenced by recent experience or by irrelevant variations in the way a task is described.

- People's judgments may be affected by fatigue or boredom.

Finally, one area where clinical judgment may be of value is in a changing environment. Actuarial models assume a stable environment, but one advantage of human judgment is the ability to detect change. Blattberg and Hoch (1990) asked supermarket managers to forecast the demand for various products. They then created a composite forecast based on the average of the managers'

judgments and the forecasts of actuarial models derived from past data. The rationale for incorporating human judgment into the forecast was that actuarial models would not be able to take into account the effects on demand of novel events, such as the behaviour of one's competitors or the introduction of new products. The composite models were more accurate than either the actuarial models or the managers working alone.

Improper linear models

Bootstrap models, random linear models, and equal weighting models As we have seen, models of judges – bootstrap models – normally outperform the judges themselves. Bootstrap models are a type of *improper* linear model, so called because they do not optimally weight the cues. Dawes (1979) describes two situations where we might wish to construct improper linear models. One situation is where we have a fairly small sample of observations and multiple regression is no longer statistically reliable. A second situation where we might wish to construct improper models is where we do not have any measurable criterion values. Dawes gives the example of entry to US graduate school, where we might wish to predict a future long-term variable called 'professional self-actualisation'. We might have a good idea of what we mean by this but no strict definition. Nonetheless, if we have cues such as students' graduate record examination, grade point average, and letters of recommendation, then we can ask staff to score candidates for professional self-actualisation, and can construct a bootstrap model with the latter variable as our criterion.

The bootstrap model is not the only improper linear model. Dawes and Corrigan (1974) examined the accuracy of two other models. For *random linear models* the weights were randomly chosen except for whether they were positively or negatively related to the criterion, and for *equal weighting models* each cue was weighted equally. When applied to five different datasets the random linear models performed about as well as the bootstrap models and the equal weighting models performed even better. Dawes and Corrigan (p.105) commented that 'the whole trick is to know what variables to look at and then know how to add'.

The lack of impact of judgment analysis

Research comparing human judgment with that of actuarial models clearly implies that human judges should be replaced by the models whenever possible. Meehl (1986, p.373) wrote that 'There is no controversy in social science that shows such a large body of qualitatively diverse studies coming out uniformly . . . as this one.'

However, this research has had negligible impact, even within the domain of clinical psychology where the statistical approach to judgment originated. For example, non-actuarial methods are preferred to available actuarial methods in the domain of brain damage assessment (Guilmette *et al.*, 1990) and interviews remain the basis of entrance into US mental health training programmes (Dawes *et al.*, 1989).

Of course, professionals in any domain may be reluctant to cede decision making to a formula because this seems to be calling into question their expertise. However, it must be remembered that their expertise is required to select and code the variables of interest. On the other hand, ceding the final decision to a formula is merely to recognise that we all have limitations in our ability to process information. Here, the evidence surely speaks for itself.

One reason why people may insist on keeping control over decisions is that they may have a selective memory for past cases. For example, people may have a good memory for favourable outcomes resulting from their own judgments, whereas they may be particularly sensitive to negative outcomes that result from an actuarial conclusion. Another reason for resistance is based on the idea that every case is unique and so statistics do not apply. Here again, we have seen that, when given a choice between accepting an actuarial conclusion or making a clinical judgment, greater inaccuracy results from the latter course of action. Unfortunately, people's confidence in their judgments may increase with the amount of information available to them but without any corresponding increase in accuracy (Oskamp, 1965).

PROBABILISTIC MENTAL MODELS

Fast and frugal heuristics

The approach of SJT is to use statistical procedures to infer what cues people are using when they make judgments. However, this approach does not tell us what is actually happening in the mind during the process of judgment. The fact that regression analysis is used to identify patterns of cue use does not mean that regression analysis is being performed in the mind during the course of judgment. The theory of *probabilistic mental models* (Gigerenzer & Goldstein, 1996; Gigerenzer *et al.*, 1991) proposes an account of the cognitive processes involved in judgment. This approach assumes that when a person is unable to distinguish between binary alternatives (for example, 'Does Bonn or Heidelberg have the larger population?') they initiate a sequential search for a cue that will provide a reason for choosing one alternative over the other. Once they have found such a cue, the process of searching is halted and the appropriate alternative is chosen.

This theory differs from the regression analysis approach, not just in its specification of the search process but in its assumption that judgment is based on just a single cue, rather than multiple cues. This approach is sometimes referred to as *one-reason decision making* (Gigerenzer & Goldstein, 1996; Gigerenzer *et al.*, 2002). The approach is also referred to as *fast and frugal*, because judgments of this sort require less time and less information than more complex procedures. The basic notion behind this approach is that people are limited-capacity processors of information.

Some fast and frugal heuristics: recognition, take the best, take the last, and minimalist

A number of *heuristics* or short cuts may be used to make fast and frugal judgments. One such short cut is the *recognition heuristic*. Suppose a person is asked whether Bonn or Heidelberg has the larger population. If she has not heard of Heidelberg but has heard of Bonn then she will answer that Bonn has the larger population. However, if she has heard of both cities or has not heard of either then it is not possible to discriminate on the basis of recognition. In this case, she will search for another cue.

In any country there will be various environmental cues that are associated with city population size. In the case of Germany, these include whether the city is the national capital, whether it has a team in the top football league, and whether the city is home to a university (Table 2.1). Each cue is merely directional, in the sense that a simple Yes/No answer is associated with population size. Some of these cues are more ecologically valid than others, meaning they are more strongly associated with city size. However, high ecological validity does not necessarily enable one

Table 2.1. *Cues, ecological validities, and discrimination rates for deciding which of two German cities has the largest population*

Cue	Ecological validity	Discrimination rate
National capital (Is the city the national capital?)	1.00	.02
Exposition site (Was the city once an exposition site?)	.91	.25
Soccer team (Does the city have a team in the major league?)	.87	.30
Intercity train (Is the city on the Intercity line?)	.78	.38
State capital (Is the city a state capital?)	.77	.30
Licence plate (Is the abbreviation only one letter long?)	.75	.34
University (Is the city home to a university?)	.71	.51
Industrial belt (Is the city in the industrial belt?)	.56	.30
East Germany (Was the city formerly in East Germany?)	.51	.27

Source: Gigerenzer & Goldstein, 1996.

to discriminate. As Table 2.1 shows, if one of the cities being compared is a national capital then this city should definitely be chosen, as the national capital is always the largest city. However, across a series of judgments about city size, where the cities are chosen at random, then the national capital cue will rarely allow one to discriminate because most comparisons will not involve the national capital. According to the take the best heuristic, people first select the most valid cue, but if that does not discriminate they move on to the next most valid cue, and so on until a cue is found that will discriminate between the options. Two other heuristics are take the last (select the cue that worked last time this type of judgment was made) and minimalist (select a cue at random).

Evidence from computer simulations shows that take the best, take the last, and minimalist compare favourably with multiple regression and other more complex procedures. Gigerenzer and Goldstein (1996) ran simulations of city size judgments that assumed varying degrees of name recognition, from total ignorance to total recognition. Averaged across trials, they found that take the best equalled multiple regression in terms of accuracy (65.8 per cent vs. 65.7 per cent respectively), but whereas multiple regression needed to consult 10 cues on average take the best only needed to look up 3. The other fast and frugal heuristics also per-

formed well. take the last looked up 2.6 cues and achieved 64.5 per cent accuracy, whilst minimalist looked up 2.8 cues and achieved 64.7 per cent accuracy (see also Gigerenzer *et al.*, 2002).

Empirical tests of the fast and frugal heuristics

Despite the success of these simulation studies, it is important to ask whether people behave in accordance with the models. In a test of the recognition heuristic, Goldstein and Gigerenzer (2002) presented pairs of German cities to students at the University of Chicago and asked them to say which was the larger of the two. They were also given a list of cities and asked to indicate which ones they recognised. On average, 90 per cent of population judgments were made in accordance with recognition. In a second study, students were again asked to choose the larger of two cities. However, the crucial comparisons in this task occurred when one city was unrecognised and the other was recognised but was known not to have a soccer team (a fact that had just been learned in a training session). People who did not place any value on recognition information should always have chosen the unrecognised city in these particular pairings. In fact, 92 per cent of inferences were made in accordance with recognition.

Both of these studies have been criticised on methodological grounds. For example, the first study does not control for any other knowledge that participants may have had about German cities. It may be that a person not only recognised Berlin (say), but also knew that Berlin is a very large city (Oppenheimer, 2003). In the second study described above, the lower level of interest in soccer among Americans may have led them to undervalue the soccer team cue when inferring city sizes (Richter & Späth, 2006). The predictive validity of the soccer team cue was also less than had been assumed in the original study (Bröder & Eichler, 2006; Newell & Fernandez, 2006).

Richter and Späth (2006, Experiment 3) asked German students to select the larger of pairs of American cities, after first learning that the presence of an international airport is a highly valid cue to city size. Their results indicate that information about the presence or absence of an airport was used together with recognition information (Figure 2.3). When the recognised city was known to have an international airport, then the unrecognised city was almost never chosen as the larger of the two. When there was no airport information provided, then the unrecognised city was chosen slightly more often. But the unrecognised city was chosen much more often when the recognised city was known not to have an airport.

Richter and Späth also found that participants used knowledge together with recognition information when making judgments about animal species' population sizes (2006, Experiment 1) and airline safety (2006, Experiment 2). Indeed, the use of recognition in relation to animal species sometimes led to biased judgments. For instance, given the pairing of an unrecognised large-population animal and a recognised small-population animal, people correctly chose the former just 33 per cent of the time. Where a high-population and a low-population animal were both

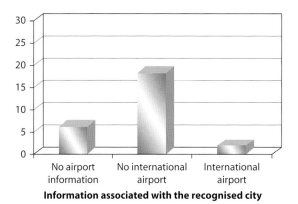

Figure 2.3. *The frequency (%) with which an unrecognised city is identified as larger than a recognised city*

Source: Richter & Späth, 2006.

recognised, but participants lacked knowledge about population size, then performance was at roughly chance level (55 per cent correct responding). Response time data from these studies also showed that people were slower to respond when recognition and knowledge were incongruent.

Similar results have been reported by Newell and Fernandez (2006), who also showed that increasing the validity of other environmental cues led to less reliance on recognition. In short, it appears that people do use recognition when making judgments but that they do not use it in the fast and frugal fashion suggested by the proponents of the recognition heuristic (Gigerenzer & Goldstein, 1996; Goldstein & Gigerenzer, 2002). In other words, people appear to use more than one reason.

Empirical evidence in relation to the take the best (TTB) heuristic is also somewhat mixed. Several studies have used a variation of a task in which participants are asked to say which of two companies' shares is likely to be more profitable, given certain items of binary information related to their financial status (for example: Is it an established company? *Yes/No*). For example, Bröder (2000) informed participants of the validity of four types of information, but on each trial the participants were required to purchase any information that they wished to see. They were only able to purchase information in the order of the cue validities, a constraint that should favour the adoption of the TTB strategy. When the cost of information was high Bröder reported that 65 per cent of people used a TTB strategy, but only about 15 per cent of people used TTB when information was cheaper or free.

Similar results have been reported by Newell and Shanks (2003, Experiment 1), who allowed participants to learn the cue validities for themselves, via feedback, during a training phase. They also found that participants were mostly unable to identify which cues had been the most useful (in both an estimation and a rank ordering task), which suggests that they did not learn the cue validities very well. A further barrier to the learning of cue validities was identified in a study where, for half of the participants, the *Yes/No* cue labels were replaced with distinct labels (for example: Where does the company have the bulk of its operations? 0 = US, 1 = UK). In the training phase, distinct labels led to the lower-value

share being chosen more often than the higher-value share, though there was no difference at the test phase.

Other studies indicate that strategy selection is quite well adapted to the environment, even if people do not always use one-reason decision making. Rieskamp and Otto (2006) have investigated how feedback affects the learning of strategies. They designed their trials such that sometimes a TTB strategy was more profitable than a weighted additive (WADD) strategy (which weighs up the pros and cons of all available information[1]). This was referred to as a *non-compensatory environment*. On other trials the reverse was the case. This was referred to as a *compensatory environment*. Across four studies they found that the WADD strategy tended to be preferred at the start of the task, but that people tended to learn to use whichever strategy was most profitable for the particular environment.

Bröder (2003) also found that people tended to learn to apply the strategy that would maximise their payoff. However, this was also moderated by intelligence (as measured by intelligence tests). Contrary to expectation, the more intelligent people did not adopt more complex strategies. Rather, the more intelligent people were more likely to adopt TTB in the non-compensatory environment. These results, together with those of Rieskamp and Otto, suggest that a compensatory strategy is the default option in probabilistic tasks like those described here. In other words, it requires a deliberate decision to ignore information and behave in a frugal fashion.

A further perspective on strategy selection has been provided by Newell *et al.* (2004). These authors note that the overall usefulness of a cue is a function of both its discrimination rate and its validity. In the example of German cities, knowing whether a city is the national capital is a highly valid cue to population size, because the capital is larger than any other city. However, this cue almost never discriminates between two alternatives because most city pairs do not include the German capital city. Therefore, the capital city cue is largely useless. In fact, discrimination and validity are negatively correlated in German cities (Gigerenzer & Goldstein, 1996).

Across several studies, Newell *et al.* examined the extent to which participants' search for information was driven by validity, discrimination rate, or *success* where 'The success of a cue is the expected proportion of correct inferences when *only that cue* can be used to make a choice' (2004, p.120). Although there was considerable variability, perhaps due to the probabilistic nature of the feedback success appeared overall to be a greater determinant of search than either validity or discrimination rate. Newell *et al.* also modelled the performance of a one-reason heuristic that they called Select The Successful (STS). They found STS to be about as accurate as TTB, only even more frugal in its information use.

Chapters 3 and 4 will explore the use of heuristics in greater detail. The fast and frugal heuristics described here have been analysed in terms of their performance over many trials, which is in keeping with the research described earlier in this chapter. However, other heuristics have been analysed in terms of the way people perform on a single trial. A common application of such heuristics is comparing people's performance on a statistical problem with an answer that is prescribed by probability theory. Nevertheless, the basic principle is the same: people use a single cue in order to make their judgment.

SUMMARY

Social judgment theory is based on the lens model of judgment, whereby the judge views the event or criterion of interest through a 'lens' of informational cues. Each cue has some degree of ecological validity; this refers to the strength of the relationship between the cue and the criterion. The accuracy of the judgment depends upon how accurately the person assesses the validity of the cues and then integrates the information.

One way of improving judgment is to replace the human judge with an actuarial model. This may be based on an optimal weighting of cues, but even improper linear models (which do not optimally weight cues) normally outperform human judges. Even bootstrap models (of the judge's own policy) normally outperform the judge that the model was based on.

Another approach to judgment is based on the notion of probabilistic mental models. Unlike signal detection theory and social judgment theory, this approach is also a theory about the cognitive processes that underlie judgment. According to this theory, people make judgments using fast and frugal heuristics. They search through cues in memory until they find a cue that enables a judgment to be made; in short, they base judgments on just a single cue. In computer simulations their accuracy approaches or equals that of multiple regression on the basis of less information. However, the evidence from psychological research is less clear.

QUESTIONS

1. What are linear models of judgment?

2. What is a bootstrap model?

3. How does clinical judgment compare with actuarial models of judgment?

4. Design a study based on the social judgment theory approach.

5. Why are people's judgments outperformed by linear models, including models of their own judgment?

6. Compare and contrast the fast and frugal heuristics approach to judgment with the regression analysis approach.

NOTE

1. More will be said about the WADD strategy in Chapter 8.

RECOMMENDED READING

Volume 2 (numbers 2–3) of the journal *Thinking & Reasoning* is devoted to the topic of social judgment theory.

Dawes, R.M., Faust, D. & Meehl, P.E. (1989). Clinical versus actuarial judgment. *Science, 243,* 1668–1673. Reprinted in T. Gilovich, D. Griffin, D. Kahneman (Eds.) (2002), *Heuristics and biases: The psychology of intuitive judgment.* Cambridge: Cambridge University Press. This paper shows how and why actuarial judgment outperforms clinical judgment.

Gigerenzer, G., Czerlinski, J. & Martignon, L. (2002). How good are fast and frugal heuristics? In T. Gilovich, D. Griffin & D. Kahneman (Eds.), *Heuristics and biases: The psychology of intuitive judgment.* Cambridge: Cambridge University Press. This book chapter gives further examples of how fast and frugal judgments can be at least as good as judgments that use more information.

Kirlik, A. (2006). *Adaptive perspectives on human-technology interaction: Methods and models for cognitive engineering and human-computer interaction.* Oxford: Oxford University Press. Alex Kirlik's book is an edited collection of chapters that apply a Brunswikian approach to human–technology interaction.

3 | Judging Probability and Frequency

CHAPTER OUTLINE

Before reading the rest of this chapter, consider the following problems (from Kahneman & Tversky, 1972):

1. A certain town is served by two hospitals. In the larger hospital about 45 babies are born each day, and in the smaller hospital about 15 babies are born each day. As you know, about 50% of all babies are boys. The exact percentage of baby boys, however, varies from day to day. Sometimes it may be higher than 50%, sometimes lower.

   For a period of one year, each hospital recorded the days on which more than 60% of the babies born were boys. Which hospital do you think recorded more such days?

2. Linda is 31 years old, single, outspoken, and very bright. She majored in philosophy. As a student, she was deeply concerned with issues of discrimination and social justice, and also participated in antinuclear demonstrations.
   Rank the following statements by their probability, using 1 for the most probable and 8 for the least probable.

   A. Linda is a teacher at an elementary school.

   B. Linda works in a bookstore and takes Yoga classes.

   C. Linda is active in the feminist movement.

   D. Linda is a psychiatric social worker.

   E. Linda is a member of the League of Women Voters.

   F. Linda is a bank teller.

   G. Linda is an insurance salesperson.

   H. Linda is a bank teller and is active in the feminist movement.

(NOTE: A BANK TELLER IS A CASHIER)

INTRODUCTION

In Chapter 2 we saw that people sometimes do not take into account all the appropriate information when making judgments and that they do not always attach the right level of importance to certain information. We also saw that people may use heuristics – short cuts – when making judgments. In this chapter I shall introduce two other heuristics that have been proposed as mechanisms for making judgments of probability or frequency. Firstly, the representativeness heuristic answers questions of probability by making an assessment of similarity. Secondly, the availability heuristic answers questions of probability or frequency by attempting to retrieve relevant examples from memory and then making an assessment of how easily those examples came to mind.

In addition, an important factor influencing the judgment of probabilities is the way that the problems are described. This is an issue addressed by support theory, discussed below, which shows that judged probabilities tend to be higher when the possible outcomes are described in greater detail.

I shall also describe an alternative approach to frequency judgment that suggests people may adopt multiple strategies. Another approach to judgment tries to account for both representativeness and availability within a model of memory; this is the MINERVA-DM model.

Finally, I shall look at the important topic of conditional probability, whereby beliefs are updated in the light of new information. In particular, I will discuss the way in which the formats of conditional probability tasks can affect performance.

THE REPRESENTATIVENESS HEURISTIC

What mental image comes to mind when you think of a computer games designer? I tend to think of a skinny, pale-skinned young man who wears glasses, trainers, and a T-shirt with a design related to science fiction or heavy metal. If you were to point out a person meeting this description and ask me what are the chances that he is a computer games designer, my snap judgment might be that the chances are quite high. However, in making such a judgment I am not actually making a judgment of probability; I am simply assessing this young man's resemblance to a stereotyped view that I possess about computer games designers. Such thinking is an example of what has been called the *representativeness heuristic*:

> *Representativeness* is an assessment of the degree of correspondence between a sample and a population, an instance and a category, an act and an actor or, more generally, between an outcome and a model. (Tversky & Kahneman, 1983, p.295)

> A person who follows this heuristic evaluates the probability of an uncertain event, or a sample, by the degree to which it is: (i) similar in essential properties to its parent population; and (ii) reflects the salient features of the process by which it is generated. Our thesis is that, in many situations, an event A is judged more probable than an event B whenever A appears more representative than B. In other words, the ordering of events by their subjective probabilities coincides with their ordering by representativeness. (Kahneman & Tversky, 1972, p.431)

Essentially, when people use the representativeness heuristic they are making a judgment of similarity. As Kahneman and Frederick (2002) put it, they are – without realising it – replacing a difficult question with an easy question. Instead of calculating a probability they are asking themselves 'Does *this* seem like *that*?' Although such heuristics can lead to error, they may often lead to judgments that are sufficient if not perfect. As Tversky and Kahneman (1983, p.296) stated: 'Representativeness tends to covary with frequency: Common instances and frequent events are generally more representative than unusual instances and rare events.' For example, the representative British or American family has two children and the representative summer day is warm and sunny.

The representativeness heuristic has been used to account for a wide variety of judgment phenomena. The ones that I discuss below are category membership, sampling, compound events, and misperceptions of randomness.

Category membership

My example above about the computer games designer involved a question of category membership. Why is representativeness likely to provide a misleading answer in this kind of judgment? The reason is that I am failing to take into account information about the proportion of people who are games designers as opposed to something else. In fact, there are many more people who are *not* computer games designers than *are*, many of whom no doubt look and dress the same way as the young man in my example. The prevalences of particular categories in the environment are known as *base rates*.

In one study, Kahneman and Tversky (1973) asked a group of students to estimate the percentage of students at their university who were enrolled in nine different fields of specialisation. These estimates reflected people's beliefs about the base rates of the specialisations. Another group was given a personality sketch of 'Tom W' and asked to rank-order each field of specialisation in terms of how similar Tom W was to the typical student in each field. A third group, composed of psychology students, was told that Tom's personality sketch had been written by a psychologist on the basis of projective tests. It was asked to rank the nine fields in order of the likelihood that Tom W was now a graduate student in those fields.

Overall, people tended to think that Tom was a student in one of the less popular courses. Moreover, these judgments were almost perfectly correlated with people's judgments of how similar Tom was to a typical student in those fields. Thus, people appeared to be neglecting base rates and relying on representativeness.

When trying to explain how people make judgments about category membership the term *representativeness* is applied in two ways:

1. a prototype (a *representative exemplar*) is used to represent categories . . . in the prediction task

2. the probability that the individual belongs to a category is judged by the degree to which the individual resembles (is *representative* of) the category stereotype. Thus, categorical prediction by representativeness involves two separate acts of substitution – the substitution of a prototypical exemplar for a category, and the substitution of the heuristic attribute of similarity for the target attribute of probability. (Kahneman & Frederick, 2002, p.73)

The first sense of representativeness, as the use of a prototype to represent a category, is referred to as a *prototype heuristic*.

Prototype heuristics also appear to be involved in other types of judgment. One such judgment is economic evaluation. For instance, Desvouges et al. (1993) found that people's willingness to donate money to help birds endangered by an oil spill was unrelated to the actual number of birds. The average amounts for saving 2000, 20,000, or 200,000 birds were $80, $78, and $88, respectively. The explanation in terms of prototype heuristics is that people create a prototypical instance, such as an image of a bird drowning in oil, in order to represent the deaths of numerous birds. This image creates an emotional response that is then mapped onto a monetary scale.

The evaluation of experiences also appears to rely on prototype heuristics. When people recall an experience that lasted over a period of time they appear not to remember every moment. Rather, they rely on a 'snapshot model'. Their judgment of the quality of the experience is based on averaging the peak moment of experience and the end moments of the experience (Frederickson & Kahneman, 1993; Redelmeier & Kahneman, 1996). Thus, patients who underwent a painful colonoscopy were more willing to go through with a second colonoscopy if the discomfort at the end of the first one was minimised, regardless of the overall duration of the experience (Redelmeier & Kahneman, 1996).

Sampling

In certain areas of life sampling is a major issue. For example, opinion pollsters need to select a group of people whose opinions will reflect those of the wider population. The size and composition of the sample they select will determine how accurately the population's opinion is reflected. Scientists also need to be sensitive to sampling issues. Newspapers often provoke 'health scares' that turn out to be based on small sample studies whose findings are not replicated when larger studies are run. According to the *law of large numbers*, the mean value of a sample is more likely to fall within a specified bound of the parent population the larger that sample is. People do show some intuitive understanding of this law.

For example, when asked to estimate the proportion of obese natives on an imaginary island in the south-east Pacific, people gave a larger estimate if they had previously encountered 20 obese islanders during their explorations, as opposed to just three, and a larger estimate if they had encountered three obese islanders rather than just one. However, the willingness to generalise also interacted in a sensible way with people's beliefs about the degree of variation in the sample. People made large generalisations, regardless of sample size, when they believed that the objects in question were homogeneous within the population. Simply encountering a single *brown* islander led to a modal generalisation of 100 per cent with regard to the colour of islanders, and the same result obtained for the electrical and combustible properties of a rare chemical element. Participants were less willing to make such a large generalisation about the colour or nesting behaviour of an imaginary bird (Nisbett et al., 1983).

However, other research indicates that, while people may be aware that a statistical mode of reasoning is appropriate, they are often unable to correctly apply this intuition and instead use the representativeness heuristic. Thus, in question 1 at the start of the chapter a smaller hospital, where fewer babies are born overall, will record more days when the proportion of male births exceeds 60 per cent as compared to a larger hospital. Consistent with the law of large numbers, the smaller hospital is likely to show larger deviations from the population figure of 50 per cent. However, most participants responded that both hospitals would record about the same number of such days.

Compound events

How did you answer question 2 at the start of the chapter? Did you rank statement H as more likely than statement F? If so, you are in good company: Tversky and Kahneman found that this ordering was made about equally by students with moderate or extensive education in statistics and probability, as well as by statistically naive students (Figure 3.1). However, this answer is also wrong. The error that people make is referred to as *the conjunction fallacy*. Probability theory tells us that the combination of two events can never be more probable than either of those two events taken singly. This is expressed by Equation 3.1:

$$(3.1) \quad P(A\&B) = P(A) \times P(B \mid A)^1$$

Or, when events A and B are independent then equation 3.2 applies:

$$(3.2) \quad P(A\&B) = P(A) \times P(B)$$

However, ranking H as more likely than F is to rate the conjunction as more likely than either of its components.

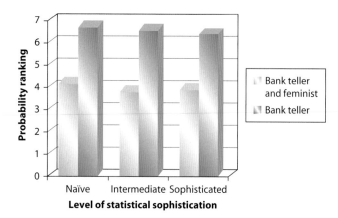

Figure 3.1. *Responses to the Linda problem in three groups with differing levels of statistical education (see problem 2 at the start of the chapter); 1 = most probable, 7 = least probable*
Source: Kahneman & Tversky 1982.

Think for a moment about statement F (Linda is a bank teller). This statement encompasses two possibilities – that Linda *is* active in the feminist movement and that she is *not* active in the feminist movement. Because it does encompass both possibilities it must therefore be more likely than the more specific statement that she is both a bank teller *and* active in the feminist movement.

Of course, the description of Linda was constructed to be representative of a feminist and unrepresentative of a bank teller. Thus, people seem to be basing their probability judgments on the basis of a similarity judgment – representativeness again. In other words, whatever occupation Linda holds we think she is likely to be a feminist. This interpretation is supported from the rankings of a separate group which was asked to assess 'the degree to which Linda resembles the typical member of that class'. Of the participants, 85 per cent showed the predicted order feminist > bank teller & feminist > bank teller.

A possible alternative interpretation of the results is that people reinterpret the statement 'Linda is a bank teller' as 'Linda is a bank teller *and not active in the feminist movement*'. However, other studies do not support this interpretation. In one study the compound statement H was removed from the list of statements for one group and C and F were removed from the list for the other group. H was still ranked comparatively higher than the other statements. In another study (Tversky & Kahneman, 1983) most people still committed the error when statement F was replaced with 'Linda is a bank teller whether or not she is active in the feminist movement'. A reduction in the error *was* observed when statistically educated students were asked to rate (not rank) the probability of only the F and F & H statements, although a sizeable minority (23/64) still made the error.

One way to reduce the incidence of the conjunction error is to provide cues to extensionality (meaning all the individual events that contribute to a probability). For example, Tversky and Kahneman presented participants with this problem:

A health survey was conducted in a sample of 100 adult males in British Columbia, of all ages and occupations. Please give your best estimate of the following values:

How many of the 100 participants have had one or more heart attacks?

How many of the 100 participants are both over 55 years old and have had one or more heart attacks?

Just 25 per cent of the participants made the conjunction error on this problem. This compared with an error rate of 65 per cent on a version in which sample size was omitted and the two questions began: 'What percentage of the men surveyed . . . ?' Thus, it seems that reference to the individual cases facilitates people's recognition of class inclusion relations. However, even frequency versions of conjunction problems, such as the above, appear not to eliminate the fallacy entirely.

Misperception of random sequences

In everyday life many of the events that we perceive or encounter are connected. For example, a traffic light switches from green to red and the nearest approaching car slows to a halt, as does the car behind, and the one behind that, and so on. As Pinker (1998, p.346) has pointed out: 'the hundredth railroad car on a passing train portends the caboose with greater likelihood than the third car'. Our minds seem well equipped for recognising or inferring connections between things. Indeed, sometimes we are too good at this, as when we see connections that are not really there (like the myriad unconnected stars, light years apart, that we perceive as Orion, the Great Bear, and so on).

This propensity can sometimes lead us badly astray, however, as the following news story from 2005 indicates:[2]

Number 53 brings relief to Italy
The elusive number 53, blamed for several deaths and bankruptcies, has finally popped up in the Venice lottery after a two-year wait.

Italians had bet more than 3.5bn euros (£2.4bn), hoping that 53 would turn up, in what became a national obsession. Last month a woman drowned herself in the sea off Tuscany after she bet the family savings on 53, Reuters reports. And police said a man living near Florence shot his wife and son and then himself because of his number 53 debts. . . .

A consumer group, Codacons, recently urged the government to ban the number 53 from the draw, to halt the country's 'collective psychosis'.

This story illustrates a phenomenon known as the *gambler's fallacy*, whereby people treat the sequential outcomes of gambling devices as non-independent. In other words, they behave as though the devices have a memory. In the case above, many people appeared to believe that the continuing absence of the number 53 made it more likely to appear on the next draw. However, on any given draw the number 53 would be no more likely to appear than any other number.

Conversely, people who play lotteries tend not to pick numbers that have recently been part of a winning combination. For example, a study of Maryland's Pick 3 lottery found that it took three months before winning numbers regained their popularity (Clotfelter & Cook, 1993; see also Terrell, 1994). Again, numbers that appeared in a recent draw are just as likely to occur again as any other number. The same is true for other gambling devices such as coins or roulette wheels, all of which lead to random, independent outcomes. A more astute lottery player might deliberately choose numbers that have recently won, on the basis that this reduces the chance of sharing the jackpot, should he or she be lucky enough to win!

Haigh (2003) observed that the first 282 draws of the British National Lottery included 132 occasions where the winning combination contained an adjacent pair of numbers. Consequently, there were fewer winners (330) than would be expected on the basis of genuinely random selection (514, given the number of tickets sold), resulting in a larger prize for those who did pick the winning combination.

There are countless other examples of people failing to appreciate the nature of randomness, such as:

- People believing that the random shuffle function on their iPod isn't working properly, because some artists seem to get played more than others (Levy, 2006a, 2006b).

- Londoners in the Second World War misperceiving random bombing patterns as deliberate targeting, because some places were bombed several times while many other places were not hit at all (Feller, 1950).

- Stock market analysts who believe that the lines on stock charts can be used to predict future movements (see Box 3.1).

BOX 3.1.   RANDOMNESS AND THE STOCK MARKET

In his book *A Random Walk Down Wall Street*, Burton Malkiel (2003[1973]) described a branch of stock market analysis known as *technical analysis*. Practitioners of technical analysis are known as *chartists* because they construct and analyse stock charts as a basis for making investment decisions. However, although stock prices tend to be on an upward trend over the long run, Malkiel noted that the next move in stock prices is largely unpredictable on the basis of past price behaviour. Thus, he put technical analysis on a par with astrology. Noting the similarity between graphs produced by coin-tossing and stock price charts, Malkiel (p.150) described a fake stock price chart that was produced by a student tossing coins, whereby each head was recorded as a half-point increase on the previous day and each tail was recorded as a half-point decrease:

One of the charts showed a beautiful upward breakout from an inverted head and shoulders (a very bullish formation). I showed it to a chartist friend of mine who practically jumped out of his skin. 'What is this company?' he exclaimed. 'We've got to buy immediately. This pattern's a classic. There's no question the stock will be up 15 points next week.' He did not respond kindly to me when I told him the chart had been produced by flipping a coin.

Along similar lines, Paulos (2003) has noted that two stock pickers who perform only at chance level are nonetheless unlikely to do as well (or badly) as each other. One of them will still outperform the other and this will, of course, probably be attributed to his ability rather than to chance (Figure 3.2). This scenario has been likened to a counterintuitive result reported by Feller (1968), who described what happens when a cumulative record of heads and tails is kept in a long sequence of coin tosses. In this situation, if – at any point in the sequence – there have been more heads than tails, then heads is said to be in the lead (and vice versa). The astonishing thing is that, in any long sequence of coin tosses, there are very few changes of lead, even though the overall proportions of heads and tails balance

out not far from 50 per cent each. In fact, the single most likely number of lead changes in a sequence of any length is zero. For a fuller description, see Haigh (2003) or Feller's original analysis. Our two stock pickers are like the heads and tails in a sequence of coin tosses. One is likely to outperform the other for much, if not all, of the time.

"I suggest you buy Acme Chemicals."

Figure 3.2. *Stock-picking*

Source: © www.cartoonstock.com

- The *hot hand fallacy*, whereby basketball fans, players, and commentators believe that a player who has just scored is more likely to score on his next attempt, and that a player who missed his last attempt is more likely to miss again next time. Gilovich, Vallone and Tversky (1985) showed that this belief was mistaken.

THE AVAILABILITY HEURISTIC

There are occasions in life when we need to try and remember how often we engage in various activities. For example, a market researcher may wish to know how often we go to the cinema in an average month or a physician may ask how many units of alcohol we consume in an average week. These judgments of *frequency* may also form the basis for estimating probabilities. For example, the probability of a motorcyclist having a fatal accident can be estimated from the frequency with which fatal accidents occur among motorcyclists.

Tversky and Kahneman (1973) proposed that such judgments were made using the *availability heuristic*:

> A person is said to employ the availability heuristic whenever he estimates frequency or probability by the ease with which instances or associations could be brought to mind. To assess availability it is not necessary to perform the actual operations of retrieval or construction. It suffices to assess the ease with which these operations could be performed, much as the difficulty of a puzzle or mathematical problem can be assessed without considering specific solutions. . . .
>
> Availability is an ecologically valid clue for the judgment of frequency because, in general, frequent events are easier to recall or imagine than infrequent ones. (cited in Kahneman, Slovic & Tversky, 1982, p.164)

As with heuristics generally, availability can lead to biases. Specifically, Tversky and Kahneman proposed that events that were encountered recently are likely to have a bigger impact on judgment, as are events that one is familiar with, as well as events for which it is easy to construct a vivid mental image.

In one study, Tversky and Kahneman presented participants with lists of names, where 19 people were famous and 20 were less well known. On half of the occasions the famous people were women and on the other half they were men. Not surprisingly, people were better at recalling the famous names. However, they also judged the class consisting of the famous names to be more frequent.

The availability heuristic can lead members of a group or team to overestimate their own contribution relative to that of others, because their own contribution comes more easily to mind. Ross and Sicoly (1979) found that husbands and wives tended to overestimate their respective contribution on a list of 20 household activities. An overall measure of perceived responsibility was shown to correlate with the number of self-generated examples of behaviour that the individual listed. Likewise, basketball players on both sides of a match tended to judge their own team as causing the crucial turning point in a game. Ross and Sicoly also showed that attributions of responsibility could be modified by manipulating the participants' focus of attention. Students who had completed a supervised BA thesis were asked either to assess their own contributions (in percentage terms) or those of their supervisor. The percentage responsibility attributed directly to the supervisor was greater than that attributed indirectly to the supervisor (obtained by subtracting the students' own percentage contributions from 100).

Recall of content versus ease of retrieval

Although the original conception of the availability heuristic stated that judgments were based on the 'ease with which instances or associations come to mind' (Tversky & Kahneman, 1973, p.208), the evidence from the early studies was actually ambiguous with regard to this assertion. These studies did not distinguish between the *ease* with which instances were brought to mind and the *number* of instances. However, subsequent research showed that judgments are affected by the ease of recall. For example, Schwarz *et al.* (1991) found that people who were asked to recall six examples of assertive behaviour subsequently rated themselves as more assertive than people who were asked to recall 12 such examples. Similarly, people who recalled six examples of unassertive behaviour rated themselves as less assertive than those who were asked to recall 12 examples. This result clearly distinguishes between the ease of recall and the content of recall, and shows that it is ease of recall that influences people's judgments.

However, when people are given a reason to discount the experience of recall then they do rely on the content of recall. Biller, Bless and Schwarz (1992; cited in Schwarz & Vaughn, 2002) required participants to recall three or nine examples of chronic diseases and then estimate their prevalence. Prevalence estimates were higher when people recalled three examples, consistent with the ease of recall explanation. However, some participants were first asked to indicate how much they knew about chronic diseases. For these participants, this cue to their lack of expertise led them to discount the ease with which they recalled examples. These people gave higher prevalence estimates when they recalled 12 examples rather than six.

The availability heuristic, like the other heuristics discussed by Kahneman, Slovic, and Tversky (1982), has received a great deal of attention over the years. However, availability has been criticised on a number of grounds. Those who hold that frequency judgments are generally quite accurate are not happy with the emphasis on erroneous judgment in the availability literature. Betsch and Pohl (2002) have also argued that availability lacks predictive validity. That is, it is not clear under what circumstances availability is to be applied. They also argue that the two mechanisms proposed by Tversky and Kahneman – (1) assessing ease of recall and (2) assessing how easy retrieval or construction of instances would be – are not clear. This criticism may hold less strongly now for assessing the ease of recall, as Schwarz's research described above examines just this issue.

SUPPORT THEORY

Support theory (Tversky & Koehler, 1994) is an important extension of the basic notion of availability. It distinguishes between *events* and descriptions of events, referred to as *hypotheses*. People judge the probability of hypotheses, rather than events, and they do this by considering the support for hypotheses. Furthermore, hypotheses can be implicit or explicit. To see how this works, consider the following study from Tversky and Koehler (1994, Study 1). They asked Stanford undergraduates to assess the likelihood of various causes of death, either described as implicit or explicit hypotheses. In this task, the category of 'other natural causes' is an implicit disjunction, because there are a number of more specific – but unstated – sub-categories that fall within it. According to Tversky and Koehler:

> When people assess their degree of belief in an implicit disjunction, they do not normally unpack the hypothesis into its exclusive components and add their support, as required by extensionality. Instead, they tend to form a global impression that is based primarily on the most representative or available cases. (1994, p.549)

Some representative data are shown in Table 3.1. For instance, participants judged that there was a .58 probability that an individual's death was due to natural causes. However, students who had been asked to assign probabilities for the categories of heart disease and cancer, as well as 'other natural causes',

estimated a total .73 probability that the individual's death was from natural causes. Thus, the support for an implicit disjunction tends to be *subadditive*, in the sense that the support is less than would be the case were the hypothesis to be unpacked into its constituent components.

Tversky and Koehler also noted that increasing support for one hypothesis does not necessarily decrease the support for competing hypotheses, and may even increase the support for all competing hypotheses, thus enhancing subadditivity (the *enhancement effect*). They described a study in which participants were asked to evaluate either the suspiciousness or the guilt of one of four suspects in a criminal case. Initial judgments were made under conditions of low information. Further evidence was then introduced that implicated each suspect to about the same degree. In the low information condition, probabilities for the four suspects summed to over 100, thus indicating that participants neglected the support for the other suspects when judging a single individual. Judgments of guilt were related to assessments of support, as expected by support theory. When the further information was provided, the probabilities for each suspect increased further, enhancing subadditivity.

MINERVA-DM: A MEMORY MODEL OF JUDGMENT

Until recently, one limitation of the heuristics approach to describing judgment processes is the lack of an integrative theory. Ideally, such a theory should give a clearer picture of how memory and judgment processes are related, and should supplement informally worded descriptions of psychological processes with a more quantitative account. One such account is the MINERVA-DM (MDM) model (Dougherty *et al.*, 1999). The brief account I provide below will focus on how this model integrates a theoretical account of memory processes with the processes of judgment; I refer readers to the original paper for the quantitative description of the theory.

MDM is a *multiple-trace memory model* that assumes that a new memory trace is created for each new event that is experienced (as opposed to updating a single memory trace each time the event occurs). Because various factors can affect the encoding of information, these traces are assumed to be degraded copies of the experienced events. In order to access memory a *memory probe* is created. The activation of memory traces by this probe produces an 'echo'; where there is only a weak similarity between a probe and a trace then the echo is weak, but where the similarity is high then a strong echo is produced. When making a judgment of likelihood, MDM calculates an 'echo intensity' that is based on the sum of the activation of all memory traces.

Suppose you wanted to estimate the relative frequency of Democrats to Republicans. You might begin by probing your memory for Democrats, resulting in an output that represents the sum of the similarities over all the traces stored in memory. Then you probe your memory for Republicans, resulting in a second

Table 3.1. *Mean probability and frequency estimates for causes of death in Tversky and Koehler's Study 1. The table compares evaluations of explicit disjunctions with coextensional implicit disjunctions*

Hypothesis	Mean estimate		Actual %
	Probability	Frequency	
Three-component P(heart disease)	22	18	34.1
P(cancer)	18	20	23.1
P(other natural cause)	33	29	35.2
Σ(natural cause)	73	67	92.4
P(natural cause)	58	56	
Σ/P	1.26	1.20	

output. Frequency estimates are attached to the outputs depending on their intensities, and these figures are then used to estimate the relative frequency.

Similarity is the basis of both MDM and the representativeness heuristic, although MDM works on the basis of instances whereas representativeness operates on the basis of similarity to a prototype. Nonetheless, Dougherty *et al.* claim to be able to account for the major judgmental biases discussed by Kahneman and Tversky. For example, they argue that the conjunction error can occur by one of two memory mechanisms. Consider the Linda problem (discussed earlier). People may construct memory probes relevant to each judgment question by using details from the vignette that appear relevant. When judging the likelihood that 'Linda is a feminist and a bank teller' the memory probe that is created contains more details relevant to 'feminist' than to 'bank teller' because it is biased by the details provided in the vignette. When judging the likelihood that 'Linda is a bank teller' the participant tries to create a probe for 'bank teller', but this probe is relatively poor on detail and so the resulting echo intensity is less. Consequently, participants judge the 'feminist and bank teller' conjunction more likely than 'bank teller' alone. Previous research has found that the conjunction error did not occur when neither the 'feminist' nor the 'bank teller' categories were detailed (Tversky & Kahneman, 1983).

However, when people have previous experience of underlying event frequencies then the conjunction error can occur in the absence of any vignette (unpublished data cited in Dougherty *et al.*, 1999). Furthermore, the extent of the conjunction error depends on the likelihood of the two constituent events. Yates and Carlson (1986) found that participants tended to rank the conjunction above *both* of its constituent events when both events were highly likely, and also when one was highly likely and the other unlikely. However, the conjunction error did not occur when both events were unlikely. This pattern of results was reproduced by Dougherty *et al.* in an MDM computer simulation. These authors suggest that when probing memory for experienced events, a conjunctive probe A ∩ B will return positive values from any memory trace that has either an A or a B component, thus exaggerating the echo intensity.

MINERVA-DM has also been used to successfully simulate availability bias and sensitivity to absolute frequencies (Dougherty *et al.*, 1999; Dougherty & Franco-Watkins, 2002). Strength of encoding is one factor that could give rise to an availability bias. People tend to give more attention to some events than to others, particularly if an event is seen as important. For example, in the 'famous names' study mentioned earlier, it is likely that the famous names received more attention and, hence, better encoding than the less famous names. This would have led to them being more easily recalled later on.

Another factor that could explain availability biases is the inability to completely discriminate between events learned in different contexts. In the famous faces study, the famous individuals would most likely have been encountered on numerous occasions prior to the study. When participants made their judgments of frequency, however, these earlier traces may well have contributed to those judgments.

The viability of MINERVA-DM's account of judgment phenomena depends on its accuracy as a model of memory. At this point it should be noted that there are alternative models of memory. For instance, Brown (2002) has proposed that frequency information can be encoded in different ways and different strategies used to estimate event frequency. In relation to encoding, he argues that repeated events that are highly distinct are more likely to be encoded as separate memory traces, whereas highly similar or identical events are more likely to be assimilated into a pre-existing scheme. The nature of the representation in turn influences the frequency estimation strategy that is used. According to this view, then, the availability heuristic is just one of several strategies for reaching judgments.

JUDGING CONDITIONAL PROBABILITY

Each of the problems in this section concerns *conditional probability*. This refers to the probability of an event given that some other event has occurred. For two events, A and B, the probability that A is true given that B is true, can be written as $P(A \mid B)$.

Conservatism

How should we go about updating our beliefs when we encounter new evidence? Bayes' theorem, described in Box 3.2, provides a way to do exactly this. The question then is *Do people adjust their beliefs as much as Bayes' theorem says they should?* To investigate whether people did respond properly to evidence, several studies by Ward Edwards and colleagues in the 1960s used the 'book-bag and poker-chip' paradigm (Edwards, 1968). In a typical study, two opaque bags each contained 100 poker chips in different proportions of red and blue. One bag contained 70 red and 30 blue chips, while the other bag contained 30 red and 70 blue chips. The experimenter would choose one bag at random and make a series of draws, taking care to replace the chip each time and shake the bag. Participants were required to say which bag they thought was being used and to give a probability. These studies indicated that people were insufficiently responsive to evidence, a phenomenon that was labelled *conservatism*.

However, research into conservatism rather 'fizzled out' (Ayton & Wright, 1994) due to the emergence of the heuristics and biases program of research and also 'disquiet over the validity of this sort of study as a model for judgment in the real world' (Ayton & Wright, 1994, p.168).[3] With regard to the latter, subtle variations in the experimental paradigm seemed to cause either increases or decreases in the level of conservatism observed. For example, participants were much less conservative when deciding whether a series of human heights was being drawn from a male population or a female population (DuCharme & Peterson, 1968). This was attributed to people's greater familiarity with the data-generating process involved in their task. Winkler and Murphy (1973) concluded that 'conservatism may be an artefact caused by dissimilarities between the laboratory and the real world'.

BOX 3.2. BAYES' THEOREM

Rational people should be prepared to revise their beliefs in the light of new evidence. Beliefs should be strengthened by supportive evidence and weakened by unsupportive evidence. In the 18th century a British nonconformist minister, the Reverend Thomas Bayes (1702–61), developed a method for revising beliefs in the light of new information (his paper on the topic was published posthumously in 1764 by his friend Richard Price). Some relevant terms to bear in mind are:

$P(H)$ This is the *prior probability*, the probability that a focal hypothesis is true prior to a particular piece of information being obtained. $P(\sim H)$ is often used to refer to the probability that the focal hypothesis is not true.[4]

$P(D\,|\,H)$ This is the probability of observing a particular datum (item of information) *if* the focal hypothesis is true. $P(D\,|\,\sim H)$ refers to the probability of observing the same datum *if* the focal hypothesis is false.

$P(H\,|\,D)$ This is the *posterior probability*, the probability that the focal hypothesis is true *given that* the datum has been observed. In other words, this is the bit that we really want to know: it is our updated belief in a hypothesis in the light of new information.

Bayes' theorem can now be stated as follows:

$$(3.3)\quad P(H\,|\,D)=\frac{P(D\,|\,H)\,P(H)}{P(D\,|\,H)\,P(H)+P(D\,|\,\sim H)\,P(\sim H)}$$

Here is a simple concrete example of Bayes' theorem based on Eddy's medical example (see main text):

$$P(ca\,|\,pos)=\frac{P(pos\,|\,ca)\,P(ca)}{P(pos\,|\,ca)\,P(ca)+P(pos\,|\,\sim ca)\,P(\sim ca)}$$

$$=\frac{0.792\times0.01}{0.792\times0.01+0.096\times0.99}$$

$$=\frac{0.00792}{0.00792+0.09504}$$

$$=0.077$$

Some authors express Bayes' theorem in the form of an odds ratio:

$$(3.4)\quad \frac{P(H)}{P(\sim H)}\times\frac{P(D\,|\,H)}{P(D\,|\,\sim H)}=\frac{P(H\,|\,D)}{P(\sim H\,|\,D)}$$

As applied to the previous data, this translates as:

$$\frac{1}{99}\times\frac{79.2}{9.6}=\frac{79.2}{950.4}$$

Thus, the odds ratio is 79.2:950.4 in favour of the growth being cancerous (i.e. it is very unlikely). To translate this back into a probability, the appropriate calculation is 79.2/(79.2 + 950.4) = 0.077.

Base rate neglect

A more realistic application of Bayes' theorem was described by David Eddy (1982). He presented 100 physicians with the following problem (slightly reworded from the original). A physician encounters a patient who has a slight lump in her breast. On the basis of previous female patients of similar age, and with similar symptoms, family history and physical findings, the physician thinks there is just a 1 per cent probability that the patient has cancer. If the woman *does* have cancer then there is a 79.2 per cent probability that a mammograph will detect this (she tests positive). If she does *not* have cancer then there is a 90.4 per cent probability that the mammograph will give her a clean bill of health (she tests negative). In this case, the woman undergoes mammography and tests positive. What is the probability that she has cancer? (Before attempting to calculate this, you might consider what your intuitive response is.)

Eddy reported that 95 out of 100 physicians estimated that there was a 75 per cent probability that the patient had cancer. This figure is nowhere near the correct answer, which can be calculated using Bayes' theorem. Sometimes it is helpful to use visual representa-

tions to help us think about difficult problems. Figure 3.3 shows a *tree diagram* that shows all the possibilities for this problem.

In this tree, <u>the nodes represent uncertainty and the branches represent the possibilities arising from the uncertainty</u>. The first set of branches show the prior probabilities (lump is cancerous or benign) and the second set of branches show the test outcomes that might arise conditional upon the presence or absence of cancer. The probabilities at the first two sets of branches are multiplied to obtain the figure shown at the leaves of the tree.

What we are concerned with is the probability that the breast lump is cancerous *given that* the test outcome was positive. Therefore, we only need to look at the leaves involving positive test outcomes (these figures are shown in bold). To obtain our posterior probability we divide the sum of these two figures into the figure associated with the focal hypothesis:

$$P(\text{Cancer}\,|\,\text{Positive})=\frac{0.00792}{0.00792+0.0954}=0.077$$

In other words, the positive test evidence should lead the physician to revise his estimate for cancer from 1 per cent to 7.7 per cent.

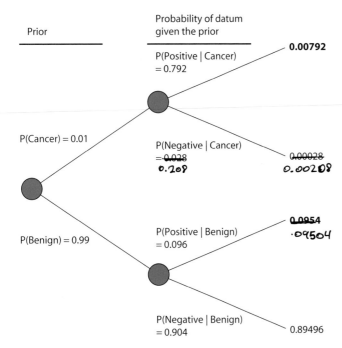

Figure 3.3. *A tree diagram representing Eddy's (1982) medical problem*

Clearly, there is a big difference between the 7.7 per cent probability and the 75 per cent that most physicians arrived at in Eddy's study.

Misunderstandings of this kind are not confined to pen-and-paper tests. Gigerenzer, Hoffrage and Ebert (1998) had a researcher pose as a client in order to obtain HIV tests at 20 German clinics. Following each test the researcher spoke to a counsellor, of whom he asked several questions in relation to the meaning of the test result. It so happens that a male from a *low-risk* group only has a 50 per cent chance of having HIV after obtaining positive diagnoses from the two available tests. This is because the tests, although highly accurate, are not perfectly accurate, and the vast majority of low-risk men do not have HIV. Thus, out of every 10,000 low-risk men tested, two will get a positive diagnosis and one of these will be wrong. However, the counsellors showed a very poor understanding of the incidence of false positives and false negatives, and most believed that a positive diagnosis meant that a client would certainly or almost certainly have HIV.

Another area where conditional probability is important is in the courtroom, especially in relation to DNA evidence. Again, there is evidence that people – including legal professionals – struggle to comprehend probabilities, but that they do better, and reach different verdicts, when evidence is presented in the form of frequencies (for an eloquent account, see Gigerenzer, 2003).

Many other studies have also reported that people fail to reason in a Bayesian fashion. The term *base rate neglect* has frequently been used to characterise the observation that base rates do not have the impact on judgments that they should have (see Koehler, 1996). One explanation of people's behaviour is that they are making an *inverse fallacy*, whereby they confuse $P(D \mid H)$ with $P(H \mid D)$. For example, the physicians in Eddy's study usually reported that they

assumed that P(cancer | positive test) was approximately equal to P(positive test | cancer). Making this inverse fallacy also entails neglecting the base rates, though Koehler (1996) has suggested that the problem is a semantic confusion rather than a misunderstanding about the role of base rates. Supporting this view, Macchi (1995) has shown that when problems are reworded to reduce semantic confusion between hit rates and posterior probabilities the use of base rates can greatly increase.

Facilitating Bayesian reasoning

Some authors have argued that rewording these kinds of problems in terms of frequencies rather than single-event probabilities can facilitate Bayesian reasoning (e.g. Cosmides & Tooby, 1996; Gigerenzer & Hoffrage, 1995; Hoffrage *et al.*, 2000). They note that our minds are shaped by the nature of the environment within which they evolve. Thus, because we encounter events in sequence it is likely that we have evolved to reason about frequencies rather than single-event probabilities (percentages and the like are relatively recent intellectual developments). For example, the following problem is a version of Eddy's medical problem only phrased in terms of frequencies (some of the numbers have been rounded up):

> 10 out of every 1000 women at age 40 who participate in routine screening have breast cancer.
> 8 out of every 10 women with breast cancer will get a positive mammogram.
> 95 out of every 990 women without breast cancer will get a positive mammogram.
> Here is a new representative sample of women at age 40 who got a positive mammogram in routine screening. How many of these women do you expect to actually have breast cancer? out of _____

On this and other Bayesian reasoning problems, Gigerenzer and Hoffrage found 46 per cent of responses could be classed as Bayesian, compared to just 16 per cent when a standard probability format was used. Cosmides & Tooby (1996) report even higher levels of Bayesian reasoning on similar problems, including 92 per cent correct responses when participants were required to mark cells in a grid that corresponded to the individuals described in the text.

Gigerenzer & Hoffrage point out that the frequency representations of these problems require a less complex cognitive process in order to arrive at a solution. Figure 3.4 shows how the information about the breast cancer problem can be represented in the form of a tree diagram. The Bayesian calculation involving frequencies (represented in lower-case) is:

$$(3.5) \quad P(H \mid D) = \frac{d\&h}{d\&h + d\&\sim h}$$

Only two numbers from this tree are involved in the calculation, which is:

$$\frac{8}{8 + 95} = 8 \text{ out of } 103$$

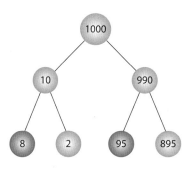

Figure 3.4. *Frequencies for the medical problem shown as a tree diagram (Gigerenzer & Hoffrage, 1995)*

However, not everyone agrees that it is the wording of problems in frequency formats that facilitates reasoning. Several authors attribute the facilitation to an increased transparency in the relations between sets and subsets. This has been referred to as the *nested sets hypothesis* (Sloman *et al.*, 2003; see also Johnson-Laird *et al.*, 1999; Macchi, 1995, 2003).

For example, Sloman *et al.* were able to facilitate performance on a conditional probability task by using fractions (for example, 'The probability that an average American has disease X is 1/1000') rather than frequencies. As they noted, a fraction need be neither a frequency nor a probability; it all depends on how one interprets it.

Some authors have reported that the facilitating effect of frequency formats are not as strong as had been previously reported (e.g. Sloman *et al.*, 2003). Other research indicates that motivation and ability factors influence the extent to which people obtain the right answer with frequency formats. Brase, Fiddick and Harries (2006) found that students at top-tier national universities outperformed those from second-tier regional universities. Also, people who were paid for their participation outperformed those who were not (these two factors did not interact).

SUMMARY

When people use the representativeness heuristic, they essentially substitute a judgment of probability with a judgment of similarity. This can lead to judgments that depart from the kind of answer that probability theory would provide. Representativeness has been applied to many judgments, including those that involve issues of category membership, sampling, compound events, and the misperception of random sequences that involve an assessment of probability. A category of representativeness known as prototype heuristics has also been applied to economic evaluation and judgments of the quality of experiences.

By contrast, the availability heuristic is based on an associative theory of memory, whereby the strength of memory associations is used to judge the frequency or likelihood of an event. The easier it is to bring instances to mind, the greater the estimated frequency

of the target event. Availability can be influenced by factors such as the recency, familiarity and vividness of instances.

According to support theory, people's judgments are based not on events, but on the support for hypotheses (descriptions of events). Less support is attached to implicit hypotheses (for example 'all natural causes of death') than to explicit hypotheses for example 'cancer, heart disease . . .'), and so estimates for implicit hypotheses tend to be subadditive.

MINERVA-DM attempts to capture all the broad phenomena of representativeness and availability within a wider theory of memory. It assumes that memory encodes all events, though sometimes in a degraded form. Judgment involves retrieving all instances that are sufficiently similar to a memory probe. The final assessment is based on the sum of activation of all memory traces. However, other memory-based accounts of judgment have been proposed that do not make the same assumptions about how memory operates. For instance, the multiple strategies perspective suggests that people may encode events in different ways and have available to them a variety of possible judgment strategies.

Conditional probability concerns judgments that take into account the relationship between belief and evidence. Bayes' theorem specifies how we should update beliefs in the light of evidence, but numerous studies have found that people appear not to be intuitive Bayesians. In particular, they often appear to neglect base rates when making their judgments. However, there is also evidence that performance can be facilitated by describing problems in terms of frequencies rather than single-event probabilities, although there is some controversy over both the extent of the facilitation and the reason for it.

QUESTIONS

1. How might prototype heuristics relate to forms of social discrimination?

2. Design a study to test whether people are more likely to commit the hot hand fallacy when excited.

3. Describe some of the ways in which Norbert Schwarz and his colleagues have distinguished between ease of recall and content of recall as influences on judgment.

4. What do you think are the advantages and disadvantages of using heuristics like representativeness and availability?

5. Describe the model of memory that underlies the Minerva DM account of judgment.

6. In their account of support theory, what do Tversky and Koehler mean by implicit and explicit hypotheses?

7. Are people Bayesian thinkers?

NOTES

1. For those unfamiliar with the notation of probability theory, please note that P(B | A) refers to the probability of B occurring *given that A occurs*. In other words, the vertical slash does not represent division.
2. At the time of writing this story was still available at http://news.bbc.co.uk/1/hi/world/europe/4256595.stm.
3. These authors point out that many of Edwards's studies actually used an 'artificial book-bag' situation, involving a display with a push-button and various lights. They note that people may have responded differently in this situation as compared to seeing a genuine book-bag!
4. Where a reasoner is aware of several explicit alternative hypotheses, the focal hypothesis may be labelled $P(H1)$ and the alternative hypotheses may be broken down into $P(H2)$, $P(H3)$, etc. Similarly, $P(D \mid \sim H)$ can also be expanded.

RECOMMENDED READING

Drummond, H. (2001). *The art of decision making: Mirrors of imagination, masks of fate.* Chichester: Wiley. This book interprets some high-profile decision disasters in terms of basic decision-making concepts such as representativeness and availability (and other ideas yet to be discussed).

Haigh, J. (2003). *Taking chances: Winning with probability* (2nd edn). Oxford: Oxford University Press. Mathematician John Haigh shows how to think rationally about chance in relation to sports and games.

Malkiel, B.G. (2003[1973]) *A random walk down Wall Street: The time-tested strategy for successful investing* (revised edn). New York: Norton. Burton Malkiel explains how an understanding of randomness can help you negotiate the stock market.

Paulos, J.A. (2003). *A mathematician plays the market.* London: Allen Lane. Another book about randomness and the stock market, by one of its victims.

Taleb, N.N. (2004). *Fooled by randomness: The hidden role of chance in life and in the markets.* London: Penguin.

4 Judgmental Distortions: The Anchoring-and-Adjustment Heuristic and Hindsight Bias

CHAPTER OUTLINE

INTRODUCTION

Consider the following questions:

- **a.** Is the percentage of African countries in the United Nations higher or lower than 25?
- **b.** What do you think the exact percentage is?

As we shall shortly see, the answer that people give to (b) is strongly affected by the figure they are asked to consider in (a), even when they believe that this figure has been randomly generated. This phenomenon has been attributed to an *anchoring-and-adjustment heuristic*, whereby people fail to make sufficient adjustment away from an initial figure that they treat as an anchor. Often, the anchors that we use are self-generated. This is because we are often faced by questions to which we think we have a rough idea of the answer, but cannot recall the exact answer. However, an initial response that comes to mind may unduly affect our final response.

A second distortion that has been observed in judgment is referred to as *hindsight bias*. This is the tendency for people to be wise after the event: when they possess some outcome knowledge they believe that the outcome was more predictable than it actually was. Note that the term *bias* refers to an erroneous outcome rather than a psychological process, although I shall examine the processes that may lead to the hindsight bias.

ANCHORING AND ADJUSTMENT

The basic phenomenon

Many types of judgment require us to produce a numerical estimate, either because there is no 'correct' answer – such as deciding the monetary value of a house – or because there is a correct answer but this is not known or does not come to mind – such as the height of K2. This section examines how people go about making estimates of this kind.

Recall the two-part question, (a) and (b), described in the introduction to this chapter. Tversky and Kahneman (1974) asked participants these questions, but with one extra element: The number mentioned in (a) was determined by spinning a wheel of fortune (0–100) in each participant's presence. They reported that the arbitrary numbers had a big effect on the estimates given in (b). For instance, the median estimates were 24 and 45 for groups that received 10 and 65, respectively, on the wheel of fortune. These authors proposed that participants were using a heuristic called *anchoring and adjustment*, according to which people make an estimate by using some starting value and then adjusting it to arrive at a final conclusion. However, people's final estimates are not sufficiently adjusted away from the initial anchor. This anchor may either be some externally generated figure (as with the wheel of fortune) or an estimate that the individual in question has generated (i.e. the first figure that came to mind).

Keren and Teigen describe anchoring and adjustment as 'more general than representativeness and availability, describing a process that applies equally well to frequency judgments, value judgments, magnitude judgments, and even causal attributions' (2004, pp.98–99). Although anchoring and adjustment was originally introduced as a heuristic like representativeness and availability, Kahneman and Frederick (2002) have subsequently proposed that it is actually rather different. Unlike representativeness and availability, anchoring and adjustment does not operate by replacing one type of judgment by a different type of judgment (for example, in the case of representativeness, replacing a probability judgment with a similarity judgment).

How robust is the effect of anchoring?

Anchoring effects have been observed in a variety of domains, including pricing (Mussweiler *et al.*, 2000; Northcraft & Neale, 1987), negotiation (Galinsky & Mussweiler, 2001), legal judgment (Chapman & Bornstein, 1996; Englich & Mussweiler, 2001), the evaluation of lotteries and gambles (Chapman & Johnson, 1994), probability estimates (see next section; Fischhoff & Beyth, 1975) and general knowledge (Jacowitz & Kahneman, 1995). In one of these studies, Northcraft and Neale (1987) demonstrated anchoring effects in the pricing estimates of estate agents. In this study, although estate agents were influenced by an external anchor the majority did not report that they had used the anchor in making their judgments. This is consistent with other research (e.g. Wilson *et al.*, 1996) and, indeed, participants have been found to use anchors even when explicitly warned not to do so (Wilson *et al.*, 1996). Englich & Mussweiler (2001) also reported that both experts and non-experts were similarly affected by an anchor, in this case with experienced judges and inexperienced law students on a legal sentencing task. The use of incentives also appears to be largely unsuccessful in reducing anchoring (Tversky & Kahneman, 1974; Wilson *et al.*, 1996; see also Chapman & Johnson, 2002, p.125). In short, such findings are consistent with the idea that people are largely unaware of the influence that anchors have on their judgments.

Even extreme or implausible anchors give rise to an anchoring effect. Strack and Mussweiler (1997, Experiment 3) gave participants general knowledge questions together with a plausible (high or low) or implausible (high or low) anchor (plausibility was rated by an independent group). An example of a comparative question with a high (low) implausible anchor is: 'Was Leonardo Da Vinci born before or after 1952 (300AD)?' After answering the comparative question participants then estimated the actual value. Implausible anchors had as big an effect on responses as plausible ones.

What are the underlying processes?

Despite the robustness of the anchoring effect, there has been little agreement as to the true nature of the underlying processes. One theory that has been proposed is that of *selective accessibility* (Strack & Mussweiler, 1997). According to this account, the comparative question task activates information in memory that is subsequently more accessible when making an absolute judgment. The comparative question refers to the initial question involving the anchor value. In the question at the start of the chapter, the comparative question is: *Is the percentage of African countries in the United Nations higher or lower than 25?*

Mussweiler & Strack (1999) suggested that people attempt to answer comparative questions by testing the hypothesis that the target's value is *equal* to the anchor. Epley (2004) listed four findings that are consistent with the selective accessibility account:

1. People attend to shared features between the anchor and target more than to unique features (e.g. Chapman & Johnson, 1999).

2. Completion of a standard anchoring task speeds the identification of words consistent with the implications of an anchor value rather than words inconsistent with it (e.g. Mussweiler & Strack, 2000).

3. The size of anchoring effects can be influenced by altering the hypothesis tested in the comparative assessment (for example, asking whether the anchor is *less* than a target value has a different effect to asking whether it is *more* than a target value).

4. People with greater domain knowledge are less susceptible to the effects of irrelevant anchors (e.g. Wilson *et al.*, 1996).

However, evidence suggests that an anchor value only reliably affects an absolute judgment if it is relevant to that judgment (Chapman & Johnson, 1994; Strack & Mussweiler, 1997). For instance, judging whether the Brandenburg Gate is taller or shorter than 150m has a considerable influence on a subsequent absolute judgment of height, but very little influence on an absolute judgment of the Gate's width (Strack & Mussweiler, 1997, Experiment 1).

One problem for the original notion of anchoring and adjustment is that the selective accessibility theory does not appear to have any need of the *adjustment* element. Although the findings are *consistent* with there being an element of adjustment, they nonetheless do not seem to require that part of the original heuristic. Rather, according to selective accessibility, an anchor activates certain information in the mind, and an absolute judgment is made based upon a portion of this activated information; it is not clear that adjustment is necessary.

However, Epley and Gilovich (2001; Epley, 2004) have made a case for 'putting adjustment back in the anchoring and adjustment heuristic'. They noted that the 'standard anchoring paradigm' is unlike many of the judgments that people make in real life. In the laboratory, the anchors that people are presented with, however, implausible, need to be taken seriously if only for a moment. But outside of the laboratory, most of the estimates we make rely upon *self-generated anchors* that we know from the outset to be wrong. We do not have to spend time and effort trying to decide whether the anchor is correct and so there is no heightened accessibility for anchor-consistent information.

Epley and Gilovich argued that insufficient adjustment rather than selective accessibility is the cause of anchoring effects when the anchor is self-generated. For example, consider the question 'When was George Washington elected president?' For many people, this is a difficult question. However, a more salient (and nearby) date in the minds of most Americans is 1776, the year of the Declaration of Independence. Thus, this date is a likely self-generated anchor when considering the question about Washington.

Epley and Gilovich (2001, Study 1) asked undergraduate students to think aloud as they tried to answer each of four questions (see Table 4.1), two of which included an experimenter-provided anchor. Of those participants who appeared to know both self-generated anchors (1492 in the case of the West Indies question), 94 per cent described a process of anchoring and adjustment in response to at least one of the anchors, and 65 per cent did so in response to both. However, for the experimenter-generated anchors, only 22 per cent of participants described an anchoring-and-adjustment process for at least one of the anchors and just 4 per cent did so in response to both.

In two follow-up studies, Epley and Gilovich asked participants to nod their heads, shake their heads, or hold their heads still while they answered a series of questions involving self-generated or experimenter-generated materials. Previous research has shown that people are more likely to accept propositions when they are nodding their heads than when they are shaking them (Wells & Petty, 1980). Thus, Epley and Gilovich thought that people in the head-nodding condition would be more willing to accept initial values that came to mind, while those in the head-shaking condition

Table 4.1. *Percentage of participants describing a process of anchoring and adjustment*[a]

Question	n	Percentage describing anchoring and adjustment
Self-generated anchor		
When was Washington elected president?	42	64
When did the second European explorer, after Columbus, land in the West Indies?	37	89
Experimenter-provided anchor[a]		
What is the mean length of a whale?	50	12
What is the mean winter temperature in Antarctica?	50	14

[a] The anchor value for the whale question was 69 feet and for the Antarctica question it was 1°F.
Source: Epley & Gilovich, 2001, Study 1.

would be more willing to reject initial values and so would produce greater adjustment. As predicted, head movements affected responses with the self-generated anchors but not with the experimenter-generated ones. With self-generated anchors, head nodding was associated with responses closest to the anchor, whereas head shaking was associated with responses furthest from the anchor (the no-head-movement condition was intermediate). Also with self-generated anchors, head nodding was associated with the quickest responses and head shaking with the slowest responses, although this was only statistically significant in one of the studies.

In a further study, Epley and Gilovich (2004) have shown that adjustments do tend to be insufficient, as proposed in the original notion of anchoring and adjustment. Epley (2004) gives three reasons why adjustment may be insufficient. First, if people simply do not know the answer then they are unlikely to adjust to it (except by accident). Second, adjustment requires attention, and hence requires cognitive resources. When there are competing demands for attention, people tend to engage in less adjustment. For instance, participants who had to memorise an eight-letter string before each question showed less adjustment (Epley & Gilovich, 2006, Experiment 2c). Thirdly, people who dislike engaging in effortful thinking tend to make less adjustment from self-generated anchors (Epley & Gilovich, 2006, Experiment 2a).

In sum, it appears that two separate processes may be at work when people try to generate uncertain estimates. When an external anchor has been provided, this activates related material in the mind that is used to produce a response. However, where no external anchor is provided, people generate their own anchor (usually some related salient figure) that they know to be wrong and which they then adjust away from.

HINDSIGHT BIAS: BEING WISE AFTER THE EVENT

Creeping determinism

The human mind exists to try and make sense of our environment in order that we can negotiate it and act upon it so as to ensure our survival. Part of the way in which we make sense of the environment is by constructing explanations for things. It is only rarely that we are able to scientifically test our explanations, and people sometimes fail to distinguish between explanations and evidence (see Chapter 5). One of the ways in which we try to make sense of the world is by interpreting the past in light of the way in which things turned out. However, one of the dangers of doing so is that we might begin to view a particular outcome as more foreseeable or inevitable than it actually was. This could have harmful consequences, such as the unfair assignment of blame for a negative outcome that was largely unpredictable, or a tendency to view criminals or the mentally ill as inevitable products of their life histories. Baruch Fischhoff (1975) referred to this hypothesised tendency as *creeping determinism*.

Two classic studies: the Gurka study and the Nixon study

Fischhoff conducted several studies to investigate the effect of outcome knowledge on uncertain judgments. In one study (Fischhoff, 1975, Experiment 1), participants received descriptions of four unfamiliar historical events, one of which concerned a British army campaign against the Nepalese Gurkas in 1814. Following each scenario four possible outcomes were described. For the Gurka scenario these were (a) British victory, (b) Gurka victory, (c) military stalemate with no peace settlement, and (d) military stalemate with a peace settlement. One group of participants was not told which of these outcomes had occurred, while four other groups were told that one of the outcomes had occurred. All participants were asked to assign probabilities to each outcome. As Figure 4.1 shows, participants who had been told about one particular outcome overestimated that outcome relative to those who had not been given any outcome information. Similar results were obtained for the other scenarios.

The term *hindsight bias* is used to describe the observation that an uncertain outcome often seems more likely *after* it is known that the outcome has occurred. Fischhoff found that hindsight bias occurred even when participants were asked to ignore outcome knowledge when making their judgments (1975, Experiments 2 and 3). He also found evidence that outcome knowledge altered people's assessment of the relevance of scenario information. For instance, in the Gurka scenario participants who were told of a British victory – including those who were told to ignore this – assigned greater importance to the fact that 'British officers learned caution only after sharp reverses', as compared to participants who

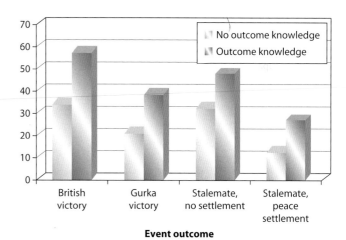

Figure 4.1. *Mean probability estimates (%) for outcomes to the British–Gurka confrontation of 1814, when an outcome was provided or not provided. There were four outcome knowledge groups, each of which was given 'knowledge' of one of the four outcomes*

Source: Fischhoff 1975.

were not provided with outcome information. In sum, people seemed to be unaware of the effect that outcome knowledge had on their judgments or, if they were aware, were unable to do anything about it.

Another classic study (Fischhoff & Beyth, 1975) was based around a contemporary event: President Nixon's historically momentous visits to China and the Soviet Union in 1972 (when the Cold War was still casting a shadow over international relations). Prior to Nixon's visits, Fischhoff and Beyth asked Israeli students to rate the likelihood of various events occurring during those visits. For instance, students who were asked about the China visit estimated things like the chance that the US would establish a diplomatic mission in Peking or meet Chairman Mao at least once, whereas students asked about the Soviet visit estimated the likelihood of events such as the establishment of a joint space programme or making a visit to Lenin's tomb. Two weeks to six months after these visits took place, the same students were asked to rate the same events, giving the same probabilities that they had given earlier on. The majority of students inflated their probabilities for events that *had* occurred and reduced them for events that *had not* occurred. This effect was particularly strong when the gap between the initial prediction and the recall task was three months or more.

The hypothetical design and the memory design

Although the bias is often associated with a distorted recollection of an earlier judgment, it is actually not necessary that an earlier judgment was made, or even that a person gave any thought at all to some outcome before it occurred. As you may have noticed, the two studies just described have different designs. The Gurka study is an example of a *hypothetical design*: the judgments of people without outcome knowledge are compared to those with outcome knowledge. The Nixon study is an example of a *memory design*: participants judge the likelihood of an outcome in ignorance of that outcome, they discover whether or not the outcome actually occurred and, finally, they try to recall their earlier judgment of likelihood. Although hindsight bias tends to be stronger in the hypothetical design (Campbell & Tesser, 1983; Davies, 1992; Fischhoff, 1977; Wood, 1978), this appears to be due to some participants in memory design studies accurately recalling their earlier judgments: Schwarz and Stahlberg (2003) found no difference in hindsight bias between the two designs once accurately recalled answers were excluded from analysis.

How robust is hindsight bias?

Although making people aware of hindsight bias does not appear sufficient to reduce it, other manipulations have been more successful (if not necessarily eliminating the bias). In one experiment, retrospective diagnoses about a neurological case study showed less hindsight bias when the neuropsychologists involved were asked to give a reason as to why each of the three possible diagnoses might be correct (Arkes *et al.*, 1988).

In another study, where participants made judgments about the outcome of psychology experiments (Davies, 1987), hindsight bias was reduced among participants who were presented with a written record of the thoughts and ideas they had generated in the pre-outcome session two weeks earlier. Slovic and Fischhoff (1977) found that asking people to engage in *counterfactual thinking* reduced hindsight bias. They asked people to rate the replicability of various possible scientific research findings. People who knew the outcomes of the original studies gave higher replicability ratings, but this hindsight bias was reduced among participants who were asked to imagine the original studies turning out differently and how they would have explained this.[1]

Cultural and individual differences

Nisbett (2003) has reviewed evidence that, compared to Westerners, East Asians[2] have a more holistic and complex view of the world generally and human behaviour specifically, which he attributes to a long tradition of thought that differs from that of the West. While there are many advantages to holistic thinking, Choi and Nisbett (2000) predicted that a downside would be a greater susceptibility to hindsight bias. Across a series of studies comparing Westerners and East Asians this is exactly what they found. They argue that complex models of behaviour are more capable of supporting post hoc explanations and, therefore, people holding such models are less likely to experience contradiction and surprise following an outcome and so more likely to show hindsight bias.[3]

Musch (2003) has provided evidence that personality differences may mediate the degree of hindsight bias. In Musch's study, personality factors played a bigger part in the hypothetical design than the memory design. He suggested that people may suppress self-presentational and other effects in the memory design if they are aware that their foresight and hindsight scores can be compared. Musch found that need for predictability was related to bias in the memory design; that is, dogmatic types who did not like ambiguity showed greater hindsight bias. With the standard hypothetical design Musch found greater hindsight bias among people who were more suggestible and people who were concerned with self-presentation.

Musch also analysed the hypothetical design in a different manner[4] designed to distinguish between actual knowledge and hindsight knowledge. Self-presentation was again a significant factor. Musch also found that a type of cognitive style known as Field Independence had an effect: people with a greater ability to break up organised stimuli into individual elements[5] showed less hindsight bias. The personality variable of Conscientiousness showed a weak relationship with each of the four factors, but was the only variable to be significantly related to both memory and hypothetical hindsight bias: greater conscientiousness was associated with greater hindsight bias. This is a somewhat puzzling finding, but perhaps those with greater levels of conscientiousness try harder to make sense of information. A sense-making account of hindsight bias will be discussed shortly.

Theories of hindsight bias

Fischhoff's (1975) preferred account of hindsight bias was that outcome information is immediately assimilated into existing memory structures. The role of memory reconstruction has been illustrated in research by Carli (1999). She presented participants with information about a romantic encounter which, the feedback group was told, led to rape. A week later, the feedback group was more likely than a no-feedback group to misrecall the details of the romantic encounter in a way that was congruent with the rape outcome. Outcome-congruent misrecall also mediated hindsight judgments. Similarly, mock-juror studies have found that jurors tend to be unable to disregard evidence that has been ruled inadmissible (Hawkins & Hastie, 1990).

Some other approaches, as described below, have not assumed that outcome knowledge is automatically assimilated into memory, but instead have theorised that hindsight bias occurs as the result of retrospectively reconstructing one's judgment. However, the difference between these two hypothesised processes may be one of degree rather than absolute. In large part, hindsight bias appears to result from cognitive processes aimed at sense-making. This is supported by the observation that unexpected outcomes lead people to engage in higher levels of sense-making activity (Hastie, 1984; Sanna & Turley, 1996; Weiner, 1985). Being able to make sense of things helps us to think and act more appropriately in the future, and in this sense hindsight bias may simply be a by-product of an adaptive cognitive process.

The idea that hindsight bias arises from sense-making cognitions is supported by investigations of those circumstances when the bias does *not* occur as well as when it does. A sense-making model proposed by Pezzo (2003) suggests that *initial surprise* at an outcome leads to sense-making activity (Figure 4.2). If the sense-making process is successful then *resultant surprise* is reduced and hindsight bias occurs. However, if the sense-making process fails then a high

Figure 4.2. *Pezzo's (2003) model of hindsight bias*

level of resultant surprise ensues and is associated with *reverse hindsight bias*, whereby the true outcome is seen as less predictable.

Reverse hindsight bias has been reported in several studies. For instance, Ofir and Mazursky (1997, Experiment 3) showed participants an undistinguished painting and told one group that it had been painted by Picasso, and another group that it had been painted by neither Picasso, Renoir, nor a 12-year-old boy; a third group was not given any information. Participants in the first two groups had to say what likelihood rating they would have given Picasso, Renoir, a 12-year-old boy, or someone else if they hadn't already been given any information about the painter's identity. They also rated their surprise about the information they had been given. Those who had not in fact received any information had to rate the likelihood associated with each option. People who were told that Picasso was the painter were rather surprised and gave Picasso a 14 per cent likelihood rating. People who were told that the painter was neither Picasso, Renoir, nor a 12-year-old boy were fairly unsurprised by this information and gave Picasso a 12.3 per cent likelihood rating. Those who were given no information at all gave Picasso a 19.3 per cent likelihood rating. These likelihood ratings are in the opposite direction of hindsight bias.

Across several studies specifically designed to test his sense-making model, Pezzo found broad support.[6] One of the tasks he used involved presenting positive, negative, or no feedback for a bogus cognitive abilities test. After receiving the performance feedback (or not, in the no-feedback group), participants were given five minutes to write down any thoughts that occurred to them. Then those in the no-feedback group were asked how well they thought they had done, and those in the feedback group how they

would have responded before receiving the feedback. Finally, a rating of resultant surprise was taken. As predicted by the sense-making model, increases in hindsight bias were associated with decreases in resultant surprise. Furthermore, participants who showed the highest levels of surprise showed a reverse hindsight bias. In the thought-listing task, people who generated more thoughts that were inconsistent with the outcome showed lower levels of hindsight bias.

In another study, Pezzo presented people with details of psychology research experiments which, for the feedback group, had outcomes that were either easy or difficult to make sense of (but which were all unexpected to some degree). For example, one *difficult* scenario stated that 'of girls who actually have sex, those who feel most guilty about it are most likely to get pregnant', whereas an *easy* scenario about who to date stated that 'for both men and women, the only factor that mattered was how physically attractive the person was'. Although overall no reverse hindsight bias was observed for the *difficult* scenarios, a considerable degree of standard hindsight bias was observed for the *easy* scenarios. Pezzo (2003, p.437) suggests that 'This finding seems to indicate that the ease with which sense can be made of an outcome, rather than "surprisingness" *per se*, is the more important determinant of hindsight bias.' The sense-making explanation of hindsight bias also appears to be consistent with the cross-cultural differences reported above, whereby East Asians appear to construct a more elaborate model of the world than Westerners, which leaves the former more vulnerable to the hindsight bias.

Consistent with the ease-of-processing idea, other research has shown that people are more confident about answers that they retrieve more quickly, whether or not they are correct (Nelson & Narens, 1990; see also Schwarz *et al.*, 1991, and Chapter 3). In a hypothetical design study involving almanac questions with numerical answers, Werth and Strack (2003) found that greater solution confidence was associated with closeness to the provided values. In a second study, the experimenters manipulated the ease of processing by making some questions easily visible (yellow question against a green background) and other questions of difficult visibility (yellow question against a red background). Answers to the easily visible questions were closer to the provided value.

Sanna *et al.* (2002) found that the generation of 10 rather than two counterfactual thoughts about the Gurka scenario led to more, not less, hindsight bias. Other evidence suggests that part of the bias that arises in memory design studies is the result of familiarity through repetition of material (see Hertwig *et al.*, 1997, on the 'reiteration effect').

SUMMARY

When making quantitative judgments people are sometimes influenced by the presence of an anchor. This may be an arbitrary value encountered during the course of an experiment, a number encountered in the natural environment (for example, a seller's price), or an initial assessment that comes to mind during the course of an evaluation. According to the original theoretical analysis of anchoring, people make an adjustment away from the anchor, but this is typically insufficient.

The anchoring effect appears to be very robust. People seem to be unaware of the effect that anchoring has on their judgments, and their judgments are not improved when monetary incentives are provided.

According to the selective accessibility account, the anchor heightens the accessibility of a small range of values in memory. According to this account, the proposal of insufficient adjustment is not needed in order to account for the judgmental errors that occur. However, other evidence indicates that adjustment does occur when the anchor is self-generated. In this circumstance, people are generally aware that their initial value is incorrect.

Insufficiency of adjustment may occur for various reasons. It may be because people simply do not know the correct answer, because there are competing demands for cognitive resources, or because people lack the motivation to engage in further thinking.

Hindsight bias is the tendency to retrospectively view events as more foreseeable or inevitable than they actually were, given that one has outcome knowledge about whether or not those events did occur. Studies of hindsight bias use either a hypothetical design, which provides or withholds outcome knowledge from different groups, or a memory design, in which the same participants give probability assessments before and after receiving outcome knowledge.

Hindsight bias can be reduced by, for example, reminding people of their earlier thoughts or asking them to engage in counterfactual thinking. There are also cultural differences, with East Asians showing more hindsight bias than Westerners, and various individual differences relating to personality.

Some theories of hindsight bias assume that memory is automatically updated in the light of outcome evidence, whereas others assume that people only engage in retrospective updating at the time of judgment. However, the difference between these two accounts may be a matter of degree rather than absolute. Another approach regards hindsight bias as a process of sense-making, and shows that people are less susceptible to hindsight bias (or show reverse hindsight bias) when it is hard to make sense of an outcome.

QUESTIONS

1. What is the selective accessibility theory of anchoring and adjustment?

2. What factors affect the level of adjustment that occurs when people use the anchoring-and-adjustment heuristic?

3. Design a study to assess the role of hindsight bias when assigning blame following some negative event.

4. Design a study of hindsight bias in relation to some forthcoming event (i.e. similar to Fischhoff and Beyth's 1975 study involving Nixon's visits to China and the Soviet Union).

5. State briefly the difference between the memory design and the hypothetical design in relation to hindsight bias.

6. Why do you think hindsight bias occurs?

NOTES

1. Counterfactual thinking does not always reduce hindsight bias. The topic of counterfactual thinking is explored further in the next section.

2. East Asians are people from China, Korea, Japan, and other countries that have been heavily influenced by Chinese culture.

3. Ji *et al.* (2000) found that East Asians are more field-dependent than Westerners, meaning that they tend to be more influenced by context when perceiving an object. Note that Musch (2003) has found that field dependence is associated with greater hindsight bias. His study is described in more detail below.

4. Musch used an intricate design in which all participants answered some questions with feedback and some questions without feedback. This allowed for a standard between-participants analysis and a within-participants analysis that controlled for the effects of knowledge (the two sets of items were equally difficult).

5. A possible role for Need for Cognition was somewhat ambiguous (this scale measures the extent to which people enjoy engaging in effortful thought).

6. The task and the analyses were considerably more detailed than is described here. I have focused on the key findings.

RECOMMENDED READING

Nisbett, R.E. (2003). The geography of thought: How Asians and Westerners think differently . . . and why. New York: Free Press. A fascinating account of cognitive differences between East Asians and Westerners.

A collection of interesting academic papers is published in a special 'hindsight bias' issue of the journal *Memory*, 11(4/5), Psychology Press, 2003.

5 | Assessing Evidence and Evaluating Arguments

CHAPTER OUTLINE

....

INTRODUCTION

....

Much of our everyday thinking consists of the generation of arguments with which we hope to convince other people of the rightness of some opinion we hold. Conversely, we often need to evaluate some argument that has been put to us. In this chapter, I shall begin by looking at what an argument consists of. Then I shall go on to discuss people's capacity for distinguishing theory and evidence, for responding appropriately to counterevidence, for finding the flaws in an argument, and for considering arguments on both sides of a topic. I shall also look at the factors that affect the way in which we process persuasion messages. Finally, I will briefly discuss the way in which people make sense of highly complex bodies of evidence.

THE STRUCTURE OF ARGUMENTS

The basic structure of everyday argument was described by the philosopher Stephen Toulmin (1958), who recognised that formal logic did not apply to most everyday arguments. In Toulmin's scheme, a person tries to establish a claim by presenting a datum or data (information) and establishing its relevance to the claim by the application of a warrant. The basic scheme, with an example, is shown in Figure 5.1a.

In Figure 5.1a, the relevance of the information that 'Dr. Jones has been working at Central University for six years' is established by the fact (the warrant) that 'academics at Central University can take a sabbatical every six years'. If the audience for this claim were to question the validity of the warrant, then the person making the claim could point out that the warrant is validated by the university's regulations. This is the *backing* for the warrant. Toulmin also developed his argument structure to take account of the possibility that claims might have to be *qualified* in the face of *rebuttal* (see Figure 5.1b). A rebuttal is an exception that weakens or overrules the claim. In the current example, the claim that Dr Jones can take a sabbatical is qualified by the term 'presumably' because of the rebuttal 'unless Dr Jones is unable to find people to cover his teaching'.

The basic structure of Toulmin's theory of arguments is like the lens model of judgment described in Chapter 2 (see Kleindorfer *et al.* 1993, pp.85–86). What are traditionally referred to as 'cues' in the lens model are 'data' in the theory of arguments, and the psychological processes referred to in the lens model as 'cue utilisation' are simply the use of warrants and backing. How the data *should* be related to a criterion is specified by a prescriptive or normative model (for more on everyday forms of argumentation, see Walton, 1989, 1996).

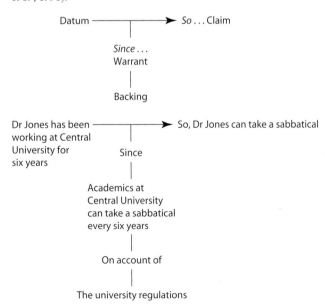

Figure 5.1a. *Toulmin's basic argument scheme in both abstract and concrete form*

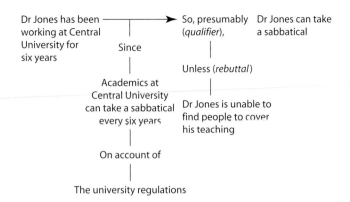

Figure 5.1b. *The concrete example of an argument from Figure 5.1a is shown here, with rebuttal and qualifier added*

Curley and Benson (1994) have proposed a theory of belief processing that is essentially a cognitive model of how arguments lead to judgments. Their model consists of a data-generation module, an argument-construction module, and a qualifier-construction module. In this model, data can either be generated from memory or obtained from the external environment. There is also an interrelationship between data and arguments: a consideration of arguments can itself prompt and guide the evocation of data, as well as be evoked by data. Data that are judged to be irrelevant are screened out and the cumulative strength of remaining arguments feeds into the strength of the final conclusion. The strength of any qualifier(s) is based on the reliability of data, the strength of individual arguments, the completeness of the evidence, and the internal coherence of different arguments.

Distinguishing between theory and evidence

The cognitive model just described is a competence model. But what are the basic *performance* findings in relation to argumentation? A key finding is that people frequently provide explanations for claims but without providing genuine evidence. Kuhn (1991) asked participants to articulate their views about the cause(s) of criminal recidivism, school failure, and unemployment. During the course of each interview session, participants were also asked to provide evidence for their views, to consider how they would respond to challenges to their views, and to consider alternative views. In general, people were able to articulate opinions on the topics in question, but at the same time they often were unable to present genuine evidence in support of their opinions. In fact, Kuhn reports that less than half the participants were able to provide genuine evidence, with most forms of evidence being what she termed pseudoevidence ('a scenario, or script, depicting how the phenomenon might occur'; 1991, p.65). Only 26 out of 160 people (16 per cent) were able to generate genuine evidence for all three topics.

Brem and Rips (2000) put a more optimistic slant on Kuhn's findings. They point out that the topics of everyday arguments are frequently very complex and that we often have neither the time nor the power to test all possible hypotheses; when we hear about young mothers who are trapped on welfare, we cannot systematically vary every aspect of their environment, or randomly assign people to poverty. (2000, p.579)

Furthermore, the media may not have provided us with all the relevant information, and even the information we have received may be hard to recall. In these circumstances the generation of an explanation can help us 'to understand a position better, identify its strengths and weaknesses, guide our search for data, and improve our ability to apply our knowledge to new situations' (2000, p.579).

Across four studies using similar materials to Kuhn, Brem and Rips found that people were better at distinguishing between explanation and evidence than one might expect from Kuhn's own study. For example, when participants were asked what would be the *ideal* evidence to convince another person of a viewpoint, they provided genuine evidence on 58 per cent of trials, as compared to 35 per cent for participants who were simply asked to provide evidence. This latter group presumably felt constrained to provide only actual evidence that they could recall. Consequently, they produced a greater quantity of pseudoevidence. In another study, participants were provided either with an explanation or with evidence relevant to various issues and asked to rate (on a 0–7 scale) how strongly that information supported a particular claim. However, whereas some people were told that very little information was available, others were told that there was a good deal of information available. Overall, participants gave higher ratings to evidence than to explanation, but they also gave explanations higher ratings in the information-poor condition than in the information-rich condition (see Figure 5.2).

A study by Sá *et al.* (2005) investigated how people of high and low cognitive ability coordinate theory and evidence. Their participants were 94 mature students, with a mean age of 32, who had returned to high school to complete their education. The researchers followed Kuhn's (1991) technique of interviewing participants on a topical issue. In this case, the issues were 'What causes children to fail in school?' and 'What causes prisoners to return to crime after they are released?' Participants also completed

measures of fluid and crystallised intelligence (combined to form a composite measure), a scale to measure actively open-minded thinking, and a scale to measure superstitious thinking.

Of particular interest was the participants' use of covariation comparison, where they implicated or called for 'some specified covariation comparison between the alleged causal antecedent and the outcome at issue' (2005, p.1153). As it turned out, people with high cognitive ability did not use this form of response any more than those with low cognitive ability, and use of covariation comparison did not correlate with any of the other measures.

However, there were individual differences on another measure of interest – the tendency to reiterate a previous causal theory or to elaborate on it. Reiteration or elaboration of a previous causal theory occurred more often among those who scored low on cognitive ability. It was also associated with superstitious thinking, but people who scored higher on actively open-minded thinking were less likely to reiterate or elaborate on an earlier theory. Actively open-minded thinking was a predictor of less reiteration or elaboration even after cognitive ability was controlled for. However, the reverse was not true: cognitive ability did not predict reiteration or elaboration once actively open-minded thinking was controlled for. Some previous studies had found that cognitive ability remained a significant predictor even after thinking dispositions had been controlled for (Sá *et al.*, 1999; Stanovich & West, 1997). However, this difference may have been because these other studies had contained instructions to engage in a decontextualised mode of thinking.

One of the questions asked by Sá *et al.* (2005) was 'Could someone prove you were wrong?' People whose responses on at least one topic were classed as an 'unequivocal no' scored lower on the cognitive ability measure, lower on the actively open-minded thinking scale, and higher on the superstitious thinking scale.

Research with 13- and 14-year-olds has also shown that the choice of explanation or evidence may be affected by the goal of reasoning (Glassner *et al.*, 2005). Questions beginning 'How do you know that . . . ?' were more likely to elicit evidence than explanations, whereas questions beginning 'Why do you think . . . ?' were more likely to elicit explanations. The authors argue that the 'How' question elicits a proof goal whereas the 'Why' question elicits an explanation goal. However, this result was based upon participants choosing from information that was provided to them. In a task where they were required to generate their own ideas for proof or explanations the pupils generated explanations more often than evidence, indicating that there may be a stronger disposition towards explanation.

Belief perseveration in the face of contradictory evidence

Many studies have investigated whether or not people respond to evidence in an appropriate fashion. A review of this literature concluded that people who hold very strong views on a topic *do not* respond appropriately to evidence that does not support their opinion (MacCoun, 1998). A classic experiment by Lord *et al.* (1979) presented participants with two purportedly authentic studies on

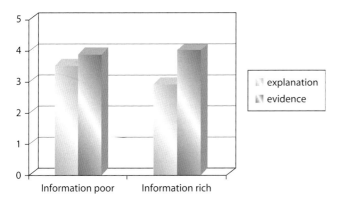

Figure 5.2. *Mean ratings of strength of support given to explanations and evidence said to be based upon little data (information-poor) or much data (information-rich). 0 represents the lowest level of support and 7 the highest*

Source: Based on Brem & Rips 2000, Experiment 2.

the effectiveness of the death penalty as a deterrent. One study indicated that there was a deterrent effect, whereas the other indicated that there was not. The prior opinions of these participants on this topic were already known, with one group being in favour of the death penalty and the other against it. Both groups of students reported that the study favouring their opinion was 'better conducted' and 'more convincing' than the other study. Lord *et al.* proposed that this result was due to the *biased assimilation* of evidence. Their participants also showed *attitude polarisation*: After reading both studies they were more convinced of the correctness of their initial opinion than they were before having read *any* evidence.

Using a range of controversial topics, Edwards and Smith (1996) were able to elucidate the nature of the psychological mechanism underlying belief perseverance. They found that (1) participants spent more time scrutinising arguments that were incompatible with their prior beliefs, (2) they generated more thoughts and arguments in response to belief-incompatible arguments than to belief-compatible ones, and (3) these thoughts and arguments tended to be refutational in nature when the presented argument was belief-incompatible. Edwards and Smith describe this process as a *disconfirmation bias* for arguments.

The biased assimilation effect is not just confined to laypersons in a given domain, but has been observed in experts. Koehler (1993) replicated the effect with experts on both sides of the extrasensory perception debate, and reported that the effect was actually stronger amongst skeptics than among parapsychologists. McHoskey (1995) found that those who held a conspiracy theory about the Kennedy assassination and their detractors both interpreted the same evidence as supportive of their views.

MacCoun's (1998) review found that the evidence for biased assimilation is more robust than for attitude polarisation, as some studies have found that the latter is limited to self-report change ratings. However, MacCoun's (1998) comment on the research is worth noting:

> Attitude polarization in response to mixed evidence, if it does exist, is a remarkable (and remarkably perverse) fact about human nature, but the mere fact that participants *believe* it is occurring is itself noteworthy. And even in the absence of attitude polarization, biased assimilation is an established phenomenon with troubling implications for efforts to ground contemporary policy debates in empirical analysis. (1998, p.267)

Belief and perception

It is also worth noting that other studies have found that our existing beliefs and commitments can affect the way in which we *perceive* events. For example, in a bad-tempered American football game supporters of Princeton (the home side) perceived many more infringements by the away side (Dartmouth) than their own side. By contrast, Dartmouth supporters perceived roughly the same number of infringements on both sides and fewer overall (Hastorf & Cantril, 1954). In another study, conducted after the 1982 Beirut massacre, it was found that pro-Arab students perceived a higher proportion of favourable references to Israel in segments of TV news than did pro-Israeli students (Vallone *et al.*, 1985). Overall, pro-Israeli students perceived the news as blaming Israel and believed that neutral viewers would become more negative towards Israel. Pro-Arab students tended to believe that the TV news excused Israel and that neutral viewers would not become biased against Israel.

Motivated reasoning

Suppose you were to read in the newspaper about some new research showing that people with your eye colour tend to have above-average intelligence and a wider circle of friends than those with a different eye colour. If you are like me, you would probably think to yourself *Cool!*, and get a faintly warm glow of superiority. On the other hand, suppose instead that the research said the opposite – that people with your eye colour tend to be below average intelligence and have fewer friends than people with a different eye colour. Most likely you would sigh and think *What rubbish! No doubt there'll be a story next week showing the opposite.*

These are exactly the kinds of reactions that people tend to give to positive and negative information relating to themselves. Positive information about intelligence, social sensitivity, professional competence, or vulnerability to future illness is perceived as more valid, accurate, and internally caused than negative information (Beckman, 1973; Ditto *et al.*, 1988; Pyszczynski *et al.*, 1985; Wyer & Frey, 1983). Negative information tends to be regarded as less valid, less accurate, and explainable by external factors.

However, it appears that people do not simply ignore information that they would prefer not to believe. We saw earlier that there is a negative argument bias for claims that contradict strong beliefs. That is, people pay a lot of attention to such arguments, trying to find a reason why they are wrong. The same seems to be true for claims that we would simply prefer not to be right. Ditto and Lopez (1992, Experiment 1) told participants that they were taking part in a study that would mimic decision making about college admissions. As part of this study, they were to work with a partner on a series of analogy problems. Before doing so, however, they needed to choose the more intelligent of two candidates to work with. In order to determine which person was more intelligent, they could look through each candidate's solutions to a previous analogies task. The solutions were more accurate for some candidates than others (positive vs. negative performance). Participants also got to see a personal evaluation of each candidate from their partner on the previous analogies task. On the basis of the evaluations, one candidate appeared to be highly likeable, whereas the other seemed disagreeable.

When the performance information was negative, participants sifted through much less information for dislikeable candidates than for likeable ones. For positive performance information, participants sifted through just as much information when the candidate was dislikeable as when the candidate was likeable.

In two further studies, Ditto and Lopez examined people's responses to positive and negative outcomes in a fake medical test. Participants were required to dip a chemically coated strip of paper in their saliva. They believed that the strip might change colour depending on whether or not they were deficient in an important enzyme. In fact the strip never changed colour. The outcome measure in the test was how long students would wait before sealing the strip into an envelope for the experimenter. People in a 'deficiency' condition were led to believe that the strip would change colour if they were *not* deficient in the enzyme. These participants waited almost 30 seconds longer before placing the strip in the envelope, compared to 'no deficiency' participants who believed the strip would change colour if they *were* deficient. Partly this was due to deficiency participants retesting themselves. In fact, 52 per cent of deficiency participants retested themselves, as compared to just 18 per cent of no-deficiency participants. Needless to say, there was no reason why the test should have been more untrustworthy in one condition than the other!

Deficiency participants also showed psychological defensiveness on some questionnaire measures taken following the testing period. Compared to no-deficiency participants, they perceived that enzyme deficiency was less serious and more common in the population. They also rated pancreatic disease (a consequence of the deficiency) as less serious and more common than did no-deficiency participants. Finally, they also saw the saliva reaction test as a less accurate indicator of their health status than did no-deficiency participants.

FINDING THE FLAWS IN ARGUMENTS

Shaw (1996) proposed that some objections to arguments are easier to make than others, because they are less cognitively taxing. In particular, it is much easier to question the truth of premises or conclusions than to attack the link between the premises and the conclusion. Questioning the premises or conclusion does not require a person to construct or evaluate mental models that represent the ways in which premises and conclusions might be linked, and it does not require them to call upon missing information that could refute the conclusion. Shaw found that student participants were more likely to attack the arguments of newspaper and magazine editorials by questioning the truth of the premises or the conclusion. She did find, however, that by drawing people's attention to the link between premises and conclusion she was able to increase the number of objections based on attacking this link.

In a second experiment, Shaw showed that it was the participants who were best able to identify the premises and conclusions in passages of natural language who were more likely to formulate objections to the link between premises and conclusions. Thus, the less able reasoners were more likely to base their objections on questioning the truth of the premises or conclusions. Similarly, people with a higher level of text comprehension are more likely to identify reasoning fallacies in everyday argument (Neuman, 2003; Neuman & Weizman, 2003).

ONE-SIDED VERSUS TWO-SIDED ARGUMENTS

Baron (1995) reported an experiment aimed at discovering whether people are more favourably disposed to arguments that consider both sides of a controversial issue (in this case abortion) or whether one-sided arguments are rated more favourably. A group of students was asked to generate arguments as if they were preparing for a class discussion. The resulting lists of arguments were then classified as one-sided or two-sided, depending on whether the students had presented arguments both pro and con. The same students were then presented with lists of arguments from 24 hypothetical other students and asked to evaluate the thinking of those students. Some of the lists contained one-sided arguments, whereas other lists were two-sided. When asked to grade the argument lists, participants gave higher grades to lists where they shared the opinion of the writer, but only if the writer had provided more arguments on that side than on the other side. Furthermore, participants gave higher grades to one-sided lists than two-sided ones, even when they disagreed with the arguments presented. When asked to justify their grades, participants frequently cited one-sidedness as a virtue. Two-sided argument lists were often seen as evidence of indecisiveness or of the writer's self-contradiction. However, sometimes participants used both one- and two-sided justifications, thus supporting an earlier suggestion (Baron, 1991) that people can hold both standards simultaneously.

Despite this tendency to prefer one-sided arguments, Baron also found that students who had themselves generated two-sided argument lists gave higher grades to the two-sided lists of the hypothetical students (individual differences in 'open-minded' thinking have also been reported by Stanovich and West, 1998). Two-sided arguments have also been observed to be persuasive in certain other contexts. Following Germany's defeat in the Second World War, Carl Hovland and his colleagues created two radio broadcasts aimed at American soldiers fighting the Japanese (Hovland *et al.*, 1949, cited in Myers, 2005). The broadcasts were intended to prevent US soldiers from assuming that the ongoing war would become easy. One of the broadcasts was one-sided and did not mention the advantage that America was now only fighting one enemy instead of two. The other broadcast did acknowledge this fact. The two-sided broadcast turned out to be most effective at persuading people who had initially disagreed with the point of view conveyed, whereas the one-sided appeal was more effective with those who already agreed. Research with simulated legal trials has also found that the defence team benefits from raising any damaging evidence before the prosecution does (Williams *et al.*, 1993). It seems that if an audience is aware that there are two sides to an argument, a person who addresses only one side may be viewed as biased and the audience may generate their own counterarguments.

BIASES IN FAVOUR OF PRIOR KNOWLEDGE OR BELIEF

Other research indicates that people find it difficult to reason from contrary beliefs. George (1995) asked three groups of people to complete two of the following three tasks:

In the *confidence* task people evaluated the truth of conditional statements such as:

If exports decrease, then unemployment will rise.

In the *entailment* task people were asked to assume the truth of the statement 'Exports decrease' and to decide whether this entailed the conclusion 'Unemployment is rising'.

In the *modus ponens* task people were presented with a complete argument:

If exports decrease, then unemployment will rise.
Exports decrease.
Conclusion: Unemployment is rising.

Participants were asked to assume the truth of the premises and then rate the truth of the conclusion. In formal logic, this argument is known as *modus ponens* and has the structure *If P then Q; P; Therefore Q*. The argument is deductively valid, so – assuming the truth of the premises – the conclusion should be accepted regardless of the believability of the premises. With *abstract* materials nearly 100 per cent of participants endorse this argument.

From Figure 5.3, we can see that the conclusion 'unemployment is rising' did not get a very strong truth rating in either the confidence or the entailment conditions. Consequently, 45 per cent of participants were unable to set aside their beliefs in the modus ponens condition, hence did not endorse the response option 'True'. Modus ponens and a number of other conditional argument forms are briefly reviewed in Box 5.1.

Other research has found that, while people tend to distinguish logically valid from invalid arguments, they also demonstrate a *belief bias*: they accept believable conclusions more than unbelievable ones, particularly with invalid arguments (for a review, see Evans *et al.*, 1993). The effect of beliefs was also evident in Kuhn's (1991) study of argument skills, discussed earlier. She found that fewer than half of the participants were able to generate a counterargument to their own views, although just over 60 per cent were able to generate alternative theories. Despite these shortcomings, Kuhn writes that 'people confidently "know" the answers to our questions, but in the naive sense of never having contemplated that the answers could be otherwise' (1991, p.265).

BOX 5.1.   LOGICAL ARGUMENTATION

A deductively valid argument is one in which, if the premises are true then the conclusion must also be true. Such arguments are said to be valid by virtue of their *form* regardless of their *content*. It may be that we disagree with the truth of the premises and the conclusion, but we should still agree that the conclusion follows logically from the information that has been stated. The two following argument forms are logically valid:

Modus ponens	**Example of modus ponens**
If P then Q.	If the light is on then Mary is at home.
P.	The light is on.
Therefore, Q.	Therefore, Mary is at home.

Modus tollens	**Example of modus tollens**
If P then Q.	If snow is falling then the weather is cold.
Not Q.	The weather is not cold.
Therefore, Not P.	Therefore, snow is not falling.

The two following argument forms are not deductively valid:

Affirming the consequent	**Example of affirming the consequent**
If P then Q.	If Fido is in his kennel then he is chewing a bone.
Q.	Fido is chewing a bone.
Therefore, P.	Therefore, Fido is in his kennel.

Denying the antecedent	**Example of denying the antecedent**
If P then Q.	If it is Sunday then Jack will wash his car.
Not P.	It is not Sunday.
Therefore, Not Q.	Therefore, Jack will not wash his car.

Many studies of people's reasoning with these argument forms have focused on abstract content, so as to exclude any effects of knowledge. Typically, 100 per cent of people endorse modus ponens and about 75 per cent of people endorse modus tollens, but about 75 per cent wrongly endorse affirmation of the consequent and 69 per cent wrongly endorse denial of the antecedent. Explanations of these findings and a discussion of research with more thematic materials can be found in Evans *et al.* (1993) and Manktelow (1999).

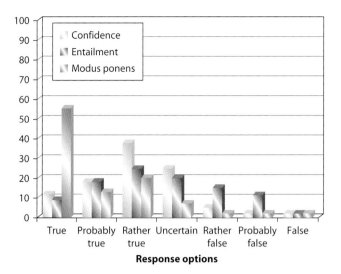

Figure 5.3. *Percentage of response choices for the three tasks related to a conditional statement* If exports decrease, then unemployment will *rise*

Source: George 1995.

While Evans and other researchers were looking at people's inability to decouple beliefs from logical thinking, other researchers were looking at the same kind of phenomenon in informal reasoning. Researchers in this tradition referred to the bias as *myside bias* (e.g. Baron, 1995; Perkins, 1985). Stanovich and West (2007) distinguish between belief bias and myside bias by suggesting that the former actually involves the inability to decouple prior *knowledge* from evaluative processing, whereas the latter involves the inability to decouple prior *belief* from evaluation. However, this seems like a minor distinction, if indeed it is a real distinction.

Stanovich and West note that studies of belief bias have found that people who score higher on measures of cognitive ability tend to show less belief bias (e.g. Stanovich & West, 1997, 1998; see also Handley *et al.*, 2004). On the other hand, studies of myside bias have found no relationship of myside bias with cognitive ability (e.g. Klaczynski, 1997; Klaczynski & Robinson, 2000). Stanovich and West (2007) suggested that a crucial difference between the different sets of studies might be that the belief bias studies have given explicit instructions to ignore prior belief and knowledge in the task. This was not the case with the myside bias studies, which are presumably more representative of real-world thinking.

PERSUASION

Under what circumstances do messages have their intended effect of persuading another person? According to the elaboration likelihood model (Petty & Cacioppo, 1986; see Figure 5.4) and the heuristic-systematic model (Chaiken *et al.*, 1989), people may process arguments along one of two routes: the *central* route or the *peripheral* route. Arguments that are processed along the central route are carefully scrutinised and may result in enduring new attitudes that are predictive of behaviour. However, arguments

that are processed along the peripheral route receive only perfunctory attention. In the latter case, the persuasiveness of a communication may be influenced by peripheral cues, such as the perceived credibility and/or attractiveness of the communicator. Such communications may result in attitude change, but this is likely to be temporary and unpredictive of behaviour. Whether a message is processed along the central or peripheral route may depend on the perceived importance of the message, the motivation of the audience, and/or the cognitive capacity of the audience.

An example of how individual and message factors may interact is provided by Mackie and Worth (1989, Experiment 2). In this study, either a positive or a neutral mood was induced in participants by presenting them with one of two 5-minute video clips: either an excerpt from *Saturday Night Live* (positive mood) or a segment on wine (neutral mood). Participants then read a 'speech' on gun control that advocated a point of view counter to that held by the participant (this had been established earlier). Half the people were told that the speech had come from an eminent legal scholar (expert source) and the other half that it had come from a university freshman (nonexpert source). For the speech itself, half the people received a version containing eight weak arguments (determined by pretesting) and half received a version with eight strong arguments. Finally, participants either saw the message for a period of 70 seconds or they had unlimited exposure to the message.

Figure 5.5a shows that, when the exposure to information was brief, people in a good mood were unaffected by the strength of arguments. They showed some attitude change, but this did not differ between strong and weak arguments. On the other hand, Figure 5.5b indicates that mood did not affect the processing of arguments when people had unlimited time to read the message. That is, strong arguments had a greater effect on attitudes than weak arguments, regardless of mood. For participants in a neutral mood, the expert and non-expert source did not differ in their effects, either with the brief presentation (Figure 5.6a) or the unlimited presentation (Figure 5.6b; the small gap between expert and nonexpert in the neutral condition is not statistically significant). However, participants in a positive mood showed greater attitude change to a brief presentation from an expert than a nonexpert (Figure 5.6a), but were unaffected by source expertise in the unlimited time condition (Figure 5.6b).

Mackie and Worth argued that positive mood had the effect of reducing cognitive capacity rather than reducing motivation (in the positive mood condition, people spent longer reading the message when given unlimited time to do so). Other researchers have noted that one's positive feelings may become linked with the message itself (Petty *et al.*, 1993).

Subsequently, Bless *et al.* (1992) noted that the studies just described did not distinguish between mood effects at the point of message encoding and mood effects at the time of judgment. This was because people gave their attitude judgments immediately after having read a short piece of text. Bless *et al.* (1992, Experiment 1) examined this issue by manipulating the point at which people's moods were manipulated. Some people had their moods manipulated prior to reading some arguments in favour of raising student services fees at their university. After reading this text, they completed a filler task that was intended to return them to a neutral

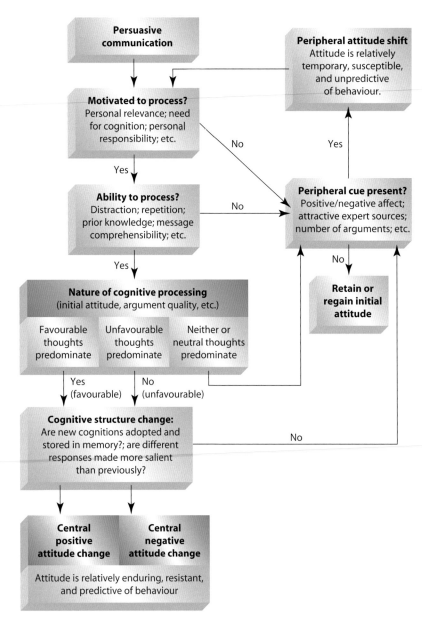

Figure 5.4. *The Elaboration Likelihood Model of Persuasion*
Source: Based on Petty & Cacioppo (1986).

state. Finally, they were asked to make an attitudinal judgment on the student fees topic. Other students did the neutral filler task prior to reading the message and were put into a positive or negative mood just prior to making their attitude judgment.

The results of this study are shown in Figure 5.7. They indicate that mood can affect attitude judgments either by influencing the encoding of the persuasive message or by influencing processes independent of the initial message elaboration. People who were in a good mood when they read the message were equally influenced by weak arguments as by strong ones, whereas people in a negative mood gave more credence to strong arguments. This replicates the earlier findings. However, when people read the initial message in a neutral state, they gave greater credence to strong arguments if they were in a *positive* mood at the time of judgment.

These results indicate that people are not merely retrieving earlier judgments when they indicate their attitudes; rather, they are constructing their judgment on the spot. Consistent with the dual-processing model, positive mood prior to reading the message appears to result in reduced elaboration of the message. Positive mood prior to judgment appears to lead people to rely on some specific aspect of the message that strengthens the impact of argument quality.

To find out what aspects of the message people were attending to, Bless *et al.* carried out a second study, which participants thought was an investigation into text comprehension. Participants read a persuasive message advocating drilling for oil off the southwestern coast of the United States. After this, some people were asked to think about the strength of the arguments they had seen,

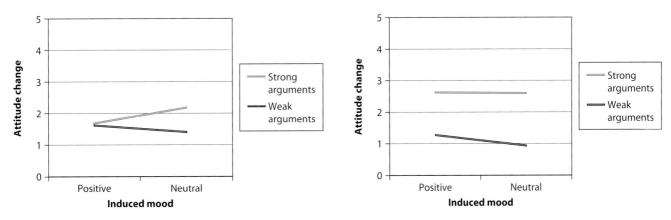

Figure 5.5. *The effect of induced mood on attitude change after reading strong or weak arguments (a) after a brief exposure time; (b) after unlimited exposure time. Attitude change was measured on a 0–9 scale*

Source: Mackie & Worth 1989.

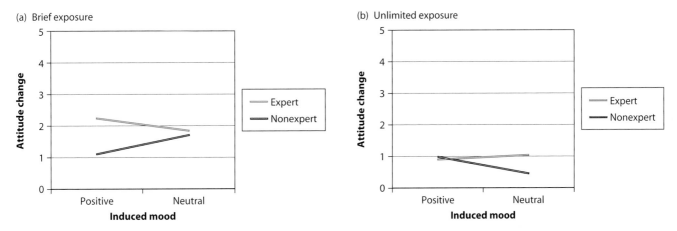

Figure 5.6. *The effect of induced mood on attitude change after reading arguments from an expert or nonexpert source (a) after a brief exposure time; (b) after unlimited exposure time. Attitude change was measured on a 0–9 scale*

Source: Mackie & Worth 1989.

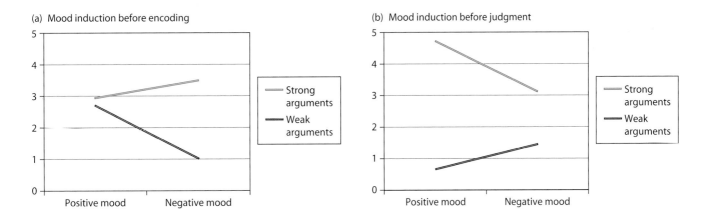

Figure 5.7. *Attitude change as a function of mood, timing of mood induction, and argument quality, (a) mood induction before encoding; (b) mood induction before judgment. 1 = strongly disapprove; 9 = strongly approve*

which was intended to create a global representation of the problem in their minds. Others were asked to think about the different arguments they had seen and how many arguments there were. This was intended to create a more detailed representation in their minds. Next, a positive, neutral, or negative mood was induced in participants. They then indicated their judgments on a nine-point scale and made a list of all the thoughts that had occurred to them while they were thinking about their answer.

People who had created a global representation of the message while in a positive mood gave more credence to strong arguments than people who had created a detailed representation. The same was true for people in a neutral mood. However, people in a negative mood barely distinguished between strong and weak arguments, regardless of whether they had created global or detailed representations. In the thought-listing task, for those who had created a global representation, positive and neutral moods led to more global thoughts being listed, as compared to those in a negative mood.

Taken together, the results from these two studies indicate that the effect of positive mood is to reduce the cognitive processing that occurs both at the encoding stage and at the evaluative stage.

EXPLANATION-BASED DECISION MAKING

The previous section looked at the conditions that can make a message seem more or less persuasive. This section asks how people might go about assessing complex information. In this regard a theory of explanation-based decision making has been proposed by Pennington and Hastie (e.g. 1993; Hastie & Pennington, 2000) to describe situations in which 'a large base of implication-rich, conditionally-dependent pieces of evidence must be evaluated as a preliminary to choosing an alternative from a set of prospective courses of action' (Hastie & Pennington, 2000, p.212).

Although in an earlier part of the chapter I distinguished between explanation and evidence, in this theory the term 'explanation-based' should not be interpreted as meaning 'lacking evidence'. Quite the contrary; it is about how people make sense of situations involving large amounts of evidence. This could include decisions about the law, engineering, medicine, politics, diplomacy, and everyday life (Hastie & Pennington, 2000).

According to this theory, decision makers begin the decision process by constructing a causal model in order to explain the available facts, and then subsequent decisions are based on this model. Much research in this domain has been conducted with mock-jurors, and the application of Pennington and Hastie's theory in this domain is referred to as the *story model*, following the observation that mock-jurors' causal models have a narrative structure (Pennington & Hastie, 1986).

Pennington and Hastie (1992) found that verdict decisions were affected by the difficulty of story construction and that stories mediated the effects of credibility information. For example, in one study (1992, Experiment 1) participants read two courtroom transcripts in which information was either arranged issue by issue or in the form of a story. The transcripts included testimony from four witnesses, one of whom gave evidence that was inconsistent with the other three. Information about the inconsistent witness was provided that either had no bearing on their credibility or which made them seem highly credible or not very credible. One case involved evidence that favoured a guilty verdict and the other case had evidence in favour of innocence.

Importantly, whether participants read the issue-based transcript or the story-based transcript did not affect how much of the case they could remember in free recall, yet recall in the form of a story was more likely among those who had read it in that form. For each case participants rated the strength of guilt or innocence on a scale running from −10 to +10. They used the same scale to rate confidence in their decision.

For each case, the rated strength of guilt or innocence was in the direction of the preponderance of evidence, but more strongly so for participants who had read the transcripts in story order. Story order participants were also more confident in their decisions. When the inconsistent witness in the case lacked credibility, that person's testimony was more likely to be discounted by participants when they had read the transcript in story order, as opposed to issue order.

In a second study (1992, Experiment 2) participants were presented with blocks of evidence. One case pointed towards the defendant's guilt, a second towards innocence, and a third was neutral. Some participants were asked to give initial guilt or innocence ratings after each block of evidence, whereas others simply gave a global rating after having received all the information. Pennington and Hastie predicted that the latter condition would be more conducive to developing a story representation of the case. As predicted, they found that participants who gave just a global rating delivered verdicts more strongly in the direction of the preponderance of evidence.

They also compared the verdict ratings delivered by the item-by-item assessors to verdict ratings derived by applying Bayes' rule to the ratings at each stage (Bayes' rule is a normative rule designed to update beliefs in the light of new evidence; see Chapter 3). They found that item-by-item participants did not sufficiently update their beliefs in the light of evidence. Rather, the previous rating appeared to serve as an anchor from which participants did not sufficiently adjust.

Further evidence for the story model comes from the finding that participants more often show false recognition of trial evidence sentences when these are compatible with the story that they have constructed (Pennington & Hastie, 1988).

The acceptability of a given story is determined by two main *certainty principles* (Pennington and Hastie, 1993). First, the *coverage* principle argues that the acceptability of a story depends on how much of the evidence it accounts for. People will have little confidence in a story that fails to account for much of the evidence. The second principle is that of *coherence*, and this depends on a story's *consistency*, *plausibility*, and *completeness*. The degree of consistency depends upon the presence or absence of internal contradictions. Plausibility depends upon the degree of correspondence between the story and the decision maker's world knowledge. Completeness depends upon whether or not the story has all the parts that the decision maker expects to constitute the structure of a story. Where more than one coherent story has been generated to explain the evidence, then their lack of *uniqueness* will reduce the decision maker's confidence in each of them.

Mulligan and Hastie (2005) have shown that information order can affect financial investment judgments. They asked participants to forecast stock prices (Experiment 1) and make long-term investment decisions (Experiment 2) on the basis of information about various different companies. Each text contained six sentences corresponding to context, problem, reaction, goal, plan and outcome. For example:

(Context-Positive)	Longsfield Technologies is a prominent company, which has been highly successful in the development of emergency medical supplies.
(Problem-Positive)	Longsfield was recently acclaimed by a prestigious publication for its advanced triage kits.
(Reaction-Negative)	Longsfield executives have said that they will continue to work toward the development of medical supply kits as they have in the past.
(Goal-Neutral)	Longsfield announced that its new customised medical kits will be ready for market by early summer.
(Plan-Negative)	Longsfield has had to make spending cuts and will be downsizing their research and development department by six per cent.
(Outcome-Negative)	Longsfield's customised medical kits are delayed in testing and will not be able to achieve their early summer release date.

Participants either received the information in a story order (as above), in reverse of story order, or in a scrambled order. Receiving the information in story order, rather than a scrambled order, led outcome information to have the biggest impact on judgments and decisions. In the scrambled orders context and problem information had a larger impact than in the story order. In concluding, Mulligan and Hastie noted that knowing what information investors possess 'may not be enough to predict their behavior. It is also necessary to know *how* they acquired that information' (2005, p.154).

SUMMARY

In Toulmin's (1958) theory of everyday arguments the relevance of data is established by warrants that link them to the claim in question. A warrant is itself established by some form of backing (usually some fact). Claims can be weakened or overturned by rebuttals, and so it is sometimes necessary to qualify one's conclusions.

This theory forms the basis of a cognitive model of belief construction proposed by Curley and Benson (1994), though everyday argumentation sometimes falls short of ideal performance in a number of ways. A key weakness of everyday argumentation is the frequent failure to distinguish between theory (sometimes referred to as 'explanation') and evidence, and to provide pseudo-evidence instead of genuine evidence (e.g. Kuhn, 1991), although Brem and Rips (2000) have shown that people are more likely to use evidence if it is easily available.

The way in which people respond to evidence depends very much on their existing beliefs and the strength of their opinion. Where people hold very strong opinions they tend to maintain their beliefs in the face of contradictory evidence. They spend little time scrutinising arguments that are consistent with their own beliefs, but a great deal of time considering arguments incompatible with their beliefs and generating refutations of those arguments (disconfirmation bias). Beliefs can also affect the way that we perceive things.

When criticising arguments, people find it easier to question the truth of the premises or conclusion than to engage in the cognitive effort of attacking the link between the two. The ability to identify flaws in a written argument is associated with individual differences in text comprehension.

Many people seem to regard one-sided thinking as a virtue and believe that two-sided arguments indicate indecisiveness. Again, though, there are individual differences in this tendency and there are also circumstances (such as the courtroom) where it is advantageous to identify the other side's evidence. There are also individual differences in people's ability to reason from premises that they do not believe.

Studies of persuasion are consistent with a dual-process model of argument processing. If the audience is not motivated, or is less cognitively able, or if the message is perceived as unimportant, then the message is processed along the peripheral route. This means it may not be properly scrutinised and the audience may be unduly influenced by irrelevant factors, such as the attractiveness of the speaker. However, messages are more likely to be processed along the central route when they appear to be important, and when the recipient is motivated and/or has high cognitive ability. This means that people, under such circumstances, are more influenced by the strength of the arguments and less by other factors.

Finally, people appear to make sense of complex information by organising it into narrative form. This theory is known as explanation-based decision making (Hastie & Pennington, 2000; Pennington & Hastie, 1993). Its application to juror decision making is known as the story model. Jurors construct stories to explain the evidence, and the acceptability of stories is determined by two main certainty principles: coverage and coherence.

QUESTIONS

1. Construct a simple argument, showing how each element fits with Toulmin's model.

2. Do you think that the use of pseudoevidence is a major problem in people's thinking?

3. Design a study to examine the phenomenon of belief perseveration.

4. How might motivated reasoning affect students' willingness to seek out and act on feedback about their performance?

5. 'Happy moods are bad for good thinking.' Discuss.

6. Give a brief account of explanation-based decision making.

RECOMMENDED READING

Kuhn, D. (1991). *The skills of argument*. Cambridge: Cambridge University Press. Deanna Kuhn's book is a detailed look at the types of argumentation deployed when discussing everyday topics. In particular, it looks at the way in which people integrate – or fail to integrate – theory and evidence during the course of argumentation.

Walton, D.N. (1996). *Informal logic: A handbook for critical argumentation*. Cambridge: Cambridge University Press. This book provides a guide to the construction of good arguments and how to criticise bad ones.

6 Covariation, Causation, and Counterfactual Thinking

CHAPTER OUTLINE

INTRODUCTION

In this chapter I shall examine some important ways in which we make sense of our world. This involves making judgments about whether or not different objects or events are associated in some way and, furthermore, making judgments as to whether one event was the cause of another event. Some theories are based on the statistical relationship between events, whereas others emphasise a role for people's interpretation of evidence, as well as their thoughts about the possible mechanisms that may relate on event to another. Finally, I shall look at the role that counterfactual thinking plays in causal judgment, as well as the functions that counterfactual thinking has in directing behaviour and mediating people's feelings.

JUDGMENTS OF ASSOCIATION

Covariation

Many of the beliefs that we acquire are as a result of our spotting a relationship, real or imagined, between variables. Suppose a branch head of an insurance company notices that older salespeople tend to sell more on average (see Figure 6.1). These two variables, age and sales, are said to *covary*. The extent of covariation can be measured statistically by a correlation coefficient r, which ranges from −1 to +1:

- +1 represents a perfect correlation whereby an increase in one variable is accompanied by a linear increase in the other, such that if the points were plotted on a graph they would all fall upon a straight line;
- 0 represents the absence of any relationship; and
- −1 is a perfect negative correlation where one variable decreases as the other increases.

The value of r for the data in Figure 6.1 is 0.926, which represents a very strong, but not quite perfect, correlation.

When two variables are correlated we cannot say for sure that one variable causes the other. In the case of the salespeople, degree of sales success does not cause age, of course, and it could be that older people have acquired better sales skills. On the other hand, perhaps customers prefer to buy financial products from older people regardless of their sales ability. Another possibility is that a selection bias is operating: Maybe young sales staff who fail to make the grade leave the job, so that only the best salespeople remain in post on a long-term basis. These explanations are not exclusive: one or more explanation could be operating, or there may be some other – as yet unidentified – explanation of the data.

Another form of covariation is where two variables are dichotomous; that is, they take on just one of two values as opposed to a range of values (see Table 6.1). For example, suppose the organiser of an office party is trying to decide whether female employees are less likely to attend than male employees. Figures are available from the previous party and show that it was attended by 20 male and 10 female employees, but not attended by 10 male employees and 5 female employees (see Table 6.2a). On the basis of these data (and in the absence of any other knowledge) one would predict that females and males are equally likely to attend the office party. This is because, for both males and females, twice as many people attended as did not attend (there were more male attendees overall, because there are more male employees in total). Researchers have frequently assumed that the appropriate measure of association for a 2 × 2 table of this sort is the phi coefficient, φ.[1] In this case φ = 0, representing the fact that there is no relationship between party attendance and sex of employee. Suppose the previous attendance data had instead been as shown in Table 6.2b.

Table 6.1.

		Is variable Y present?	
		Yes	No
Is variable X present?	Yes	a	b
	No	c	d

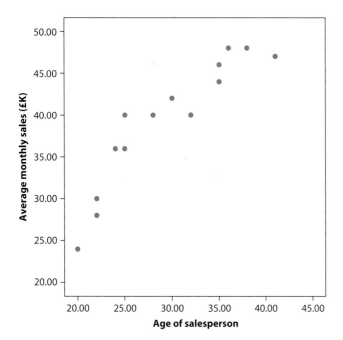

Figure 6.1. *A hypothetical relationship between salespersons' ages and average monthly sales*

Table 6.2a. *The number of male and female employees who attended the last office party*

		Attended office party?	
		Yes	No
Sex of employee	Male	20	10
	Female	10	5

Table 6.2b. *Revised figures for the number of male and female employees who attended the last office party*

		Attended office party?	
		Yes	No
Sex of employee	Male	8	22
	Female	12	3

These data indicate that more female employees attended the party than males ($\varphi = .506$). However, further investigation would be necessary in order to establish *why* this was the case.

Illusory correlation

One of the most frequently documented biases in covariation judgment is known as *illusory correlation*. This occurs when people see a correlation where none exists. One factor that can lead to illusory correlation is a high outcome base rate, a phenomenon that has parallels in Pavlovian learning (Vallée-Tourangeau *et al.*, 1998). Another factor relating to illusory correlation is prior belief. In one early study, Loren Chapman (1967) presented participants with a series of word pairs on a large screen. On the left side of the screen people saw either *bacon, lion, blossoms*, or *boat*. On the right side of the screen they saw *eggs, tiger*, or *notebook*. Although each left- and right-side word was paired equally often, people overestimated how often they saw *bacon-eggs* and *lion-tiger*.

Loren and Jean Chapman (1967, 1969, 1971) found that many clinical psychologists had false beliefs about the ability of projective tests to identify aspects of their patients' personalities. For example, the Draw-a-Person test asks patients to draw a human figure. Most clinicians in the Chapmans' study believed that there was a link between aspects of the drawings and their patients' personalities. For example, they believed that patients who were suspicious of others would draw figures with atypical eyes. Actually, the test is useless, though when naive college students were presented with randomly paired drawings and descriptions they reported the same illusory correlations as the clinicians.

The Chapmans reported similar results for the Rorschach inkblot test, in which patients are asked to say what they 'see' in an inkblot. According to the 32 clinicians studied, the five most common responses by homosexual men were (1) human or animal anal content, (2) feminine clothing, (3) male or female genitalia, (4) humans with sex confused, and (5) humans with sex uncertain. In fact, these responses do not distinguish between homosexual and heterosexual men. There are also two Rorschach cards where homosexual men do tend to respond differently. They more often report seeing monsters on Card IV and a figure that is 'part animal' and 'part human' on Card V. However, only two of the clinicians ever listed one of these valid cues.

A group of laypeople who were asked to report which of the cues came to mind when thinking about homosexuality rated the invalid cues as 'moderately strong' but the valid cues as just 'very slight'. Another group of laypeople were shown Rorschach cards that had homosexual 'symptoms' (e.g. 'has sexual feelings towards other men') or neutral symptoms (e.g. 'feels sad and depressed much of the time') written on one part of the card. Another part of the card recorded valid and invalid cues to homosexuality, as well as some 'filler' cues. The card series was constructed so that there was no correlation between symptoms and responses. However, the naive participants 'detected' the same illusory relationships reported by the clinicians: they associated the invalid cues, but not the valid or filler cues, with the homosexual symptoms.

Biased attention to certain types of information

Another bias that has been observed in covariation assessment is that people do not treat the four cells in Table 6.1 as equally important. Smedslund (1963) noted that people place too much importance on the co-occurrences of the two variables (the *a* cell) and concluded that 'normal adults with no training in statistics do not have a cognitive structure isomorphic with the concept of correlation' (p.172). However, this conclusion underestimates people's ability to distinguish relationships between variables, as demonstrated in the research described earlier. Subsequent research shows that the impact of the different cells on judgments follows the ordering $a > b \approx c > d$ (e.g. Kao & Wasserman, 1993; Levin *et al.*, 1993; Lipe, 1990; Wasserman *et al.*, 1990). In particular, this ordering shows that the joint presence of variables has the biggest impact on judgments and the joint absence has the smallest effect.[2]

McKenzie and Mikkelsen (2007) have proposed a model of covariation assessment that accounts for both the effects of prior belief and the differential impact of the four cells. They argue that participants, when presented with a laboratory task, do not merely attempt to *describe* a relationship between variables, as the experimenter intends; rather, they use their world knowledge to help them *induce* a conclusion about a possible relationship. The role of prior beliefs is normatively justifiable, and Bayes' Theorem (see Chapter 3) provides a method for updating beliefs in the light of new evidence. McKenzie and Mikkelsen's argument also utilises the *rarity assumption*, the idea that a variable that can either be present or absent tends to be absent more often than present (e.g. Anderson, 1990; McKenzie *et al.*, 2001). In short, when one already believes that two variables are much more likely to be absent than present, then further evidence of absence is not particularly informative. However, to encounter a conjunction of the variables would be surprising, hence informative, causing a bigger impact on one's judgment.

In a test of the Bayesian model, McKenzie and Mikkelsen (2007, Experiment 2) asked participants to select from the records of former high school students in order to help determine whether there was a relationship between students' 'emotional status' and whether or not they dropped out of school. In fact, few high school students are emotionally disturbed and few students drop out. Information about these two variables was framed differently across two conditions. In the *presence rare* condition participants were told that the records contained information about whether students were emotionally disturbed (Yes or No) and whether they had dropped out (Yes or No). The Yes/Yes combination in this condition represents a rare outcome and corresponds to cell *a* in Table 6.1. By contrast, cell *d* represents a common outcome.

In the *absence rare* condition participants were told that the records contained information about whether students were emotionally healthy (Yes or No) and whether they had graduated (Yes or No). The Yes/Yes combination in this condition also corresponds to cell *a* in Table 6.1, but now represents a common outcome, whereas cell *d* is the rare outcome.

Participants were presented with the 'randomly sampled' files of two former students, one of which corresponded to cell *a* and one to cell *d*, and asked to select the student that showed stronger support for a relationship between emotional status and high school outcome. As predicted by the Bayesian model, participants selected the cell *d* information much more frequently in the *absence rare* group than in the *presence rare* group.

Another group of participants received basically the same kind of task, only with abstract information to prevent the effect of prior knowledge. Very few people selected the cell *d* observation. This is consistent with the idea that people assume rarity unless they have information to the contrary.

JUDGMENTS OF CAUSATION

The Power PC theory

The coefficients *r* and φ are bi-directional in that they measure the dependence of event A on event B and the dependence of B on A. In some situations, researchers are more interested in a one-way dependence between cue A and outcome O. For this situation, the statistic ΔP is utilised. This calculates the probability of O occurring in the presence of cue A minus the probability of O occurring in the absence of cue A:

(6.1) $\Delta P = P(O \mid A) - P(O \mid {\sim}A) = a/(a+b) - c/(c+d)$

In Table 6.2, if we were interested in the extent to which being male predicts party attendance, then the relevant calculation would be

$8/(8+22) - 12/(12+3) = -.533.$

This calculation represents the probability of men's party attendance minus the probability of women's party attendance. The result is a negative contingency indicating that party attendance by men is less likely.

It should be noted that ΔP simply measures the degree of association between observed data, whereas a judgment about causality involves inferences that go beyond the data. For this reason and others (see e.g. Shanks, 2004), Cheng (1997) proposed the Power PC theory as a normative model of causal judgment. Where C is the target cause and E the effect, the extent to which a target cause facilitates an effect is determined by:

(6.2) $p = \dfrac{\Delta P}{1 - P(E \mid {\sim}C)}$ (Facilitative power)

According to this equation, a candidate cause is judged to have more causal power as $P(E \mid {\sim}C)$ increases. However, if $P(E \mid {\sim}C) = 1$ then no conclusion about causality can be inferred as the ratio is undefined. For preventative causal relationships the equation is:

Table 6.3. *Mean judgments of contingency*

P(E|C)	P(E|~C)				
	0.00	0.25	0.50	0.75	1.00
1.00	0.85	0.52	0.37	0.13	−0.03
0.75	0.65	0.43	0.16	0.06	−0.12
0.50	0.37	0.19	0.01	−0.19	−0.34
0.25	0.12	−0.10	−0.14	−0.37	−0.58
0.00	−0.08	−0.45	−0.51	−0.66	−0.75

Source: Wasserman *et al.* 1993, Experiment 3.

(6.3) $p = \dfrac{\Delta P}{P(E \mid {\sim}C)}$ (Preventative power)

In this case, people increase their estimates of preventative power as $P(E \mid {\sim}C)$ decreases.

A common research design in this area has been to study how well people learn the relationship between variables over a series of trials. In one study (Wasserman *et al.*, 1993) participants were asked to assess the extent to which pressing a telegraph key (cause C) caused a white light to flash (effect E). Depending upon the condition, pressing the key always, sometimes, or never made the light flash The probabilities for the light flashing after a key press, $P(E \mid C)$, are shown in Table 6.3. Again depending upon the condition, the light always, sometimes, or never flashed in the *absence* of a key press. These probabilities, $P(E \mid {\sim}C)$, are also shown in Table 6.3 The pairings of $P(E \mid C)$ and $P(E \mid {\sim}C)$ gave rise to a total of 25 conditions. Each condition lasted for one minute. If a participant did not press the key within a one-second interval then the light would flash with probability $P(E \mid {\sim}C)$. After completing each condition participants rated the causal effect of the key press on a scale from −100 ('prevents the light from occurring') to +100 ('causes the light to occur'), with 0 representing the absence of any effect.

The results of the study show that the participants were extremely sensitive to the conditional probabilities (Table 6.3). Consider the situation where a key press always caused the light to flash ($P(E \mid C) = 1$). In this situation people should have given a judgment of +100, indicating that a key press always causes the light to occur. However, with each increase in the likelihood of the light flashing in the *absence* of a key press ($P(E \mid {\sim}C)$), people's judgments of causality decreased.

The data indicate that people's judgments do not conform to the Power PC model. For example, in situations where $P(E \mid C) = 1$ people's judgments vary from +85 when $P(E \mid {\sim}C) = 0$, to +13 when $P(E \mid {\sim}C) = 0.75$, despite the fact that $p = 1$ in each condition. In fact, people's judgments are closer to Δp than to p (Shanks, 2004).

Most other studies have also found that people's judgments are closer to Δp than to p (Shanks, 2004). For example, in Lober and Shanks (2000, Experiments 1 and 2) p was held constant while ΔP

was varied. Contrary to the Power PC theory this manipulation led to differences in people's causal judgments. When participants were presented with summary information rather than a trial-by-trial presentation (2000, Experiments 4 and 5), participants' estimates were even more closely related to ΔP. Other researchers have also found that people are more sensitive to contingency information presented in a summary format (Kao & Wasserman, 1993; Ward & Jenkins, 1965). Lober and Shanks did conduct one trial-by-trial experiment, however, where they found that people's judgments varied as ΔP was held constant and p manipulated, consistent with the Power PC theory, although a summary version (2000, Experiment 6) did not replicate this finding.

Rescorla–Wagner theory

Lober and Shanks argue that all of these findings are consistent with a version of the Rescorla–Wagner theory of learning (Rescorla & Wagner, 1972). This is a descriptive theory that explains how associations develop between representations of stimuli over a series of exposures to those stimuli. In short, exposure to stimuli causes a change in associative strength that depends upon (a) the rate of learning, and (b) the difference between the maximum possible associative strength (*asymptote*) and the current strength. As applied to causal learning tasks, the Rescorla–Wagner theory can be expressed in the equation:

(6.4) $\Delta V = \alpha\beta(\lambda - \sum V)$

where ΔV represents the change in the associative strength between cause and effect (or cue and outcome), λ is the maximum possible associative strength, $\sum V$ is the associative strength on the current trial, and α and β are learning rate parameters representing the associability of the cause and effect (or cue and outcome) respectively.[3] As well as explaining many effects in animal learning, Rescorla–Wagner theory also accounts for many effects in human causal learning. Nonetheless, there are findings that the theory cannot comfortably accommodate without modification and there are also other models that have been proposed (seven models are reviewed in Perales & Shanks, 2003).

Several studies have also noted the existence of subgroups among participants who adopt different judgment strategies. Lober and Shanks (2000, Experiment 2) observed a small minority of participants who behaved exactly as predicted by Power PC theory: post-test questioning revealed that they realised that the difference between $P(E\,|\,C)$ and $P(E\,|\,\sim C)$ was uninformative when $P(E\,|\,C)$ was 1.0. Furthermore, all participants in this study, and most in Anderson and Sheu (1995), said that they were trying to compute and compare $P(E\,|\,C)$ and $P(E\,|\,\sim C)$. The latter study also identified a minority who reported calculating only $P(E\,|\,C)$. This led Anderson (2000, p.357) to write:

> Subjects behaved in a rather conscious hypothesis-testing manner, which happened to be mimicked by the Rescorla–Wagner theory. It is quite plausible that lower organisms are incapable of such conscious calculations but do behave in accord with the Rescorla–Wagner theory.

Evidence and causal mechanisms

Clearly, not all causal judgments are made on the basis of a long series of learning trials (as I hope a moment's thought should confirm). Accordingly, some researchers have taken a different approach to the study of causal judgment. For example, Schustack and Sternberg (1981) gave people causal scenarios like the one below:

A market analyst noted that among cosmetic manufacturers:

In Company 1
The office staff of the company organized and joined a union. The company's major product was under suspicion as a carcinogen.
There was a drastic drop in the value of the company's stock.

In Company 2
The office staff of the company did not organize or join a union. The company's major product was under suspicion as a carcinogen.
There was a drastic drop in the value of the company's stock.

In Company 3
Illegal campaign contributions were traced to the company's managers.
The company's major product was not under suspicion as a carcinogen.
There was no drastic drop in the value of the company's stock.

What is the probability that for some other cosmetic manufacturer, stock values would drop drastically if the company's major product were under suspicion as a carcinogen?

Schustack and Sternberg reported that people used five types of evidence when making their judgments. First, the hypothesis that a target event causes a particular outcome is confirmed by the joint presence of the event and the outcome (the event is sufficient for the outcome). Second, the hypothesis is disconfirmed by the presence of the target event and the absence of the outcome (the event is not sufficient for the outcome). Third, the hypothesis is disconfirmed by the absence of the target event and the presence of the outcome (the event is not necessary for the outcome). Fourth, the hypothesis is confirmed by the joint absence of target event and outcome (the event is necessary for the outcome). Fifth, the target hypothesis is disconfirmed by the strength of alternative hypotheses.

Other researchers have noted that, when people think about causation, they are not merely interested in the extent to which events covary; rather, they are particularly interested in the specific mechanism(s) that leads to an outcome. In fact, spotting covariance relationships without understanding causal mechanisms can have particularly unfortunate consequences (Box 6.1). Ahn *et al.* (1995, Experiment 1) presented participants with sentences such as 'Flight 921 crashed in Lincoln, Nebraska last winter.' They were given the opportunity to ask any questions they liked in order to

BOX 6.1. IDENTIFYING COVARIANCE RELATIONSHIPS WITHOUT UNDERSTANDING CAUSAL MECHANISMS – THE CASE OF CARGO CULTS[4]

Since the late 19th century, Melanesia has experienced a number of movements known as cargo cults. Although these have mostly died out now, they originally developed among some groups of islanders after they encountered outsiders for the first time. What typically happened was that after a period of contact with the newcomers, the islanders eventually realised that these people were not gods, but that their power came from their equipment (or 'cargo'). They did not understand anything of Western manufacturing and often did not believe what the visitors told them about the origin of these goods. Subsequently, the islanders would reconstruct symbols that they associated with the newcomers in the belief that these would lead to the appearance of cargo.

The best-known examples of this occurred during and after the Second World War, when many American troops were stationed in Melanesia during their campaign against Japan. Many islanders had never seen either Westerners or Japanese before, and were astonished to see the arrival of huge quantities of clothes, medicine, canned food, tents, weapons, and so on to feed and equip the military personnel. After the war, the Americans abandoned their airbases and the cargo no longer arrived from the skies.

In order to facilitate the arrival of cargo, the islanders reconstructed the artefacts they had seen the Americans use and also imitated their practices. They would build a hut by the side of a landing strip and sit a man in it (the 'controller') wearing wood-carved 'headphones' with bits of bamboo sticking out of them like antennae. They would light signal fires by the side of the runway and wait for the aircraft to arrive. Sometimes they would create their own landing strips in the hope of attracting more planes. They would also march up and down holding twigs for rifles, wearing military-style insignia, and with the letters 'USA' painted on their bodies.

In short, the cargo cults associated the paraphernalia of the visitors with the arrival of the cargo, but without correctly understanding the mechanism by which the cargo arrived. They seemed to have believed that the cargos were actually gifts from the gods as a reward for various ritual practices (such as marching in uniform).

The Nobel prize-winning physicist Richard Feynman famously compared astrology, various kinds of mysticism, and other pseudo-sciences to the cargo cults, coining the term 'cargo cult science'. He regarded research into these areas as having many of the trappings of science but without the rigour (Feynman, 1986).

help figure out the cause of the event and, finally, to state the most likely cause of the event. About two thirds of participants asked questions that were concerned with causal mechanisms, and very few asked covariation-type questions (even when instructions attempted to prompt such questions). Accordingly, 83 per cent of final explanations were mechanism explanations. In another study (1995, Experiment 4), Ahn *et al.* presented people with various combinations of covariation and mechanism statements relating to events, for example:

Kim had a traffic accident last night
Kim is near-sighted and tends not to wear her glasses while driving.
Traffic accidents were much more likely last night than on other nights.

Participants were asked to rate the extent to which each factor was responsible for the target event (in this case, Kim's traffic accident). Results showed that a factor was assigned a stronger causal status when it was supported by mechanism information.

Fugelsang and Thompson (2003) found that quantitative co-variation data had a different effect on people's causal beliefs as a function of (a) people's initial beliefs about a candidate cause, and (b) whether people had previously been exposed to mechanism information or non-quantitative covariation information (this simply stated that previous research had found a correlation between candidate cause and outcome). For people previously

exposed to non-quantitative covariation information, subsequent quantitative information had equal impact on people who had a high or a low belief in the causal effect of some factor. However, for people previously exposed to mechanism information, quantit-ative covariation data had a bigger impact when the candidate was already considered highly believable. Furthermore, introspective ratings showed that participants had a reasonable awareness of the impact of covariation data on their judgments, but very little awareness (if any) of the impact their own prior beliefs had.[5]

Fugelsang and Thompson argued that the first stage of causal judgment involves the search for a plausible mechanism. This search is basically a useful heuristic that results in a manageable number of causal candidates for which covariation is considered. If a plausible mechanism can be identified then covariation information is given more weight. However, where people are asked to judge an unbelievable causal candidate, they may introduce more plausible alternatives into their choice set. This will then dilute the effect of covariation data on the unbelievable candidate. The fact that people are largely unaware of the impact of their own prior beliefs is consistent with the notion that causal beliefs are recruited automatically and that their application may be outside the reasoner's conscious control (see also White, 1989).

Another study of causal reasoning (Fugelsang & Dunbar, 2005) found that different areas of the brain were activated when theory and data were inconsistent compared to when they were consistent. Consistent theory and data referred either to (1) plausible theory and strong data, or (2) implausible theory and weak data. Similarly, inconsistent theory and data referred either to (1) plausible theory and weak data, or (2) implausible theory and strong data. Using functional magnetic resonance imaging (fMRI), the authors found that theory–data consistency was associated with activation in brain regions associated with learning and memory, including the caudate[6] and parahippocampal gyrus. By contrast, theory–data inconsistency activated areas associated with error detection and conflict monitoring, including the left dorsolateral prefrontal cortex, dorsal regions of the anterior cingulate cortex, and the precuneus.

Mental models and mental simulation

Related to the notion that people may consider plausible mechanisms underlying causality is the notion of *mental simulation*. The philosopher Kenneth Craik (1943) proposed that people's understanding of the external world is represented in internal models (what we now call *mental models*). These models enable us to predict the outcomes of actions by running a mental simulation of reality. However, the accuracy of one's predictions will depend on how accurately one's mental model depicts reality.

For instance, people have different ideas about how thermostats work (Kempton, 1986). One view of the thermostat is that it controls the relative proportion of the time that the heating is on. Another view is that the thermostat controls how much heat is produced. Both of these mental models predict that in order to heat a room most quickly you need to turn the thermostat up to maximum. In fact, neither model is correct. The thermostat simply turns the heating off or fully on. When the heating is on, it stays on until the temperature reaches the temperature setting on the thermostat. Then it turns the heating off. As Norman (2002[1988], p.38) has pointed out, we do not have any direct evidence of how a thermostat works. All we know is that, if our room is too cold, then we turn up the thermostat and eventually we feel warmer.

Several studies have found that asking people to imagine or explain a causal scenario increases the perceived probability of that scenario (Carroll, 1978; Gregory *et al.*, 1982; Koehler, 1991). However, the perceived probability may be reduced when people also consider alternative scenarios. Dougherty *et al.* (1997) asked people to read a story about the death of a firefighter tackling a blaze. Although the story did not mention the cause of death, the text made smoke inhalation sound like the most salient cause. Participants were asked to rate the likelihood of this cause and to list all the thoughts and ideas they had considered while thinking about this question. As predicted, people whose thought listings indicated a single causal scenario gave a higher probability to death by smoke inhalation than did people who produced more than one causal scenario.

A further study investigated how the likelihood of alternative causes affected the generation of scenarios. Focal scenarios were judged most likely when alternatives were made unlikely in this way (and judged least likely when alternatives were made likely).

Thought-listing revealed that people were most likely to consider alternative causes when those alternatives were made likely. When they were made unlikely, people still considered those alternatives but then rejected them (counterfactual thoughts about the alternatives were most frequent in these circumstances). Dougherty *et al.* suggested that the MINERVA-DM model (see Chapter 3) may account for their findings. Specifically, they argued that people probe memory with the various causal scenarios they consider. The likelihood of the focal scenario depends on how many scenarios are considered and the similarity between these and any instances stored in memory. More detailed scenarios will increase the similarity between the memory probe and stored instances.

COUNTERFACTUAL THINKING

Counterfactual thinking and causation

In Chapter 5 we saw that asking people to imagine how events might have turned out differently can sometimes lead to a reduction in hindsight bias. This kind of thinking – thinking about alternatives to past events – is called counterfactual thinking. It is another of the ways in which we try to make sense of things. In particular, counterfactual thinking is important for judgments of causation (Mackie, 1974). When making a judgment about whether A causes B, it is not enough that we repeatedly observe that B follows A, but we also make a judgment about whether B would have occurred in the absence of A.

One of the most common triggers for spontaneous counterfactual thinking is *negative affect*. For example, the worse that parents feel shortly after the death of a child (whether from exceptional or unexceptional circumstances), the more they report counterfactual thinking over a year later (Davis *et al.*, 1995). Another trigger for counterfactual thinking is *outcome closeness*, which is the perceived nearness to some outcome occurring. For instance, a traveller who misses his plane by five minutes is more likely to generate counterfactual thoughts than one who missed his plane by an hour (e.g. Kahneman & Tversky, 1982).

Normality and mutation

Once counterfactual thinking is activated, the construction of a counterfactual depends on forming a mental representation of *normality* and then *mutating* the exceptional event in order to reconstruct normality (Kahneman & Miller, 1986). For instance, in a study by Kahneman & Tversky (1982) participants learned that Mr Jones had been killed by a drunken driver while on his way home. People who were told that Mr Jones had left work on time but taken a different route home from usual said that he would still be alive if he had gone home by his usual route. People who were told that he had left work early but travelled by his usual route said that he would still be alive if he had left work at his usual time. Thus, in both cases people tended to mutate the exceptional event.

Some authors have reported that counterfactuals are more likely to involve actions than inactions. For example Kahneman & Tversky (1982) presented participants with the following scenario:

> Mr Paul owns shares in company A. During the past year he considered switching to stock in company B, but he decided against it. He now finds out that he would have been better off by $1200 if he had switched to the stock of company B. Mr George owned shares in company B. During the past year he switched to stock in company A. he now finds that he would have been better off by $1200 if he had kept his stock in company B. Who feels greater regret?

Of the participants, 92 per cent said that Mr George would feel greater regret. However, the existence of counterfactual thinking was not measured directly in this study, a criticism which has been applied to several other studies of action–inaction (for a review see Roese, 1997). Another factor affecting the content of counterfactual thoughts is *controllability*. Antecedents that are perceived to be more controllable appear to be more mutable (Miller *et al.*, 1990; N'gbala & Branscombe, 1995).

The functions of counterfactual thinking

Roese (1994) has proposed that counterfactual thinking is functional in at least two ways: it has a *preparative function* (helping us to avoid the recurrence of negative outcomes) and an *affective* function (making us feel better). Frequently, it is the failure to achieve some goal that leads to negative affect. This in turn often activates *upward* counterfactual thinking – that is, thoughts about how things could have been better. For example, after doing badly in an exam Mike thinks to himself 'If only I hadn't gone out drinking the night before I would have got a better grade.' This is an example of a *subtractive* upward counterfactual, because the conditional removes the factual antecedent in order to reconstruct reality. More useful from the preparative viewpoint are *additive* upward counterfactuals that provide a new antecedent, for example, 'If I had studied harder then I would have got a better grade.' Counterfactuals can also involve *downward* comparison, for example, 'If I had not set my alarm clock I would have missed the exam altogether' (downward and subtractive), or 'If I had drunk any more the night before I would have been too sick to make the exam' (downward and additive).

The preparative value of upward counterfactuals was shown by Roese (1994, Experiment 2). Students were asked to list their thoughts about a recent exam that had gone badly; they also completed a mood questionnaire and, finally, they rated their future intentions as regards studying, consulting with professors, and attending lectures. Compared to a control group who had not listed their thoughts, students who listed the kind of positive behaviours that would have led to better performance (upward counterfactuals) also showed stronger intentions to perform success-facilitating behaviours in future. By contrast, students who listed the kind of behaviours that would have made things worse (downward counterfactuals) showed no greater intentions compared to the control group. On the other hand, people who generated downward counterfactuals reported more positive feelings on the mood scale.

There was no effect of additive vs. subtractive counterfactuals in this study, but this was examined further in another study where actual future behaviours were assessed, rather than just intentions. In this study participants were awarded points for solving a series of anagrams on a computer. They were able to make decisions about various aspects of the task: the gap between presentations, the topic area, and difficulty level. Participants were told that the solution of difficult anagrams would be rewarded with bonus points, but in fact all participants received fairly difficult anagrams and no bonus points were awarded. After completing 10 anagrams participants were told their true score, but they were also told that the average score was 53 points higher than their own score and that they were ranked 37 out of 45 participants. Except for a control group, participants were then asked to list their thoughts, as in the previous study. Finally, participants completed a second set of 10 anagrams. People who had listed upward counterfactuals performed significantly better on the second set of anagrams than people who listed downward counterfactuals (who performed about the same as the control group). Additive counterfactuals were associated with better performance than subtractive counterfactuals (that were non-significantly lower than the control group).

In these studies participants were instructed to list particular types of counterfactuals. In reality, though, individuals choose to construct one type or another. There may be a trade-off when we do this (Roese, 1994). Should we generate downward counterfactuals and make ourselves feel better, at least in the short term? Or should we generate upward counterfactuals and be better prepared for other events in the long-term?

SUMMARY

Studies of covariation judgments have found that people sometimes perceive an illusory correlation; that is, a relationship where none exists. This is particularly the case were people have prior beliefs about the events in question. People also seem to attend more to certain relevant items of information than others: notably, they place more emphasis on the joint presence of two events rather than other possible conjunctions. Nonetheless, there may be a normative justification for this.

Many studies of causal judgment have presented people with a series of paired events that requires them to judge whether one event was the cause of the other. Two prominent theories of such judgments are the Power PC theory and the Rescorla–Wagner theory. The evidence for both is mixed, and there is evidence for the existence of different judgment strategies among participants.

Other researchers have focused more on the way that people interpret evidence, particularly evidence about causal mechanisms. Some research indicates that people are more likely to use covariation information if they have already identified a plausible causal mechanism.

People may also engage in mental simulation when thinking about possible causes. In fact, simply thinking about a causal scenario can increase the likelihood that people attach to that scenario. The MINERVA-DM model proposes that people compare scenarios with instances stored in memory. A more detailed scenario is likely to enhance the match with stored instances, thereby influencing the judgment of likelihood.

People's judgments of causality may also be affected by their mental models. People's mental models are often incomplete or incorrect and can have an unfortunate effect on behaviour. For instance, people often have an incorrect understanding of how thermostats work, leading them to operate the device incorrectly.

Counterfactual thinking also seems to play a role in causal judgment. It is typically triggered by negative affect, often following an exceptional event. Thinking about how things might have happened differently may have the function of making people adapt their behaviour towards a more successful outcome in future situations. It also appears to help people moderate their feelings after an event.

QUESTIONS

1. Design your own study to investigate the phenomenon of illusory correlation.

2. In relation to causal judgment, what is meant by 'facilitative power' and 'preventative power'?

3. Evaluate the Power PC theory of causal judgment.

4. What role do people's beliefs about mechanisms play in causal judgment?

5. Briefly outline the concept of mental models in relation to causal judgment.

6. According to Roese, what are the functions of counterfactual thinking?

NOTES

1. $\varphi = \dfrac{ad - bc}{\sqrt{ab + cd + ac + bd}}$

2. Vallée-Tourangeau *et al.* (1998) have noted the way in which many textbook accounts of covariation assessment present oversimplified accounts that frequently suggest people's judgments are *only* based on cell A. They also note weaknesses in Smedslund's original research and report a modified replication that obtained more positive results.

3. The Greek letters used in this equation are pronounced as follows: Δ = delta, α = alpha, β = beta, λ = lambda, and Σ = sigma.

4. The description here is largely based on the accounts at http://en.wikipedia.org/wiki/Cargo_cult (retrieved 12 Feb. 2007) and by Glines (1991).

5. There is considerable evidence that people lack insight into the cognitive processes that underlie their judgments. Thus, they may also be unaware of external, as well as internal, influences on their judgments. Our explanations for our judgments and behaviours are essentially post hoc rationalisations. This important topic will be explored in more depth in Chapter 15.

6. The caudate is part of a structure known as the basal ganglia. Its role in learning and intuitive thinking will be further discussed in Chapter 15.

RECOMMENDED READING

Norman, D.A. (2002). *The design of everyday things*. New York: Basic Books. Originally published in 1988 as *The psychology of everyday things*. This is one of my favourite books. It is the kind of book that really does make you see the world in a different way. Norman also talks about the idea of mental models, which is one of the ideas I have described in this chapter.

Roese, N. (1995). *What might have been: The social psychology of counterfactual thinking*. Mahwah, NJ: Erlbaum.

7 Decision Making under Risk and Uncertainty

KEY TERMS

Allais paradox
ambiguity aversion
certainty effect
coefficient of variation
cumulative prospect theory
decision by sampling
decision field theory
disappointment
expected utility
expected value
framing effects
functional magnetic
    resonance imaging (fMRI)
ignorance aversion
loss aversion
possibility effect
priority heuristic
probability weighting
    function
prospect theory
reflection effect
risk sensitivity
St Petersburg paradox
source preference
subadditivity
two-stage model
value weighting function
Weber's Law

CHAPTER OUTLINE

Before reading any further, please give your responses to the following problems (for numerical outcomes, just assume that the units are the major units of your own national currency).

Problem 1
Which would you prefer:

A. A certain gain of 3000   B. An 80 per cent chance of gaining 4000, otherwise nothing

Problem 2
Which would you prefer:

A. A 0.1 per cent chance of gaining 5000   B. A certain gain of 5

Problem 3
Which of the following situations would you prefer:

Situation A:
100 million for certain

Situation B:
A 10 per cent chance of 500 million
An 89 per cent chance of 100 million
A 1 per cent chance of nothing

Problem 4
Which of the following situations would you prefer:

Situation C:
An 11 per cent chance of 100 million
An 89 per cent chance of nothing

Situation D:
A 10 per cent chance of 500 million
A 90 per cent chance of nothing

Problem 5
In addition to whatever you own, you have been given 1000. You are now asked to choose between:

A. A 50 per cent chance of 1000, otherwise nothing.   B. 500 for certain

Problem 6
In addition to whatever you own, you have been given 2000. You are now asked to choose between:

C. A 50 per cent chance of losing 1000, otherwise nothing.   D. Losing 500 for certain.

INTRODUCTION

Each problem shown above is a *risky* decision. Technically speaking, this means that particular outcomes occur only with a stated probability. Most economic and psychological accounts of risky decision making have taken a quantitative approach, and assume that when people make risky decisions they are trying to maximise something such as expected value or expected utility. However, economic theories fail to capture much of human decision-making behaviour. By contrast, prospect theory is a modification of expected utility theory that accounts for many of the violations of that theory.

Following on from prospect theory, I take a short excursion into the neuroscience of valuation to show how brain-imaging research is producing findings that relate to cognitive theories about decision making, including prospect theory.

In most everyday decisions probabilities are unknown. I describe two approaches to decision making under uncertainty. One of these is a two-stage model that combines support theory with a later development of prospect theory, known as cumulative prospect theory. The second approach is referred to as risk sensitivity theory, and has developed from the literature on optimal foraging in animals.

Many other theories of decision making have been proposed, some of them in opposition to prospect theory and some as a supplement to it. Process models of decision making are concerned with the stages of thinking that lead up to a decision. Two examples I describe here are decision field theory and the priority heuristic.

DECISIONS UNDER RISK (1): EXPECTED VALUE THEORY AND EXPECTED UTILITY THEORY

Value, utility, and the St Petersburg paradox

The start of this chapter showed a number of decision problems involving described probabilities and monetary outcomes. According to *expected value theory* the optimum action on such problems can be determined calculating the value of each possible outcome and weighting those outcomes by their probability of occurrence (i.e. multiply the outcomes by their probabilities). Then you choose the course of action with the highest *expected value*. For example, which of the following gambles would you prefer?

1. A 70 per cent chance of £100, otherwise nothing.

2. A 35 per cent chance of £250, otherwise nothing.

According to the criterion of expected monetary value, Gamble 2 is the better bet because it has an expected value of £87.50 (.35 × 250) whereas Gamble 1 has an expected value of £70 (.7 × 100).

However, Daniel Bernoulli (1954[1738]) observed that people do not behave as though they are maximising expected value. He described a game known as the St Petersburg paradox. Suppose I toss a fair coin and keep on tossing it until it lands on heads. If it lands on heads on the first toss, the game ends and you win one euro. If it does not land on heads until the second toss, then the game ends on the second toss and you win two euros. If it lands on

heads on the third toss then the game ends and you win four euros. With every toss that the game continues the amount that I must pay you doubles. The question is, how much would you be willing to pay me in order to participate in this game?

Based on the concept of expected value you should be willing to pay me quite a large sum of money because the game itself has *infinite* expected value.[1] Bernoulli argued that a point would come in the game where further tosses of the coin would barely add to the *utility* that would accrue if the game ended at that point (where utility refers to pleasure or usefulness).

This idea – referred to as diminishing marginal utility for gains – is shown graphically in Figure 7.1. As a person's wealth increases, each extra unit of money adds utility but by less than the previous unit. This means that more wealth is always better, but by the same token an increase in wealth that would make a poor person very happy will not have the same utility for someone who is very wealthy. The property of diminishing marginal utility is consistent with Weber's Law, a psychological law that is normally applied to judgments of physical magnitude (see Box 7.1).

Bernoulli's theory explains why even bets are unattractive. Suppose two men are playing a game of chance in which there is

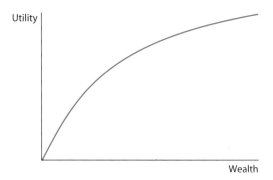

Figure 7.1. *The utility of wealth*
Source: Bernoulli 1954[1738].

BOX 7.1.   WEBER'S LAW AND THE UTILITY FUNCTION

One intriguing aspect of Figure 7.1 is that this curve resembles the curves that are produced in magnitude estimation studies. For example, if we are asked to judge the heaviness of various weights, and our estimates are plotted against the actual weights, then we get a graph rather like Figure 7.1. That is, as the weights become heavier we are less able to accurately assess further increases. If, instead of plotting the raw amounts, we plot the logarithm of the magnitude estimate against the logarithm of the stimulus intensity we get a straight line. The relationship between magnitude estimate and stimulus intensity is that of a *power law*, as described by the equation $P = KS^n$, whereby perceived magnitude, P, equals a constant , K, times the stimulus intensity, S, raised to a power, n.

Some studies have asked people to make direct comparisons between two stimuli. Suppose George is asked to hold a weight in each hand. If he can tell the difference between a weight of 100 grams and a weight of 102 grams, but not a smaller

difference, then his *difference threshold* for a 100 gram weight is 2 grams. However, George is unable to tell the difference between a 200 gram weight and a 202 gram weight, which is also a difference of 2 grams. In fact, his difference threshold for a 200 gram weight turns out to be 4 grams.

For each comparison, if we divide the difference threshold by the stimulus weight, we get the same figure:

$2/100 = 0.02$ and $4/200 = 0.02$

The relationship between difference threshold and stimulus magnitude is known as *Weber's Law* and the constant that results is known as *Weber's Fraction* (after Ernst Weber, 1795–1878; see Goldstein, 2007). The observation that the utility function in Figure 7.1 resembles judgments about other stimuli suggests that people respond to money in the same way that they seem to respond to sensory stimuli.

---

a 50/50 chance of winning or losing. Each man is worth £10,000 and each bets £5000 on the game. For each man there is a 50/50 chance of ending up worth either £15,000 or £5000, with the expected outcome being (£15,000 + £5000)/2 = £10,000. Thus, the expectation is one of no change. However, the utility curve says that the loss of £5000 has greater negative utility than the gain of £5000 has positive utility – that is, the potential loss looms larger than the potential gain. Therefore, most people would be unwilling to take the bet – they are risk averse.

Whereas expected value theory says that rational decision makers should weight monetary outcomes by the probability of their occurrence, expected utility theory says that rational decision makers should weight the utilities of outcomes by their probability of occurrence. The concept of utility has the advantage of being applicable to things other than money, although it has the disadvantage of not being directly measurable. Nonetheless, techniques do exist for eliciting people's utility functions (e.g. Goodwin & Wright, 2004). The notion that people *are* utility maximisers has become widespread in economics and in evolutionary biology.

Three failures of expected utility theory

Risk-seeking versus risk-averse behaviour Although the utility function in Figure 7.1 suggests risk aversion, utility theory allows that some people may have a different utility function. Nonetheless, they are still considered rational as long as they attempt to maximise expected utility. In practice, though, people are widely assumed to be risk averse. However, contrary to this assumption, research reported by Kahneman and Tversky (1979,

1992) has indicated a fourfold pattern of risk attitudes depending on whether outcomes are gains or losses, and whether probabilities are small or medium-to-large.

Problems 1–6 below, first mentioned at the start of the chapter, are taken from Kahneman and Tversky (1979). The numbers in round brackets read as (outcome, probability) and the numbers in square brackets are the percentage of people choosing each option. In Problem 1, most people prefer a sure gain of 3000 over an 80 per cent chance to gain 4000. The expected value of the risky option is 3200, which is more than for the sure thing, hence people are risk averse in their choice. However, when the outcomes are losses rather than gains people mostly choose the risky option rather than the sure loss (Problem 1'). In this case, the risky option has the worse expected value (−3200) hence the majority choice is risk-seeking.

These two problems involve large probabilities. However, when the probabilities involved are very small (Problems 2 and 2'), then people are risk-seeking for gains and risk averse for losses.

Problem 1 | Problem 1'

	(4000, .80) < (3000)			(−4000, .80) > (−3000)	
N = 95	[20]	[80]	N = 95	[92]	[8]

Problem 2 | Problem 2'

	(5000, .001) > (5)			(−5000, .001) < (−5)	
N = 72	[72]	[28]	N = 72	[17]	[83]

Kahneman and Tversky (1992) confirmed this pattern of responses in a series of two-outcome gambles where there were no sure things (each outcome being probabilistic). Thus, the assumption of risk aversion is not supported.

The Allais paradox: evidence that people do not maximise expected utility Another problem with expected utility theory is that people do not always choose decision options that maximise expected utility. This was demonstrated by Allais (1953, 1990). Consider again Problems 3 and 4 from the start of the chapter:

<u>Problem 3</u>
Which of the following situations would you prefer:

Situation A:
100 million for certain

Situation B:
A 10 per cent chance of 500 million
An 89 per cent chance of 100 million
A 1 per cent chance of nothing

<u>Problem 4</u>
Which of the following situations would you prefer:

Situation C:
An 11 per cent chance of 100 million
An 89 per cent chance of nothing

Situation D:
A 10 per cent chance of 500 million
A 90 per cent chance of nothing

Most people say that they prefer A to B in Problem 3 and D to C in Problem 4 (Slovic & Tversky, 1974). However, this is not a choice that would be made by someone maximising utility. Why is this? Firstly, bearing in mind that there is no utility for a zero outcome we can express the preference for A over B as follows:

$$u(100 \text{ million}) > 0.89\, u(100 \text{ million}) + 0.1\, u(500 \text{ million})$$

Subtracting 0.89 u(100million) from both sides of the inequality leaves us with:

$$.11\, u(100 \text{ million}) > 0.1\, u(500 \text{ million})$$

However, if we describe the preference for D over C in the same fashion, we now get the reverse inequality:

$$.11\, u(100 \text{ million}) < 0.1\, u(500 \text{ million})$$

In fact, what I have just shown is that options C and D in Problem 2 are actually obtained by subtracting an 89 per cent chance of 100 million from both A and B. The fact that preferences change when a common element is removed from A and B violates an axiom of expected utility theory, known as Savage's (1954) sure-thing principle (see Box 7.2). This says that people's choices should be based upon those attributes of options that *differ*: attributes that are the same in both options should not affect choice. The

BOX 7.2.   THE ALLAIS PARADOX AND SAVAGE'S SURE-THING PRINCIPLE

Another way of thinking about the Allais problem is to imagine the situations as lotteries in which the probabilities are represented by numbered balls (Table 7.1). A person taking part in one of these four lotteries would simply be choosing a ball at random from an urn. The interesting column in Table 7.1 is the last one, showing the outcome that would occur if a person were to select a ball numbered between 12 and 100 inclusive (representing 89 per cent probability). In Lottery A, a player would win 100 million if they picked a ball from 12 to 100, or any other ball besides. Similarly, in Lottery B a player will also win 100 million if they pick any ball from 12 to 100. Thus, when deciding whether to play Lottery A or B a person should not consider what might happen if they pick a ball from 12 to 100 because the outcome would be the same in each case (the sure-thing principle).

Now consider Lotteries C and D. Once again, for balls 12 to 100 the outcomes are identical for each lottery, except that now the outcome is to win nothing. Again, balls 12 to 100 do not need to be considered when deciding which lottery to play. However, if you now blank out this last column in Table 7.1 (equivalent to applying the sure-thing principle) you will see that the choice between A and B is exactly the same as the choice between C and D.

Rather than conclude that people are irrational, Allais himself seems to have regarded the 'anomalous' preferences as so compelling that he drew the conclusion that it is the theory, rather than people, that is at fault. Student participants do not find Savage's axiom especially compelling. A study reported by Slovic and Tversky (1974) found that most people continued to make paradoxical choices even after they had heard arguments advocating Savage's position. In a second study people heard arguments both for and against the sure-thing principle *prior* to making a choice. More people rated the Allais argument as more compelling than Savage's (51 per cent vs. 42 per cent). Curiously, given the preference for Allais's argument, more people made choices consistent with the sure-thing principle (61 per cent) rather than inconsistent with it (35 per cent). However, comments by some subjects indicated that their choices satisfied the sure-thing principle because they felt Allais's recommendation was too conservative, and not because they found Savage's argument more compelling.

Table 7.1. *The Allais paradox represented as a lottery*

	Ball numbers		
	1	*2–11*	*12–100*
<u>Situation 1</u>			
Lottery A	100 million	100 million	100 million
Lottery B	Nothing	500 million	100 million
<u>Situation 2</u>			
Lottery C	100 million	100 million	Nothing
Lottery D	Nothing	500 million	Nothing

preference pattern in Allais's problem also indicates, of course, that people are not maximising expected utility.

Kahneman and Tversky (1979) described performance on the Allais problem as representing a *certainty effect*. In other words, a switch from certainty to uncertainty (or vice versa) exerts a particularly large effect on people's preferences.

Evidence that people do not integrate prospects with existing assets A third way in which expected utility fails to describe how people think about decisions is its assumption that they integrate possible outcomes (prospects) with their current assets. Kahneman and Tversky presented two different groups of participants with one of the following problems:

Problem 5
In addition to whatever you own, you have been given 1000. You are now asked to choose between

A.   (1000, .50),   and   B. (500)
N = 70   [16]   [84]

Problem 6
In addition to whatever you own, you have been given 2,000. You are now asked to choose between:

C.   (−1000, .50),   and   D. (−500)
N = 68   [69]   [31]

The choice percentages shown in square brackets show a reflection effect. However, a person behaving according to utility theory should either choose A and C or B and D. Utility theory says that we should integrate decision outcomes with our current assets. If we do this we see that the outcomes for both A and C are (2000, .50; 1000, .50) and the outcomes for B and D are (1500). It seems that people are not integrating their assets and outcomes in this way, a phenomenon that Kahneman and Tversky refer to as the *isolation effect*.

DECISIONS UNDER RISK (2): PROSPECT THEORY

The value function and the probability weighting function

Prospect theory can be considered as a psychological variant of subjective expected utility theory. The process of considering a decision begins with an *editing stage*, in which decision makers structure the decision problem in such a way as to simplify subsequent evaluation and choice (the *evaluation stage*). One important way in which they do this is by coding potential outcomes as gains and losses relative to some reference point. This reference point is often the status quo, but may also be an expectation or an aspiration – an important difference from utility theory, in which potential outcomes are always evaluated in relation to the current

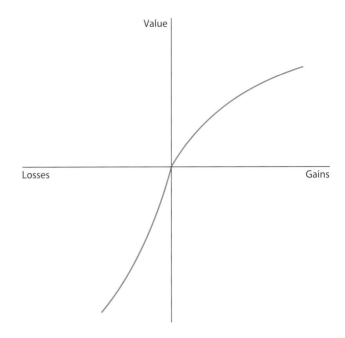

Figure 7.2. *A hypothetical value function in prospect theory*

asset position. The demonstration of the isolation effect shows that people do not always integrate potential outcomes with existing assets, as required by utility theory. The nature of the reference point – and hence, whether outcomes are evaluated as gains or losses – can also be affected by the description of the problem (see the section below on *framing effects*).

At the *evaluation phase*, both a value function and a weighting function are applied to prospects. The S-shaped curve in Figure 7.2 is a representation of the value function (value is pretty much the same as utility, except for its being assessed relative to a reference point). This curve is said to be concave for gains and convex for losses, capturing the notion that people are more sensitive to changes occurring near the reference point than to those further from it.

In discussing the utility function in expected utility theory, I noted that losses loom larger than gains (the reason that people usually turn down even bets). In prospect theory, the cause of this phenomenon is reflected in a steeper curvature of the value curve for losses compared to gains. However, as we have already seen, in prospect theory possible changes in fortune are not necessarily evaluated in relation to current assets. Thus, a potential objective gain of a certain amount could still be evaluated as a potential loss if it falls short of an aspiration or expectation. Furthermore, according to prospect theory initial losses are felt more keenly than subsequent losses of the same amount – this does not follow from expected utility theory.

Prospect theory also adopts a decision-weighting function, π (Figure 7.3). One reason that this is needed is to account for the large effect on preferences when outcomes switch from certain to uncertain (the *certainty effect*), as in the Allais paradox. On that particular problem, the switch from certainty to uncertainty led to a preference reversal. The weighting function is also needed to account for the big impact that small probabilities have on preferences (perhaps accounting for the popularity of lottery tickets and insurance).

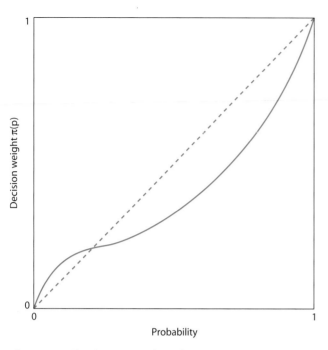

Figure 7.3. *The decision weighting function in prospect theory*

The weighting function has a reverse S-shape[2] that shows how stated probabilities are transformed, such that decisions are highly affected by small probabilities, whereas they are much less sensitive to medium-to-high probabilities (except at the boundary of uncertainty and certainty). There is evidence that the curvature of the weighting function is more pronounced when outcomes arouse affective feelings. For example, Rottenstreich and Hsee (2001) found that people attached greater value to shifts from certainty to a 99 per cent probability when outcomes were (for example) electric shocks rather than cash penalties. By contrast, people attached little value to the difference between a 99 per cent chance of an electric shock and a 1 per cent chance, whereas they attached considerably more value when the difference involved the chance of a financial penalty.

In general, weighted probabilities sum to less than 1, a property that is referred to as *subcertainty*. It should be noted that the decision-weighting function is not a measure of what people believe the probabilities to be. After all, in the problems shown above the probabilities are actually stated for the participants. Decision weights simply measure the *impact* that probabilities have on decisions.

Prospect theory not only explains a wide range of phenomena observed in laboratory experiments, but has also been applied to a range of real-world settings (Box 7.3). In this sense, it is the most

BOX 7.3.   APPLICATIONS OF PROSPECT THEORY

Applications of prospect theory have been investigated in many domains, both in the laboratory and in real-world settings. These will be explored in more depth in the next chapter, but a number of illustrative phenomena are described below.

As we saw earlier, the overweighting of low probabilities helps explain the popularity of both lotteries and insurance. Similarly, it turns out that there is a bias towards betting on long-shots in horse races; that is, the percentage of time that long-shots win is less than the percentage of money bet on them (Camerer, 2000). There is also an end-of-the-day effect in horse racing, whereby betters tend to shift their bets away from favourites and towards longshots in the last race of the day (Ali, 1977; McGlothlin, 1956). Expected utility theory cannot easily explain this shift, because a bettor who integrated his wealth would not treat the last race of the day as any different from the first race of the next outing. However, prospect theory assumes that people have a minimal target (or reference point) of breaking even at the end of the day. Anything below this target is regarded as a loss and triggers risk-seeking behaviour in an attempt to break even. Diminishing sensitivity to successive losses means that the cost of the last bet is relatively trivial compared to what has already been spent.

A similar targeting effect has also been observed in New York Cab drivers (Camerer *et al.*, 2000). According to standard labour-supply theory, drivers should maximise their profits by working longer on good days and quitting earlier on bad days. In fact, for drivers with several years' experience there was no correlation between daily wage and hours worked, whereas inexperienced drivers quit earlier on good days. Thus, inexperienced drivers fail to maximise their earnings because they quit once they have met their daily target. Over time, these drivers either quit or shift towards driving about the same number of hours each day.

Daily targeting of this sort is computationally simpler than taking the longer perspective. It also helps mitigate certain self-control problems. For example, a driver who takes a longer perspective on his earnings might be tempted to quit early today and make up for the shortfall tomorrow. However, when tomorrow arrives he might be tempted to do the same again, thus getting into an endless cycle of putting off the hard work until some future time.

Several authors (reviewed in Camerer, 2000) have observed a *disposition effect* in investment. This refers to a tendency of investors to hold on for too long to stocks that have lost value, but to sell stocks that have risen in value. The disposition effect has been demonstrated experimentally and in real-life settings, and appears to be a consequence of loss aversion: investors are more sensitive to their losses than to their gains, and are more willing to gamble to recoup those losses. Of course, it could be that investors hold on to failing stocks because they expect them to 'bounce back'. However, Odean (1998) reported that one year after winning stocks had been sold, they were still outperforming the losers that had been retained.

successful account of human decision making so far proposed. Nonetheless, other research has identified some aspects of decision performance that appear to conflict with prospect theory (e.g. Birnbaum, 2006; see also the section on *risk sensitivity theory* below). Some researchers have also criticised prospect theory for its lack of detail about the underlying cognitive processes (see the final section below on *process theories of decision making*).

Framing effects in decision making

According to the invariance axiom of utility theory *The outcomes and associated probabilities are all that is required to determine a decision maker's preference between uncertain events*. In other words, irrelevant changes of wording in the description of a decision should not affect our preferences regarding that decision. We have already seen that people violate this principle, however (Problems 5 and 6 above). By coding the same outcomes as either a gain or a loss, it is therefore possible to change the way that people evaluate those outcomes.

In another demonstration of framing, Kahneman and Tversky (1984) asked their participants to imagine that the USA was preparing for the outbreak of an unusual Asian disease, expected to kill 600 people. Two alternative programmes for combating the disease had been proposed, for which the exact scientific estimate of the consequences were as follows:

If programme A is adopted, 200 people will be saved (72 per cent)

If programme B is adopted, there is a one third probability that 600 people will be saved and a two thirds probability that no people will be saved (28 per cent)

The numbers in parentheses represent the proportion of respondents choosing each option and indicate that most people preferred option A, which could be characterised as a riskless option as it guarantees that 200 people will be saved. In comparison, the possibility of loss for option B makes the gamble unattractive.

However, other participants were presented with the same scenario and asked to choose between option C and option D:

If programme C is adopted, 400 people will die (22 per cent)

If programme D is adopted, there is a one third probability that nobody will die and a two thirds probability that 600 people will die. (78 per cent)

Of course, programmes C and D are actually the same as programmes A and B except that now the outcomes are framed in terms of the numbers of lives that might be lost. We can see that now the risky option (D) is more popular than the riskless option.

One early study reported that experts were also susceptible to framing effects. McNeil *et al.* (1982) found that both physicians and laypeople altered the choice of surgery or radiation therapy as a treatment for lung cancer depending on whether likely outcomes were described in terms of survival rates or mortality rates. Nonetheless, in actual medical situations this type of framing effect appears not to be robust and other factors appear to be more important (Christensen *et al.*, 1995; Siminoff & Fetting, 1989; for a review of medical decision making see Hamm, 2003). However, in the financial domain framing effects appear to be much more robust. Richard Thaler (1980) noted that lobbyists for the US credit card industry had an interesting response when it appeared that a bill would be passed to allow stores to charge higher prices to credit card users. They preferred that this price difference be described as a cash discount rather than a credit card surcharge. Similar findings will be discussed further in the next chapter.

There is some evidence that positive and negative framing are associated with different levels of cognitive processing. Dunegan (1993, Experiment 1) presented a project-funding scenario to 128 members of an international company engaged in the development of high-technology engineering systems. The scenario tested the extent to which participants would be willing to jeopardise their ability to fund certain opportunities by allocating further funding to an existing project that was already behind time and over budget, but which could most likely still be successfully completed. The positive frame stated that *Of the projects undertaken by this team, 30 of the last 50 have been successful*, and the negative frame stated that *Of the projects undertaken by this team, 20 of the last 50 have been unsuccessful.*

Dunegan found that the negative framing group allocated less money on average to the current project and they rated themselves as less likely to actually fund such a request. In addition, the negative framing group perceived greater risk, were more disappointed in the project, and were more concerned about minimising losses. These measures, together with some others, accounted for a significant proportion (45 per cent) of the variance in funding allocations among the negative framing group, but were not predictive of funding allocations in the positive framing group. A follow-up study, using students, found that people in the negative framing condition had a greater disparity between their images of the current state and their images of the goal state. Dunegan argued that the negative framing condition induced a negative affective state, leading to a more controlled mode of cognitive processing.

Consistent with the idea that negative frames lead to more cognitive processing, other studies have found that negative frames are associated with a slower response time (Payne *et al.*, 1993; Gonzalez *et al.*, 2005). In the study by Gonzalez and colleagues, student volunteers responded to a series of framing problems while inside a functional magnetic resonance imaging (fMRI) scanner. As usual, the predominant choices were the sure-thing option in the positive frame and the risky option in the negative frame. For positively framed problems less brain activity was evident when the sure-thing option was chosen than when the risky option was chosen. For negatively framed problems there was no difference in brain activity for the sure-thing and risky options.

Gonzalez *et al.* found that risky choices were associated with higher levels of activity in brain regions associated with imagery and working memory function (specifically, the frontal and parietal lobes).[3] They suggested that there is an interplay between affect and cognition in framing problems. That is, people generally try to minimise cognitive processing but when a problem induces negative feelings then the level of cognitive processing increases. Thus, in the positive frame the sure-thing option tends not to arouse negative feelings and is relatively quickly accepted. However, in the negative frame both options arouse negative feelings and lead to more processing.

Another fMRI study of framing has also indicated a role for affective influences (De Martino *et al.*, 2006). This study endowed participants with an amount of money and then asked them to choose between a sure thing (gain or loss, where the loss was less than the endowment, hence an overall gain was involved) or a risky option involving a chance to keep all or lose all. Choice of the sure thing in the gain frame and the gamble option in the loss frame were both associated with greater amygdala activity. This is an area of the brain associated with affective processing. However, when people made choices that ran counter to their general tendency – typically, choosing the gamble in the gain frame and the sure thing in the loss frame – there was increased activity in the anterior cingulate cortex (ACC), an area believed to be responsible for conflict monitoring and cognitive control. Taken together, these results indicate opposing influences between an emotional amygdala-based system and an analytic ACC system.

Indications of dual-processing mechanisms are consistent with the evidence that framing effects are moderated by cognitive ability and cognitive motivation. For example, in one study smokers at a public event read smoking-cessation messages that were either framed in terms of the lives that could be saved if smokers quit the habit or in terms of the numbers that would die if smokers continued to smoke. They were then asked about their own intentions to quit. People who enjoyed engaging in effortful thinking were unaffected by the framing manipulation, but less motivated thinkers registered a greater intention to quit after reading the gain-framed message (Steward *et al.*, 2003). In another study, Stanovich and West (1998) found that students of higher cognitive ability – as indicated by their SAT scores – were less susceptible to framing on the Asian disease problem described above.

Rationales for the value and probability weighting functions

Although the value function and probability weighting functions account for a great deal of decision behaviour, it is not clear why these functions are the way they are. However, the concept of declining marginal utility (see Figure 7.1 and the top right-hand section of Figure 7.2) has a parallel in nature. For example, Harder and Real (1987; see also Real, 1996) showed that the rate of net energy gain to bees shows diminishing returns as the nectar reward size increases. Plotted graphically, this is of the same form as Figure 7.1.

Evidence that people may be sensitive to the structure of gains and losses in the environment has been provided in a theory of *decision by sampling* (Stewart *et al.*, 2006). This theory was inspired by other approaches that involve memory sampling, such as the MINERVA-DM theory that we encountered in Chapter 3. According to this theory, when we are faced with a decision problem involving monetary amounts and probabilities (for example), we compare these attribute values with previously encountered values sampled from memory. The contents of memory are, in turn, assumed to reflect the structure of the world.

Stewart *et al.* investigated the frequency with which differing monetary amounts were manually entered into or withdrawn from people's bank accounts. Both credits and debits were found to follow a power law. There were many small gains and losses, and relatively fewer larger gains and losses. Stewart *et al.* argue that the preponderance of small gains and losses means that these are more frequently sampled from memory, hence people are more sensitive to smaller outcomes. This is consistent with the curvature of the value function in prospect theory. There were also relatively more small losses compared to small gains. This asymmetry is consistent with the observation that losses loom larger than gains.

Other evidence points towards probabilities being compared with attribute values being retrieved from memory. For instance, larger working memory spans correlate with less subadditivity in probability judgments (Dougherty and Hunter, 2003a, 2003b). Stewart *et al.* also review several sources of evidence indicating an S-shaped function for probabilities whereby both smaller and larger probabilities are over-represented in the environment relative to middle-range probabilities. For example, Gonzalez and Wu (1999) conducted a study to investigate the shape of the probability weighting function. When the relative ranks of these probabilities were plotted against the probabilities themselves the result was an S-shaped curve, indicating that small probabilities are overestimated and large probabilities underestimated.

THE NEUROSCIENCE OF VALUATION

Montague (2006) has made the point that mobile organisms need to have an internal model of the world, and that this requires assigning values in order that goals can be chosen and prioritised, and so feedback can aid learning. Furthermore, it is computationally more efficient to have a single mechanism for valuing different types of goals and stimuli:

> Without internal currencies in the nervous system, a creature would be unable to assess the relative value of different events like drinking water, smelling food, scanning for predators, sitting quietly in the sun, and so forth. To decide on an appropriate behaviour, the nervous system must estimate the value of each of these potential actions, convert it to a common scale, and use this scale to determine a course of action. This idea of a common scale can also be used to value both predictors and rewards. (Montague & Berns, 2002, p.276)

Studies of primates have shown that midbrain dopaminergic neurons[4] play a crucial role in the valuation of rewards and in developing expectancies (e.g. Romo & Schultz, 1990). For example, when a monkey receives an unexpected squirt of juice there is a sudden activity 'spike' in dopamine neurons in the ventral tegmental area. If, however, the monkey receives a series of trials on which the juice squirt is preceded by a flash of light one second earlier, then the dopamine spike eventually stops appearing after the reward but instead appears after the light flash. Once the light–juice relationship has been learnt, any occasional non-appearance of the squirt following the light results in a fall in dopamine activity below the normal baseline.

With human participants, the dopamine system responds not just to actual rewards but to symbolic information. For instance, young men show a greater dopamine response to pictures of sports cars, which have a high status, than to other types of cars (Erk et al., 2002). In another series of studies (McClure et al., 2004), a cup of Coke led to greater brain activity when the cup was labelled 'Coke', and to greater liking, than when the cup was unlabelled (even though participants could not be absolutely certain that they were really drinking Coke). This brand name effect did not work for Pepsi: brain activity and liking were not increased when a Pepsi drink had a Pepsi label attached to it (even though people did not have a preference between Pepsi and Coke in a blind taste test).

These kinds of studies indicate that a single mechanism is used for evaluating different kinds of stimuli. Furthermore, both people and non-human primates develop expectations based on experience and evaluate outcomes in relation to those expectations. In the case of people purely symbolic information can also be rewarding.

Other studies have examined people's responses to gambles. Breiter et al. (2001) used fMRI to examine activity in brain regions into which dopaminergic neurons project – namely the orbito-frontal cortex, the nucleus accumbens, the amygdala, the sub-lenticular extended amygdala (SLEA) of the basal forebrain, and the hypothalamus – and which project back to the area from which these projections arise. During a 'prospect' phase participants saw an arrow spin around a disk divided into three regions representing different monetary outcomes. When the arrow stopped on one of the three regions, that area began to flash, marking the start of the 'outcome' phase. Three spinners were used, each of which had zero as one of its outcomes. A good spinner had two positive outcomes in addition to the zero outcome, a bad spinner had two negative outcomes, and an intermediate spinner had a positive and a negative outcome.

During the prospect phase, the SLEA and the orbital gyrus appeared to track expected value: they both showed the greatest activity in response to the good spinner and the least activity in response to the bad spinner. Responses to actual outcomes increased monotonically with value in the nucleus accumbens, SLEA, and hypothalamus.

Another aspect of decision behaviour that has been investigated with fMRI is loss aversion. Tom et al. (2007) reported evidence that this phenomenon is not the result of negative affect. When participants were asked to accept or reject gambles involving a 50/50 chance of gaining one amount or losing another, brain areas associated with negative emotions showed no increase in activity as the size of potential losses increased. Rather, the processing of gains and losses occurred mainly in the same brain areas (the ventral striatum and ventromedial prefrontal cortex), indicating an aggregate representation of decision utility. Activity in these areas decreased as potential losses increased. Loss aversion in behaviour was strongly correlated with neural loss aversion.

However, Shiv et al. (2005) did find evidence for the role of emotions in myopic loss aversion. In myopic loss aversion people

who are faced with a series of bets do not think about their long-run potential gains and losses, but instead evaluate bets one at a time, thus continually rejecting advantageous gambles due to the possibility of a loss. The Shiv et al. study was slightly different from that of Tom et al.. Whereas Tom et al. did not resolve the gambles during the process of scanning, Shiv et al. did do so. Furthermore, each gamble was the same. Specifically, participants played 20 rounds in which the choice was always whether to invest $1 in a gamble offering a 50 per cent chance of gaining $2.50 and a 50 per cent chance of gaining nothing. The optimal strategy is, of course, to invest in each gamble. The participants were people with damage to brain areas involved in processing emotion (the target patients), patients with brain damage in non-emotion areas, and normal controls. The most optimal players were the target patients. They invested 84 per cent of the time, compared to 61 per cent for the brain damage controls, and 58 per cent for the normal controls. All three groups of participants tended to invest on the earliest rounds, but for both groups of control patients this declined across the course of the rounds. This decline occurred regardless of the experience of winning or losing rounds, although losing appeared to make people even less likely to invest.

DECISION MAKING UNDER UNCERTAINTY

As we have seen, prospect theory posits a weighting function that transforms stated probabilities. However, for most events that we encounter in real life there are no stated probabilities. In this section I shall describe two approaches to uncertain decisions, one based upon an extension of prospect theory and another based upon a model of decision making from the literature on behavioural ecology.

Support theory and cumulative prospect theory: a two-stage model of decision making

To explain uncertain decision making, Kahneman and Tversky (1992) developed a modified version of prospect theory, known as cumulative prospect theory. Later, this was combined with support theory (Tversky & Koehler, 1994; see Chapter 3) into a two-stage model (Fox & Tversky, 1998; see also Fox & See, 2003).

In the two-stage model, people first form an assessment of the probabilities of uncertain events. Secondly, they apply a weighting to these probabilities, adjusted for their own perceived knowledge of the domain in question. These weights are then combined with the output of prospect theory's value function. Consistent with support theory, Fox and Tversky (1998) found that participants priced prospects higher when they were given a more specific description. For example, participants judged a 78 per cent likelihood that *a team* from the Eastern Conference would win the National Basketball Association's 1996 playoffs. However, a separate group of participants assigned a 90 per cent probability that *one of the four leading teams* from the Eastern Conference would win the playoffs. This ordering of likelihoods is the reverse of what should rationally be the case: the four leading teams are merely a subset of the Eastern Conference so it is less likely that the winner of the playoffs will be among them than among the entire Eastern Conference.

Other participants were asked to state their certainty equivalent for a prospect that offered $75 if one of these events came about.[5] The median certainty equivalent was lower for the prospect of an Eastern Conference team winning ($50) than for one of its four leading teams winning ($60). These certainty equivalents are indicative of the weightings that people attach to these events and, as with the group who assessed likelihoods, they are the opposite of what should be rationally expected.

The weightings that people attach to judged probabilities are also modified to take account of people's perception of their knowledge about the domain in question. This accounts for the phenomenon of *ignorance aversion*. Heath and Tversky (1991) found that people preferred to bet on vague events that they felt knowledgeable about rather than chance events that they considered equally probable. For example, people who felt knowledgeable about football preferred to bet on uncertain football events rather than chance events. However, when people lacked knowledge of football they preferred to bet on chance events.

Figure 7.4 is a visual representation of Fox and Tversky's (1998) two-stage model of uncertain decision making. This incorporates both the value function and the decision-weighting function from prospect theory, except that decision weighting is now influenced by judged probabilities and modified by the decision maker's attitude towards the source of uncertainty.

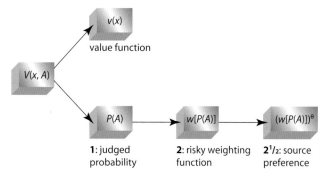

Figure 7.4. *Visual depiction of the extended two-stage model. $V(x, A) = v(x) (w[P(A)])^{\theta}$, where $V(x, A)$ is the value of the prospect that pays $x if event A obtains (and nothing otherwise), v(.) is the value function for monetary gains, P(.) is judged probability, w(.) is the risky weighting function, and θ is the source preference parameter.*

Source: Fox & See, 2003.

Risk-sensitivity theory

Research into optimal foraging in animals has focused closely on animals' experience of their environments. This literature has given rise to a class of normative models known as risk sensitivity theories which, as we shall see shortly, have also been applied to humans. These theories 'construe risk-sensitivity as the response of organisms whose goal is the maximization of Darwinian fitness in stochastic environments' (Weber *et al.*, 2004, p.430).

Consider an animal that is foraging for food. It has the choice between two food sites. Both sites offer the same level of food on average, except that over time one site shows a lot more variation around this average than does the other site. What should the animal do? The *energy budget rule* (Caraco, 1980; Stephens, 1981) says that the animal's decision should depend on its current energy state. If the animal requires few resources, then it is better off going to the low-variation site, where it will most likely satisfy its requirements, before turning its attention to other matters (such as mate acquisition). If it goes to the high-variation site there is a greater chance that it will not be able to satisfy its food requirements. On the other hand, if the animal's food requirements exceed the average amount offered at the two sites, then it is better off following the risky strategy of choosing the high variation site. There, at least, a higher possibility exists of obtaining the necessary resources. Note that this prediction differs from the widespread assumption in the human research literature that people prefer certainty over ambiguity (Ellsberg, 1961; Slovic & Tversky, 1974).

The energy budget rule also predicts how organisms should behave where time delays are involved. It takes time to travel to a food source, so in choosing between two equivalent food locations an animal needs to take into account its current energy requirements and the nature of the delay in reaching each location. The energy budget rule predicts that an organism should prefer a fixed delay over a variable delay when the animal will not starve during the fixed delay period (holding food equivalent across delays). However, if the organism *is* likely to starve before the fixed delay expires, then it should opt for the variable delay because this offers the only possibility of staying alive long enough to obtain food.

Supporting the energy budget rule, Caraco found that wild-caught birds behaved in exactly this fashion when two seed sources were arranged in a laboratory setting (Caraco, 1981, 1983; Caraco *et al.*, 1980). The energy budget rule has also predicted foraging behaviour in several other species (Kacelnik & Bateson, 1996). However, not all studies have provided supportive evidence (Kacelnik & Bateson, 1996; Shafir *et al.*, 1999). One problem appears to be that it is difficult in practical terms to operationalise an animal's energy budget, because there are many things that may affect this such as ambient temperature, predation risk, and so on (see Pietras *et al.*, 2003, and also Soto *et al.*, 2005). Recognising these difficulties, two different approaches have developed, as described below.

One approach focuses on studying human participants in order that variables of interest are more tightly controlled. In one study human participants undertook several blocks of trials within which they had to try and earn points – to be translated into cash – within a limited time period (Pietras *et al.*, 2003; see also Pietras &

Hackenberg, 2001). They did this by choosing one of two flashing keylights to press. Pressing a keylight five times consecutively would turn off the other keylight, and after a delay the chosen keylight would stop flashing but stay illuminated, indicating that it had been chosen. One keylight had a fixed delay of 10 seconds, the other key had an equiprobable delay of 2 seconds or 18 seconds. A counter visible to the participants kept a record of the cumulative delay time. At the end of each block, if the cumulative delay did not exceed a certain threshold then the participant would be rewarded with 10 points (worth 25¢).

During positive budget conditions, the threshold was set at 50 seconds, so exclusive preference for the fixed option would always result in points earnings, whereas exclusive preference for the variable option would only result in earnings half the time. During negative budget conditions the threshold was set at 40 seconds or 32 seconds, so that exclusive preference for the fixed option would never result in points earnings but exclusive preference for the variable option would result in earnings with $p = 0.19$. Pietras et al. found that participants strongly preferred the fixed delay and variable delay, respectively, under these conditions. They also found that people were sensitive to the specific outcomes that they encountered; for example, under the negative budget people might switch to the fixed option if they had been fortunate enough to experience several short delays with the variable keylight.

Another study introduced the concept of *need* into simple gambles involving ambiguity (Rode et al., 1999, Experiment 4). In this experiment participants aimed to blindly draw a threshold number of black balls from a box in order to gain a chance of winning a prize. Participants could choose to draw from a *risky* box with a specified number of black and white balls or from an *ambiguous* box with an unknown distribution of black and white balls. Within the conditions of the experiment the threshold number of black balls was varied, as was the known distribution of black and white balls.

Participants were considerably more likely to select the ambiguous box when the threshold exceeded the expected value of the risky box than when it did not. People were also sensitive to probabilities: they increasingly chose the ambiguous box as the probability of drawing black from the known box fell.

Other studies indicated that ambiguity aversion does not depend on the direct comparison of an ambiguous and a known option (Rode et al., 1999, Experiments 1 and 2) and that people avoid options with high outcome variability regardless of whether probabilities are explicitly stated or not (Experiment 3). Overall, these results are consistent with optimal foraging theory.

A second approach to risk sensitivity has recognised that many studies have not taken into account individuals' *perceptions* of variability or risk. For instance, a price reduction of $100 sounds great when buying a $200 pen, but trivial when buying a $20,000 car (Weber et al., 2004). This is consistent with our earlier discussion of the utility function and Weber's Law.[6] The *relative* variability of risky choice alternatives can be measured by dividing the standard deviation of outcomes by their mean (For those who haven't studied statistics: the standard deviation is simply a particular measure of variation. Don't worry if you're unfamiliar with this.) The resulting measure is referred to as the *coefficient of variation* (CV). As well as having greater psychological plausibility, the CV has the advantage of being dimensionless; that is, the unit of measurement is cancelled out, so it is possible to make comparisons across different domains (this approach is interesting in light of the evidence that humans and other animals use a single internal scale for value; see the earlier section on the neuroscience of valuation).

In a review of animal studies, Shafir (2000) found that the CV was a better predictor of risk sensitivity than was variance. Weber et al. (2000) reviewed human studies of decision making and found that the CV was a slightly stronger predictor of risk taking than was variance or standard deviation in both the gain domain and the loss domain. However, the results were not as strong as for the animal studies, possibly because the human studies did not call upon personal experience with the domain. To address this problem, Weber et al. examined choice behaviour in a card game where participants could choose cards from a constant payoff deck and a variable payoff deck. They found that risk aversion increased with the CV, but showed no relationship with the variance of outcomes. Expected value also predicted choice proportions, but CV predicted above and beyond expected value.

In summary, risk sensitivity theory offers an interesting perspective on decision making that differs from expected utility theory and prospect theory in that people are concerned with the variance of some outcome rather than some average value. However, there has still been relatively little research with human participants, although some of the early results described here are encouraging.

PROCESS MODELS OF DECISION MAKING

Some authors have tried to say more about decision making as a process. In *decision field theory* (Busemeyer & Johnson, 2004) the deliberations of a decision maker involve switching attention between alternatives and thinking about their consequences. In doing so, an overall feeling of desirability in relation to each action accumulates. Once a threshold is passed, then the successful action is chosen. Busemeyer and Johnson show how their theory provides an alternative account of many of the phenomena that prospect theory was designed to explain.

By contrast, Birnbaum (e.g. 1997, 2006) has identified several new paradoxes that are not accounted for by cumulative prospect theory, but which he explains in terms of a transfer of attention exchange (TAX) model.

In the rest of this section I shall describe in some detail another attentional account of decision making under risk. This account has been proposed by Brandstätter et al. (2006). These authors suggested that people apply a simple heuristic when choosing in a described decision task. They refer to this as the *priority heuristic*. This heuristic is based on the following steps:

- *Priority Rule.* Go through the reasons in the order: minimum gain, probability of minimum gain, maximum gain.

- *Stopping Rule.* Stop examination if the minimum gains differ by 1/10 (or more) of the maximum gain; otherwise, stop examination if probabilities differ by 1/10 (or more) of the probability scale.

- *Decision Rule.* Choose the gamble with the more attractive gain (probability).

In cases where the prospects are all negative, these rules are the same except that 'gains' are replaced by 'losses'.

To see how the priority heuristic works, let us revisit the Allais paradox (Problems 1 and 2 from earlier in the chapter).

<u>Problem 1</u>
Which of the following situations would you prefer:

Situation A:
100 million for certain

Situation B:
A 10 per cent chance of 500 million
An 89 per cent chance of 100 million
A 1 per cent chance of nothing

<u>Problem 2</u>
Which of the following situations would you prefer:

Situation C:
An 11 per cent chance of 100 million
An 89 per cent chance of nothing

Situation D:
A 10 per cent chance of 500 million
A 90 per cent chance of nothing

In Problem 1 the decision maker's aspiration level is 50 million; that is, one tenth of 500 million (the maximum gain). The minimum outcomes are zero (in B) and 100 million (in A). Because 100 million exceeds the aspiration level the sure thing in Situation A is chosen.

In Problem 2 the minimum gains are both zero (with probabilities of .89 and .90), thus they fall short of the aspiration level. The maximum gains are 100 million (in C) and 500 million (in D). Therefore, the priority heuristic predicts the choice of D.

The priority heuristic also predicts the reflection effect, as well as the observation of risk aversion for low probability losses and risk seeking for low probability gains. Furthermore, Brändstatter *et al.* showed that the priority heuristic outperformed prospect theory, as well as several other theories and heuristics, when used to predict choices on a series of gambles taken from the literature, as well as randomly chosen gambles. Finally, the authors conducted a study in which participants' response times were recorded on a series of choices of gambles. This found that response times were longer for problems where the priority heuristic predicted that more reasons would need to be examined.

Although these data are impressive, they must nonetheless be regarded with some caution. For example, the stopping rule seems fairly arbitrary, although the authors justify it on the basis of certain numbers being prominent within the decimal system. Indeed, animals have also been observed to violate the utility axioms on a version of Allais's problem (Battalio *et al.*, 1985; Kagel *et al.*, 1990), yet they are not – presumably – operating according to a decimal system. The response time data may also be interpretable in terms of a different process than a search for reasons. For instance, it may relate to a process involving decision weighting. There are also phenomena that the priority heuristic does not address, such as framing effects, the influence of affect on the weighting of probabilities, and some of the real-world phenomena that prospect theory successfully predicts.

SUMMARY

Faced with a choice between risky prospects, expected value theory states that each potential outcome should be weighted by the probability of its occurrence. The expected value of any given alternative is the sum of its weighted outcomes. The rational decision maker should choose the alternative with the highest expected value.

Bernoulli's St Petersburg paradox demonstrated a problem with the concept of expected value, leading him to develop the idea that what people are actually trying to maximise is expected utility. In the 20th century, a series of axioms was developed, which were said to underpin expected utility theory. A rational decision maker should follow these axioms if he wishes to make decisions consistent with his beliefs.

However, much psychological research has found many instances where people do not behave according to the axioms of expected utility theory. Prospect theory was developed as a theory of how people actually make decisions between two alternatives under risk. It recognises that the reference point against which gains and losses are defined may be an aspiration or expectation rather than the status quo. Furthermore, small probabilities tend to be overweighted in decision making, whereas medium-to-high probabilities are underweighted.

Key to any decision making is the concept of valuation. Recent evidence indicates that a single internal scale is used for valuing different types of outcomes, potential outcomes, and predictive cues. The brain's dopamine system appears to be the mechanism underlying the valuation process.

In order to explain decision making under uncertainty cumulative prospect theory was developed, and then combined with support theory into a two-stage model. People make an assessment of probability, which is then weighted and modified according to the decision maker's own knowledge of the domain in question. An alternative approach to uncertain decisions comes from optimal foraging theory. This specifies that choices are determined by a combination of the need of the decision maker, the mean expected outcome of each option, and the variance of each option's outcomes.

Finally, some approaches to decision making place greater emphasis on the stages of processing involved. One such approach is decision field theory, which emphasises switches in attention over time between different elements of the decision problem. Another approach is that of the priority heuristic, which argues that decisions under risk do not involve the computation of expectations; rather, people give sequential attention to outcomes and probabilities according to an order of prioritisation.

QUESTIONS

1. Do you think it makes sense for people to be more sensitive to losses than to gains? Why?

2. In what ways have people been observed to violate expected utility theory?

3. Compare and contrast prospect theory with expected utility theory.

4. What is the energy budget rule?

5. Construct alternative forms of a message framed, alternately, as a gain and a loss. The message could be – for example – a political communication or an advert for a product.

6. Design a study to test whether loss aversion is acquired through learning.

7. Evaluate two alternative approaches to utility theory and prospect theory.

NOTES

1. The expected value is $(1/2 \times 1) + (1/4 \times 2) + (1/8 \times 4) + (1/16 \times 8) + \ldots = \infty$

2. Readers who refer back to the early writings on prospect theory will spot that visual representations of the probability weighting function are not a reverse S-shape, but more of a simple curve. However, an in-depth study by Gonzalez and Wu (1999) indicates that reverse S-shape better captures the weighting function.

3. Even more specifically, the main areas involved were the Right-dorsolateral prefrontal cortex, the Right-intraparietal sulcus, and the Left-intraparietal sulcus.

4. Dopamine is a type of neurotransmitter, that is, a chemical 'messenger' that passes from one nerve cell (neuron) to another.

5. The certainty equivalent is the amount of money that a person would be willing to accept for certain rather than gamble. In this case, a person's certainty equivalent is the amount of money she would be willing to accept rather than obtain $75 only if the relevant National Basketball Association event comes about.

6. Try not to confuse Ernst Weber, the discoverer of Weber's Law, with Elke Weber, whose research is referred to in this section!

RECOMMENDED READING

Montague, R. (2006). *Why choose this book? How we make decisions.* London: Dutton. A very readable account of how expectations and learned values are represented in the brain.

8 | Preference and Choice

CHAPTER OUTLINE

INTRODUCTION

Traditional economic theory assumes that individuals know better than anyone else what is good for them and act accordingly. The idea that people are rational actors implies that they should follow the axioms of rational choice. However, this is often not the case. In the first part of this chapter I describe some of the research that shows how people violate these axioms and why. Then I go on to look at several decision biases that are associated with 'mental accounting', the way in which people think about financial activities. In a third section I look at some issues concerned with the desire for choice and how people respond to complex choices. It turns out that simply desiring choice can sometimes be disadvantageous. People may also choose from a variety of strategies for making choices, depending on the complexity and importance of the decision. However, having greater choice does not necessarily lead to greater satisfaction. Finally, I look in greater depth at an aspect of choice that runs through most of the chapter – the role of emotion.

THE CONSTRUCTION OF PREFERENCE

According to rational choice theory, people have preferences that are *revealed* in their behaviour. However, a considerable body of psychological research indicates that people construct their preferences during the process of thinking about choice (see Lichtenstein & Slovic, 2006). This can lead to the violation of rational norms as described below.

Violations of transitivity

Table 8.1 shows how five hypothetical college applicants rate on the attributes of intellectual ability, emotional stability, and social facility. Tversky (1969) presented people with each possible pairing of the five applicants, except that the data were shown in the form of bar graphs. They were told that:

> The college selection committee is interested in learning student opinion concerning the type of applicants that should be admitted to the school. Therefore, you are asked to select which you would admit from each of several pairs of applicants. Naturally, intellectual ability would be the most important factor in your decision, but the other factors are of some value, too. Also, you should bear in mind that the scores are based on the committee's ranking and so they may not be perfectly reliable. (E. Shafir, 2004, p.442)

Tversky found that most people preferred A to B, B to C, C to D, and D to E. By the axiom of transitivity, this means that the participants should also have preferred A to E, but in fact they mostly preferred E to A. When interviewed, not only did none of the participants realise that their preferences were intransitive, but when they were informed of this some denied it was possible and asked to see the experimenter's record. However, the vast majority of participants said that 'people are and should be transitive' (E. Shafir, 2004, p.455).

Table 8.1. *Ratings of five applicants on three dimensions*

Applicant	Intellectual ability	Emotional stability	Social facility
A	69	84	75
B	72	78	65
C	75	72	55
D	78	66	45
E	81	60	35

Source: Tversky, 1969.

It appears that people simplified this task by overlooking the small differences in intellectual abilities between A and B, B and C, C and D, and D and E, and choosing on the basis of the larger differences on other attributes. However, when A and E were compared they noticed the much larger difference in intellectual ability.

Although such simplifications do not maximise expected utility, this particular 'cost' is most likely outweighed by the benefit of less and faster computation. However, in principle it would be possible to take advantage of another person's intransitivity to their cost (Tversky, 1969).

It has been argued that evolution is unlikely to select against occasional intransitive choice behaviour. Animals have to make a range of multiattribute choices, for which it helps to have fast, efficient choice mechanisms, but it seems unlikely that their natural environment provides the conditions for intransitivity to occur. However, in controlled studies animals too have been observed to make intransitive choices (e.g. Bernard and Giurfa, 2004; S. Shafir, 1994).

Violations of procedure invariance

Response mode compatibility In a series of studies Slovic and his colleagues found that the attractiveness of gambles depends on the question that people are asked about them (e.g. Lichtenstein & Slovic, 1971; Slovic & Lichtenstein, 1968). When asked to choose between pairs of gambles with a similar expected value, they tend to choose the gamble with the highest probability but lower potential payoff. However, when asked how much they would be willing to pay for any individual gamble, or how much they would sell such a gamble for, their stated amounts are related more to the potential outcomes rather than the probabilities. This kind of cognitive processing leads to preference reversals, with high-outcome/low-probability gambles being assigned higher prices but low-outcome/high-probability gambles being chosen when the two types of gambles are paired. Such preference reversals were even found when gambles were played for real money on the floor of the Queens Casino in Las Vegas (Lichtenstein & Slovic, 1973).

Later research showed that the primary cause of preference reversals in these studies is the overpricing of bets with a high payoff (Tversky *et al.*, 1990). It seems that people focus on the features of the task that are compatible with the response mode. Non-matching task features have less impact on judgment because they require extra cognitive effort in order to be mapped onto the response scale. This explanation is referred to as the *compatibility hypothesis* (Lichtenstein & Slovic, 1973; see also Tversky *et al.*, 1990; and Slovic *et al.*, 1990).

Further evidence for compatibility was provided by Slovic *et al.* (2002). One group of participants was asked to rate the attractiveness of a 7/36 chance to win $9. Another group was asked to rate a modified version of this gamble to which a small loss had been added:

7/36 chance to win $9
29/36 chance to lose 5¢

This inferior bet was rated as more attractive than the version where no loss was involved. Slovic *et al.* (2004) argued that it is quite difficult to assess the attractiveness of $9 in isolation, whereas the payoff is more compatible with the attractiveness scale when the small loss is added.

Also supporting the compatibility hypothesis is the observation that people who exhibit the predicted reversal spend longer thinking about pricing than about choice (Schkade & Johnson, 1989). Also, fewer preference reversals occur with problems involving nonmonetary bets (Slovic *et al.*, 1990).

The prominence hypothesis Consider the following example of a preference reversal (Tversky *et al.*, 1988). In one scenario, Israeli participants were told that the transport ministry was trying to reduce traffic fatalities from the current level of 600 casualties per year. Some people were asked to choose between the following two options (the percentage choosing each is shown in parentheses):

Programme X: 500 casualties   Cost $55 million   (67 per cent)
Programme Y: 570 casualties   Cost $12 million   (33 per cent)

As you can see, most people preferred the more expensive programme that led to fewer casualties. Other people were presented with the same options, except that there was a missing value that they had to fill in to make each option equivalent. For example:

Programme X: 500 casualties   Cost $?
Programme Y: 570 casualties   Cost $12 million

In order that Programme X is equivalent to Programme Y, it should be assigned (on average) a value of at least $55 million. Anything less than this would imply that people should not be choosing Programme X in the choice task. Nonetheless, the typical matching value was *less* than $55 million, and only 4 per cent of participants gave a value higher than this.

Because safety is regarded as the most important attribute, most people use this as the basis for choice. However, such *qualitative* reasoning cannot be used to complete the matching task; this actually *requires* that people engage in *quantitative* reasoning.

This phenomenon has been formulated as the *prominence effect* (Tversky *et al.*, 1988): the more prominent attribute will weigh more heavily in choice than in matching. Simplifying strategies of this sort enable people to resolve conflicts and are easier to justify than more complex procedures.

Separate versus joint evaluation Imagine two possible scenarios for choosing a new stereo. In one scenario you are at an electronics store making direct comparisons between models. You have narrowed the choice down to two models (A and B) and are comparing various attributes, perhaps even listening to the same piece of music played on each stereo one after the other. In the other scenario, you spend some time evaluating model A at one particular store. Bearing this model in mind as a possibility, you then decide to wander to the only other store nearby, where you spend some time evaluating model B.

Table 8.2. *Mean willingness-to-pay values for the two dictionaries in the dictionary study*

Evaluation mode	Dictionary A	Dictionary B
Joint	$19	$27
Separate	$24	$20

Source: Hsee, 2000.

Chris Hsee (1996) has shown that these two modes of evaluation – joint versus separate – can lead to different outcomes. Consider the following two second-hand music dictionaries:

	Dictionary A	Dictionary B
Year of publication	1993	1993
Number of entries	10,000	20,000
Any defects?	No, it's like new	Yes, the cover is torn; otherwise it's like new

One group of students was informed about both these alternatives and asked how much they would be willing to pay for each dictionary, bearing in mind that they were planning to spend between $10 and $50. The remaining students were only told about one dictionary and asked how much they would be willing to spend.

As Table 8.2 shows, people were willing to pay more for Dictionary B under joint evaluation, but more for Dictionary A under separate evaluation. Hsee proposed the *evaluability hypothesis* to account for these results. He argued that such reversals occur when one of the attributes of an object is hard to evaluate independently, but the other attribute is relatively easy to evaluate independently. This was supported by a further study where the two objects of choice were CD changers. These differed in terms of CD capacity and sound quality, where the latter was indexed in terms of percentage scores for total harmonic distortion (THD). In one version of the study participants were told that the THD ratings for most CD players ranged from .002 per cent (best) to .012 per cent (worst). This range information was expected to make it easier for participants to evaluate the CD changer in the separate evaluation condition. In the other version of the study, participants were not provided with this information. As predicted, separate and joint evaluations only led to preference reversals among participants who were not provided with the range information for THD.

Hsee suggests that people may make choices that they later regret if they use the wrong mode of evaluation. Imagine a person is carefully comparing the sound quality of two sets of speakers in an audio store. After much thought, he decides to purchase the speakers that, in his opinion, have a slightly better sound quality than the other set. However, after a couple of weeks of having the speakers in his living room, he is struck by how visually unattractive they are, and can't help remembering how much nicer the other set had been. Worse, he realises that he is not getting any satisfaction from the fact that the sound quality of his chosen speakers is marginally better; the small difference he perceived in the audio store is no longer salient when listening at home. In fact, if he had evaluated the two sets of speakers separately, he would almost certainly have not noticed the difference in sound quality.

Choice strategies

We have seen that people use simplifying procedures in determining their preferences. In fact, there are quite a few potential *strategies* for making choices, and these are typically divided into two broad classes: *compensatory* and *non-compensatory*. Compensatory strategies involve tradeoffs whereas non-compensatory strategies do not.

Consider the *weighted additive* (WADD) *rule*. This is a fully compensatory strategy. The decision maker scores each alternative on each relevant attribute. The attributes themselves are weighted according to their importance. Multiplying the scores by the weightings and summing across attributes provides an overall score for each alternative. For decisions under risk, probabilities are taken into account, so decision makers may use the expected value or expected utility rules.

It is the most accurate choice strategy but also the most effortful precisely because it does use all the information available, makes tradeoffs, and evaluates every alternative. Other strategies are not as accurate but have the benefit of requiring less cognitive effort. For example, with the *elimination-by-aspects* strategy the decision maker first identifies the most important attribute and selects an aspiration level for this. Any alternative that fails to meet this threshold is eliminated from the choice set. If two or more alternatives remain in the choice set at this point, then the process is repeated using the second most important attribute, and so on until one alternative remains.

A decision maker can rely on a single strategy or use different strategies in combination. A person's repertoire of strategies depends upon factors such as age, experience, and formal training and education (Payne *et al.*, 1993), thus there are individual differences in the availability of strategies. The selection of a particular strategy is contingent on a combination of task factors and personal factors. This is consistent with our earlier observation that preferences are *constructed* rather than revealed during the process of choice. In general, people desire the best or most accurate outcome from a decision, but they also wish to expend the least effort possible in making the decision. These two aims are often incompatible. For example, achieving accuracy when there are multiple alternatives with multiple attributes will require a considerable degree of cognitive effort. Other task aspects that might call for effortful processing are the importance of the decision and whether or not the decision maker is accountable to others.[1]

Computer simulations and other experimental studies reviewed by Payne *et al.* have shown that less effortful strategies can often be surprisingly accurate, though no single heuristic is accurate across all contexts (1993, p.131). They also examined combinations of strategies, noting that elimination-by-aspects combined with the weighted additive rule worked well in all task conditions, whereas elimination-by-aspects combined with the majority of confirming dimensions heuristic was much less efficient. Some less effortful strategies have also been found to be more advantageous when

making decisions under time pressure, because there is not enough time to apply the more complex rules (Payne *et al.*, 1988).

Context-dependent preferences

The theory of rational choice assumes that people try to maximise value when they choose between options. An assumption of this theory is that the preference between options does not depend on the presence or absence of other options. Suppose Bob prefers stereo system A to stereo system B. If we now add stereo system C to the set of options, Bob should still prefer A to B, regardless of where C ranks in his preferences. This principle is called the *independence of irrelevant alternatives*. It also follows that the 'market share' of an option cannot be increased by enlarging the choice set (a property known as *regularity*).

In fact, several studies have demonstrated violations of regularity (e.g. Huber *et al.*, 1982; Simonson & Tversky, 1992). For example, Simonson and Tversky gave participants descriptions and pictures of five microwave ovens taken from a catalogue. They were asked to scrutinise these carefully and to familiarise themselves with the options available on the market. Subsequently, one group of people was asked to choose between X and Y below, whereas another group was given a choice between X, Y, and Z:

X.   Emerson
     (0.5 cu. ft.; regular $109.99; sale price 35 per cent off)

Y.   Panasonic 1
     (0.8 cu. ft.; regular $179.99; sale price 35 per cent off)

Z.   Panasonic 2
     (1.1 cu. ft.; regular $199.99; sale price 10 per cent off)

Because the Panasonic 1 and Panasonic 2 were quite similar, the lower discount on the latter made it seem like a poorer option. However, it was not clearly inferior to the Emerson. Nonetheless, adding the Panasonic 2 to the choice set actually reduced the market share of the Emerson and increased the market share of the Panasonic 1 (Figure 8.1), thus violating the property of regularity. The observation that the popularity of an option can be increased

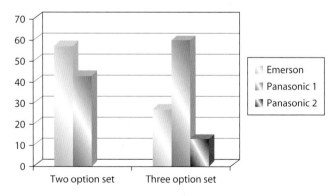

Figure 8.1. *The percentage of people choosing microwave ovens from a two-option set and a three-option set*
Source: Simonson & Tversky, 1992.

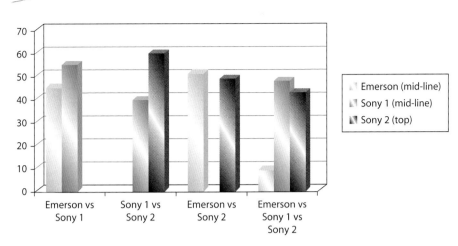

Figure 8.2. *The percentage of participants choosing particular models of cassette player in two-option or three-option choices*
Source: Simonson & Tversky, 1992.

by enlarging the choice set is referred to as the *asymmetric dominance effect* (or *attraction effect*).

In the study just described, the effect occurs as a result of 'local context'; that is, even though participants had familiarised themselves with an overall market of five options, the asymmetric dominance effect occurred due to the specific subset of choice options that was actually presented (the local context). Simonson and Tversky (1992) have also shown that 'background context' can affect choice. In this situation, a choice made earlier can affect a subsequent choice.

In other choice situations a *compromise effect* has been observed as a result of *extremeness aversion*. According to prospect theory (Kahneman & Tversky, 1979, 1992), people evaluate outcomes as gains or losses from a reference point that is normally the status quo. A general property of this value function is that people are loss averse, and that losses loom larger than gains. In some situations, choice options may be evaluated in terms of their advantages and disadvantages relative to each other, in which case the disadvantages will loom larger than the advantages. This being the case, options with extreme values are likely to be less attractive than options with intermediate values. For example, when asked to choose between cameras varying in quality and price, a $170 camera and a $240 camera were equally popular in a binary choice, but the $240 camera was the most popular choice when a $470 camera was added to the set of options.

Extremeness aversion can also give rise to *polarisation*. When disadvantages loom larger than advantages on just one attribute, then the introduction of a third option will produce a bias against one of the extreme options but not the other. Simonson and Tversky provided participants with details of three AM-FM cassette players, including photographs, information on features, brand names and prices. These can be summarised as:

X.   Emerson
      (mid-line; $39.99)

Y.   Sony
      (mid-line; $64.99)

Z.   Sony
      (top; $149.99)

In binary choices, the Emerson was about as popular as each of the Sony models. However, in the trinary set only 9 per cent chose the Emerson, with each of the Sony models being about equally popular (Figure 8.2).

In all the examples presented in this section, participants were always required to choose one of the products. In real life, a person usually has the option to defer choice. Tversky and Shafir (1992) showed that choice conflict led to a greater tendency to defer choice. When given the opportunity to defer a hypothetical choice between a $99 Sony CD player and a $169 Aiwa, 46 per cent of participants postponed the decision. However, when the only model on offer was the $99 Sony, 66 per cent of participants chose this rather than deferring the decision. Furthermore, 73 per cent of people chose a $99 Sony when the only other product was an *inferior* $105 Aiwa (24 per cent deferred and 3 per cent chose the Aiwa). This last example shows that it is not the mere presence of two products that leads to conflict. Rather, the conflict arises when there is not a clear reason to choose between options.

MENTAL ACCOUNTING

In the previous chapter, I noted that prospect theory has provided explanations for a variety of financial behaviours, including the tendency of bettors to switch to longshots on the day's final race and of inexperienced New York cab drivers to quit work once they had reached the day's target income. Prospect theory has influenced much theorising about the way that people think about money, or *mental accounting*. Thaler (1999) defines mental accounting as 'the set of cognitive operations used by individuals and households to organise, evaluate, and keep track of financial activities'. The reference to 'financial activities' in this definition may be unnecessarily restrictive. As some of the examples in this section show, various human activities may be thought about in the same way that we think about money.

The endowment effect

The loss aversion implied by prospect theory's value function suggests that people should find it hard to part with things that they own. This *endowment effect* suggests that people may tend to overprice items that they are trying to sell. In one study (Kahneman *et al.*, 1990), students were randomly assigned to three groups. One group, the sellers, were given a coffee mug and asked whether they would be willing to sell it at a series of prices between $0.25 and $9.25. A second group, the buyers, were asked whether they would be willing to purchase a mug at the same set of prices. Consistent with the endowment effect predicted by loss aversion, the sellers set a higher median price ($7.12) than the buyers ($2.87). However, we cannot truly say that the sellers are overpricing their mugs unless we have some independent valuation of the coffee mugs. This valuation was provided by a third group, the choosers. This group was asked to choose, for each of the prices, whether they would rather have the cash or a mug. The median price of the choosers was $3.12, which is much closer to that of the buyers, thus supporting the idea that the sellers were overpricing a mug that they had only just been endowed with.

Some authors have argued that the endowment effect arises from using one-shot experiments with naive participants, and claim that experience in a market setting reduces the effect (e.g. Coursey *et al.*, 1987). Kahneman *et al.* (1990) included studies where advanced undergraduate students participated in a series of markets, but they found that the endowment effect persisted. More recently, however, List (2004) reported results from a field study carried out at a sportscard show in a large city in the southern USA. The study examined the willingness to trade coffee mugs and luxury candy bars of a similar financial value. He found that a reluctance to trade one's endowment was common among non-dealers, whereas no such tendency was observed among dealers (who, a survey confirmed, had much more trading experience).

One practical implication of the endowment effect arises in relation to the use of *contingent valuation* for measuring the value of public goods. In a typical application of contingent valuation, relevant stakeholders are asked how much they would be willing to pay in order to improve some aspect of the environment (or reduce the damage to it). Alternatively, they might be asked how much they would be willing to accept in order to allow some damage to occur. Willingness to pay (WTP) and willingness to accept (WTA) ought to be equivalent, but people frequently give much higher prices for WTA than for WTP. This is consistent with loss aversion: WTA is associated with giving up a public endowment, and this loss translates into a higher valuation of the good in question. On the other hand, WTP is associated with prevention of damage or improvement. Because this is experienced as a gain, the value attached to it is not as high.

Discrepancies between WTP and WTA tend to be larger for goods that are hard to value, such as environmental services (Baron, 1997). Stated values are also associated with people's feelings. In a laboratory study that measured WTP and WTA for lottery tickets, positive feelings were associated with WTP judgments and negative feelings were associated with WTA judgments (Peters *et al.*, 2003). More highly positive feelings were associated with higher WTP prices and more highly negative feelings were associated with higher WTA prices. Furthermore, comments made by buyers and sellers showed that they focused on different aspects of the situation. Buyers more than sellers tended to mention that there was only a small chance of winning, whereas sellers tended to mention that they *might* win; in other words, buyers tended to focus on probability whereas sellers tended to focus on the outcome.

Status quo bias, omission bias, and action effects

The endowment effect is a reluctance to trade objects that one owns. A related effect is that of *status quo bias*, or the preference for remaining in one's current state. Johnson *et al.* (1993) carried out an experiment that investigated people's willingness to change the nature of their auto insurance policies. This preceded an actual change in the insurance laws of Pennsylvania and New Jersey that provided the opportunity for a quasi-experimental follow-up. The change in the law allowed insurance companies to provide consumers with the option of a reduced right to sue accompanied by cheaper auto insurance.

The experimental study was conducted with university employees. A 'Full Right' group was told that the state's standard insurance policy had no restrictions on the bearer's right to sue for pain and suffering. Participants were asked whether they would forgo their right to sue in exchange for a 10 per cent reduction in their insurance premium. If they were unwilling to give up the right to sue for a 10 per cent reduction, they were asked what percentage reduction would be enough to make them give up the right to sue. In the 'Limited Right' condition, the standard auto insurance policy was described as restricting the right to sue and participants had the option to acquire the right to sue in exchange for an 11 per cent increase in their premium (equivalent to the 10 per cent decrease in the Full Right group). If 11 per cent was too much, then they were asked to indicate the percentage increase that would be acceptable to acquire the right to sue. A 'Neutral' group was not told what the standard policy was, but participants were asked to state their choice and to indicate the premium difference that would make the options equally attractive.

If people were making this decision on purely economic grounds, then there should not be any difference between the programmes chosen by each group. However, people's responses tended towards the status quo, consistent with the prediction of loss aversion (Figure 8.3). As it happens, the status quo bias was even larger in real life. Changes to the insurance laws in Pennsylvania and New Jersey permitted companies to offer Limited Right policies. However, in New Jersey the default policy is the Limited Right policy, so motorists have to acquire the right to sue actively. In Pennsylvania the situation is the reverse: the default policy is the Full Right policy. Data published in 1992 showed that only about 20 per cent of New Jersey motorists acquired a Full Right policy, whereas 75 per cent of Pennsylvania motorists retained their Full Right policy.

Ritov and Baron (1992) have proposed an alternative account of the status quo bias. They argue that a different kind of bias is

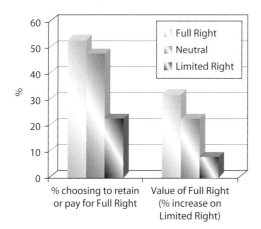

Figure 8.3. *The percentage of participants retaining or acquiring a more expensive Full Right insurance policy (left-hand bars), and the percentage extra value of that policy above a Limited Right policy (right-hand bars). The differently shaded bars represent the current standard policy*

Source: Johnson *et al.*, 1993.

actually at play: the *omission bias*. Omission bias arises when people are reluctant to risk a negative outcome as the result of performing an action. Whereas maintaining the status quo is often associated with doing nothing, in other situations a person might need to act in order to maintain the status quo if, for example, he knows that change will occur in the absence of such action. Ritov and Baron presented people with scenarios in which a negative outcome occurred. The scenarios varied in terms of whether a person had acted in order to maintain the status quo, acted to effect change, had maintained the status quo by not acting, or had allowed change to occur by not acting. For example, the following scenario describes a situation where a person maintains the status quo by acting, and a negative outcome results:

> Henry owns shares in Company A. During the past year his investment manager asked him whether he would object to switching to stock in Company B. Henry objected and got to keep his shares in Company A. Now he finds out that he would have been better off by $1200, if he had switched to the stock of Company B.

In line with earlier findings (Kahneman & Miller, 1986), participants thought that bringing about negative change through action was worse than maintaining the status quo through inaction. However, people also thought it was worse to maintain the status quo through action than to bring about change through inaction.

Omission bias could be harmful in many ways. For instance, when told about a hypothetical disease that could kill 10 out of 10,000 children, many people were unwilling to administer a vaccine that itself could kill 5 out of 10,000, despite the overall benefit this would bring (Ritov & Baron, 1990).[2] People often justified this reluctance on the grounds that they did not want to cause the death of any children, or even a single child.

Omission bias has been linked to the concept of 'protected values', values that people protect from tradeoffs (Fiske & Tetlock,

1997), such as the unwillingness to take any action that might harm a child no matter what the potential benefit. However, studies of moral norms in relation to environmental behaviour have found that protected values can also be associated with a commitment to action (e.g. Black *et al.*, 1985; Cialdini *et al.*, 1990; Hopper & Nielson, 1991; Stern *et al.*, 1993). People with strong views on the protection of the environment often perceive a moral obligation to act.

However, studies of omission bias are typically framed in such a way that respondents do not have the opportunity to express commissions. Tanner and Medin (2004) presented participants with a series of hypothetical environmental problems where they were asked to choose between taking an action or not taking an action. For different problems, acting or not acting were associated either with certain outcomes (for example, 'the health of 480 [out of 720] children will be damaged for sure') or risky outcomes (for example, 'there is a one third probability that the health of none of the 720 children will be damaged, and a two thirds probability that the health of all of them will be damaged'). Also, whereas the options just described are negatively framed, in some versions the options were positively framed (for example lives saved, rather than lives damaged). Participants also answered a series of questions designed to measure protected values (for example, 'People should only undertake this action if it leads to some benefits that are great enough').

In this study, participants with strong protected values were unaffected by the framing manipulation; they selected action more often than no-action regardless of positive or negative framing, and regardless of whether the act had certain or risky outcomes. However, for participants with low protected values the results were different. For positively framed outcomes, no-action was preferred when it was associated with a risky outcome. In the negative frame, no-action was preferred when it was associated with a certain outcome.

The sunk cost effect

If you go to the cinema but find that the movie you are watching is really boring, what do you do? Do you walk out or do you sit through to the end? If you sit through to the end when there are more enjoyable things you could be doing, then you may be committing a *sunk cost error*. According to Arkes and Blumer (1985), the sunk cost effect 'is manifested in a greater tendency to continue an endeavour once an investment in money, effort, or time has been made'. From the point of view of economic theory, this is an error because the only thing that should matter is a consideration of potential future costs and benefits.

Arkes and Blumer demonstrated the pervasiveness of the sunk cost effect across a series of studies. For example, they examined how frequently people visited the Ohio University Theatre after purchasing tickets that were either sold at full price ($15), at a $2 discount, or at a $7 discount, according to a random schedule. More visits to the theatre were made in the first half of the season, when presumably the original purchase was still fairly fresh in people's minds, and during this period people who had bought the full-price tickets attended more often than people who had purchased the discounted tickets.

Sunk cost thinking can lead people to throw good money after bad, leading to an *escalation of commitment* (e.g. Staw, 1976). This has important implications for business and public policy decisions. For example, sunk cost thinking reduces decision makers' willingness to cancel big-budget projects that are going badly, or their willingness to bring soldiers home from a war zone where no clear victory is in sight.

Thaler (1980) explained the sunk cost effect in terms of prospect theory. He suggested that expenditures are not automatically felt as a loss, but in circumstances where they are then people act in such a way as to attempt to recoup the loss. For instance, purchases made for immediate consumption (such as buying lunch) are not in any way 'painful'; indeed, there is probably some net benefit. Similarly, purchasing items that will be consumed in the future, such as theatre tickets, is also probably pain-free; one is exchanging money for an asset that will be experienced as a benefit at the moment of consumption (there may also be a tingle of anticipation). However, expenditures without associated benefits, either due to unanticipated circumstances or one's own failure to take advantage of an asset, may be experienced as a loss, and the bigger the expenditure the bigger the pain of that loss.

Where people can act to prevent or to recoup a loss they are likely to do so. Thus, people who (on a random basis) paid full price for their season tickets to Ohio University Theatre went to the theatre more often, because not attending would have elicited a greater sense of loss compared to those who received discounted tickets.

According to Arkes and Blumer, 'prospect theory does not specify the psychological basis for the findings that sure losses are so aversive and sunk costs are so difficult to ignore' (1985, p.132). They suggested that people have an aversion to being wasteful or being seen to be wasteful (see also Arkes, 1996; Arkes & Ayton, 1999). However, to my mind it is not clear that this 'Do not waste' heuristic so much explains the aversiveness of losses as merely redescribes them. Perhaps people develop a rule about not wasting *because* they are averse to losses. It is also not clear to what extent people really are averse to waste. Evidence suggests that people are only really influenced by sunk costs when they attend to readily computable units of measurement within a mental account. Monetary expenditures on specific items often fall into this category. However, Soman (2001) found that people were unaffected by sunk costs involving *time*, except where time could be assessed against some more readily accountable unit.

It appears that ordinary monetary sunk costs do not last indefinitely. In the theatre study, people who had purchased season tickets attended less during the second half of the season and there was no effect of ticket price during this later period. Similarly, Gourville and Soman (1998) found that individual attendance at a health club was greatest during the period in which the dues were paid, but then swiftly fell away until the next payment period. Gourville and Soman used the term *payment depreciation* to refer to the declining relevance of an earlier expenditure.

There is some evidence that having an education in economics reduces the frequency with which sunk cost thinking occurs. Larrick *et al.* (1990) found that economics professors, as compared to professors of biology or the humanities, were more likely to report failing to use items they had purchased, and were more likely to abandon some activity before completion, such as dropping a research project that was not proving worthwhile or failing to

watch a movie until the end. They also found that naive students who underwent half an hour's training on normative principles performed more successfully up to a month later, compared to untrained students, on a subsequent decision-making test.

Transaction utility

During a recent trip to a cinema in London's West End, I purchased a bottle of Italian beer for £3.50. At my local off-licence in London's East End, the same bottle would have cost me £1; indeed, I would be unwilling to purchase from my off-licence if it cost substantially more. So why was I willing to pay more at the cinema? Thaler (1999) suggests that there are two kinds of utility associated with a purchase: *acquisition utility* and *transaction utility*. Acquisition utility is simply the value of a good relative to its price, whereas transaction utility is the perceived value of the 'deal'. The deal is the difference between the amount paid and the 'reference price' for the good, where the reference price is what you would expect to pay in a given context. The West End of London tends to be expensive, because many tourists go there, and cinemas generally tend to sell refreshments at high prices because they have a captive audience (does anybody take their own beer to the cinema?); therefore, the reference price that I have for beer purchased there is higher than the reference price in the less salubrious area where I live.

The validity of my anecdotal example could be questioned, because the places in which I consume the beers is different (cinema versus my home), therefore the consumption experience may be different. However, Thaler (1985) held the consumption experience constant in a study where he asked people how much they would be willing to pay to drink a bottle of beer while lying on a hot beach. Half the participants were told that their friend would go to a fancy resort hotel to buy the beer, and the other half were told that their friend would go to a run-down grocery store. The median prices that people were willing to pay (in 1984 prices) were $2.65 (resort) and $1.50 (store), indicating that people had a different reference price depending on the place of purchase – even though the consumption experience was the same. Economically, this is irrational.

Budgeting

Thaler (1999) noted that we can categorise money at three levels. Firstly, there is our income which, broadly speaking, consists of regular income, irregular income, and windfalls. Secondly, there is our wealth, which might consist of our pensions, current account (or checking account in the USA), insurance plans, and so on. Thirdly, there are our expenditures, such as money spent on food, housing, and so forth. In economics, it is assumed that these different accounts are substitutable, or *fungible*, meaning that money can be moved between the different accounts. However, people tend not to think like this. For example, a person might be willing to spend $50 on a sweater after having previously spent $50 on theatre tickets, but not after having spent $50 on slacks.

People generally set budgets for expenditure prior to actually spending their money. Because we cannot be sure how many spending opportunities we will be faced with in a given time period, we sometimes overestimate or underestimate the money required for a particular account. Consequently, we overconsume some goods and underconsume others.

Heath and Soll (1996) suggest that people use similarity judgments and categorisation to *post* items to a particular budget. To test this idea, they investigated underconsumption across the categories of entertainment, food, and clothes. To use their example, suppose Susan normally spends $50 per week on entertainment. We now need to assess the effects of Purchase (P), Satiation (S), and Income (I) on her spending behaviour.

Suppose she makes a $20 expenditure. How much is she now willing to spend on entertainment? If the $20 was spent on a sports ticket, then she says she is likely to spend $32 on entertainment, thus P = 50 − 32 = 18. If, in fact, she receives the sports ticket as a gift, then because of the effects of satiation she is not now willing to spend the full $50 on entertainment, but is still willing to spend $42, so S = 50 − 42 = 8. Lastly, if Susan spent the $20 on an unexpected parking fine then she is now willing to spend $45 on entertainment, so I = 50 − 45 = 5.

To assess Susan's level of underconsumption we calculate P − S − I, which is 18 − 8 − 5 = 5. In other words, Susan spends less on entertainment after having already spent money on entertainment, compared to having already spent money in some other category. Heath and Soll's participants were asked exactly these kinds of questions and they found a widespread tendency to underconsumption. Furthermore, there was a typicality effect: a previous expenditure on a highly typical category member, as compared to a less typical category member, reduced the amount that people were willing to subsequently spend in that category (typicality was independently assessed). For instance, more people underconsumed entertainment after purchasing a $20 sports ticket (highly typical) than after purchasing $20 worth of party snacks (not so typical).

Kahneman and Tversky (1984) provided further evidence that people's choices are affected by the organisation of expenditures into *topical* mental accounts. Suppose you are in a store, considering a purchase. You discover that you could save $5 by taking a 20-minute drive to a different store. Would you do this? If people think about this problem in terms of a *minimal mental account*, then the only thing that should matter is the $5 saving, not the type of purchase. A second possibility, assumed by economic theory, is that people use a *comprehensive account* that considers current wealth, future earnings, and the possible outcomes of other probabilistic holdings. However, the evidence suggests that people evaluate the choice using a *topical mental account*, within which outcomes are considered in relation to a reference point that is determined by the context. Kahneman and Tversky presented people with one of two versions of the following problem (one version has the figures in parentheses):

> Imagine that you are about to purchase a jacket for $125 ($15) and a calculator for $15 ($125). The calculator salesman informs you that the calculator you wish to buy is on sale for $10 ($120) at the other branch of the store, located 20 minutes' drive away. Would you make the trip to the other store?

Most people were willing to make the trip to save $5 on a $15 calculator, but not to save it on a $125 calculator.

The following example is also from Kahneman and Tversky (1984):

Problem 1 ($N = 200$):
Imagine that you have decided to see a play and paid the admission price of $10 per ticket. As you enter the theatre, you discover that you have lost the ticket. The seat was not marked, and the ticket cannot be recovered.

> Would you pay $10 for another ticket?

> Yes (46 per cent)   No (54 per cent)

Problem 2 ($N = 183$):
Imagine that you have decided to see a play where admission is $10 per ticket. As you enter the theatre, you discover that you have lost a $10 bill.

> Would you still pay $10 for a ticket for the play?

> Yes (88 per cent)   No (12 per cent)

In this example, people are less likely to purchase a new ticket after having lost the old one, because the two expenditures come from the same topical mental account. Losing a $10 bill is less painful because it is most likely considered part of our general wealth account rather than part of our budget for entertainment.

Hedonic framing and the hedonic editing hypothesis

Consider the following two scenarios, adapted from Thaler and Johnson (1990):

Scenario 1
Suppose Mr A wins $25 in an office lottery, and on the same day wins $50 in another office lottery. Now consider Mr B, who wins $25 in an office lottery and, two weeks later, wins $50 in a second office lottery. Who do you think would be happier, Mr A or Mr B?

Scenario 2
Suppose Mr A receives a $20 parking ticket and, on the same day, receives a bill for $25 from the registrar because a form was filled in improperly. Now consider Mr B, who receives a $20 parking ticket and, two weeks later, receives a bill for $25 from the registrar because a form was filled in improperly. Who is more unhappy, Mr A or Mr B?

In thinking about these problems, we are asked to consider (a) whether it is better to have one large gain or two equivalent smaller gains, and (b) whether it is worse to have one large loss or two equivalent smaller losses. Thaler (1985) proposed that people might cognitively separate or integrate gains and losses in such a way as to maximise their happiness (the *hedonic editing hypothesis*). Based on the curvature of the value function in prospect theory, he derived four principles of hedonic framing:

1. Segregate gains (because the gain function is concave).

2. Integrate losses (because the loss function in convex).

3. Integrate smaller losses with larger gains (to offset loss aversion).

4. Segregate small gains (silver linings) from larger losses (because the gain function is steepest at the origin, the utility of a small gain can exceed the utility of slightly reducing a large loss).

Consistent with the hedonic editing hypothesis, Thaler and Johnson (1990) found that 63 per cent of participants thought that Mr B would be happier in Scenario 1 above (25 per cent thought Mr A would be happier). However, for Scenario 2, which concerns losses, the results did not support the hypothesis: 75 per cent of participants thought that Mr A would be more unhappy (17 per cent said Mr B would be). Across a range of materials, Thaler and Johnson found that people preferred to separate losses rather than integrate them, though where it was possible to combine a small loss with a larger gain then they did so. Thaler argues that, with the exception of multiple losses, the rules of hedonic framing are a good description of how people would like to have the world organised. He suggests that 'loss aversion is even more important than the prospect theory value function would suggest, as it is difficult to combine losses to diminish their impact' (1999, p.188).

Further evidence of hedonic editing can be found in studies of choices between indulgences and cash or necessities. Cash itself is fungible, so can be spent on luxuries, necessities, or savings. Therefore, given the choices between cash and a luxury, or cash and necessities, in each case people should generally prefer the cash. However, if people receive cash they may feel obliged to add it to their savings or to spend it on necessities, despite the fact they would get greater enjoyment from the indulgence of a luxury (a holiday, a fancy dinner, etc.). But when given advance choice between cash or luxury, people might opt for the latter, because this precommitment to indulgence ensures that they will not end up adding the cash to their general pool of money.

For instance, Kivetz and Simonson (2002, Study 2) gave three different groups of participants one of the following choices, which they could receive if they won a (hypothetical) lottery: (1) a cash prize of $80, or a massage or facial (valued at $70); (2) a cash prize of $80 or $70-worth of credit towards grocery bills; (3) a massage or facial worth $70, or $70-worth of credit towards grocery bills. As predicted, participants made intransitive choices. Specifically, 25 per cent preferred the massage or facial to the cash, only 9 per cent preferred the grocery credit to the cash, but 63 per cent chose the grocery credit over the massage or facial.

WANTING CHOICE AND COPING WITH IT WHEN YOU GET IT!

Suppose you want to see a particular movie that is showing at both a single-screen cinema and at a multiplex near you. Where would you go? It is likely that many people would choose to go to the multiplex simply because it offers choice. Indeed, experimental evidence suggests that both people and animals prefer choice over no-choice. It may be that people are predisposed to opt for choice because keeping our options open can often deliver us with better outcomes. However, sometimes people can be induced to opt for choice over no-choice, even when this cannot improve their outcome. This effect has been referred to as *the lure of choice* (Bown et al., 2003).

Sometimes people may be less satisfied when they opt for choice rather than no-choice (Gilbert & Ebert, 2002). Photography students who had been given the opportunity to change their minds about one of two prints they had chosen liked their prints less, several days later, than students who had not been given the option to change their mind. However, they themselves failed to anticipate this reduction in liking. Nonetheless, in another study (Gilbert & Ebert, 2002, Study 2b), 66 per cent of participants said they would prefer to be in a condition where they had the opportunity to change their mind (in this case, about a choice of art poster). In other words, most people chose to be assigned to a condition that would result in the least satisfaction.

One of the features of modern consumer societies is that we are faced by more and more choice. In his 1970 classic *Future Shock*, the futurologist Alvin Toffler used the term 'overchoice' to describe the situation in which the proliferation of consumer options, as well as the increasing number of decisions that it is necessary to take in a modern society, would actually pose a problem for people's ability to make those choices. The observation that heuristics can be quite effective for laboratory decisions – often about monetary gambles – might suggest that people are easily able to navigate a world in which many decisions must be made and where consumer options proliferate. However, other research suggests that Toffler's warning may have been quite prescient.

A series of studies reported by Iyengar and Lepper (2000) tested a *choice overload hypothesis*, according to which the provision of extensive choices, whilst initially desirable, would ultimately reduce people's motivation to engage with choice. Their first study was conducted in a field setting. Draeger's Supermarket is an upmarket grocery store in California. It offers an enormous array of products, and provides tasting booths in which customers are frequently offered sample tastes from the produce available. On two consecutive Saturdays two researchers, dressed as store employees, set up a tasting booth and invited passing customers to 'come and try our Wilkin and Sons jams'. The tasting-booth display was rotated on an hourly basis between a limited-selection display (6 flavours of jam) and an extensive-selection display (24 flavours of jam).

Of 242 customers who passed the extensive-selection display, 145 (60 per cent) stopped at the booth, whereas of 260 customers who passed the limited-choice selection only 104 (40 per cent) stopped. Of the people who did stop and taste some jam, one might expect that more jam would be tasted in the extensive-selection condition; in fact, there was not a significant difference between the conditions. However, in the limited-choice condition 31 (30 per cent) of the consumers purchased some jam, whereas just 4 (3 per cent) customers purchased jam in the extensive-choice condition. One limitation of this study was that the consumers were self-selecting in each condition. However, Iyengar and

Lepper reported similar results in experimental settings where they assigned people to different conditions.

In a series of studies, Schwartz and his colleagues used questionnaire measures to divide people into maximisers and satisficers. Maximisers were consumers who wanted to choose the best possible product, whereas satisficers were simply interested in finding something good enough to satisfy them. Schwartz et al. (2002, Study 2) found that maximisers showed greater regret about recent purchases they had made. It seems that people who tend to give consideration to multiple alternatives are more likely to continue pondering non-chosen alternatives after a choice has been made, worrying that they did not make the right choice. Maximisers also tended to compare themselves with others. When they compared themselves with people who had done worse they did not appear to feel any happier, whereas making comparisons with people who had done better made them feel less happy.

These social comparison effects were also confirmed experimentally (2002, Study 3), using a task in which participants were asked to work on anagrams alongside another person working independently on the same task. The other person was actually a confederate of the experimenter, and deliberately appeared to solve problems either faster or more slowly than the real participant. Maximisers rated their own abilities as much poorer, and they experienced more negative affect, after they had worked alongside a faster peer. By contrast, they showed little response to working alongside a slower peer. Satisficers' self-ratings showed little sensitivity to working alongside either slower or faster peers.

Schwartz et al. have also noted a link between mental wellbeing and individual differences in choice behaviour (2002, Study 1). Across several samples,[3] a tendency to maximise was associated with a tendency to experience more regret and depression, less optimism, less happiness, lower self-esteem, and less life satisfaction. Maximising also showed a small association with a tendency to perfectionism. Maximising was not, however, associated with neuroticism. Consistent with the experimental research described above, statistical analyses indicated a possible mediating role for regret between maximisation and depression, and between maximisation and happiness.

EMOTION AND CHOICE

There is an increasing recognition of the role that emotion plays in choice behaviour and our response to choice. Several sections of this chapter have referred to certain aspects of this topic. For example, emotion affects the extent of the endowment effect, with sadness actually leading to a reverse endowment effect. In the section on mental accounting I referred to the *hedonic editing hypothesis* – the idea that people 'cognitively separate or integrate gains or losses in such a way as to maximise their happiness'. We have also seen that people who try to maximise during choice are more likely to worry afterwards that they did not choose the best outcome, and thereby experience regret. People also sometimes forgo good opportunities if they anticipate there is a possibility of regret (Tykocinski & Pittman, 1998; see also Chapter 10).

Many of our likes and dislikes are often not consciously arrived at, but are quite intuitively determined. This includes things like visual art, music, and food. If pressed, we can of course come up with reasons as to why we do or don't like these things, though these may simply be post hoc rationalisations rather than genuine reasons. In fact, simply asking people to provide reasons for their choices in these domains may actually lead to poorer-quality choices being made. For example, students who were asked to list reasons for liking or disliking various jams were more likely to disagree with expert jam tasters than students who simply stated their preferences (Wilson & Schooler, 1991). Similarly, people who provide reasons for an (intuitively determined) choice may subsequently indicate less satisfaction with their choice (Wilson et al., 1993). Such results are consistent with the idea that two systems are involved in thinking: a deliberative, analytical system, and a fast, intuitive system. In the studies just described, it appears that the normal operation of the intuitive system is disrupted and overridden by the analytical system when a person is asked to provide reasons for an intuitive preference.

Slovic et al. (2002) have reviewed a series of studies supporting the existence of an *affect heuristic*, whereby preferences and choices may be determined by a simple feeling of 'goodness' or 'badness' that is taken to represent the positive or negative quality of a stimulus. For instance, Slovic et al. (1991; see also Peters & Slovic, 1996) asked people to generate images of cities and states, using a word-association technique. Participants then rated how positive or negative each image was. The averaged ratings were clearly associated with people's stated preferences for those cities or states.

Several studies show that people's evaluations of an attribute can be strongly affected by representing that attribute as a proportion or percentage of something. This is referred to as *proportion dominance*. In the studies reviewed at the start of this chapter, we saw that the rated attractiveness of a gamble is determined mainly by the probability involved rather than the monetary payoff. These results can be interpreted in terms of proportion dominance. For instance, consider how attractive a 7/36 chance of $9 is. In assessing this, people know where the probability of 7/36 lies on the probability scale. However, there are no obvious boundaries to help define how good or bad an outcome of $9 is. Slovic et al. (2002) report that this gamble was made more attractive, when a small *loss* was added (i.e. a 7/36 chance of winning $9, but a 29/36 chance of losing 5¢). This is because the small loss helps bring the value of $9 into sharper focus.

People's responses to life-saving interventions can also be dramatically affected by proportion dominance. In a study on airport safety, people were more willing to pay for a programme to save 98 per cent of 150 lives than for a programme to save 150 lives in total (Slovic et al., 2002; see also Fetherstonhaugh et al., 1997). Whereas it is not clear how to assess the value of saving 150 lives, 98 per cent is very close to the high end of the probability scale, so is clearly good.

More trivially, people placed more value on a 7 oz helping of ice cream, in which the ice cream was brimming over the top of a small carton, than they did on an 8 oz helping of ice cream in a very large carton (Hsee, 1998).

It is clear from these and other studies that people's judgments may sometimes be at fault due to the application of the affect heuristic. In particular, we may be vulnerable to the way in which others frame information so as to trigger affective feelings. Slovic *et al.* (2002) list various examples from the world of entertainment and marketing: entertainers who change their name to a more pleasing one; background music in movies; smiling models in mail-order catalogues; and the labelling on food products, such as '98 per cent fat-free'. In other circumstances, it might be desirable if we could trigger more affective responses. For example, young smokers find it hard to worry about risks that are perceived to be far into the future. Likewise, we are often more responsive to the suffering of one identified person than we are to the suffering of hundreds of thousands; indeed, merely adding statistical information to information about an identified individual can *reduce* people's willingness to help (Jenni & Loewenstein, 1997; Kogut & Ritov, 2005a, 2005b; Small & Loewenstein, 2003). Similarly, where wrongdoing is concerned we are more punitive with regard to an identified individual than with regard to unidentified individuals (Small & Loewenstein, 2005).

SUMMARY

People do not appear to behave according to the principles of rational choice. They make intransitive choices, they make different choices depending on how they are required to indicate their preferences (a violation of procedure invariance), and their choices are also affected by the presence of irrelevant alternatives. Importantly, these results indicate that people are not 'revealing' their preferences during the process of choice but, rather, they are 'constructing' them.

Mental accounting refers to the way in which people think about financial activities. Many of the insights in this domain come from prospect theory. For instance, consistent with loss aversion, people appear to overprice goods that they currently possess (the endowment effect), though this is also moderated by a person's emotional state at the time. There is also evidence that people separate or integrate gains and losses so as to maximise their happiness (the hedonic hypothesis). Like the other research presented in this chapter (and in this book generally), this strand of research indicates that people are using cognitive simplifications that may be quite useful, but which sometimes may act against their own interests.

In general people prefer having choice to no-choice. However, sometimes the existence of choice acts as a 'lure' such that people may end up choosing an option that they may not otherwise have chosen. Having choice does not necessarily lead to greater satisfaction. Similarly, having less choice and using simpler strategies are often associated with greater subsequent satisfaction. Having greater choice or using an analytical choice strategy can prompt subsequent feelings of regret in relation to the options that were not chosen.

Finally, choices involve emotional content, such as the experience of liking or disliking, or of regret (anticipated or experienced). Indeed, preferences and choices may often be determined by the application of the *affect heuristic*, a simple feeling of goodness or badness in relation to a stimulus that drives one's judgments and behaviour.

QUESTIONS

1. Design a novel sunk cost experiment.
2. Explain the concept of underconsumption and overconsumption.
3. Discuss the status quo bias, omission bias, and action effects.
4. Would it be advantageous to always use the weighted additive strategy when making choices?
5. 'Preferences are constructed rather than revealed.' Discuss.
6. Do you think maximisers would be happier with their choices if they learned to satisfice instead? How would you test this idea?
7. How might an intransitive thinker be turned into a 'money pump'?
8. What are 'protected values'? Give an example from everyday life.

NOTES

1. Accountability may or may not lead to more effortful processing (see the discussion in Payne *et al.*, 1993, pp.254–255). For instance, a decision maker who knows what the audience wants to hear might behave as a 'cognitive miser', whereas a decision maker who does not know the views of his audience may think more carefully.
2. Sunstein (2005) notes that people are far more troubled by the idea of euthanasia (which many governments prohibit) than they are by the withdrawal of life-saving equipment. For example, a doctor who administers a lethal injection to a patient is seen as causing that death through his own action, whereas the withdrawal of life-saving equipment may be seen as 'allowing nature to take its course'.
3. The participants, all recruited in the US and Canada, included students from three universities, health care professionals, commuters, and jurors-in-waiting. In total, there were 1747 respondents. Some samples filled out more questionnaires than others, so my generalised summary here does not actually apply to every single participant.

RECOMMENDED READING

Gilbert, D. (2006). *Stumbling on Happiness*. London: Harper Press. This is a marvellously well written popular science book in which Daniel Gilbert examines the topic of affective forecasting. Winner of the UK Royal Society's science book prize.

Payne, J.W., Bettman, J.R. & Johnson, E.L. (1993). *The adaptive decision maker*. Cambridge: Cambridge University Press. This academic book summarises much of the authors' own research on choice strategies.

Schwartz, B. (2004). *The paradox of choice*. New York: HarperCollins. Barry Schwartz contends that when it comes to choice more is not necessarily better.

9 | Confidence and Optimism

KEY TERMS

calibration
confidence intervals
confirmation bias
direct support model
ecological models
egocentrism
focalism
foxes
hard-easy effect
hedgehogs
hot air hypothesis
illusion of control
noise-plus-bias model
optimistic bias *or* unrealistic
   optimism
overconfidence
overprediction
probabilistic mental models
random support theory
reference group neglect
strength-and-weight model
underconfidence
underprediction

CHAPTER OUTLINE

In 1984, The Economist asked four European former finance ministers, four chairs of multinational firms, four Oxford students, and four London garbage collectors to predict the next decade's inflation, growth rates, and sterling exchange rates. Adding up scores ten years later, the garbage hauliers tied the company bosses for first place, and the finance ministers finished last. (Myers, 2002, p.158)

INTRODUCTION

The previous chapters in this book have shown that people are frequently mistaken in the judgments that they make. However, the studies cited thus far have not asked people how confident they were about the correctness of their answers. In fact, there is a great deal of research that suggests people are *overconfident* in their judgments, believing themselves to be right about things more often than they are. They also tend to think that they are able to perform skilled behaviours more accurately than they actually can. Relatedly, people are frequently *overoptimistic* about the future, at least in relation to events – good or bad – that may happen to them. This generally rosy view of the world, at least insofar as it relates to ourselves (as opposed to other people) may also affect the commitments that we make and, thus, our ability to achieve our goals. In this chapter, I shall examine the evidence for overconfidence and overoptimism, some possible causes, and our ability to plan for the future.

ASSESSING CALIBRATION (1): STATING PROBABILITIES

Consider the following question (from Lichtenstein *et al.*, 1982):

'Absinthe is (a) a precious stone; (b) a liqueur'. On the following scale, what is the probability that your answer is correct:

50%   60%   70%   80%   90%   100%

On a two-alternative forced choice problem like this one, participants understand that one of the answers *is* correct. Therefore, the probability scale can begin at 50 per cent, which indicates guessing between the two. Other variations on the task would require the use of a full-range (0–100 per cent) scale, for example:

- *No alternatives*: 'What is absinthe?' The respondent gives an answer and rates its probability of being correct.

- *One alternative*: 'Absinthe is a precious stone. What is the probability that this statement is true?'

- *Three or more alternatives*: 'Absinthe is (a) a precious stone; (b) a liqueur; (c) a Caribbean island; (d). . .'. Here, the respondent can either select their favoured alternative and rate its probability of being true, or they can assign probabilities to each alternative.

In what follows I shall focus mostly on the two-alternative forced choice task, as this has received the bulk of researchers' attention in the literature. Let us consider what it means to be well calibrated on this type of task. Suppose out of 100 general knowledge questions, there were 20 where I rated the probability of my being right as 50 per cent (i.e. guessing). If this numerical assessment of my own confidence is correct, then I should expect to answer half those questions (10/20) correctly. Then, suppose there were 10 questions where I rated the probability of my being right as 60 per cent. If I am perfectly calibrated, then I would expect to answer 6 out of those 10 questions correctly. And so on across the rest of the probability scale. Needless to say, for all the questions where I rated the probability of a right answer as 100 per cent I should answer the question correctly.

Overconfidence

As it turns out, people appear to be rather poorly calibrated. Many authors have reported that people are generally *overconfident* when answering general knowledge questions (for a review, see Lichtenstein *et al.*, 1982). Overconfidence is often illustrated with calibration curves like the one shown in Figure 9.1. The identity line shows how people's responses would look if they were perfectly calibrated. However, actual responses typically fall below the identity line. You may be wondering at this point whether overconfidence would disappear if one of the other

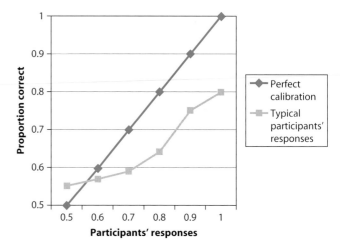

Figure 9.1. *A typical calibration curve for half-range, general knowledge items*

methods above were used. The answer would appear to be 'No'. Fischhoff *et al.* (1977) investigated the use of questions using no alternatives, one alternative, and two alternatives. They also investigated the use of both half-range and full-range probability scales, and the use of odds instead of probabilities as the mode of response. Overconfidence occurred with each of these methods.

Attempts to reduce overconfidence through feedback have met with mixed results, and it is not obvious that the methods would easily transfer to natural settings (see Lichtenstein *et al.*, 1982, pp.320–321). Likewise, greater motivation may not improve calibration. Sieber (1974) gave two groups of students a test, telling students in one group that this was their mid-term examination (high motivation), and telling those in the other group that the test was to help coach them for their mid-term exam (lower motivation). Although performance did not differ between the two groups, students who thought they were taking their mid-term exam showed significantly greater overconfidence.

A search for confirming reasons? One proposed explanation for overconfidence is that it arises from a biased search of memory. Koriat *et al.* (1980) proposed that calibration tasks involved three stages of processing: (a) memory is searched for relevant information and an answer is chosen; (b) the evidence is assessed and a feeling of certainty develops; and (c) this feeling is translated into a numerical response. Koriat *et al.* investigated the possibility that a biased search at the first of these stages might be the cause of miscalibration. That is, they believed that people might exhibit a *confirmation bias*, whereby they seek information that confirms their answer but neglect information that might be inconsistent with their answer. They noted that when participants were asked to write down reasons relating to their responses in a two-alternative task, they mainly tended to produce reasons that confirmed their response. In a follow-up study, participants were asked to generate reasons in accordance with one of three conditions: (1) one argument *against* their chosen answer; (2) one argument *for* their chosen answer; and (3) one argument for and one argument against their chosen answer. However, realism was only improved among those people who generated one argument against their response, and the reduction in overconfidence was extremely small.

In a follow-up study involving a forecasting task, Fischhoff and McGregor (1982) failed to find any effect of disconfirming evidence. In two experiments, Allwood and Granhag (1996) looked at the effects of self-generated arguments versus experimenter-provided arguments, as well as *self-contained* arguments versus two related arguments where one argument opposed the other. None of these led to any major reductions in overconfidence, although experimenter-provided arguments against an answer led to a slight reduction compared to a control group (in which no arguments were generated or provided). Experimenter-provided arguments where one of the arguments supported the answer actually led to greater overconfidence, even though this argument was paired with an opposing argument.

Rather more convincing evidence for a biased processing of arguments has been presented by Tetlock (2005). His participants were expert political forecasters – people who made a living by commenting or providing advice on significant political and economic trends. From the late 1980s to the mid-1990s (and beyond in a few cases), these experts made forecasts about the political and economic situations of many countries. They gave numerical probabilities for their forecasts and were also asked to explain the thinking behind two of their judgments (one inside their own area of expertise and one outside).

When the objective frequency of certain types of political events was compared with experts' probabilities, the experts were shown to be hugely overconfident. Although the experts were better calibrated than a comparison group of undergraduate students, they were outperformed by both crude and sophisticated algorithms. For example, simply assigning high probabilities to the continuation of recent trends was more accurate than the judgments of the experts. Forecasters were more overconfident about judgments in their own area of expertise than in other areas. In particular, they tended to overpredict change; that is, they used the extreme end-points of the probability scale (0 to 1) more often, so made more 'big' mistakes. Judgments about their own area of expertise led to a production of more causal arguments than judgments in other areas – based on an analysis of verbal protocols – and these arguments were lopsidedly in favour of the future perceived as most likely. These findings support what Tetlock calls the 'hot air hypothesis'.

Based on questionnaire measures, Tetlock also divided participants into *hedgehogs* and *foxes*:

> The intellectually aggressive hedgehogs knew one big thing and sought, under the banner of parsimony, to expand the explanatory power of that big thing to 'cover' new cases; the more eclectic foxes knew many little things and were content to improvise ad hoc solutions to keep pace with a rapidly changing world. (2005, pp.20–21)

Although both hedgehogs and foxes tended to overpredict change, Tetlock found that hedgehogs did so *more than foxes*. This was the case when predicting both change for the better and change for the worse. The thinking of foxes showed more integrative complexity (for example grappling with tradeoffs), and this made them less likely to use the end-points of the probability scale. These fox–hedgehog differences could not be attributed to differing political views, as hedgehogs were more likely to be firmly placed on either the political left or the right whereas foxes were more often political 'centrists'.

Probabilistic mental models Other authors have taken the view that people may not be as poorly calibrated as much of the research makes them appear. Proponents of *ecological models* (as termed by McClelland and Bolger, 1994) assume that people are well adapted to their environment; as such they extract and store information about the frequency of events in the environment; and then they use these stored frequencies when making probability judgments. According to ecological models, the mis-calibration of judgment that is so frequently observed in studies results from people being asked to make single-event probability judgments, rather than frequency judgments, about a series of questions that are unrepresentative of the environment. This general approach was developed independently by Gigerenzer *et al.* (1991) and Juslin (1993, 1994).

To illustrate, let us look at the theory of *probabilistic mental models* proposed by Gigerenzer *et al.* They ask us to consider the question:

Which city has more inhabitants:

(a) Heidelberg
(b) Bonn?

In their theory, people first try to construct a *local mental model*. A local mental model contains information that enables the person to either retrieve the answer or to derive the answer through logical reasoning. For example, if the person simply remembers that Bonn has over 290,000 inhabitants whereas Heidelberg has between 100,000 and 200,000, then she can simply state – with 100 per cent confidence – that Bonn has the most inhabitants.

However, if a person cannot answer the question in this way then she constructs a probabilistic mental model (PMM). The PMM contains a reference class of relevant objects; in the current example that might be *All German cities with a population of 100,000 or more*. The PMM also contains the target variable *population size*. It also contains *probability cues* and *cue validities*. The probability cues are features of the environment that are predictive, to some extent, of the target variable. For instance, in Germany cities that have a football team in the Bundesliga (Germany's premier league) tend to be larger than cities that do not have a team in the Bundesliga. Thus, a person who knows that one city has a football team in the Bundesliga and another does not will conclude that the city with a team has a larger population. If both cities have a team in the Bundesliga or if neither does, then this cue is useless for distinguishing the two, and so another cue must be found. Different cues have different predictive validities. The confidence that a person has in her answer depends on the validity of the cue used in making the judgment. If no cue can be found, then the person simply guesses and gives a confidence level of 50 per cent.

PMM theory predicts two circumstances where people will demonstrate good calibration. Firstly, they should be well calibrated when making confidence judgments about a set of questions that is *representative* of the environment. To test this, Gigerenzer *et al.* (Experiment 1) randomly selected 25 cities from the 65 German cities that have populations above 100,000. They then constructed all 300 possible pairings of these cities, asked participants to say which city had the most inhabitants, and asked them to rate their confidence about each pairing. There was no overconfidence on this task.

The second circumstance where people should be well calibrated is when making *frequency judgments* about experimenter-selected general knowledge questions. On this kind of task, the reference class is different. The appropriate reference class becomes *previous general knowledge tests I have taken*. Because most people have experience of answering general knowledge questions, they should have a reasonable idea of how well they typically do. Across 350 such questions, after each block of 50 questions Gigerenzer *et al.* asked people to say how many they thought they had answered correctly. Their calibration was very good: on average people missed the true frequency by about one question in each block of 50.

PMM theory also predicts the circumstances where both overconfidence and underconfidence should occur. Overconfidence results when people give confidence judgments about unrepresentative (and difficult) sets of questions. However, general knowledge questions that are actually quite easy can lead to reduced overconfidence or even *underconfidence*; the differential performance on hard and easy questions has been noted in previous research and is known as the *hard-easy effect* (see Lichtenstein *et al.*, 1982).[1] Underconfidence also results when people make frequency judgments about naturally sampled questions (representative set). Both predictions were confirmed in Gigerenzer *et al.*

PMM theory can also account for the failure of previous studies to find a debiasing effect of asking people to provide reasons for their choice of answer. Firstly, people are assumed to always search for a confirming cue to back up their answer, even in control conditions where they are not required to write down their reasons. Secondly, if required to write down a reason *against* their selection, the search for a disconfirming cue will take place after a confirming cue has already been found. Furthermore, the ongoing search for cues is as likely to find another confirming cue as a disconfirming one. Every time this happens, confidence will increase. It also means that the search for a disconfirming cue must continue. However, if people follow the Take The Best heuristic (see Chapter 2), then the progressive search for more cues will only turn up cues with lower ecological validity. Thus, on average the requirement to produce an argument against one's answer is not expected to decrease one's confidence.

The strength-and-weight model Griffin and Tversky (1992) proposed a *strength-and-weight model* to explain observed patterns of overconfidence and underconfidence. 'Strength' refers to the extremeness of available evidence, and 'weight' refers to the predictive validity of that evidence. To use their example, consider a letter of reference written by a professor on behalf of a student. A letter that speaks in glowing terms of the student is said to be high in strength. However, if the professor actually barely knows the student, then the letter carries little weight.

Griffin and Tversky proposed that people tend to focus mostly on the strength of evidence, perhaps making some (probably insufficient) adjustment in response to the weight (if known). Thus, the process of confidence judgment is essentially one of applying the representativeness heuristic coupled with anchoring and adjustment. Overconfidence occurs when high strength is combined with low weight, and underconfidence occurs when low strength is combined with high weight.

In an experiment to test this theory, participants were asked to make predictions about random pairings of American states. Three types of prediction were required, and concerned population size, high school graduation rates, and the difference in voting rates between the two previous presidential elections. It was expected that people would be (1) both accurate and confident about population judgments, (2) much less accurate and confident about voting rates (as it was expected that people would not be knowledgeable about this topic), and (3) inaccurate *but confident* about education. This last prediction was made on the basis that people would have good knowledge about the universities and cultural events within a state, and would use these cues to guide their judgment, whereas these cues are not very predictive of high school graduation rates. These predictions were supported, with chance levels of accuracy for both voting rates and high school graduations, but with greater confidence about the latter.

The strength and weight model has been referred to as a *direct support model*, in reference to support theory (Tversky & Koehler, 1994), because of the assumption that support – or strength of evidence – for a focal outcome, relative to its alternative, is what determines confidence (Koehler *et al.*, 2002).

Stating probabilities: an assessment of the competing views One thing that is quite clear from the research into two-alternative half-range tasks is that we cannot draw strong conclusions from studies where the questions were not randomly sampled (though in the real world, of course, there is no guarantee that a question will be representative of its domain!). People are not well calibrated, but there does not appear to be general overconfidence (e.g. Juslin *et al.*, 2000). Despite the results reported by Griffin and Tversky in support of their strength-and-weight model, the review by Juslin and colleagues of studies that used random sampling found that the estimated percentage correct roughly equalled the actual number of correct answers. Other studies have investigated calibration in multiple domains and found that the degree of over- or underconfidence varies from one topic to another (Juslin *et al.*, 1997; Klayman *et al.*, 1999).

Despite the important influence of the ecological approach, some questions remain. One such issue concerns the exact nature of the psychological processes involved. For example, in Chapter 2 we saw evidence that people may not always use one-reason decision making as claimed by the theory of probabilistic mental models. If this is correct, then it also calls into question that theory's account of confidence judgments. Also, there are cross-cultural differences in overconfidence on two-alternative half-range tasks (see below), which any theory of confidence judgments should explain.

Tetlock's research into expert political judgment also appears to be inconsistent with the ecological arguments proposed by Juslin and Gigerenzer. Political forecasters were better calibrated than undergraduate students, but were still considerably overconfident, and were outperformed by both crude and sophisticated algorithms. Most forecasters produced more than one causal argument for their judgments, and the more one-sided the pattern of arguments the more overconfident they tended to be. However, arguments that showed more integrative complexity – that is, more qualifications and tradeoffs – were associated with less overconfidence.

Cross-cultural differences

A number of studies have looked to see whether overconfidence differs from country to country. Before we look at this literature, try answering the following question (from Yates *et al.*, 1996):

> [I]magine that we randomly sample 1000 undergraduate students at universities in the United States and another 1000 at universities in Taiwan. We ask each student to respond to a large number of general knowledge items like the [two-alternative problems seen earlier]. Of course, in each place the items are in the native language (English in the United States and Chinese in Taiwan). The subject matter of the items would be equally familiar to people in both countries, too.
>
> Where would you expect the overconfidence to be greater? (check one):
>
> _____ Overconfidence greater in Taiwan
> _____ Overconfidence greater in the United States
> _____ Overconfidence the same in Taiwan and the United States

When this question was posed to students in Taiwan and in the US, 64 per cent of Taiwanese thought that Americans would show greater overconfidence, as did 61 per cent of Americans themselves. Just 20 per cent of Taiwanese and 9 per cent of Americans thought that Taiwanese students would show greater overconfidence. In fact, the reverse appears to be true: the Taiwanese show greater overconfidence than Americans (Lee *et al.*, 1995; Yates *et al.*, 1990). In fact, many Asian populations show greater overconfidence than Western ones. The Chinese show more overconfidence than Americans (e.g. Yates *et al.*, 1989), and respondents from Hong Kong, Indonesia, and Malaysia show more overconfidence than British respondents (Wright *et al.*, 1978). However, Lee *et al.* (1995) found that Singaporean respondents showed about the same level of overconfidence as Americans; they also found that the Japanese showed less overconfidence than Americans (Yates *et al.*, 1989, reported about the same level of overconfidence between Americans and Japanese respondents).

Yates *et al.* (2002) have reviewed various possible explanations for Asian–Western differences and largely rule out the possibility that different groups may have received questions of different difficulty, or that different nationalities may have been using the response scales in different ways. One possible contributor to cross-national differences in overconfidence is a difference in the recruitment of arguments. A study reported by Yates *et al.* (2000; cited in Yates *et al.*, 2002) asked participants to list arguments for and against each of the alternative answers presented to them. Japanese participants listed more arguments against their chosen alternative than did the Americans who, in turn, listed more such

arguments than Chinese participants. Another possible explanation, suggested by Wright and Phillips (1980) is that Chinese, Malaysian, and Hong Kong respondents may tend to view the world in non-probabilistic terms. Thus, these nationalities tend to produce more 100 per cent judgments in calibration studies than do Westerners or the Japanese. Wright and Phillips's Asian respondents also produced more 'Don't know' answers in response to open-ended questions such as 'Will you catch a head cold in the next three months?'

ASSESSING CALIBRATION (2): CONFIDENCE INTERVALS

Before reading any further, try the following test (updated from Russo and Schoemaker, 1989[2]):

> For each of the following ten items, provide a low and high guess such that you are 90 per cent sure the correct answer falls between the two. Your challenge is to be neither too narrow (i.e. overconfident) nor too wide (i.e. underconfident). If you successfully meet this challenge you should have 10 per cent misses – that is, exactly one miss.

		90% confidence range	
		LOW	HIGH
1.	Martin Luther King's age at death	_____	_____
2.	Length of the Nile River	_____	_____
3.	Number of countries that are members of OPEC	_____	_____
4.	Number of books in the Old Testament	_____	_____
5.	Diameter of the moon (in miles or kilometres)	_____	_____
6.	Weight of an empty Boeing 747 (in pounds or kilograms)	_____	_____
7.	Year in which Wolfgang Amadeus Mozart was born	_____	_____
8.	Gestation period (in days) of an Asian elephant	_____	_____
9.	Air distance from London to Tokyo (in miles or kilometres)	_____	_____
10.	Deepest (known) point in the ocean (in feet or metres)	_____	_____

Answers in both imperial and metric units are given at the end of the chapter.

If your two estimates in each of the above questions accurately reflected a 90 per cent confidence that the true answer lay between them, then the correct answer should lie between the two estimates for nine out of the 10 questions. If this is the case, then you can consider yourself to be 'well calibrated'. If, like most people, you entered the correct answer between the two estimates for fewer than nine questions, then you were overconfident in your responses. Russo and Schoemaker administered the test to over 1000 people and reported that fewer than 1 per cent of respondents answered nine or more items correctly.

Overconfidence on interval tasks turns out to be substantial. For example, Russo and Shoemaker (1992) asked business managers to give intervals for a range of topics. When asked to give 90 per cent confidence intervals, their ranges contained the correct answer between 42 per cent and 62 per cent of the time, depending on the topic and the participant group. Ranges of 50 per cent contained the correct answer about 20 per cent of the time.

Confidence interval judgments appear to be quite insensitive to different instructions. Teigen and Jørgensen (2005, Experiment 3) found that 90 per cent and 50 per cent confidence intervals were both associated with 23 per cent hit rates. Participants who were asked to give any intervals that they felt like generated a similar size interval to these other two conditions and obtained a similar hit rate (27 per cent). When this group was asked to rate their confidence that their intervals contained the correct answer, the mean response was 42 per cent.

In another experiment (2005, Experiment 4), participants were asked to give *improbably* high and low figures. These improbable intervals were associated with higher hit rates of about 65 per cent, yet despite the instruction to set an improbable interval participants gave a confidence rating of only 75 per cent.

Nonetheless, within this overall pattern of insensitivity to task instructions there were certain variations. When the task involved estimating historical dates (2005, Experiment 3), events in the more distant past were associated with increasing intervals. When the task involved estimating capital cities' population sizes (Experiment 4) there were both over- and underestimations, though overestimations (mainly of small capitals) were two to three times more common. An overestimation bias may be due to the fact that known cities tend to have larger populations than unknown cities.

Soll and Klayman (2004) present evidence that overconfidence arises on interval tasks partly as a result of 'noise' (random error) and partly as a result of a tendency to seek confirming evidence for one's judgments (*confirmation bias*). Let us consider the issue of noise first, as it is not obvious why random error should cause overconfidence. Soll and Klayman ask us to imagine that Serge is trying to estimate the year of Charles Darwin's birth. Because Serge cannot remember the exact year, there is a range of possibilities. In Figure 9.2, the years towards the centre of the range are considered highly likely by Serge, but as the dates move away from this area then Serge's estimated likelihoods decrease. In other words, Serge's range of probabilities forms a normal (bell-shaped) distribution.

Suppose Serge is trying to set an interval such that there is an 80 per cent chance that Darwin's date of birth lies within it. If Serge were perfectly calibrated then he would set interval I. As it happens, though, he is prone to random error in setting his interval, which means that he is just as likely to set his interval too narrow (interval J) as he is to set it too wide (interval K). However, the area under the curve that is excluded by interval J (the dark blue area) is greater than the interval added by interval K (the light blue area). This translates into 14 per cent overconfidence for

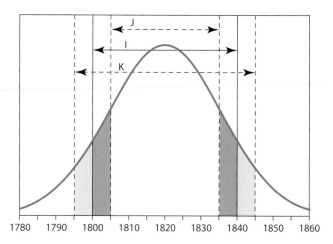

Figure 9.2. *A hypothetical subjective probability function for an estimate of the year Charles Darwin was born. Intervals J and K represent opposite 10-year errors in estimating the interval, I, that contains 80 per cent of the probability*
Source: Soll & Klayman 2004.

interval J and 9 per cent underconfidence for interval K. Clearly, over a series of such judgments random error will give the appearance of an overconfidence bias. If overconfidence is indeed the result of random error in setting intervals, it does not actually require that people have subjective probability distributions in their minds, simply that they have a general notion that some answers are more probable than others.

Across three studies, Soll and Klayman examined whether people's confidence intervals were consistent with those that would be produced by a combination of basic accuracy plus random error. They began by estimating subjective probability distributions for participants based on their intervals. Across all answers in a given domain they averaged the difference between the median of the interval and the true answer. They also calculated the mean expected absolute difference that would occur if the participant's end-points were the 10th and 90th percentiles of a normal distribution. The ratio of the expected to the actual deviation represents the extent to which a person is well calibrated or not. Soll and Klayman found a high degree of overconfidence. In other words, mere random error was not enough to explain miscalibration.

Further analyses examined variation in responding within participants, between participants, and between different domains. These analyses showed that some apparent overconfidence was actually due to noise. However, the contribution of noise was actually quite small, indicating that most miscalibration was due to genuine overconfidence.

The anchoring-and-adjustment heuristic provides a potential explanation for overconfidence in interval tasks. When answering a question, people may first generate an estimated answer that serves as an anchor, then adjust away from that in order to set the intervals. However, as adjustment is typically insufficient people's intervals are too small. One finding argues against this explanation. Soll and Klayman found that when people were explicitly asked to set a median value between their intervals, they actually set wider intervals rather than narrower ones (see also Juslin *et al.*, 1999). An alternative account, proposed by Soll and Klayman, is based on the idea that people sample information from memory when they set intervals in a confidence task. Such samples may be biased, yet people tend to treat them as more reliable than they actually are. However, taking a wider sample of information reduces the degree of bias. This is what happens when people are asked to state a median judgment as well as an interval.

Finally, it is worth noting that for the two studies where Soll and Klayman recorded the sex of their participants (2004, Studies 1 and 3) men were found to be more overconfident than women; that is, they set narrower confidence intervals but were not more accurate. A number of other studies have also reported men to be more overconfident than women (see the section below on *Overconfidence in investment behaviour*). One speculation about this is that expressions of confidence tend to be accorded greater attention compared to more equivocal judgments, as Tetlock's research (described earlier) has shown. As men tend to be more status-oriented than women, it is possible that such conveying of confidence is one way to achieving status.

BEING BETTER THAN OTHER PEOPLE

Other cross-cultural research has indicated that there may be more than one form of overconfidence. Lee *et al.*'s (1995) study not only asked participants to engage in a general knowledge confidence task, but also asked them to engage in an assessment of peer comparison. They were told that they were among a sample of 100 students at their university who had been ranked on some skill or personal characteristic, such as writing effectiveness, influence on other people, or interest in sports. Their task was to estimate their percentile ranking. On this task, Americans showed *greater* overconfidence than the Chinese in Taiwan, the Japanese, Singaporeans, and Indonesians. The Japanese and Singaporeans showed slight underconfidence. On items that were neutral as far as self-esteem was concerned, all participants showed underconfidence.

Kruger and Dunning (1999) have also looked at people's self-appraisals relative to others. In different experiments, they presented participants with questions requiring logical reasoning abilities, a knowledge of grammar, and an understanding of humour. After completing the tests, participants were asked to estimate how many items they had got right and to compare their performance to those of their peers. On each test the majority of students placed themselves above the 50th percentile among their peers. More alarmingly, the poorest performers showed the greatest discrepancy between their estimated and actual position among their peers. Those in the bottom quartile (scoring on average at about the 12th and 13th percentile) believed their performance to be at about the 60th percentile in the class. There was one exception to the general overestimation of abilities: students in the *top* quartile estimated their percentile performance to be slightly lower than it actually was.

It might be questioned whether these results are a regression effect, whereby both the best and the worst performers tend to place themselves closer to the mean than they actually are. However, Kruger and Dunning provided experimental evidence of the reality of the effect. Four to six weeks after the grammar study, the top- and bottom-quartile performers took part in a second phase of the study. They were presented with the original responses from five other people, asked to review these, and to then reassess their own performance. The top-quartile students, who had originally underestimated their performance relative to their peers, now evaluated themselves more realistically (i.e. in an upward direction). However, the bottom-quartile students did not alter their inflated appraisals of themselves.

Kruger and Dunning argue that a person's very lack of skill in a particular domain means that he or she is unable to accurately assess their performance in that domain. However, they also showed that both skill and self-assessment can be improved. In a final study, they presented people with a set of problems based on Wason's (1966) selection task, after which people made the usual self-assessments. Half of the participants were then given a training pack on logical reasoning, while the others completed a filler task. On a subsequent set of logical problems, the people who had received training not only gave more accurate responses, but also gave much more accurate assessments of their own performance.

A different account of these results is based on a *noise-plus-bias* model (Burson *et al.*, 2006; see also Krueger & Mueller, 2002). This model suggests that people of all skill levels lack knowledge about how they compare to others, hence their judgments are noisy. They are also equally prone to overestimating their percentile ranking on tasks perceived as easy and equally prone to underestimating their ranking on tasks perceived as hard. Burson *et al.* note that this model predicts that the more skilled performers should be better judges of their percentile only on tasks that are easy; on difficult tasks they should be worse judges of their percentile.

This is exactly what they found in a series of studies where the difficulty of the tasks was manipulated. Furthermore, although Kruger and Dunning had argued against the operation of regression to the mean in their studies, Burson *et al.* suggested that this might nonetheless have played a role. To eliminate the potential for regression effects, their third study adopted a split-sample method. Participants were asked to complete either an easy or a difficult word task. For instance, some people were presented with the ten-letter word *typewriter* and given three minutes to find four-, five-, or six-letter words within this. This was an easy task. In the difficult version, a word such as *gargantuan* was used.

After this initial task, participants estimated their percentile ranking, gave a rating of difficulty, and also completed an unrelated questionnaire. Then they were presented with a second ten-letter word and again asked to find other words within this. After this second task, they again estimated their percentile ranking of performance, gave a difficulty rating, and they were also asked how good they were in general at finding four-, five-, or six-letter words in general on this type of game.

Three analyses are relevant here. The first analysis simply looks at the participants' percentile rankings in relation to the quartiles of actual performance. Secondly, participants were also divided into quartiles according to their performance on the *first* task and their percentile rankings for the second task were then analysed. The third analysis did the reverse: participants were divided into quartiles according to performance on the second task and their percentile rankings for the first task were analysed. Burson *et al.* found that the magnitude of miscalibration was less in the two split-sample analyses than in the overall analysis. This shows that when performance and calibration are both measured within the same task the results *are* affected by regression to the mean.

HOW WELL CALIBRATED ARE OUR JUDGMENTS ABOUT BEHAVIOUR?

Overconfidence in investment behaviour

There is considerable evidence that we are not merely over-confident about our knowledge, but also about the way we act upon the world. One example of this is trading on the stock market. Traders who are overconfident are likely to trade more, but because transactions also incur costs, the more transactions that take place the more costs are incurred. However, there is evidence that, even aside from transaction costs, overconfident traders may still perform more poorly. Odean (1999) notes that overconfident investors may not merely overestimate the precision of the information signals they receive, but they may also systematically misinterpret them. If this is the case, then they are likely to make poorer trades even after transaction costs are taken into account. Odean examined 10,000 randomly chosen active customer accounts from a nationwide (US) discount brokerage house. Average percentage returns were recorded for three periods: 84, 252, and 504 days following purchases and sales of securities. In all three time periods, the securities that were purchased underperformed the ones that were sold (over a one-year horizon the average return to a purchased security was 3.3 per cent less than to a security that was sold).

Of course, there are a variety of reasons why investors may trade, such as to meet liquidity demands. To control for a variety of motivations, Odean also examined trades where a purchase was made within three weeks of a sale, because such transactions are unlikely to be made by cash-strapped investors. Again, he found that the returns to purchased securities were poorer than to those that had been sold (over a one-year horizon, securities that were purchased underperformed those that were sold by nearly 5 per cent).

Odean points out that people intending to purchase a security are faced with a formidable challenge, due to the huge number of available prospects. In order to deal with this people may tend to direct their attention to securities that have performed very well or

very badly (these are also more likely to be discussed in the media). However, when looking for a security to sell people are considering a much smaller set (i.e. what they already own). Nonetheless, in other ways selling is a difficult task. The rational investor needs to consider any tax gains or losses from selling and balance this against the expected future returns from other securities. The evidence suggests that people actually tend to take a simpler approach: as mentioned in Chapter 7, people tend to sell their winning investments and hang on to the losing ones, consistent with loss aversion.

Several authors have noted that self-serving attributions are greater for men than for women (e.g. Beyer, 1990; Deaux & Farris, 1977); in other words, men take more credit for their successes, whereas women are more likely to cite luck or other factors. Furthermore, men tend to be more overconfident than women (Lundeberg *et al.*, 1994), especially in domains that are perceived to be masculine (Beyer & Bowden, 1997; Deaux & Emswiller, 1974; Lenney, 1977). In a highly uncertain, male-dominated environment such as the stock market, where the quality of feedback is poor, it is reasonable to expect that men will exhibit greater overconfidence than women, resulting in more trades and perhaps poorer overall performance. Barber and Odean (2001) found exactly this. In a study of data from 35,000 broker accounts they found that men traded 45 per cent more often than women and underperformed the market by 2.65 per cent (compared to women's 1.72 per cent underperformance).

Skill, egocentrism, and the illusion of control

A survey of 3000 new business owners found that they rated an 81 per cent probability of success for their own business, though when asked about businesses like theirs they gave a probability of 59 per cent (Cooper *et al.*, 1988). These results are indicative of considerable overconfidence, given that roughly two thirds of new businesses fail within four years (Dun & Bradstreet, 1967; Dunne *et al.*, 1988), and 79.6 per cent fail within 10 years (Dunne *et al.*, 1988). One possible explanation as to why so many people try to enter a market where failure is likely is that these entrepreneurs believe themselves to have a particular skill but neglect to realise that they are competing with others who also possess that skill.

Camerer and Lovallo (2000) labelled this belief *reference group neglect*. They quote Joe Roth, the chairman of Walt Disney Studios, who was asked why it is that so many big-budget movies are released on the same weekends:

Hubris. Hubris. If you only think about your own business, you think, 'I've got a good story department, I've got a good marketing department, we're going to go out and do this.' *And you don't think that everybody else is thinking the same way.* In a given weekend in a year you'll have five movies open, and there's certainly not enough people [movie-goers] to go around. (*Los Angeles Times*, 1996, quoted in Camerer & Lovallo, 2000, p.422, emphasis added)

To test the reference group neglect hypothesis, Camerer and Lovallo recruited two groups of students to a study that offered some monetary payoff at the end. One group was recruited through the usual general recruiting instructions. Participants in the other group were specifically informed that their skill in sports or current events trivia would affect their payoff.

The basic idea behind the game was that participants made a series of decisions about whether or not to enter a market, where the possible payoff depended partly on how many other people were in that market. The game took place over several rounds, and each round was assigned a market 'capacity' of two, four, six, or eight people. The payoff to each entrant was a share of a fixed sum ($50), the size of which depended on the market capacity, on how many other people entered the round, and on a personal ranking. This ranking was either determined randomly or was based on their skill in sports or trivia. Everybody took part in a series of rounds based on a random ranking and a series based on a skill ranking. The quiz that determined the skill ranking took place at the end of the experiment, so people did not know their skill ranking beforehand.

In each round people made a private forecast of how many people they thought would enter and received $0.25 for each correct forecast. They also had to privately decide whether to enter themselves. At the end of each round, participants were told how many people had entered. Figure 9.3 shows the average payoff across rounds, depending upon the nature of the recruitment instructions and the type of ranking. The game was more profitable for participants in the random condition than for those in the skill condition. Furthermore, the difference between the random and skills conditions was considerably larger under the self-selection recruitment instructions than under regular instructions. This finding is indicative of reference group neglect.

As a further test, Camerer and Lovallo also used participants' forecasts of how many people would enter each round in order to compute the average *expected* payoff for each round. This analysis controlled for the possibility that players were simply underforecasting how many people would enter each round. They found that most players expected the average profit to be less in skill periods than in random periods. As Camerer and Lovallo (2000, p.421) put it, most people seemed to be saying 'I expect the average entrant to lose money, but not me!'

Similar results have been reported in a series of real and imagined competitions conducted by Windschitl et al. (2003). These authors used the term *egocentrism* to describe what is essentially reference group neglect. They found that when a competitive task was made easier for all competitors, people believed that their own chances had improved relative to those of their competitors. Likewise, when a competitive task was made harder, people thought their chances had fallen relative to those of their competitors. Windschitl et al. also found a moderating effect of *focalism*. Focalism is the tendency to overweight assessments related to the focal outcome. When participants were asked to assess the chances of their competitor, the shared-circumstance effect was significantly smaller (though still in the direction of egocentrism).

Windschitl et al. note that egocentrism and focalism may have various effects on people involved in competition. These processing biases may help determine whether or not someone decides to enter a competition, how hard they try, and the resources they invest, the strategy they use, and the emotions they experience. Furthermore, people are likely to resist rule changes that lower or restrict everybody's performance, but to embrace rule changes that benefit the performance of all competitors.

In general, people seem to be overconfident about their abilities in domains where they perceive some control. For instance, McKenna (1993) asked people about their perceived risk of accident when they were either the driver or the passenger of a car. People rated themselves as more at risk when they were the passenger than when they were the driver. However, even as the driver they felt they were just as at risk as their peers from hazards that were perceived as uncontrollable, such as black ice, tyre punctures, or brake failure. In other circumstances, people may be quite poor at even distinguishing controllable from uncontrollable events, and may adopt a skill orientation for events that are actually determined by chance alone (Langer, 1975; see also Box 9.1).

Perceptions of control may not be the whole story when it comes to overconfidence in behaviour. For instance, in one study bus drivers were generally overconfident about their ability to drive a bus through a gap of varying widths (the gap was between two 6-foot-high wooden posts). However, when the task was made very easy the drivers were somewhat underconfident (Cohen, Dearnaley & Hansel, 1956, cited in Harvey, 1994). Note that this task also involved the estimation of frequencies, because, for each gap, the drivers had to predict how successful they would be out of five attempts. In another study, Cohen and Dearnaley (1962, cited in Harvey, 1994) found that football players, at professional, university, and school level, were overconfident about their ability to kick the ball into the goal from various distances up the pitch. The only exception was at the shortest distance (20 feet), at which point players were very slightly underconfident.

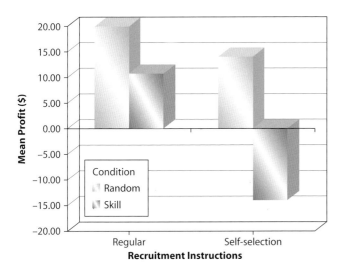

Figure 9.3. *Average industry profit from a market entry game*
Source: Camerer & Lovallo, 2000.

BOX 9.1. THE ILLUSION OF CONTROL IN FINANCIAL TRADERS

Fenton-O'Creevy *et al.* (2003) investigated the hypothesis that the performance of professional traders would be affected by an *illusion of control*. This is a phenomenon whereby people over-estimate the extent to which they are in control of certain events. Indeed, people often seem to believe that they can exert control over chance events (Langer, 1975). Their participants were 107 financial traders from four City of London investment banks. Just two participants were female, which – the authors reported – is reflective of the male-dominated nature of the trading environment. The total annual remuneration of these traders was positively associated with their education, experience, and job level.

In the task, the traders were required to press three computer keys in order to maximise a fluctuating index that was shown on the screen. They were told that the movements of the index were partly random but that the three keys might exert some effect – but with a time lag – on its movements. In fact,

the changes in the index were determined by a random walk overlaid upon an underlying rising trend. The first two rounds of the game were set up so that the participants gained points, whereas in round 3 they lost points, and in round 4 their scores stayed constant (though with some small random variation).

After each round, participants were asked to rate their success in raising the index, and the four ratings were combined to give a measure of the illusion of control. Illusion of control showed a negative correlation with traders' annual earnings: The greater the illusion, the less a trader earned. In addition, the job performance of each trader was independently rated by a senior manager from their company. This showed that the profit contribution of traders, as well as their analytical ability and risk management ability, was negatively associated with illusion of control. There was no association, however, between rated people skills and illusion of control.

FEEDBACK AND SELF-ASSESSMENT

In order for people to learn from experience, it is important that they get relevant and prompt feedback. Unfortunately, this is not always the case. In the stock market, for example, short-term movements of share prices are not a reliable guide to the underlying health of a company (or to the stock market in general); thus, the fact that my shares rose shortly after I purchased them is not a reliable indicator of my ability to spot good investments. Any other volatile environment is likely to produce the same problem of ambiguous short-term feedback.

Dunning (2005) has described some other potential problems with feedback. For instance, feedback may be *hidden*: thus, after behaving badly at an office party a worker may never find out how many people decided not to invite him to subsequent parties. Feedback may also be *absent*: in some countries people rarely get punished for dropping litter, whether by overt punishment or mere expressions of disapproval. People who drop litter may thereby underestimate the extent to which people disapprove of this behaviour. Feedback may be *probabilistic*: in many contexts there is not a direct correspondence between choosing the right action and getting rewarded for it. A motorist who obeys the speed limit through a small village may find herself being hooted by the impatient driver behind. Feedback may also be *incomplete*: even if we know the consequences of actions we have taken, we do not know how things would have turned out if we had behaved differently. If I appoint Jim to a vacant position, I do not get to find

out how things would have been had I appointed Mary instead. Finally, feedback may be *biased*: people are rather disinclined to pass bad news to others, and may even distort feedback so as to make it seem more agreeable.

Even when people receive clear and unambiguous feedback, we still sometimes fail to take the appropriate messages on board. For example, we tend to pay more attention to positive co-occurrences of actions and outcomes than we do to combinations involving non-occurrences of one, other, or both. Sports men and women often develop superstitions, whereby they link a successful outcome with some irrelevant action they performed before the event in question. They then feel the need to perform that action before subsequent events. Presumably, some of them drop the superstition when it fails to 'work', though it may also be the case that they identify some other action as the cause of the failure, and thereby add to the superstition.

Other errors of thought may lead to the neglect or cognitive distortion of feedback. People sometimes create self-fulfilling prophecies, whereby they seek evidence that can only confirm their theories, no matter how accurate or inaccurate those theories may be. For example, teachers who were told that some of their students were late bloomers found that those students performed better as time passed. In fact, the students labelled as late bloomers had been randomly selected, so their improved performance was presumably due to the way that the teachers treated them (Rosenthal & Jacobsen, 1968).

Hindsight bias is another barrier to learning from feedback. As we saw in Chapter 4, in the light of feedback people often mis-remember (or reconstruct) their earlier judgments, such that they believe they foresaw the future more accurately than they actually did. People also tend to seek out feedback that fits their self-image and they also tend to misremember feedback in a way that fits their self-image (see Dunning, 2005 for a review). Similarly, as with the traders mentioned earlier, people – especially men – tend to attribute positive outcomes to their own actions, and negative outcomes to other people or other external factors. Dunning also notes that people tend to accept positive feedback uncritically, whereas they scrutinise negative feedback. They also tend to perceive their positive actions as central and stable aspects of the self, whereas their negative actions are fleeting and unrepresentative. Failures may be construed as 'near successes'!

EXPERIENCE, EXPERTISE, AND THE CALIBRATION OF JUDGMENT

On various different types of judgment, some studies have not been particularly encouraging about experience and expertise.[3] For example, having experience with a task actually exacerbates unrealistic optimism about project completion time (see Chapter 10). Odean's research into investor behaviour, described earlier, also showed that stock market traders exhibit overconfidence, to the extent that one author has written: 'In contrast to an approach that accepts expert decisions as the standard, Odean shows us that experts have no expertise other than their ability to charge investors fees for their collectively useless and harmful advice' (Bazerman, 2001, p.354).

We have also seen that political experts are poorly calibrated to the extent that greater accuracy can be achieved by simply assuming that recent trends will continue. Despite this, Tetlock (2005) found that the most sought-after experts were more overconfident than their colleagues outside the limelight. It may be that overconfident experts 'may be more quotable and attract more media attention' (2005, p.63) or, alternatively, overconfident experts may be more likely to thrust themselves forward.

However, other findings have been more positive about expertise, although this tends to depend on the particular domain of judgment. The review of calibration studies by Lichtenstein et al. (1982) examined experts in several domains. Among these, weather forecasters using the full range of probabilities were found to be surprisingly well calibrated about their predictions. One study in particular has frequently been cited. A series of 24,859 precipitation forecasts, made in Chicago over a four-year period, showed excellent calibration (see Murphy & Winkler, 1977). Another study showing good calibration involved expert bridge players (Keren, 1987). It is notable that judgment in these two domains is characterised by rapid, accurate, and unambiguous feedback.

However, subsequent research has indicated that the extent to which weather forecasters are well calibrated actually depends on the frequency with which the forecast event occurs (i.e. the base rate). The base rate for rain in Murphy and Winkler's (1977) analysis was about 25 per cent. However, when trying to predict a less frequent event, extreme storms, which have a base rate of 13 per cent, forecasters were not well calibrated (Winkler & Poses, 1993). There was also an unusual pattern related to the size of the area being forecast: forecasters tended to over-use high probabilities for small areas (where storms are rare) and to underuse high probabilities for larger areas (where storms are more common). In other words, the forecasters seemed to be exhibiting base rate neglect.

Random support theory

Other studies of forecasters also support this base rate effect. Koehler et al. (2002) have reviewed some of these studies, as well as other expert judgments in the domains of medicine, the law, business, and sports. To explain the results of these studies (all using full-range probabilities), Koehler et al. developed a theory related to Griffin and Tversky's strength-and-weight model. This is the *random support theory* (RST), according to which 'probability judgments reflect the balance of evidence captured by underlying distributions of support for correct and incorrect hypotheses' (2002, p.688). Koehler et al. described three parameters that underlie the predictions of the model:

> Alpha (α): the judge's *discrimination ability*, defined as the difference in support for correct and incorrect hypotheses, indexing the quality or 'weight' of the evidence.
> Sigma (σ): the *extremity* of the judge's responses, defined as the tendency to depart from the base-rate value, indexing the perceived strength of the evidence.
> Beta (β): the differential support received by the focal hypothesis; among other things, β can be viewed as an index of a judge's sensitivity to the outcome base rate. (2002, p.688)

RST, like the strength-and-weight model, assumes that people make case-based judgments. In other words, people seek support for the case at hand but tend to neglect wider considerations such as evidence strength and base-rate information. In other words, σ and β do not vary as much as they should, or may even remain constant, across different domains of judgment.

Supporting this account, Koehler et al. observed, in the medical domain, that when discriminability and base rate were both high (for example, Intensive Care Unit survival), physicians' judged probabilities were too low relative to outcome frequency (underprediction). On the other hand, when discriminability and base rate were both low (for example, pneumonia), their judged probabilities were too high (overprediction). Calibration was considerably better when the discriminability was high and the base rate low (for example, streptococcal throat infection).

Like the strength-and-weight model, RST also predicts that people's judgments may be affected by personal experience or the availability of cases in memory. Thus, Koehler et al. cite a study showing that personal experience with a patient (relative to written descriptions) can increase overprediction (Bobbio et al., 1992). Another study they cite found that the availability of cases of bacteremia in physicians' memories correlated with their judged probability of bacteremia (Poses & Anthony, 1991).

OPTIMISTIC BIAS OR UNREALISTIC OPTIMISM

Optimistic bias research is concerned with people's judgments of how likely it is that some uncertain event will happen to them in the future. For a series of positive and negative potential life events, Weinstein (1980) asked students to rate how likely it was that these events would happen to them, and how likely it was that they would happen to their average classmate. Respondents thought that it was more likely that good things would happen to themselves, and that bad things were less likely to happen to themselves. This result has subsequently been much replicated.

The accuracy of people's predictive judgments regarding themselves can be assessed by waiting to see whether or not the target event does occur (within some reasonable period of time). However, such longitudinal studies are rare for obvious reasons. More typically, one of two other procedures is used. Firstly, people may be asked to rate their own chances relative to those of the average person (direct measure). Secondly, people may be asked to make separate likelihood judgments for themselves and for the average person (indirect measure). Optimistic bias has been reported with both types of measure, but they may not be measuring the same thing. It seems that the direct measure tends to focus one's attention mainly on oneself, whereas the indirect measure focuses attention both on self and other by virtue of its separate questions (Aucote & Gold, 2005; Covey & Davies, 2004; Eiser et al., 2006).

Actually, one variation on the optimistic bias measure is to adopt a comparison other than 'the average person'. Alternatives that have been used include the 'typical other person' (e.g. Perloff, 1987), '(most) people they know' (e.g. Drake, 1984), or 'other students at the same university and same sex' (e.g. Weinstein, 1980). Optimistic bias has been observed using each of these alternatives. However, optimistic bias does not appear to occur when participants compare themselves to a good friend (Perloff & Fetzer, 1986).

As with self-assessments of behaviour, the illusion of control appears to play a large part in generating optimistic bias. This relationship was confirmed in a meta-analysis of 27 samples, although there were also moderating effects of participant nationality, student status, risk status, and the type of optimistic bias measure used (Klein & Helweg-Larsen, 2002).

It is interesting to note that positive illusions are associated with mental well-being (see Taylor & Brown, 1988). They are associated with happiness, the ability to care for others, and the ability (and enthusiasm) to engage in productive work. In particular, people who have a strong sense of personal control, self-efficacy, and other positive beliefs tend to respond better to the kinds of stressful situations that could tip some people towards depression. This includes having the motivation to take positive action when adverse situations occur. Furthermore, different emotions have different effects on people's risk judgments and their optimism. Lerner and Keltner (2001, Study 3) induced the emotions of fear, anger, or happiness in their participants. When questioned about life events that were unambiguous in terms of their certainty and controllability, only the 'happy' participants were optimistic, whereas the fearful and angry participants were about equally

pessimistic. However, for events that were ambiguous in terms of their certainty and controllability, the angry and the happy participants were about equally optimistic, whereas only the fearful participants were pessimistic.

On the other hand, there is a concern that optimistic bias may represent a barrier to effective risk communication, and that unrealistically optimistic people may fail to protect themselves against a hazard. In line with this concern, studies attempting to reduce people's optimistic biases have not always been successful (e.g. Weinstein & Klein, 1995). It may be that there are optimal levels of positive illusions, such that a mild optimistic bias is associated with positive mental and physical health, but that both the inability to deceive oneself and extreme levels of optimism are associated with worse mental and physical outcomes (Baumeister, 1989).

SUMMARY

The accuracy of people's confidence in their knowledge has been measured in several different ways. In particular, the two-alternative forced choice test has been widely used. Many of these studies have found people to be overconfident in their knowledge. One early account of this phenomenon suggested that people tended to only search for reasons that could confirm their answer, thus neglecting arguments against it. However, the empirical evidence for this theory is not very strong.

In fact, it is not entirely accurate to characterise people as overconfident. A full explanation of people's performance on calibration tasks actually needs to also account for the hard-easy effect, whereby overconfidence is most pronounced on difficult tasks but people are less overconfident, and often underconfident, on easy tasks. Two prominent theories that try to explain such results are the theory of probabilistic mental models and the strength-and-weight model.

Other relevant phenomena include (1) the observation of cross-cultural differences in calibration and (2) the assessment of oneself as being better than most others. Cross-cultural differences do not appear to be due to artefacts such as national biases in the way people use response scales. However, although some explanations have been mooted it is probably fair to say that we do not yet have a good understanding why the cross-cultural differences exist.

Most people seem to assess their performance on tasks as better than that of most other people, the one exception being the top performers who actually slightly underestimate themselves relative to others. The evidence indicates that the very lack of a skill in some domain hinders the ability to accurately assess oneself in that domain. Fortunately, education on a particular topic seems to improve not just performance, but also the accuracy of self-assessment relative to others.

People also seem to be imperfectly calibrated with regard to judgments of their behaviour, as well as their knowledge. Overconfidence and the hard-easy effect have been observed in various domains. Overconfidence may be explained, in large part by the illusion of control, although this does not explain the existence of underconfidence on easy tasks. On skill-based tasks where people are pitted against others, people may suffer from reference group neglect, whereby they underestimate the extent to which other people may have the same skills as themselves. Overconfidence may also be created and maintained through self-serving attributions and imperfect feedback.

Studies of expertise have shown mixed results when it comes to calibration. Weather forecasters were once thought to be extremely well calibrated, but more recent evidence shows that this is not always the case. In fact, their calibration performance appears to depend on the base rates of the target event. To account for this, and calibration in other types of experts, random support theory has been developed.

Finally, when people imagine how likely it is that good or bad (uncertain) events will happen to them in the future, they are optimistically biased. They think good things are more likely to happen to them than to others, and bad things are less likely to happen to them than to others. Illusion of control appears to play a large part in this, though there are other factors too. Mood state affects both beliefs about controllability and the level of optimism. Despite some of the advantages of being optimistic, a central concern of such research is that people may fail to protect themselves against certain hazards.

ANSWERS TO THE TEST ON PAGE 97

(1) 39 years; (2) 4187 miles or 6738 kilometres; (3) 11 countries (as of 2006, at the time of writing); (4) 39 books; (5) 2160 miles or 3476 kilometres; (6) 390,000 pounds or 176,901 kilograms; (7) 1756; (8) 645 days; (9) 5959 miles or 9590 kilometres; (10) 36,198 feet or 11,033 metres.

QUESTIONS

1. If you were going to ask people to provide confidence judgments what do you think would be the best way of asking for such judgments and why?

2. How might focalism and reference group neglect (egocentrism) lead to overconfidence?

3. Evaluate theories of performance on confidence tasks that require stated probabilities.

4. How would you expect anxiety and happiness to affect confidence and calibration? Design an experiment to test this hypothesis.

5. Compare and contrast Kruger and Dunning's (1999) 'incompetence' model of inflated self-assessments with the noise-plus-bias model of Burson *et al.* (2006).

6. Several studies indicate that men are more overconfident than women. Why do think this is and how would you go about testing your explanation?

NOTES

1. Aside from the confidence–frequency distinction and the issue of representative vs. selected sampling, Peter Juslin and his colleagues have highlighted some other measurement problems that could give rise to the artifactual appearance of overconfidence and the hard-easy effect (Juslin *et al.*, 2000). For example, a person who is perfectly calibrated, but who shows some random noise in his confidence judgments, will nonetheless give the appearance of the hard-easy effect. To illustrate, note that, for a given confidence category, over/underconfidence is assessed by subtracting the proportion of correct answers from the subjective probability. Therefore, when the proportion of correct answers is 0.5, calibration must range between perfect calibration (0.5 − 0.5) and 0.5 overconfidence (1 − 0.5). When the proportion of correct answers is 1, then calibration must range between perfect calibration (1 − 1) and −0.5 underconfidence (0.5 − 1). However, a perfectly calibrated person who makes some random error in his confidence assessment will appear to be underconfident on the easy items and overconfident on the harder items. This is because at the ends of the probability scale there is only one direction in which the errors can go.

2. The number of countries in OPEC has changed since Russo and Schoemaker originally published this test.

3. Often, an expert is assumed to be someone with a great deal of experience. However, experience alone does not always confer the ability to make accurate and calibrated judgments. This raises the question of what an 'expert' actually is, but I shall not explore this further here.

RECOMMENDED READING

Dunning, D. (2005). *Self-insight: Roadblocks and detours on the path to knowing thyself.* New York and Hove: Psychology Press. The title says it all. This is a very readable account of the topic of self-insight.

Fenton-O'Creevy, M., Nicholson, N., Soane, E. & Willman, P. (2005). *Traders: Risks, decisions, and management in financial markets.* Oxford: Oxford University Press. This is an interesting account of risk perception, risk taking, optimistic bias, illusion of control, and personality profiles of financial traders.

Tetlock, P.E. (2005). *Expert political judgment: How good is it? How can we know?* Princeton and Oxford: Princeton University Press. How accurate are professional economic and political forecasters? Are they overconfident? Tetlock's book is an impressive study of experts over a period of years.

10 | Judgment and Choice over Time

CHAPTER OUTLINE

INTRODUCTION

Many of our judgments and decisions have a time element involved in them. Sometimes this is something we are explicitly aware of, and at other times it is something left implicit. One fairly explicit judgment about time is the setting of deadlines, which requires some assessment of how long we think it will take us to complete a task. Similarly, we often form an intention to carry out some task, though we often fail to actually do so. How strong is the link between intention and action, and why are we sometimes deceived by our own intentions? Choice itself often involves some kind of tradeoff between the present and the future, as when we make a decision about whether to spend or save money. Finally, good decision making requires that we can predict how we will feel about potential outcomes. As we shall see, people are often quite inaccurate in predicting how they will feel. In this chapter, I shall look at each of these areas of judgment and choice across time.

DEADLINES

I love deadlines. I like the whooshing sound they make as they fly by. (Douglas Adams, author of **The Hitchhiker's Guide to the Galaxy** *and other books)*

Hofstadter's Law: Everything takes longer than you think, even when you take into account Hofstadter's Law. (Hofstadter, 1980, p.152)

In the previous chapter we saw that people are often overconfident and optimistic. The planning of projects is one area where people appear to be optimistic: we frequently underestimate the time it will take to complete projects. This applies to individuals, organisations, and governments; indeed, public life is full of examples of big projects being completed late (and usually over budget).

In one study, psychology students were asked when they expected to submit their honours thesis, and were also asked when they thought they would submit if 'everything went as poorly as it could'. Only 30 per cent of students submitted their thesis by the predicted time. The average completion time was 55 days, 22 days longer than predicted. This was also seven days longer than the prediction made under the worst-case scenario. Nonetheless, estimated completion times did correlate with final completion times, so people's estimates were not uninformative – just generally optimistic. Students also showed a high level of confidence in their duration estimates (Buehler *et al.*, 1994, Studies 2 and 3). Many other studies have found optimism about task completion using a variety of tasks (many studies are listed by Roy *et al.*, 2005a, 2005b).

Surprisingly, this lack of realism appears not to be moderated by dispositional optimism, self-esteem, or non-clinical depression (see Buehler *et al.*, 2002). Likewise, people with a disposition towards procrastination do tend to complete work later, and are aware of their problems with time management, but show roughly the same levels of optimistic bias to non-procrastinators (Lay, 1986). Optimistic bias appears to be greater in the most motivated people (Buehler *et al.*, 1997), whether the motivation is monetary or simply the emphasised desirability of early completion. It is also greater among people who have *more* experience with the task in question (Boltz *et al.*, 1998; Hinds, 1999). Buehler *et al.* (2002) also report some unpublished results suggesting that the underestimation of project completion times may be stable across cultures. They found that both Canadian and Japanese participants showed optimism about task completion. This was despite the fact that the Japanese students, unlike the Canadians, did not try to 'explain away' past prediction failures through external attributions; rather, they tended to attribute the cause of past failures to themselves.

Kahneman and Tversky (1979; Kahneman & Lovallo, 1993) suggested that when people estimate how long a project will take they think about the task at hand and construct a scenario of how they expect progress to develop. This scenario tends to involve a series of steps that lead to a successful conclusion. This way of thinking is optimistic because people fail to imagine the kind of problems that might throw the project off course (essentially, this is another example of the focalism bias described in the previous chapter). As other research has shown, simply imagining how a scenario might unfold can lead people to increase their belief that the scenario *will* unfold that way (Koehler, 1991). According to this view, we might expect people's estimates to be infused with a dose of realism were they to consider previous projects of a similar kind. This latter approach is referred to as the 'outside view', whereas the typical approach that people take is referred to as the 'inside view' (or *planning fallacy*).

However, even when people do consider past cases they may still make optimistic estimates (e.g. Buehler *et al.*, 1994, Study 4). One reason is that people tend to view each case as unique, thus reducing the relevance of past instances. Thus, students are optimistic about completing their projects on time, even while admitting that they struggled to complete previous projects on time. Roy *et al.* (2005a) propose another, though not mutually exclusive, reason why people may not always be appropriately influenced by past experience. They suggest that people actually misremember how long previous projects took, such that they believe these tasks took less time than they actually did (see also Griffin & Buehler, 2005; Roy *et al.*, 2005b).

It may also be that people downplay the significance of previous experience when they do not like the implications for the current case (Buelher *et al.*, 2002). Other people's experiences may also fail to impact on our current estimates, because we tend to attribute others' outcomes to their personal dispositions (Jones & Nisbett, 1972), and because we are less certain about what really happened when we consider other people's experiences.

GOOD INTENTIONS

In the previous section we looked at people's ability to accurately estimate how long it will take to carry out some project. However, prior to engaging in some action comes the intention to do so. One strand of research has examined how well people's intentions predict their behaviours. This topic is particularly important in the domain of health research, where the concern is to identify and overcome the factors that prevent individuals from taking exercise, using condoms, having breast examinations, and so on.

One prominent theory that has been developed to link beliefs to behaviour is Ajzen's (1985, 1988) *theory of planned behaviour* (Figure 10.1). This theory links three factors to intentions, which are then linked to behaviour. Although stronger intentions are associated with a greater likelihood of carrying out an action, the relationship is far from perfect. Current intentions typically account for about 20–40 per cent of variance in behaviour. There are many factors that affect the relationship between intentions and behaviour, including knowledge, ability, resources, opportunity, and personality (Sheeran, 2002). Sheeran also found that the strength of the intention–behaviour relationship varies between domains, and is also stronger in relation to specific behaviours as opposed to broader behavioural goals.

Another factor that may mediate the relationship between intentions and behaviour is temporal distance. According to *construal level theory* (Liberman & Trope, 1998; Trope & Liberman, 2003),

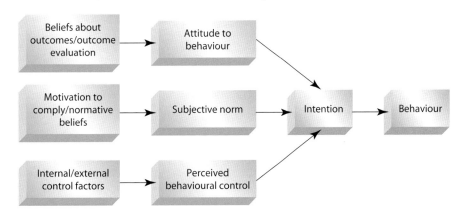

Figure 10.1. *Ajzen's theory of planned behaviour*

distant future events are construed at a higher level than near future events. Thus, people's preferences regarding distant future events are more strongly affected by high-level considerations, whereas their preferences regarding near-future events are more strongly affected by low-level considerations. For instance, one study (Liberman & Trope, 1998) described a forthcoming guest lecture as either interesting or uninteresting and as being given at a convenient or inconvenient time. When asked to rate their interest in attending the lecture in the near or distant future, the described interest level had a bigger influence on preference as temporal distance increased, whereas the convenience of the timing had less influence as temporal distance increased.

Situational factors, known as 'channel' factors (Lewin, 1951), can increase the likelihood of an intention being carried out. In one classic study, students received a persuasive appeal to take part in a tetanus inoculation program (Leventhal *et al.*, 1965). Some of these students were provided with a map of the campus that showed the location of the health centre. Although all students reported strong intentions to be inoculated, those who received the map were much more likely to actually do so.

Consistent with the strength-and-weight model of confidence (Griffin & Tversky, 1992; see previous chapter), people's predic-

tions about their own future behaviour may be erroneous because they place too much weight on the strength of their intentions, while underweighting predictive factors unrelated to current intention strength. In one study (Koehler & Poon, 2006, Study 1), students at the University of Waterloo rated the strength of their intentions to give blood at a forthcoming clinic. They also rated the probability that they would actually donate blood, and they indicated their agreement with a series of unexceptional statements about blood donation (for example, 'More Canadians should donate blood'). Some people rated their agreement with these statements prior to making their predictions and rating their intentions; for others, rating the statements followed the predictions and intention ratings. As expected, doing the agreement rating task *first* led to an increase in prediction ratings and intention strength, but did not lead to a significant increase in the number of people who actually donated blood. The average probability for blood donation was 43 per cent, whereas just 20 per cent of respondents reported actually giving blood.

In a subsequent study (Koehler & Poon, 2006, Studies 2 and 3), participants recruited for a future web-based study (see Figure 10.2) predicted a higher likelihood of their taking part when they were told that their participation was very important (as opposed to

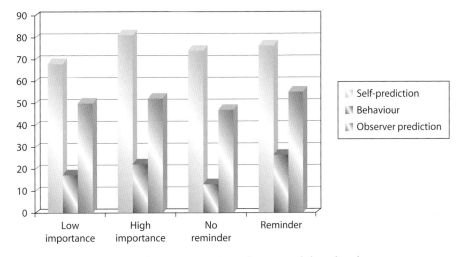

Figure 10.2. *Predictions and actual proportions of participants taking place in a web-based study*
Source: Koehler & Poon, 2006, Studies 2 and 3.

merely 'helpful'), but were no more likely to actually take part. A second manipulation involved promising (and sending) an e-mail reminder to half the students just before the study was due to take place. This manipulation had no effect on predicted rates of participation, but it did significantly increase the rate of actual participation from 13 per cent to 26 per cent. Finally, independent observers who had each seen the responses of a single participant (though not that person's self-prediction) were asked to predict whether that person had taken part. Their predictions were not influenced by the importance manipulation, but they were affected by the reminder manipulation. Thus, the observers were more sensitive to the factors affecting participants' behaviour than the participants themselves.

CHOICE OVER TIME

Time preference

There is considerable evidence that people prefer immediate rewards to delayed rewards. As we shall see shortly, many people prefer to take money now rather than to receive a slightly larger amount a month from now. One symptom of this in everyday life is the failure of many people to save sufficiently for their retirement. This tendency to prefer rewards now rather than later is known as *time preference* (Frederick *et al.*, 2002). This seems to be widespread in intertemporal choice (Figure 10.3), though there are exceptions as we shall see. In the 19th century the economist John Rae (1834) proposed various psychological motives underlying behaviour. These included:

- the desire to contribute to society (the 'bequest motive')
- having the intellectual ability to reflect and act prudently (self-restraint)
- the excitement produced by the prospect of immediate consumption
- the discomfort of deferring gratification.

These motives can be distilled into a theory whereby (1) people only care about their immediate utility, except where there is utility from the anticipation of future consumption, and (2) people do not like the self-denial required in order to delay gratification. These two broad factors may both differ among individuals. For instance, some people may be better than others at imagining future consequences, although it was also suggested that people might suffer a systematic tendency to underestimate future wants (Böhm-Bawerk, 1889).

Subsequently, Paul Samuelson (1937) developed the *discounted utility model* (DU model), an attempt to provide a generalised quantitative model of intertemporal choice. The central feature of this model was a discount rate that attempted to encompass all the psychological factors that had previously been proposed. In other words, the discount rate was a single parameter that determined the relative weight that a person would attach to his well-being in different time periods. In monetary terms, if I am indifferent between £100 now and £150 in a year's time, then my discount rate is 50 per cent. Although Samuelson made no claims for the model's normative or descriptive validity, the DU model was quickly adopted by economists as their standard for analysing intertemporal choice (Frederick *et al.*, 2002). Indeed, there are reasons why people should discount the future (Baron, 2000, pp.471–472), such as the fact that the future is always uncertain (for example, 'How long will I live?' 'Is the economy going to collapse?').

As it happens, the DU model does not provide a very good description of actual behaviour. The most frequently documented violation of the model is the fact that discount rates do not remain constant over time (e.g. Chapman, 1996; Redelmeier & Heller, 1993; Thaler, 1981; Thaler & Shefrin, 1981). Thaler (1981) found that, on average, people were indifferent between $15 now and $20 in one month (345 per cent discount rate); $50 in one year (120 per cent discount rate); and $100 in ten years (19 per cent discount rate). This pattern of declining discount rates is known as *hyperbolic discounting*.

Hyperbolic discounting also leads to a kind of preference reversal, known as *dynamic inconsistency*. Suppose I prefer to have £200 in a year's time to £100 nine months from now. However, on a shorter timescale I also prefer to have £100 in a month's time to £200 four months from now. In other words, even though there is a three-month difference in both choices, I prefer the smaller reward when it is near but not when it is further away. This kind of reversal has been observed in many studies (e.g. Kirby & Herrnstein, 1995; Solnick *et al.*, 1980). These studies have presented people with synchronous choices, but they also imply that someone who prefers £200 in a year to £100 in nine months will prefer the £100 if presented with the same choice in eight months' time. Dynamic inconsistency has also been observed in pigeons (Ainslie & Herrnstein, 1981; Green *et al.*, 1981).

There are also many other behaviours that are inconsistent with the DU model (for a review, see Frederick *et al.*, 2002). For

Figure 10.3. *Time preference: people tend to prefer utility now to delayed utility.* © Matt Feazell

instance, gains are discounted at a higher rate than losses, and small outcomes are discounted more than large ones. One interesting 'anomaly' relates to the *assumption of consumption independence* that underlies the DU model. This assumption states that a preference for one consumption profile over another should not be due to any periods in which consumption is identical in the two profiles. To test this assumption, Loewenstein and Prelec (1993) presented participants with the following pair of sequences.

Imagine that over the next five weekends you must decide how to spend your Saturday nights. From each pair of sequences of dinners below, circle the one you would prefer. 'Fancy French' refers to a dinner at a fancy French restaurant. 'Fancy Lobster' refers to an exquisite lobster dinner at a 4-star restaurant. Ignore scheduling considerations (e.g. your current plans).

Options	first weekend	second weekend	third weekend	fourth weekend	fifth weekend	
A	Fancy French	Eat at home	Eat at home	Eat at home	Eat at home	[11%]
B	Eat at home	Eat at home	Fancy French	Eat at home	Eat at home	[89%]

Options	first weekend	second weekend	third weekend	fourth weekend	fifth weekend	
C	Fancy French	Eat at home	Eat at home	Eat at home	Fancy Lobster	[49%]
D	Eat at home	Eat at home	Fancy French	Eat at home	Fancy Lobster	[51%]

Note that the consumption at the fifth weekend is identical for A and B, and is identical for C and D. Thus, this period should not be instrumental in affecting preferences. Therefore, someone who prefers B to A should also prefer D to C. However, as shown by the bracketed choice percentages, a significant number of people choose B over A and C over D.

Two tendencies appear to be at play in these patterns of preferences. Firstly, Option A represents a declining sequence whereas Option B is an improving sequence. Research indicates that people prefer improvement over decline, even where the declining sequence is more beneficial overall (e.g. Hsee *et al.*, 1991). Secondly, in Option C the consumption profile is more spread out than in Option D. Evidence suggests that people prefer to spread consumption over time. For example, another study by Loewenstein and Prelec asked three groups to imagine they had been given two $100 coupons that could be spent on fancy restaurant dinners, and were asked when they would choose to used them (excluding special occasions, such as birthdays). One group was told that the coupons could be used at any time; a second group was told that the coupons had to be used within four months; and a third group was told that the coupons had to be used within two years. People who were given two years to use the vouchers spread their consumption over longer periods than both the four-month group and those who were not given a time limit (Figure 10.4).

Explanations of time preference

In the following sections, I review a number of explanations for people's time preferences. Some of these hark back to the different

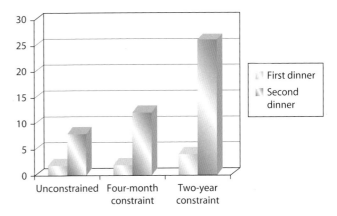

Figure 10.4. *The median number of weeks into the future that two dinners were scheduled, under conditions of no time constraint, a four-month constraint, or a two-year constraint*
Source: Loewenstein & Prelec, 1993.

motives that were proposed prior to the development of the DU model. Recent reviews of the literature (e.g. Frederick *et al.*, 2002; Read, 2004) note that these explanations are not mutually exclusive and that a variety of mechanisms and motives may be involved in intertemporal choice.

Self-awareness, commitment, and self-control

First you will raise the island of the Sirens,
those creatures who spellbind any man alive,
whoever comes their way. Whoever draws too close,
off guard, and catches the Sirens' voices in the air –
no sailing home for him, no wife rising to meet him,
no happy children beaming up at their father's face.
The high, thrilling song of the Sirens will transfix him,
lolling there in their meadow, round them heaps of corpses
rotting away, rags of skin shrivelling on their bones . . .
Race straight past that coast! Soften some beeswax
and stop your shipmates' ears so none can hear,
none of the crew, but if you are bent on hearing,
have them tie you hand and foot in the swift ship,
erect at the mast-block, lashed by ropes to the mast
so you can hear the Sirens' song to your heart's content.
But if you plead, commanding your men to set you free,
then they must lash you faster, rope on rope.
(Circe's warning to Odysseus in Homer's **Odyssey***, Book XII*[1]*)*

Evidence that people do have some insight into their future behaviour comes from examples of commitment, as indicated in Homer's story of Odysseus and the Sirens. In following Circe's instructions, Odysseus makes a commitment that saves his life and that of his crew.

A particularly dramatic example from everyday life has been described by Schelling (2006, p.63). Pregnant women sometimes ask medical staff to not administer anaesthesia during the delivery of their baby. Physicians often propose placing a facemask beside the patient so that she can inhale nitrous oxide if she needs it, but some women ask that this should not be done. They fear that if it is available then they will use it, so they want that opportunity to be withheld from them. Some women who make this request have experienced asking for and receiving anaesthesia in earlier deliveries. They have experienced the pain and expect to ask for relief, but they also expect to regret this if they do so. Therefore, they commit themselves in advance to not having anaesthesia available. This poses an interesting ethical and practical dilemma for hospitals and physicians.

One less dramatic form of commitment that I regularly make is not purchasing biscuits when I buy groceries. From experience, I know that I find it very hard to exercise restraint when I have biscuits in my house – I will easily eat the entire packet within two days. However, I do not feel such visceral *wanting* when I am in the supermarket, so it is easy not to buy them. Sometimes people's future actions fall short of their intentions despite their having made a commitment. For instance, many people wish to get fit but are not confident that they have the willpower to exercise regularly. They therefore join a gym, on the basis that they will want to exercise in order to justify their membership payments. This is essentially using a sunk cost as a form of commitment. However, as we saw in the previous chapter people attend the gym less as more time passes since the previous payment.

In one study of commitment (Ariely & Wertenbroch, 2002), students had to write three short papers for a class. One group of students had evenly spaced deadlines imposed upon them by the instructor. Those in the other group were allowed to set their own deadlines, although they did not have to do so and were free to submit all three papers at the end of the semester if they so wished. For both groups, 1 per cent was deducted from the grade if a paper was submitted late. In the free-choice group, most students did choose to set themselves deadlines. However, few of these set deadlines that were evenly spaced, and they performed worse than those with evenly spaced deadlines. This suggests that they did not fully anticipate the difficulty of completing their work.

As noted in Chapter 8, people may also precommit to indulgence. When choosing in advance between possible lottery prizes, a significant proportion choose luxuries over cash, because making this choice relieves them of the obligation to save the cash (if won) or spend it on necessities. In line with construal level theory (see earlier in this chapter), people are more likely to commit to indulgence for outcomes that are further into the future than for those that are imminent. More distant and lower-probability commitments, respectively, are less concrete and therefore easier to make. Kivetz and Simonson (2002) found that genuine lottery participants, who indicated their preferred prize in advance, were more likely to choose an $80 facial or massage over $85 in cash when the lottery draw was in 14 weeks', rather than one week's, time.

There is evidence that impulse control is associated with higher levels of intelligence, as Rae suggested back in the 19th century. A study conducted by Walter Mischel during the 1960s investigated the ability of 4-year-olds to delay gratification (Mischel *et al.*, 1989; Shoda *et al.*, 1990). The children were presented with a marshmallow and told that they could either eat it right there and then, or they could wait until the experimenter had run an errand, in which case they could have *two* marshmallows. Some children grabbed the marshmallow the moment that the experimenter left

the room (to return about 15–20 minutes later). Other children waited for a while, but then gave in to their impulses. But some children managed to resist entirely and were rewarded with two marshmallows.

The children who waited often used a variety of strategies to try and divert their attention from the marshmallow. They would talk to themselves, try to sleep, play games, rest their head in their arms, or even cover their eyes so they didn't have to look at the marshmallow. Years later, Mischel tracked down these children as adolescents. The longer children had managed to resist temptation at age 4, the better adjusted they were in almost every way. They were more socially competent, cognitively able, self-assertive, and better able to face up to challenges. On the other hand, the children who had grabbed the marshmallow were more likely to be deficient in these same qualities, including being prone to jealousy, envy, and bad temper. They were also still unable to delay gratification. Other research has shown that self-discipline is a stronger contributor to academic performance than IQ (Duckworth & Seligman, 2005; see also Hogan & Weiss, 1974; Wolfe & Johnson, 1995). Furthermore, a study that measured the discount rates of students found that higher discount rates were associated with lower grade point average (Kirby *et al.*, 2005).

Frederick (2005) has also reported that people who score lower on a measure of cognitive reflection rated themselves as more impulsive than the average person, whereas the most reflective people rated themselves as less impulsive than average. On hypothetical choices, the least reflective people were also less likely to choose the larger delayed reward over an immediate reward, although this effect diminished or disappeared for delays of 10 years or more, or where the delayed reward was paid in instalments over a period of time.[2]

However, it should also be noted that attempts at self-control can sometimes backfire. Baumeister and Vohs (2003) found that dieters who had resisted an initial temptation to grab some snacks later ate more ice cream in an ice cream taste test. They also gave up earlier when faced with a difficult intellectual problem. Perhaps the act of resisting the initial temptation 'used up' their ability to resist later on, or possibly the consumption of ice cream was seen as a reward for their earlier resistance.

Visceral influences Visceral influences are another factor that may affect intertemporal choice. These are physiological states such as hunger, sexual desire, cravings, and so on, that can pose a challenge to our attempts at self-control (Loewenstein, 1996). Because such states are transient, predictions about future states can be erroneous because we tend to project our current state into our prediction (Van Boven & Loewenstein, 2003), a phenomenon known as *projection bias*. In particular, the temporal proximity of a reward can activate visceral states (e.g. Laibson, 2001; Loewenstein, 1996), as may the spatial proximity of a reward, or indeed various other cues that are associated with the reward. Visceral factors can lead people to make choices they regret (Hsee & Hastie, 2006), as in the case of a teenage girl who does not take protective measures prior to visiting her boyfriend, because she is not aroused and does not anticipate engaging in sexual activity. Once with her boyfriend, however, she becomes aroused and does engage in sexual activity, possibly with undesired consequences.

Savouring and dread Whereas the DU model assumes a constant discount rate for gains, in reality people sometimes prefer to defer their gains. Also, they sometimes prefer to accept losses earlier rather than later. These two patterns of behaviour can be explained, respectively, in terms of the utility of anticipating pleasant outcomes and the disutility of dreading unpleasant outcomes. Evidence for these influences was obtained from a study by Loewenstein (1987), in which people were asked to specify the maximum amount of money they would pay in order to obtain or avoid various outcomes:

a. obtain $4

b. lose $4

c. lose $1000

d. receive a (non-lethal) 110-volt shock

e. obtain a kiss from the movie star of your choice.

Participants made their judgments for outcomes that occurred immediately, as well as following delays of 24 hours, three days, one year, and 10 years. For the kiss from the movie star, people were willing to pay the most to receive this in three days' time, thus indicating that it was something they would look forward to. On the other hand, people were willing to pay more to avoid the electric shock if it was going to occur in one year or 10 years, rather than in the immediate future. This implies that the shock is something that they would dread. The monetary amounts, however, seemed to be discounted in the usual fashion.

Mental accounting Mental accounting may also play a role in intertemporal choice. Prelec and Loewenstein (1998) have suggested that there is a disutility or 'pain of paying' associated with payments for immediate consumption. When payment precedes consumption, the pain of paying is offset by the anticipation of future consumption. On the other hand, at the point of consuming people only think about current and future payments. According to this view, different ways of paying may lead to different decisions. For instance, for one-off consumption experiences, such as holidays, people are likely to prefer to pay in advance. However, where something is consumed over a period of time, such as a consumer durable like a car, people may prefer to spread their payment across time.

Another aspect of mental accounting concerns *diversification bias* (Read & Loewenstein, 1995). This refers to the tendency to spread out benefits and burdens. For example, one study (Simonson, 1990) offered students free snacks that they could choose from a menu presented to them. One group made one choice per week for three weeks, and the snack was delivered at the end of that class each week. A second group made all their choices simultaneously in advance, and again received the snack at the end of the class each week. A third group also made their choices simultaneously in advance, and received those choices at the end of the first class (this condition controlled for satiation). Students in both the simultaneous-choice groups selected a wider variety of different snacks than the students who made a single choice each week. This can be considered as a forecasting error: when choosing in advance we erroneously think we will get bored with repeated consumption of the same item. Another study

(Kahneman & Snell, 1992) found that people's liking of yoghurt increased after they had eaten it every evening for eight days, whereas they themselves had predicted that they would like yoghurt *less* after this period of consumption.

Reference points and loss aversion A prospect theory-type value function can also explain some phenomena in intertemporal choice. One prediction is that the compensation that people demand in return for the delay of some benefit exceeds what they would be willing to pay in order to speed up the receipt of that benefit by the same amount of time. For instance, Loewenstein (1988) found that people were willing to pay $0.25, on average, to speed up the receipt of a $7 gift certificate from four weeks to one week. However, they required $1.09 to compensate for delaying the receipt of the certificate from one week to four weeks. This is what would be expected if speed-ups and delays are treated, respectively, as gains or losses from a reference point, in combination with a prospect theory-type value function that produces loss aversion. Similarly, this also predicts a greater discount rate for gains than losses, as the proportional change from (say) −£5 to −£10 is less than the change from £5 to £10.

Such a value function also explains why there is a greater discount rate for smaller amounts. For example, the shape of the function means that there is a greater proportional change between £100 and £200 than there is between £10 and £20. Therefore, a person should have a smaller discount rate for larger outcomes, because they will be more willing to wait. Similarly, the shape of the function is consistent with a greater discounting of gains than losses.

However, just as the DU model cannot account for all the phenomena, neither does a prospect theory-type value function. For example, dynamic inconsistency cannot be accounted for.

The evolutionary perspective Several authors have noted that time preference in both humans and non-humans appears to make sense from an evolutionary point of view (e.g. Robson, 2002; Rogers, 1994; Sozou & Seymour, 2003; Trostel & Taylor, 2001). They link time preference to reproductive concerns. As individuals age, their fertility declines. Furthermore, mortality rates increase sharply in old age as the body's very capability to repair age-related damage declines (Sozou & Seymour, 2003). Indeed, there is evidence that the ageing process itself is the result of selection for genes that have a positive effect early in life and a detrimental effect later. Mortality rates also vary with the degree of external hazard (for example, predation, aggressive rivalries over mating opportunities). These factors imply that delayed rewards will be of lower value because (a) there is a chance the individual may die before the reward is received, and (b) even if the individual does not die, his or her fertility will have declined by the time the reward is received.

Sozou and Seymour have modelled these assumptions mathematically. They noted that, with an uncertain environmental hazard rate, declining fertility with age, and increasing mortality with age, it should be expected that time preferences will be lowest in middle age. Their explanation (2003, p.1052) is that:

1. The young adult acts as if there may be no tomorrow, i.e. the environmental hazard rate may be high. Hence its time-preference rate is high.

2. The middle-aged adult knows that the environmental hazard rate is low. At the same time, its rate of physiological decline is still fairly modest. Thus, it can take a long-term view and its time-preference rate is low.

3. The old adult knows that the environmental hazard rate is low, but its physiological state is deteriorating rapidly, with declining fertility and increasing mortality. It therefore knows that there is no tomorrow.

At a superficial level, much consumption in modern humans may not appear to be about reproduction, survival, or helping one's kin. However, at a deeper level of analysis many aspects of consumption relate in some way to reproduction, from the clothes that one wears to the car that one drives. Also, 'Other forms of "visceral" pleasure – eating, drinking, partying, etc. – are proxies for reproduction, and should be subject to broadly similar forms of time-preference function' (Sozou and Seymour, 2003, p.1052).

Consistent with evolutionary ideas about time preference, it has been found that women with lower life expectancy tend to reproduce earlier. Wilson and Daly (1997) investigated a number of factors related to reproductive timing in 77 neighbourhoods of Chicago. Firstly, they found that higher homicide rates were associated with lower life expectancy, *excluding deaths by homicide*. Secondly, life expectancy plus economic inequality predicted homicide rates even more strongly. Criminal activity itself appears to be 'an outcome of steep future discounting and escalation of risk in social competition' (1997, p.315) among people with poor prospects. Thirdly, Wilson and Daly looked at the 10 neighbourhoods with the highest life expectancies, the 10 neighbourhoods with the lowest, and the 10 nearest the median. In particular, they looked at age-specific birth rates as a function of life expectancy. As Figure 10.5 shows, declining life expectancy was associated with declining age of motherhood.

Geronimus (1992, 1996) found that young mothers in American urban ghettoes often reported that becoming pregnant was an active decision in anticipation of early 'weathering' (physical

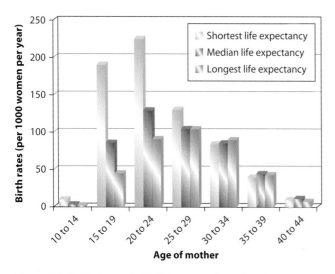

Figure 10.5. *Birth rates in 30 Chicago neighbourhoods as a function of life expectancy*

decline) and poor health, and expressed the wish to have children while still young and fit. Even when teenage pregnancy is not the result of a deliberate decision, actually seeing the pregnancy through to a birth *is* deliberate. In the UK, girls from the poorest socioeconomic backgrounds have the highest rate of pre-18 pregnancies and the lowest rate of pre-18 abortions (Lee *et al.*, 2004). Furthermore, in deprived areas the parents of pregnant teenagers, as well as other adults, are more likely to express anti-abortion attitudes than are adults in wealthier areas. By contrast, girls in wealthier families are more likely to have an abortion, and express their desire to further their education, get a good job, and/or postpone motherhood until they have found a man whom they would regard as a suitable father.

AFFECTIVE FORECASTING

Accurate decision making requires that we have a pretty good idea how certain outcomes will make us feel. Unfortunately, evidence has been accumulating that we often inaccurately predict how we (or others) are feeling or will feel in the future. Kahneman (1994) has distinguished between *decision utility* and *experience utility*. Decision utility is a decision maker's utility at the time of making a decision, and reflects her assessment of the options at the point of making the decision. Experience utility reflects a person's experience of the consequences of the decision. However, for the reasons discussed below it seems that these two utilities are often not well matched. Consequently, people may fail to choose what makes them happy (Hsee & Hastie, 2006).

Mispredicting happiness

> *Future, n. That period of time in which our affairs prosper, our friends are true and our happiness is assured. (Ambrose Bierce, The Devil's Dictionary)*

> *The grass is always greener on the other side. (proverb)*

A study reported by Schkade and Kahneman (1998) found that people in the American Midwest and in California all tended to believe that Californians were more happy than people in the Midwest. However, ratings of happiness from both groups actually showed no difference. Each group believed that factors such as the climate and culture would have a bigger impact on the other group's happiness than it actually did.

Cohn (1999, cited in Kahneman, 2000) asked people to estimate the mood states of lottery winners and paraplegics either one month or one year after the transitional event. People who were not personally acquainted with a lottery winner or paraplegic estimated that they would be just as happy or miserable, respectively, a year after the event as compared to a month after the event. People who were personally acquainted with them, however, made an adjustment for time, predicting that lottery winners would be less happy a year later and that paraplegics would be less unhappy a year later. This, in fact, is closer to the truth. One classic study (Brickman *et al.*, 1978) found that lottery winners, after a period of time had passed since their win, were not greatly happier than paraplegics (though they were somewhat happier on average). After highly salient events, people appear to adjust quite quickly to their original state. This phenomenon has been referred to as a *treadmill effect* (e.g. Brickman & Campbell, 1971).

People seem to fail to account for treadmill effects, however, when they predict the happiness of themselves or others. Rather, their judgments may be biased by focalism, or a focusing illusion; that is, the tendency to focus on a central event while neglecting relevant contextual factors. In the case of lottery winners and paraplegics, there are many different factors that affect mood on a day-to-day basis, but laypeople do not think of these when trying to assess how a lottery winner or paraplegic might be feeling. Similarly, Midwesterners trying to imagine life in California tend to think about the weather and culture, neglecting the fact that people quickly adjust to these and that there are many other things that influence their general happiness.

Other evidence indicates that a biased recall of the past may contribute to erroneous predictions of future feelings. One example of this is the 'peak–end' effect, described in Chapter 3. Focalism can also lead to a biased recall of past events. Americans who were surveyed prior to the 1996 presidential election predicted that they would be much happier following a Clinton victory than they actually were immediately after Clinton had won. However, when surveyed three months after Clinton's win the same people recalled having been happier right after the election than they actually had been at the time (Mitchell *et al.*, 1997). In focusing specifically on the target for recall (Clinton's victory, in this case) people neglect many of the other situational factors that may have contributed to their mood at the time.

Another factor contributing to erroneous affective forecasting is the fact that we sometimes fail to learn from our experiences. Following a negative event, people often 'explain away' that outcome in a way that is favourable to themselves (the phenomenon of *immune neglect*). For example, students who failed a test tended to denigrate the test in order to make themselves feel better. When they predicted how they would feel if they did poorly on a future test, they expected that they would not feel particularly unhappy. Thus, they used their interpretation of the first test to account for how they might feel in future (Wilson *et al.*, 2001).

Mispredicting regret

Regret is associated with counterfactual thinking (Kahneman & Miller, 1986). It is a negative emotion that we experience when we realise that our circumstances would be better if we had behaved in a different way. Choices may be affected by the anticipation of regret. For example, Tykocinski and Pittman (1998) identify a phenomenon they call *inaction inertia*. They found that people who had just missed an excellent consumer opportunity, such as a cheap holiday, were less likely to grab that opportunity if it was made available again at a slightly less generous (but still good) price. They felt that they would regret the fact that they hadn't take advantage the first time around.

However, other research indicates that people may actually experience less regret after a negative event than they would expect to experience. Daniel Gilbert and colleagues (2004) conducted a clever series of studies to examine forecast and experienced regret. In one study, they approached passengers on a subway train and asked them to predict how they would feel if they missed a train by one minute (narrow margin) or by five minutes (wide margin). A second group of passengers were approached in the station itself after they had actually just missed their train by about one minute or five minutes. People predicted that they would feel more regret if they missed a train by a narrow margin than a wide margin; however, people who actually had missed their train by a narrow margin did not experience significantly more regret than those who missed it by a wide margin. Indeed, the forecasters overestimated the extent of regret that would be felt in the narrow-margin group.

Follow-up studies found that people expected to blame themselves more for missing a train by a narrow margin than a wide margin. However, self-blaming by people who *had* missed a train was no more prevalent under a narrow margin than a wide margin. Also, forecasters overestimated the degree of self-blaming that would occur in either condition. In fact, people who had missed a train tended to blame someone or something else, for example, 'I would not have missed the train if all the gates were opened instead of just one' (2004, p.349). This is another instance of immune neglect.

SUMMARY

Various studies have found that people are frequently too optimistic about the time it will take them to complete a task. Motivation and experience actually seem to be associated with less realism regarding completion times. The planning fallacy is a prominent explanation for such optimism. This suggests that people tend to take the 'inside view' of a task, focusing on how the various steps of a plan will lead to success, but neglecting to take into account past experience and the various things that could interfere with task completion. It may also be that people misremember how long previous tasks actually took.

People also seem to focus too much on their own intentions when predicting the likelihood that they will carry out some future action. They neglect predictive factors that are unrelated to intention strength. Also, when thinking about distant future events people focus on higher-level attributes (such as how interesting a forthcoming talk is expected to be), but when thinking about imminent events they focus on feasibility (for example, how convenient is the timing of the talk?).

In many domains people prefer immediate rewards to future rewards. The discounted utility model proposes that people discount future rewards at a constant rate. However, for monetary outcomes hyperbolic discounting (i.e. declining discount rates with increasing time) appears to be a more accurate description of behaviour. In some circumstances people actually prefer to delay rewards rather than have them immediately. This, and other intertemporal choice phenomena, has given rise to a number of theories. These theories are not all mutually exclusive, and it is likely that several mechanisms and motives are involved.

Finally, a growing strand of research has been concerned with people's ability to predict their own feelings. Indeed, knowing how we will feel about something is essential for accurate decision making. Nonetheless, because of biased recall of past experiences, focusing illusions, immune neglect, and other cognitive processes, people often mispredict their own feelings. Thus, they may often fail to choose what could make them happy.

QUESTIONS

1. What factors may make people overly optimistic about deadlines?

2. Explain dynamic inconsistency.

3. What would life be like if people tended to prefer rewards in the future to immediate or imminent rewards?

4. Which account, or combination of accounts, do you find most convincing as an explanation of time preference?

5. Discuss the pros and cons of commitment and self-control in future-oriented decision making.

6. Why do people seem to be rather poor at predicting their future feelings?

7. How do you think life might be if there were no treadmill effects?

NOTES

1. Robert Fagles' translation, published in 1996 by Penguin Books. See Sources and Credits, page 209.

2. These results are discussed in more detail in Chapter 15, where I talk about individual differences more generally.

RECOMMENDED READING

Gilbert, D. (2006). *Stumbling on happiness*. London: Harper Press. This is a marvellously well written popular science book in which Daniel Gilbert examines the topic of affective forecasting. Winner of the UK Royal Society's science book prize.

Sanna, L.J. & Chang, E.C. (2006). *Judgments over time: The interplay of thoughts, feelings, and behaviors*. Oxford: Oxford University Press.

11 Dynamic Decisions and High Stakes: Where Real Life Meets the Laboratory

INTRODUCTION

Many decisions in the 'real world' are interdependent. They take place in an environment that changes over time, and are either due to events outside our control or result from previous actions that we ourselves have taken. This kind of decision making is known as *dynamic decision making* or DDM (Brehmer, 1992; Edwards, 1962). Examples of dynamic decision situations include managing factory output, air traffic control, firefighting, and driving a car. Dynamic decisions are typically more complex than most of the decisions that have been considered so far in previous chapters. Experimental research into dynamic decision making uses laboratory surrogates for real-life situations, typically observing the extent to which novices are able to learn to control a particular system and investigating the factors that underlie learning.

However, even though DDM tasks aim to be as realistic as possible they still differ from real-life tasks in various respects. In particular, the stakes are typically higher in real-life tasks, and the expertise of the decision maker has often been acquired over a period of years rather than minutes, hours, or days. Thus, in this chapter I shall examine decision making in both dynamic laboratory tasks and in everyday situations.

DYNAMIC DECISION MAKING

The Beer Distribution Game

How do people control dynamic, complex, real-world systems? The need to answer this question gave rise to the development of DDM as a research area (Brehmer, 1992; Edwards, 1962). As an introduction to the idea of dynamic decision making, let us consider the Beer Distribution Game (Sterman, 1989a). This simulates the manufacturing and distribution of beer (though it could be any commodity). Four players represent the supply chain of manufacturer, distributor, wholesaler, and retailer. Each player begins the game with an inventory of 12 cases of beer, as represented by chips on the board. The game starts with the retailer turning over a card that specifies a level of consumer demand. The retailer then submits an order to the wholesaler, who in turn submits an order to the distributor, who in turn submits an order to the manufacturer (the brewer). *These orders are the only communications that are allowed between the players.* Once the brewer receives his order he then ships beer to the distributor. When the distributor receives the beer he then ships to the wholesaler, who ships to the retailer, who sells it to the consumers. The next round of the game begins after the orders have been shipped.

There are some other factors that complicate the task. One important factor is that there is a time delay between placing an order and receiving the beer. This makes it difficult for players to know how much beer they should keep in their inventories. For example, while the retailer (or someone else in the chain) is waiting for one consignment of beer to arrive he might receive another order. He does not want to run out of beer, because if he does there is a fine of $1 per case (representing angry customers and lost sales). Therefore, he might wish to keep enough beer in his inventory just in case unexpected orders arrive. On the other hand, he has to incur a charge of $0.50 per case to hold beer in inventory.

The initial level of demand is for four cases per week, and remains so for the first few rounds. In fact, for the first four weeks each person in the chain beneath the manufacturer is directed to order four cases, thus maintaining equilibrium while the players get used to the task. Starting with the fourth week, players can order any non-negative quantity that they wish. In the fifth week, customer demand jumps from four cases per week to eight, and stays at this level for the rest of the game. Only the retailer ever gets to see the level of customer demand, but not even he can know in advance what the demand will be.

How do players react to this jump in demand? According to traditional economic theory, after a few turns of the game during which players make some adjustments, they should eventually settle into an equilibrium whereby everyone is ordering eight cases and everyone's inventories remain at a constant level. However, this is not what happens in reality. Instead, players overreact by ordering too much. Perhaps the retailer orders 12 cases; the wholesaler responds by ordering 16 cases, and the distributor by ordering 20. Because of the delays in the system, players may notice that their existing inventory is running out as new orders come in, so they place more large orders. Then, as large supplies of beer begin to flow back down the supply chain, players find that they have too much inventory. They respond to this by cutting their orders drastically, sometimes to zero. Instead of settling into an equilibrium, the beer 'industry' experiences oscillating waves of over-ordering and under-ordering; that is, costly cycles of boom and bust.

According to Sterman (1989a), players' behaviour is driven by the anchoring-and-adjustment heuristic. Instead of making difficult calculations about inventory, time delays, and so on, they anchor on a recent pattern of orders and inventory levels and base their next order on this. However, the application of this heuristic in an environment with time delays leads to the cyclical pattern of over- and under-ordering.

Sterman (1989a) noted that players' emotions run high during the debriefing period following the game. People are frustrated at their inability to control the system and often report feelings of helplessness. They 'feel themselves to be at the mercy of forces outside their control' (p.335). Apart from the retailers, most players believe that the customer demand was oscillatory, and blame this perverse demand pattern for their own poor performance. Sterman adds:

> Many participants are quite shocked when the actual pattern of customer orders is revealed; some voice strong disbelief. Few ever suggest that their own decisions were the cause of the behaviour they experienced. Fewer still explain the pattern of oscillation in terms of the feedback structure, time delays, or stock and flow structure of the game. (1989a, p.336)

There are many different kinds of DDM tasks of varying levels of difficulty. Although performance on these tasks does not always fall into the cyclical pattern observed in the Beer Distribution Game, people generally perform well below the optimum level, sometimes dramatically so. For example, in one study participants who were attempting to fight forest fires frequently allowed their headquarters to burn down (Brehmer & Allard, 1991). In another study, participants who were playing the role of a physician frequently allowed their patients to die while they were waiting for the results of tests that were actually non-diagnostic (Kleinmuntz & Thomas, 1987). Even where people do demonstrate improved performance across trials on a task, they may nonetheless be unable to verbalise the strategy they are following (Berry & Broadbent, 1984). In other words, the learning is implicit rather than explicit.

In order to maintain experimental control over a dynamic system of interest while also keeping a degree of realism, DDM researchers have implemented dynamic tasks in computer simulations that are often referred to as *microworlds*. Microworlds enable researchers to investigate a variety of factors, such as cognitive ability, type of feedback, timing of feedback, strategy use, and knowledge acquisition.

The characteristics of a dynamic decision environment

The primary characteristics of a dynamic decision environment are dynamics, complexity, opaqueness, and dynamic complexity

(Gonzalez, Vanyukov, *et al.*, 2005). The *dynamics* of the system refers to the dependence of the system's state on the state at an earlier time. This is influenced by factors beyond the decision maker's control (exogenous factors) and by the actions taken by the decision maker (endogenous factors). In a dynamic system, a positive feedback loop is one in which the loop is self-reinforcing or self-amplifying, such as the accrual of interest within a savings account. A negative feedback loop is a self-correcting or self-dampening loop, such as the way that eating assuages hunger and thereby leads to less eating (Gonzalez, Vanyukov, *et al.*, 2005).

Complexity, loosely speaking, refers to the number of interacting or interconnected elements within a system that can make it difficult to predict the behaviour of that system. However, it is difficult to provide a clear definition of complexity. Firstly, system components can vary in terms of how many components there are, the number of relationships between them, and the nature of those relationships. Thus, there is not a straightforward mapping between these factors and task difficulty. Secondly, the complexity of a system may also be a function of the decision maker's ability.

Opaqueness refers to the invisibility of some aspects of the system (Brehmer, 1992). Again, this is hard to define exactly as it may depend on the decision maker's knowledge about a system.

Dynamic complexity refers to the way in which decision makers are able to use system feedback in order to control the system, given the interplay of the previous factors. Diehl and Sterman (1995) highlight three elements of a system's feedback as particularly important. Firstly, opaqueness within the system can give rise to unexpected side effects. Secondly, the relationship between variables may be non-linear (hence harder to comprehend). Thirdly, delays in feedback may make it harder for a decision maker to understand and control a system.

MENTAL MODELS, FEEDBACK, FEEDBACK DELAYS, AND RECOGNITION PROCESSES

Mental models and feedback

People represent dynamic decision tasks, as well as their environment generally, in the form of mental models (see Chapter 6). These are representations of the environment, typically incomplete, that aid our understanding of the current and future states of the world and enable us to act accordingly. Unfortunately, gaps or errors in our mental models sometimes only become apparent when interaction with the world leads to unexpected events (e.g. Besnard *et al.*, 2004).

Although feedback interventions are generally considered to benefit performance on a task, this is more so for simple tasks than for complex ones, for tasks requiring low cognitive ability, and for well-practised tasks (Kluger & DeNisi, 1996). In a study of decision support for dynamic tasks, Gonzalez (2005a) found that the provision of feedback was an inferior way of trying to aid learning and performance, compared to the viewing of a highly skilled operator's decision behaviour during a trial. This study utilised the Water Purification Plant (WPP) microworld shown in Figure 11.1,

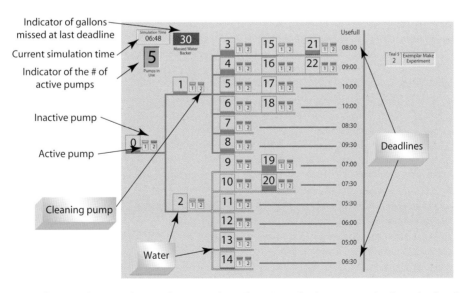

Figure 11.1. *The Water Purification Plant simulation. This screenshot is from Gonzalez (2005a, p.146), where the description states: 'The simulation time is 6:48, the operator has missed 30 gal water, and 5 pumps (the maximum number possible) are active. Water enters from outside the system and moves continuously through the open pumps from left to right toward the deadline column. The operator decides when to open and close pumps while simulation time is running.'*

in which participants attempt to empty water from various tanks that are linked together in chains. Some chains are longer than others and this affects how long it takes to pump water out of the system. Furthermore, not all the water pumps can be activated at once, and pumps cannot be used again within 10 minutes following a period of use. During the simulation, participants are given deadlines to empty the water from various chains.

Participants spent two days undertaking practice trials under one of the following conditions: *control* participants only received feedback about the total amount of water left in the system after *all* deadlines had expired; people in a *feedback* condition received detailed information about the water left in the system after each separate deadline; in the *self-exemplar* group people ran one trial under the control condition and then viewed a replay of that trial; in the *feedback-exemplar* group people received both detailed feedback and replayed their previous trial; and in the *expert-exemplar* condition people ran one trial under the control condition and then replayed the trial of a highly skilled participant.

As expected, the performance of all groups improved across trials. However, in the early stages of learning, people in the feedback condition actually showed poorer learning than the control participants, although they did catch up later during the training period. Apart from the inferiority of the feedback group at the start, all groups except the expert-exemplar group performed at about the same level throughout practice and testing (no decision support was given during the testing trials). By contrast, the expert-exemplar group began to outperform the other groups midway through the practice trials, and this superior performance continued throughout the testing period. Its members made better use of the water pumps during the test phase, they made fewer decisions overall throughout practice and testing, and their decisions were more similar to those made by the expert.

Given that the expert-exemplar group did not see the expert's behaviour during the test phase, its members' superior performance here cannot be due to them copying the expert. One possibility is that they developed a better understanding (mental model) of the task overall which guided their behaviour. Another possibility is that instances of the expert's performance were stored in memory, retrieved when a similar situation was recognised, and fine-tuned with practice (see the section on *Theories of learning*, below).

The effect of feedback delays

A major contributor to suboptimal performance on dynamic decision tasks is the misperception of feedback. For example, delays in feedback make it harder for people to establish relationships between their actions and the outcomes of those actions. This is exacerbated by the occurrence of side effects as the result of exogenous events, including random perturbations of the system. We saw earlier that feedback delays on the Beer Game led to severely suboptimal performance in the form of systematic and expensive oscillations.

Diehl and Sterman (1995) systematically varied feedback delay in a stock adjustment task. Participants were required to maintain a stock inventory at a target level while minimising the costs arising from changes in production. In each time period they were able to review their inventory levels, sales, production, and costs. From the easiest to the hardest task conditions, participants incurred higher costs than would have been expected under an optimal rule, though – with the exception of the hardest condition – they did better than would have been the case if they had exerted no control at all. In particular, under all gain conditions participants incurred higher costs as the feedback delay increased.

Diehl and Sterman also examined the length of time that participants spent on each decision they made. Gains and delays had no systematic effect on the time spent on decisions, indicating that greater complexity did not lead to greater effort. Furthermore, degree of effort was not associated with level of performance. These results might be partly explained by individual differences between participants. Indeed, an analysis of notes made by participants during the trials indicated that there may have been differing levels of sophistication. Some people only attended to their inventory, whereas others considered both the inventory and change in inventory (indicating an understanding of the relationships between production and stock). At the highest level of sophistication, some participants attended to inventory and *expected* change in inventory.

Their notebooks also indicated a number of different strategies. The 'act and wait' strategy involved making no changes to production until the results of a previous change had become apparent. Others began by making a careful analysis of the system, but resorted to an inventory-only strategy when their decisions resulted in instability. Others abandoned control in the face of oscillations, in the hope that the system would settle down (one person wrote: 'I can't believe this is happening' before giving up on calculations and resorting to the inventory-only strategy). Diehl and Sterman concluded that participants suffered from two types of misperception of feedback: they were insufficiently aware of the structure of feedback within the system, and they were unable to infer the consequences of the feedbacks and time delays.

Other evidence indicates that the learning acquired on DDM tasks is most applicable *locally*; that is, following training, people show improved performance on situations that resemble those encountered during training, but tend to fare less well in situations that are dissimilar to training (e.g. Gibson *et al.*, 1997).

Results like those described in this section indicate that people do not appear to vary their strategies in DDM tasks in the way that might be expected according to the adaptive decision maker hypothesis (described in Chapter 8). Other DDM results also run counter to this hypothesis. For example, studies involving health management tasks have found that even experienced participants tend to spend too much time collecting information from diagnostic tests, leading to worse outcomes than if they had simply treated the patient without test information (Kerstholt, 1994, 1996; Kleinmuntz, 1985; Kleinmuntz & Thomas, 1987).

Recognition

The idea of the local applicability of learning suggests that people are more likely to recognise situations when they are similar to those they have previously encountered. The role of similarity relations in recognition has been investigated by Gonzalez and Quesada (2003). Their participants engaged with the Water

Purification Plant task, mentioned earlier. The authors used a numeric formula to assess the degree of similarity between two trials. In this formula, two variables affected the overall similarity: the time at which a decision was made and the amount of water in the tank at the time of decision. Similarity was a good predictor of people's performance. It was also possible to distinguish good and poor performers according to the similarity of their decisions: from the very beginning, good performers showed higher decision similarity. Recognition of similarity was also affected by complex interactions between task features. In particular, participants learned to intervene later in shorter chains (with tighter deadlines) and sooner in longer chains (with later deadlines).

THEORIES OF LEARNING IN DYNAMIC DECISION-MAKING TASKS

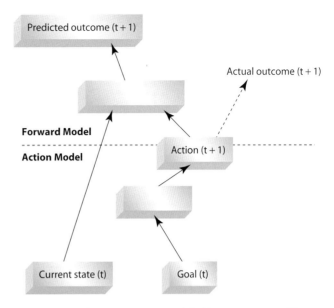

Figure 11.2. *The connectionist model of learning proposed by Gibson et al., 1997*

Various accounts have been proposed with regard to learning in dynamic systems (see e.g. Busemeyer, 2002). One way to represent learning is in the form of a *production system*. A production system is a set of *production rules* that relate to a particular task. These are rules that specify the conditions under which particular actions are to be executed. Essentially, a production rule says *If you recognise situation S, then carry out action A.* Anzai (1984), for example, implemented a set of production rules within a computer simulation, based on the think-aloud protocols of participants who had engaged in a DMM task (steering a ship through a series of gates). The simulation did a reasonable, though not perfect, job of reproducing the strategies used by the participants (who differed in their level of experience).

Another type of theory assumes that specific *instances* or *exemplars* are stored in memory (e.g. Dienes & Fahey, 1995). Whenever an action leads to a successful outcome, then both the initial situation and the response to that situation are stored together in memory. Stored instances are more likely to be retrieved if they are similar to the current situation, together with the associated response.

Another account of learning is provided by *connectionist* theory (sometimes referred to as *parallel distributed processing*, or PDP). Connectionist models consist of interconnected units. The connections between units have a strength, or weighting, that depends upon previous experience. Thus, the output of a given unit depends upon the output of a previous unit weighted by the strength of the connection with that unit. Gibson *et al.* (1997) found that the connectionist model in Figure 11.2 did a good job of predicting responses on Berry and Broadbent's (1984) Sugar Production Factory task.

This model, in fact, involves two connectionist submodels. The action submodel in the bottom half takes the current goal and the current state of the environment and feeds them into a hidden layer of units that computes a weighted sum of the inputs and then feeds this into a nonlinear logistic function (see Gibson *et al.*, 1997

for the full details). The output is an action that produces an outcome. The representations of current state and action feed into another layer of hidden units in the prediction submodel[1] that lead to a prediction of the outcome that the action will achieve.

Given that the environment itself does not specify how a decision maker should modify his actions, how does correction take place within this model? Firstly, an error signal is derived by comparing the predicted outcome with the actual outcome. This error signal is propagated back through the network in order to adjust the connection weights between the layers of the prediction submodel. This improves the model's ability to predict how actions will affect the environment. Secondly, another error signal is derived by comparing the actual outcome with the goal. This error signal is also back-propagated to the prediction submodel (holding the connection weights constant) to determine how changing the action would change the error. This information is then used by the action submodel to adjust its connection weights, so as to bring the output of an action closer to the intended goal.

Gonzalez, Lerch, *et al.* (2005) have proposed that learning on dynamic tasks occurs through the accumulation and refinement of instances (*instance-based learning theory*, or IBLT). An instance consists of environmental cues (the *situation*), the set of actions that are applicable to the situation (the *decision*), and the evaluation of the goodness of a decision in a particular situation (the *utility*). Thus, the accumulation of instances is the accumulation of situation-decision-utility (SDU) triples.

When faced with a particular situation people are likely to retrieve similar instances, or SDUs, from memory. Thus, in a typical situation people assess the utility of an action by combining the utility of similar instances retrieved from memory. However, in atypical situations people fall back on heuristics to evaluate the potential success of an action. Alternative actions are evaluated sequentially, and after each evaluation the decision as to whether or not more alternatives should be evaluated is determined by a *necessity level.* Necessity may be subjectively determined by the decision maker's own preferences or by exogenous factors such as lack of time. Once a decision has been made, the outcome of the decision acts as feedback that may be used to modify the utility value of the original SDUs.

In short, IBLT consists of five learning mechanisms: (1) instance-based knowledge; (2) recognition-based retrieval; (3) adaptive strategies; (4) necessity; and (5) feedback updates. Gonzalez, Lerch, *et al.* implemented their theory in a series of computer simulations, using the Water Purification Plant microworld mentioned earlier. In these simulations they varied parameters, such as the rules for searching and the provision of feedback, and examined how the resultant patterns of performance matched with human data. Interestingly, the best fit to human data was obtained with a model that did not learn on the basis of results (no feedback mechanism), though this was not the model that produced the best overall performance! However, the comparisons in this study were to aggregate human data. In reality, there is evidence for consider-able individual differences in behaviour on dynamic tasks.

INDIVIDUAL DIFFERENCES IN DYNAMIC DECISION MAKING

Performance on DDM tasks shows considerable inter-individual variability, and one might expect that much of this can be attributed to differences in cognitive ability among people. However, many studies have failed to find an association between performance on intelligence tests and performance on DDM tasks (Brehmer, 1992; Rigas & Brehmer, 1999). This appears to be due to the difficulty of obtaining reliable performance measurement on DDM tasks.[2] As we have already seen, there are a number of structural factors that may contribute to the complexity and dy-namic complexity of a DDM task, and these may differ between tasks. Some tasks also may not have an optimal solution.

Later studies have shown that where reliable measurement can be obtained, then performance on intelligence tests does relate to DDM performance. Rigas *et al.* (2002) obtained reliable perform-ance scores from two tasks whose requirements were somewhat similar (though not identical). Participants engaged in each task several times, during the course of which the task parameters were varied. They also completed a non-verbal test of general intelli-gence (Ravens Advanced Progressive Matrices, or APM; Raven, 1976). People who scored highly on APM were more likely to do better in both tasks. Furthermore, there was an even stronger correlation between the two microworlds: people who did well on one also tended to do well on the other. Finally, the authors found that the best prediction of performance in one microworld was obtained by incorporating both the APM scores *and* the performance level in the other microworld. In short, these results support the contention that low reliability in previous studies can

account for their failure to find an association between intelligence and DDM performance. Similar results have been obtained by Gonzalez, Thomas, *et al.* (2005).

Cognitive ability also interacts with the nature of the workload. In a study involving the WPP task, Gonzalez (2005b) found that: (a) low-ability participants were outperformed by high-ability par-ticipants on both practice and test trials, and (b) when the practice trials were made particularly demanding – either by having more trials of shorter duration or by having participants perform two independent tasks concurrent with the WPP task – then the low-ability participants showed no improvement between the practice and test trials.

Similar results were reported by Gonzalez (2004), who also pro-vided evidence that low-ability participants increasingly relied on heuristic responding across a series of fast trials, whereas their use of heuristics appeared to decrease across slow trials. This suggests that a few slow practice trials are more beneficial than a larger number of fast trials, because they enable people to acquire more complex and useful knowledge. High-ability participants showed less use of heuristic responding across trials in both time conditions, but generally made less use of heuristics in the slow condition.

EVERYDAY DECISION MAKING

In this section I am going to focus rather more on decision making in the real world. This does not preclude discussing some research that occurs in the laboratory, but the research tends to be much more broadly conceived, in the sense that researchers are often concerned with a wide array of processes, such as goal-setting, planning, perceptual and attentional processes, comprehension processes, forecasting, attending to feedback, and so on. In par-ticular, expertise tends to be a central focus of much research.

In what follows I will examine three factors that influence everyday judgments and decisions: expertise and situation aware-ness, individual differences, and stress. Then I shall go on to look at the specific approach of naturalistic decision making and the theories associated with this.

Expertise and situation awareness

Situation awareness is

> the perception of the elements in the environment within a volume of time and space, the comprehension of their meaning and the projection of their status in the near future. (Endsley, 1988, cited in Endsley, 2006)

In fact, a major difference between people with differing degrees of expertise in a domain is the extent of their situation awareness (but see Box 11.1). For example, experienced motorists, and motorists with advanced training, engage in a more effective and

BOX 11.1.   DECISION MAKING PRIOR TO RECREATIONAL AVALANCHE INCIDENTS

On January 12, 1993, three skiers left Vail Ski Area headed for the backcountry. The avalanche hazard was posted as high for that day, but the three friends had just completed an avalanche course and were confident they could find safe powder skiing beyond the area boundaries. They had been warned about the unstable conditions by the Vail ski patrol, and as they passed the avalanche warning signs at the backcountry access gate, they saw all around them evidence of the danger: a dozen fresh slides on nearby slopes, collapsing and cracking in the snow under their skies, and heavy drifting on unstable slopes already loaded almost to the breaking point.

In their quest for untracked powder they descended, as a group, into a steep, wind-loaded gully – a classic terrain trap. The avalanche they triggered caught all three skiers, deeply burying and killing one of them. (from McCammon, 2001)

As described in the incident above, avalanche awareness is not a guarantee of safety in the mountains. In fact, one review of avalanche accidents, in which all the victims were 'avalanche-aware', found that 83 per cent (34/41) of the accidents were due to decision-making errors as opposed to aspects of the terrain or snowpack.

Even those with advanced training may overlook, or fail to act on, environmental cues that indicate an avalanche risk. McCammon (2002) analysed over 600 recreational avalanche incidents drawn from the Colorado Avalanche Information Center, as well as records published elsewhere. These involved 1180 people in total.

Based on the presence or absence of various hazard indicators (for example avalanches within the area in the last 48 hours, above-freezing air temperatures or rain at the time of the incident), McCammon was able to construct hazard scores for all but 24 of the incidents. He also categorised each party according to the skill level of their most experienced member (no avalanche training; 'avalanche aware'; basic training; advanced training). When moving through familiar terrain, groups without advanced training exposed themselves to just as much hazard as they did in unfamiliar terrain. However, groups with advanced training exposed themselves to significantly less hazard when moving through *unfamiliar* terrain, but to just as much hazard as the other groups when moving through *familiar* terrain. It is not clear whether the highly trained parties failed to recognise the hazards in unfamiliar terrain, or whether

they recognised them but continued regardless; but either way their familiarity with a slope was more likely to override the benefits of their knowledge and experience. McCammon suggests that a *familiarity heuristic* is in operation: we tend to believe that our behaviour is correct to the extent that we have done something before.

McCammon has also identified two other factors that sometimes negate the effects of training. Firstly, he suggests that we tend to believe that a behaviour is correct to the extent that other people are engaged in it. This is the *social proof heuristic*, and we are particularly likely to use it in situations of uncertainty. McCammon found that parties with either basic or advanced avalanche training exposed themselves to higher hazard levels if they had encountered similar others just prior to the accident. Untrained parties were unaffected by their encounters with others, but exposed themselves to a similarly high level of hazard, whereas trained parties who *had not* encountered similar others exposed themselves to less hazard.

The second factor that can negate training is the *commitment heuristic*: 'the tendency to believe that a behaviour is correct to the extent that it is consistent with a prior commitment we have made' (2002, p.4). For untrained groups, hazard scores were the same for highly committed groups and less committed groups (as defined by stated goals or obvious motivations due to approaching darkness or similar constraints). However, trained groups who were highly committed exposed themselves to greater hazard than less committed groups.

Such findings are consistent with other evidence that a combination of information plus skills training is not always enough to make people change their behaviour (McCammon, 2004). McCammon and Hägeli (2004) examined several avalanche-related decision-making frameworks in terms of how well they would have identified conditions in past accidents and the proportion of accidents that would have been prevented. They found that the most effective decision-making method was also the simplest. It involved simply adding up a number of 'obvious clues'. Other methods involved the application of severity weightings or the balancing of different variables within an equation. It should be emphasised, of course, that an ideal comparison of such methods would involve predictive testing rather than retrospective application to past data. Nonetheless, the results are highly suggestive.

efficient search for hazards (Horswill & McKenna, 2004). Consequently, motorists with over 10 years of driving experience are faster to respond to hazards than are drivers with less than three years of experience (McKenna & Crick, 1991).

One of the ways in which expertise enables greater situation awareness is through the automatisation of certain behaviours. For instance, when we first learn to drive we need to devote a great

deal of conscious attention to the most basic behaviours, such as depressing the clutch, changing gear, and so on. Because our attentional capacity is quite limited, novice drivers often focus on basic behaviours and neglect certain aspects of the environment. By contrast, experienced motorists do not need to devote much conscious thought to the basic behaviours involved in driving; these have become quite automatic. This frees up some of their mental workspace for scanning, interpreting, and predicting the environment. However, these activities require controlled cognitions and are easily disrupted if attention is redirected to another task, such as taking a call on a mobile phone (e.g. Strayer & Johnston, 2001).

The definition of situation awareness given above indicates that it is not enough to merely perceive the relevant aspects of our environment; accurate decision making also depends on interpreting our perceptions correctly and using the resultant mental model to accurately anticipate future events. For example, seagoing vessels display lights at night in order that other vessels can determine what type of craft they are and in which direction they are heading. Nonetheless, they are sometimes misinterpreted and the misinterpretations are sometimes fatal (e.g. Burns, 2005).

Endsley (2006) has reviewed several studies of pilots and army platoon commanders in relation to their situation awareness. In one study of pilots, the least experienced (general aviation pilots) described themselves as passive recipients of information and tended to focus on information in their immediate environment. Intermediate experience (line pilots) was associated with seeking out information and interpreting it, and high experience (line check aircrew) was associated with being proactive and considering a large number of details and complex relationships (Prince & Salas, 1998). In general, greater levels of experience were associated with more pre-flight planning and preparation, including information gathering (for similar results see Jensen et al., 1997).

A second study reviewed by Endsley (2006) concerned the performance of novice and experienced infantry platoon commanders in a virtual reality battle simulator (Strater, Endsley, et al., 2001). The more experienced platoon leaders showed greater perceptual-level awareness (identifying the location of their own troops and the enemy troops). They also showed greater comprehension of the situation (identifying the strongest enemy and the greatest enemy threat). Further research showed that new platoon leaders also had difficulties projecting future situations, even though they may have understood the current situation (Strater, Jones, et al., 2001). This was reflected in problems such as a lack of contingency planning, poor responses to unexpected events, and poor time management.

Individual differences in everyday decision making

In the section on dynamic decision making we saw that intelligence appears to predict performance once reliable DDM performance measures can be obtained. Is the same true for the real world? A great deal of research has been devoted to answering this question, although this research has long been a part of mainstream psychology rather than a recent offshoot of decision research. In fact, performance on intelligence tests is a very strong and reliable predictor of job performance (Furnham, 2005). Furthermore, the more complex the job, the better the predictive value of IQ (Hunter & Hunter, 1984; Salgado et al., 2003). IQ is a better predictor of job performance than any other known variable, including personality factors. In fact, some authors doubt that measures of personality add any predictive value at all beyond that measured by IQ (e.g. Menkes, 2005).

Despite the predictive value of IQ measures, there are at least a couple of caveats worth mentioning. Firstly, although IQ is a strong predictor of school and college performance, self-discipline is an even better predictor of academic performance among adolescents (Duckworth & Seligman, 2005). Secondly, Sternberg and his colleagues (Hedlund et al., 2006; Sternberg, 1997) have argued that intelligence tests can better predict job performance if they include measures of *practical intelligence*. These are measures of practical skills rather than abstract thinking. Perhaps more importantly, Hedlund et al. (2006) found that the gender and ethnic differences that are observed on traditional IQ tests were either absent or greatly reduced on their tests when practical measures were included.

Another source of individual difference research is the examination of different decision *styles*, typically assessed using questionnaire measures. Two styles that are often measured are reflective and intuitive or spontaneous, but others include internalising and externalising (e.g. Coscarelli, 1983a, 1983b; Johnson, 1978; Niles et al., 1997), locus of control (Friedrich, 1987), and dependent and avoidant (Scott & Bruce, 1995).

However, conclusive findings have not been forthcoming. One problem is that different studies identify different styles. Also, it is not clear in these studies whether the styles can be distinguished from abilities.[3] More importantly, most such studies merely claim to identify styles from questionnaire measures but do not actually investigate real-world performance.

One exception is a study by Scott and Bruce (1995), which included a workplace outcome measure for one group of respondents. These were 189 engineers and technicians from the research and development department of a US industrial firm. The managers of these employees were asked to rate them on five measures of innovative behaviour, and these were subsequently aggregated into a composite measure. They also gave a single rating for the overall innovativeness of each employee. The results showed that innovation was less likely with a rational decision-making style, but was somewhat more likely with an intuitive decision-making style.[4]

Stress, judgments, and decision making

It is probably fair to say that stress is generally regarded by most people as a bad thing. Thus, stress is widely held to have a negative impact on judgments and decisions. In reality, the evidence to date is less clear-cut. Firstly, there are multiple possible 'stressors' – factors that may disrupt performance. For example, one book about stress and judgment (Hammond, 2000) lists 49 stressors in the index, including cold, continuous work, financial risk, sleep loss, and time pressure. These different stressors may have different effects on the human cognitive system. Secondly, the research evidence about the effects of stress does not tell a consistent story. Although stressors sometimes lead to worse performance, they also sometimes have no effect or can even lead to better performance. Thus, Hammond notes that theories of the effects of stress on judgment tend to have 'escape routes' to account for the negative results.

Bearing this in mind, there is no clear story I can tell here about stress. However, I shall briefly consider one particular stressor: sleep deprivation. In some occupations this is a major concern for job performance. One such occupation is the military, and lack of sleep has been implicated in several military tragedies. For example, during a 'friendly fire' incident in Operation Desert Storm, American fighter pilots attacked and destroyed ground vehicles from their own unit. The pilots had become confused and spatially disorientated after failing to update positional references. They had also had very little sleep in the previous 24 hours (Belenky *et al.*, 1994). A similar failure to update maps, coupled with a general failure to attend to urgent tasks, has been observed in soldiers after working for about 36 hours as part of a realistically simulated military operation (Bandaret *et al.*, 1981).

The effects of sleep deprivation are varied and complex (Harrison & Horne, 2000). Sleep deprivation has been shown to lead to poorer performance on tasks involving cognitive speed, psychomotor skills, visual and auditory attention, and short-term memory. However, there may be a confounding effect to do with how monotonous and lacking in novelty a task is. Certainly, Kjellberg (1975, 1977) has shown that the less interesting a particular task is, the faster the effects of sleep deprivation set in. However, even with dull tasks, the effects of sleep deprivation can be overcome by motivating participants by providing them with the results of their performance (Wilkinson, 1965) or financial reward (Horne & Pettitt, 1985), or increasing the rate of stimulus presentation (Corcoran, 1963).

These latter results might indicate that more complex tasks are resistant to the effects of sleep deprivation, but matters are actually not quite so straightforward. This is well illustrated in a study by Harrison and Horne (1999). Participants engaged in a marketing strategy simulation game that became increasingly difficult as time progressed, with participants facing problems in finding a place for their product in a near-saturated market. Participants who had undergone 36 hours' sleep deprivation were unable to cope with the task, becoming insolvent or near-insolvent. They relied on previously successful decisions that were no longer appropriate and failed to innovate in critical situations. By contrast, the same participants were unaffected by sleep deprivation when required to complete a complex 30-minute critical reasoning task, designed to assess their ability to assimilate and understand large amounts of complex written information.

Harrison and Horne (2000) have reviewed the literature on sleep deprivation and complex tasks. Most of the studies involved two or three nights' sleep deprivation. They found that fatigue had a detrimental effect in the following areas:

- Appreciating a complex situation while avoiding distractions
- Keeping track of events, developing and updating strategies
- Thinking laterally and being innovative
- Assessing risk – anticipating a range of consequences
- Maintaining an interest in the outcome
- Controlling mood and 'uninhibited' behaviour
- Showing insight into one's own performance

- Remembering 'when' something happened rather than 'what' happened
- Effective communication.

In terms of stress more generally, Hammond (2000) suggested that we cannot predict what effect a stressor might have unless we have a theory about the cognitive processes required to undertake different types of task. In other words, whereas some tasks require an intuitive mode of thought, others elicit a more analytical way of thinking. These different modes of thinking may be affected differently by the various possible stressors. For example, because intuitive thought is quick by its very nature, it is unlikely to be affected by time pressure, whereas time pressure may have a bigger effect when a task requires analytical thinking.

NATURALISTIC DECISION MAKING

What naturalistic decision making is and how it is studied

Many researchers who are concerned with everyday decision making now identify themselves as part of a distinct academic framework, referred to as *naturalistic decision making* (NDM). NDM is 'an attempt to understand how people make decisions in real-world contexts that are meaningful and familiar to them' (Lipshitz *et al.*, 2001). NDM is less concerned with psychological processes at the moment of choice, and more concerned with the processes leading up to the moment of choice. This means studying the processes of planning, perception, comprehension, and forecasting. Indeed, the scenarios and cognitive processes investigated in NDM often have as much in common with problem solving as they do with traditional conceptions of decision making. Most of the research into NDM has focused on workplace performance, though some NDM research has been laboratory-based. Much of this work is therefore concerned with expertise and the elicitation of knowledge from experts. The study of experts precedes the development of NDM as a distinct field of research, but the two clearly overlap.

In the past, attempts to elicit knowledge from experts relied on unstructured interviews. These were not very profitable and led to a bottleneck in the development of expert systems (Schraagen, 2006). However, under the heading of *Cognitive Task Analysis*, a variety of new techniques have been developed. These include the use of concurrent verbal reports and the critical decision method. This latter technique involves the telling and retelling of a previously encountered situation, usually unusual or challenging, that involved a 'critical decision(s)'. During the retelling, the interviewer guides the expert with a series of prompts and very specific probe questions. The technique results in a detailed timeline of events that includes observations, options, actions, and so on. The resulting case studies are often useful as training materials.

Another technique has been to give the expert a head-mounted video camera in a real or simulated environment. After the event, the individual involved talks through the event with an interviewer while watching a video replay. At the first stage, the person relives and recalls the event from an 'inside' perspective, trying to recall all the thoughts that occurred at the time. At the second stage, the person recalls the event from an 'outsider' perspective, while watching the replay and listening to the recording of the first recollection. At this stage the interviewer can also ask focused questions based on the responses that were given during the first recall session (Omodei *et al.*, 1997).

Several theories of NDM have been proposed, of which I discuss two in some detail below. Firstly, image theory has been proposed as a theory of both personal and organisational decision behaviour (Beach, 1990). Much of the empirical work inspired by image theory has concerned how people select the options that they later choose between. In fact, according to image theory the construction of a choice set is driven less by the selection of options and primarily by the rejection of options that are inconsistent with our basic values.

Secondly, much of the research that has been reported under the NDM banner has been concerned with the nature of expertise and with high-stakes decisions made under severe time pressure. Thus, firefighters, pilots, and battlefield commanders have all featured prominently in NDM studies (see for example the collections by Zsambok & Klein, 1997, and Flin *et al.*, 1997). The theory of recognition-primed decision making proposes that people in such pressured situations use their experience to generate just one option. They mentally simulate what will happen if they follow this course of action, and only generate other options if they identify a serious problem.

Two theories of naturalistic decision making

Image theory *Image theory* is a theory of how people's knowledge guides their decision making. It proposes that knowledge is partitioned into three schematic knowledge representations or *images* (see Figure 11.3). These images constitute a person's decision *frame*.

The *value image* refers to the basic beliefs, values, morals, and ethics of a person. They can be thought of as a set of principles that guide behaviour.

The *trajectory image* represents a person's agenda of goals for the future, and may be determined by one's principles, by problems encountered in the environment, or both. Goals may vary in the extent of their concreteness, and it may be harder to tell when more abstract goals have been achieved. However, surrogate events may serve to indicate when a more abstract goal has been achieved. For instance, if your goal is to 'become famous', then the receipt of fan mail may suggest that this goal has been achieved.

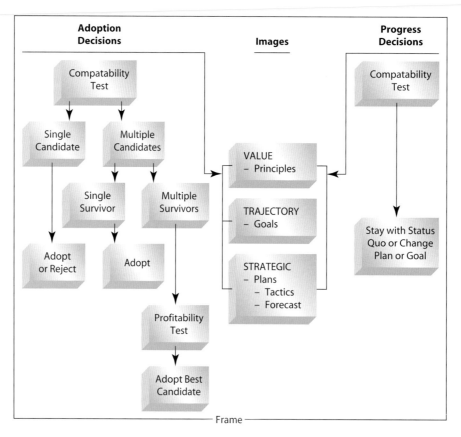

Figure 11.3. *Image theory*

The *strategic image* represents a person's plans for achieving their goals. The concrete behaviours that are considered in relation to the implementation of the plan are referred to as *tactics*, and the imagined scenario that tries to anticipate the outcome of the tactics is referred to as the *forecast*.

In image theory, decision makers are only willing to consider decision options that are compatible with their value image. Options that are not compatible are screened out via a *compatibility test*. This test looks for violations of a decision maker's standards. Violations are all or nothing, and if the total number of violations exceeds some *rejection threshold*, then the option is rejected from the choice set. In other words, screening is non-compensatory; attributes that violate a decision maker's standards are not compensated for by more positive attributes.

The compatibility test is also applied when making decisions about progress. During the implementation of a plan, an individual must assess whether or not that plan is making progress towards the achievement of the relevant goal. If it is not, then the existing plan must be amended or a new plan adopted.

Evidence for the compatibility test in pre-choice screening has been provided by Beach and Strom (1989). In a hypothetical job search, during which participants read about various characteristics of potential jobs, options were eliminated from consideration once participants had encountered approximately five characteristics that violated their standards. Non-violations played virtually no role at all in the screening process. A later study, involving a hypothetical choice of apartment, found that the information used to decide whether or not to visit an apartment had no effect on subsequent rental decisions, which were based on new information (Van Zee *et al.*, 1992).

One gap in image theory is that there is no specification of how people decide to stop searching for information on candidates that have not been rejected (Beach, 1990, p.76). One obvious 'stopping rule' would be to quit collecting information just before net costs (in terms of time and effort) begin to outweigh the benefits. However, such a calculation is a compensatory process that goes against the basic idea of screening, which is that it is a non-compensatory process (Harvey & Bolger, 2001).

In fact, Harvey and Bolger found evidence that compensatory processing does occur in screening. In a variation on the apartment choice task participants first rated several rooms, after which they had the option to buy information (using points) about the quietness of any rooms they wished, and after they had as much information as they wanted they rated the rooms again. Finally, they chose a room. If the room was better than the current room then they were credited with points. Contrary to what image theory predicts, attractiveness was clearly related to the expected points score but not to the compatibility score. Furthermore, people were more likely to collect information that was associated with a higher number of expected points, indicating that their viewing decisions were part of a compensatory choice process. Finally, the post-viewing expected points score was a much better predictor of choice that the compatibility score.

According to image theory, when a choice set consists of multiple items people apply a *profitability test*. They choose from a repertoire of choice strategies on the basis of their expectations about the benefits and costs associated with those strategies. There

is plenty of evidence that people do adopt various strategies during choice (see Payne *et al.*, 1993; Chapter 8).

Image theory has also been proposed as a theory of how organisational decisions are made. Just as individuals have certain principles and goals, so do organisations. The organisational equivalents of the value, trajectory, and strategic images are, respectively, the organisation's *culture*, *vision*, and *strategy* (Beach & Connolly, 2005). However, there has not been a great deal of research into the organisational version of image theory (though Beach and Connolly review several relevant studies).

In summary, image theory provides an intuitively appealing account of decision making, in particular through its attempt to link people's values to the decisions they make. At the same time, while image theory has been promoted as a model of naturalistic decision making, supporting evidence from real-life situations is lacking. In addition, given the centrality of images within the theory there has been relatively little exploration of these, nor is it entirely clear how images *should* be studied (Beach & Connolly, 2005, p.171). As we have seen, there is nothing in image theory that specifies when people should stop searching for information about options, and there is also some clear evidence against the theory.

Recognition-primed decision making Klein (1998) describes a study in which fireground commanders were interviewed about non-routine experiences ('critical incidents'). Rather than comparing multiple options, it was expected that commanders would only consider two options when under time pressure. Contrary to this expectation, commanders frequently reported that they did not compare *any* options at all. Indeed, some commanders reported that they did not make 'decisions' at all. What they actually did was to use their experience to generate a single option. In other words, they were able to recognise even non-routine situations as an example of a prototype, and based on this recognition they normally generated a single response that was acted upon.

Based on this research, Klein developed the *recognition-primed decision* (RPD) model. This is specifically a theory about decision making in high-stakes, time-pressured situations. As shown in Figure 11.4, recognising a situation as prototypical involves the identification of relevant cues that aid situational understanding, the development of expectancies and suitable goals, and the identification of a typical course of action. Having identified a typical course of action, decision makers do not compare this to some other course of action. Instead, they evaluate this option using mental simulation; that is, they imagine how a situation is likely to play out if they were to adopt this course of action, and only if they identify some problem do they generate a further option.

Is it the case that the single option generated under time pressure is the best option? In earlier research, Klein and colleagues had noted that chess masters made better moves than class B players when under 'Blitz' conditions (six seconds per move; see Calderwood *et al.*, 1988). However, to determine the quality of the *first* move considered, a subsequent study asked stronger and weaker chess players[5] to think aloud while they considered four mid-game positions that were presented to them (Klein *et al.*, 1995). As expected, the first moves considered by players tended to be stronger than later moves that they considered.

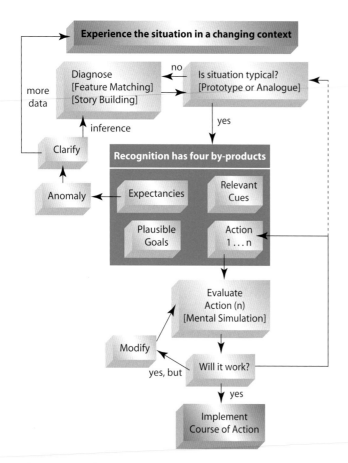

Figure 11.4. *The recognition-primed decision model*
Source: Klein, 1998.

rapidly as typical of various prototypes, using representativeness and availability heuristics, and are able to evaluate the courses of action suggested by these prototypes by conducting mental simulations, using the simulation heuristic, without having to compare options. (Klein, 2001, p.114)

One limitation of the RPD model is that it has been specifically designed for decisions made under time pressure. Not all naturalistic decision making occurs under such pressure, however. For example, aircrew rarely have to make decisions under time pressure, except where their own failure to act appropriately has created that pressure. Orasanu and Fischer (1997) argue that aircrew may respond to a problem by seeking information. Where they believe they have sufficient information they may follow a procedural rule or, in the absence of such, may generate and choose among different courses of action. This requires more cognitive effort and so is more vulnerable to stressors, particularly among less experienced crew (e.g. Stokes & Kite, 1994). On the other hand, where time is very limited and risk is high, crews may feel the need to act regardless of whether they believe they understand the situation properly. Orasanu and Fischer have incorporated this approach into a modified version of the RPD model.

Another domain that requires high-stakes decision making, but not always under time pressure (at least, no *perceived* time pressure) concerns the assessment of avalanche likelihood in wilderness environments. In this domain, there is evidence that certain contextual factors can cause people to fail to apply expert knowledge that they possess. This type of observation is less easily explained within the current specification of the RPD model.

SUMMARY

Dynamic decision making research examines people's behaviour in microworlds; simulated environments in which people typically try to control a complex system in which initial decisions may affect later decisions. Often there are feedback delays that might impair the participant's ability to construct an accurate mental model of the system. An example of this is Sterman's Beer Distribution Game.

On some tasks, people do learn to exert a certain degree of control over the system, but performance is usually far from optimal, and people may find it hard to explain their behaviour. Also, people often waste time seeking useless information. Such behaviour would appear to run counter to the adaptive decision maker hypothesis. Explanations of learning in dynamic decision-making tasks include the use of production rules, the retrieval of instances or exemplars, and connectionism.

At least some of the variability in performance on these tasks may be due to individual differences in intelligence. Recent research suggests that the early failure to find any such differences was due to the unreliability of performance measures.

Other researchers have looked at everyday decision making. Such research tends to be more broadly conceived than laboratory decision making, involving a much wider range of cognitive

The RPD model has been studied in various domains, including health care, design, and electronic warfare (for a review see Ross *et al.*, 2006). It has interesting implications for training people in decision skills. Rather than teach people a domain-general approach to analytical decision procedures, the RPD model suggests that people should engage in deliberate practice within their specific domain of interest. By engaging in multiple simulations or scenarios, novices can learn to identify relevant cues, generate expectations, and identify goals and typical actions. Through the use of feedback, and comparisons with other people, they can learn the limitations of their mental models and the courses of action that they consider. This approach explicitly recognises the tacit nature of much knowledge.

Some authors within the NDM approach have written quite critically of some mainstream decision-making concepts (criticising the mainstream is often the case with a new field trying to carve a niche for itself). However, Klein himself regards his approach as blending three of Kahneman and Tversky's (1982) heuristics, i.e. representativeness, availability, and simulation. He writes:

Instead of seeing these as biases, I have found it more useful to see them as strengths that permit skilful decision making in field settings. Experienced decision makers are able to categorize situations processes. One strand of research examines the relationship between expertise and situation awareness. Other researchers have looked at the effects of sleep deprivation on decision making.

Job performance is known to be associated with intelligence, which suggests that the individual differences found on dynamic decision-making tasks generalise to the real world. It is as yet less clear whether there are decision-making styles that play a major role in everyday decisions.

Some decision researchers who are interested in real-world contexts now identify themselves as working within a field called naturalistic decision making. This chapter has reviewed two theories of NDM: image theory and the recognition-primed decision model. Both theories propose a role for knowledge in guiding decision behaviour. Image theory proposes that people screen out decision options that violate their basic values. By contrast, the RPD model is an attempt to explain how critical decisions are made under time pressure and stress. When experts, such as fire commanders, recognise a situation as prototypical they often use their knowledge to generate a single course of action.

QUESTIONS

1. What are the features that characterise dynamic decision situations?

2. Design a study to investigate individual differences in situation awareness (choose a domain other than those mentioned in this chapter).

3. Do a literature search on other theories of naturalistic decision making and write an evaluative report on these.

4. Design a study to compare the influences of intelligence and personality on decision making.

5. Describe three theories of learning in dynamic decision-making tasks.

6. Discuss the role of feedback in dynamic decision-making tasks.

7. Evaluate the recognition-primed decision model.

NOTES

1. Gibson *et al.* (1997) use the term *forward submodel*, but I have used the term *prediction submodel* as I find it more descriptively appealing. Similarly, Gonzalez (2005a) has referred to the forward submodel and the action submodel, respectively, as the judgment submodel and the choice submodel.

2. Reliability has two meanings. One aspect of reliability is the extent to which measures are internally consistent. Different measures can be said to be reliable if they are accurately measuring the same variable. The other aspect of reliability is the extent to which the same outcome is achieved when the same measurement is taken on more than one occasion (test-retest reliability).

3. In Chapter 15 we shall see evidence that more intelligent individuals are more reflective.

4. For reasons that were not explained, data were not available for the avoidant and spontaneous styles.

5. The stronger players had ratings between 1700 and 2150, and the weaker players had ratings of 1150 to 1600.

RECOMMENDED READING

Hutchins, E. (1995). *Cognition in the wild*. Cambridge, MA: MIT Press. This book is an in-depth study of the relationship between thought and the environment within which thinking takes place. The author is an anthropologist and an open-ocean racing sailor, and draws upon his knowledge of ship navigation to explore human cognition.

Klein, G. (1998). *Sources of power: How people make decisions*. Cambridge, MA: MIT Press. This is perhaps the most influential book on naturalistic decision making.

12 | Risk

INTRODUCTION

How do you feel about nuclear power? X-rays? Do you smoke, drive, take illegal drugs? Have you been mountain climbing, or would you like to? The study of risk can be quite perplexing. People are often quite willing to accept certain types of risks, but get quite angry about other risks that actually pose less of a threat. It is also a curious paradox of progress, at least in the developed world, that new technologies often make us feel more at risk, while at the same time providing us with lifestyles and lifespans that previous generations could never have imagined.

In this chapter, I shall examine the factors that influence our judgments of risk. As we will see, early cost-benefit analyses of what is regarded as an acceptable level of risk quickly gave way to psychometric analyses. This latter technique has found that people have a range of interrelated intuitions that can be grouped into two dimensions. We shall also look at the influences on risk judgments from emotional factors, social factors, personality, sex, race, and expertise.

THE REVEALED PREFERENCES APPROACH TO RISK

In a 1969 *Science* article Chauncey Starr posed the question, 'What is our society willing to pay for safety?' To answer this question he applied cost-benefit analysis to various technologies and behaviours. As an example of the kind of figures he used (which involved various assumptions), here are the types of data used for assessing motor-vehicle travel:

> The calculation of motor-vehicle fatalities per exposure hour per year is based on the number of registered cars, an assumed $1\frac{1}{2}$ persons per car, and an assumed 400 hours per year of average car use . . . The figure for annual benefit for motor-vehicle travel is based on the sum of costs for gasoline, maintenance, insurance, and car payments and on the value of the time savings per person. It is assumed that use of an automobile allows a person to save 1 hour per working day and that a person's time is worth $5 per hour. (pp.1237–1238)

Starr plotted the level of risks to benefits for various technologies/activities, where risk was defined as the probability of fatalities per person-hour of exposure, and benefit per person was measured on a dollar scale. The ratio of risks to benefits differed for various activities. On the assumption that these figures were a reasonably accurate reflection of people's tolerance for various risks, people appeared willing to accept voluntary risks (for example, smoking, hunting) that were about 1000 times greater than involuntary risks (for example, electric power). Starr also suggested that benefit awareness, as estimated from the level of advertising, increased the levels of risk that the public were willing to accept.

Using his methodology, Starr thought currently accepted levels of risk could be used to predict the risks that would be accepted from other sources (for example, acceptance levels for coal-burning power plants could be used to predict the acceptable level of risks from nuclear power stations).

THE PSYCHOMETRIC APPROACH TO RISK

The two dimensions of risk

Starr's methodology was based on the notion that people's preferences are *revealed* in their behaviour. This idea was questioned in Chapter 8. In particular, it is also questionable whether people's behaviours are based on a rational assessment of costs and benefits. Other authors have examined people's *expressed preferences* in relation to risks and benefits. Fischhoff *et al.* (1978) asked members of the Oregon League of Women's Voters and their spouses (a thoughtful and influential group of private citizens) to rate various technologies/activities for risk, benefit, and maximum level of acceptable risk. They also asked them to rate each item on various risk characteristics: voluntariness of risk, immediacy of consequences, whether the persons exposed have a knowledge of the risks, whether the risks are known to science, the extent of control that a person has over the risk, newness of the risks, whether the risk kills people one at a time or in large numbers, whether the risk is one that arouses dread, and the likelihood that the consequences will be fatal.

There were high intercorrelations between the various risk factors. Using the technique of factor analysis, Fischhoff *et al.* found that two basic dimensions appeared to underlie the perceived relationships between these risk factors. One of these factors can be termed *dread risk* and the other *unknown risk*. Dread risk is associated with the feeling of dread, and with a number of other factors such as catastrophic consequences and fatal consequences. Unknown risk is associated with factors such as being novel, unobservable, and having delayed consequences. A similar study found that the single factor 'number of people exposed' emerged as a third dimension (Slovic *et al.*, 1980). Nonetheless, two underlying dimensions seem to capture most of the variation in responding, a finding that has also been replicated in other countries (e.g. Brun, 1992; Teigen *et al.*, 1988; Vlek & Stallen, 1981). Figure 12.1 shows how these two dimensions map onto a number of risks.

Factors underlying the two dimensions

Voluntary versus involuntary risks Starr's 1969 paper hypothesised that voluntariness mediated perceived risk–benefit relationships. To test this idea, Fischhoff *et al.* (1978) dichotomised their items into the 15 most voluntary and 15 least voluntary risks. Contrary to Starr's hypothesis, the relationship between perceived risks and perceived benefits did not differ for voluntary and involuntary risks. However, in terms of what was regarded as an acceptable level of risk, people were willing to tolerate a higher level for risks that they saw as voluntary. Nonetheless, the extent to which a risk is seen as involuntary also correlates highly with other factors, such as lack of control, global catastrophe, inequity and catastrophe (Slovic *et al.*, 1980). This raises the possibility that it is these other factors that impact on people's judgments, and not involuntariness per se. Indeed, when these factors were removed statistically, voluntariness no longer related to acceptable risk.

Catastrophic potential Slovic *et al.* noted that respondents seemed to show little concern about the risks from diagnostic X-rays, despite the fact that the invisible and irreversible contamination that they produce can lead to cancer and genetic damage. By contrast, people believed that nuclear power posed a greater risk of death than any of the other hazards that they were asked to consider. This perception was linked to the perceived potential for disaster. Presumably, it is – at least in part – the concern about

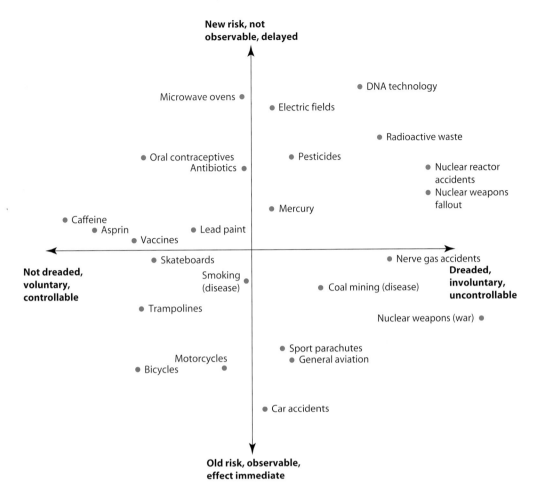

Figure 12.1. *The two-dimensional factor structure*
This is a simplified graphic that does not show all of the risks that have been reported in such studies.

catastrophic potential that lies behind public opposition to nuclear technology.

Slovic *et al.* also pointed out that it is very difficult to demonstrate the improbability of catastrophic accidents because doing so requires vast amounts of data. What little evidence there is may be interpreted within the framework of a person's prior beliefs. Furthermore, certain types of accident, when they occur, may have *signal value* – that is, they may be interpreted in terms of an increased likelihood of similar events in the future and, thus, the need for corrective action. This hypothesis was supported by a questionnaire study that showed certain types of events to be regarded as more informative than others. Consider the following two scenarios. In one, a dam collapse kills 40 people. In the other, a partial core meltdown at a nuclear reactor kills one person inside the plant, but the radiation is contained and does not reach the external environment. The judged levels of grief and suffering were about the same for both incidents (4.9 vs. 4.5 on a seven-point scale). However, the nuclear accident was seen as more informative and more worrying, and people thought that there was a greater need for awareness and a greater effort needed to prevent recurrence.

Known versus unknown risks People tend to be more concerned about unknown risks than known risks. When risks are unknown it is likely that people fear the worst. When people first became aware of HIV/AIDS in the 1980s, almost nothing was known about how the disease was spread, about how many people had the illness, or what the chances were of acquiring it. It is probably fair to say that public concern in Western countries was far greater in those early days than it is now, when we know more about HIV, how to avoid it, and what can be done to assist those who have acquired it.

It is sometimes argued that we should respond to new risks by applying the *precautionary principle*. This is sometimes formulated in different ways, for example:

In order to protect the environment, the precautionary approach shall be widely applied by States according to their capabilities. Where there are threats of serious or irreversible damage, lack of full scientific certainty shall not be used as a reason for postponing cost-effective measures to prevent environmental degradation. (The United Nations *Rio Declaration on Environment and Development*[1])

[I]f an action or policy might cause severe or irreversible harm to the public, in the absence of a scientific consensus that harm would not ensue, the burden of proof falls on those who would advocate taking the action. (Wikipedia)[2]

In practice, the precautionary principle – at least in its most stringent formulations – is controversial. Opponents argue that it is a major hindrance to desirable development (or would be, if applied). Thus, supporters of genetically modified (GM) crops point to the huge benefits that this technology could bring to the world's poor and hungry. Opponents of GM crops say that the major beneficiaries of GM would be the multinational corporations that make them, with great risk to the environment.

Finally, one likely factor in people's concerns about unknown risks is the *ignorance aversion* that we encountered in Chapter 7. Recall that not only do people prefer to bet on events that they feel knowledgeable about (which would be perfectly rational), but they prefer to bet on vague events that they feel knowledgeable about rather than chance events that they consider equally probable.

Perceptions of control People are willing to accept a higher level of risk for things that they perceive they have control over. However, as we saw in Chapter 9, people typically perceive themselves as having more control than they actually do (including the perception of control over chance events). This can lead to unrealistic optimism, whereby people believe that good things are more likely to happen to them than to other people and bad things are more likely to happen to other people than to them.

It is likely that there are both advantages and disadvantages to the illusion of control and optimistic bias. Without striving, there can be no achievement, but without the belief that one has some control then striving will not occur. However, when one strives for something a negative outcome is always a possibility. In some domains, negative outcomes may mean physical harm. For instance, a motorist who has an unrealistic perception of his level of control may kill himself (and others) through dangerous driving.

Other intuitions about risk

Naturalism: nature knows best One quite common intuition is that 'natural is good' (e.g. Baron, 1998). Thus, 45 per cent of the general public in Oregon agreed that 'Natural chemicals, as a rule, are not as harmful as man-made chemicals.' Of the same group of respondents, 49 per cent blamed agricultural pesticides for causing malformations in newly born children in a (hypothetical) small community. For a sample of professional toxicologists these percentages were just 13 per cent and 6 per cent, respectively (Kraus *et al.*, 1992).

The naturalism heuristic is perfectly understandable; after all, our very survival is based on the consumption of the water, fruit, vegetables, and meat that our environment provides us. However, the products of the natural world are not always benign. Plants did not evolve because they wanted us to eat them; on the contrary, many plants have their own defence mechanisms against consumption. This is thought to be why people have an aversion to

bitter-tasting foods: the aversion is an evolved mechanism to alert us to the possible presence of toxins (Soranzo *et al.*, 2005). However, the same aversion may act against the interests of contemporary humans by making us reluctant to eat foods containing nutrients that combat heart disease and cancer.

We may overestimate the extent to which the natural world is benign. Some of the foodstuffs we consume now are only safe because conscious or unconscious domestication has made them so. Earlier in human history these foods were extremely dangerous. For example, wild almonds contain a chemical called amygdalin, which breaks down to create the lethal poison cyanide. A snack of wild almonds can kill someone who ignores the bitter taste. Diamond (1998) has described how domestication gave rise to the non-lethal sweet almond. It so happens that the occasional almond tree contains a mutation in a single gene that prevents them from synthesising amygdalin. In the wild, these trees die without leaving progeny because birds discover and eat all their seeds. However, when early farmers discovered these trees they would plant the seeds in their orchards, thus beginning the spread of sweet almond trees.

Ames and Gold (1990) have described plants and animals as being in an 'evolutionary war'. Plants have developed natural pesticides to prevent their being eaten, but animals have also developed defences against certain toxins. Thus, people are quite well protected against low doses of carcinogens. This is just as well, since about half the natural chemicals that have been tested on rodents have been found to be carcinogenic. This is about the same proportion as for synthetic chemicals, yet many more synthetic chemicals have been tested overall than natural ones. Of the 27 natural pesticide rodent carcinogens that had been identified by 1990, one or more had been found in the following foodstuffs: anise, apple, banana, basil, broccoli, Brussels sprouts, cabbage, cantaloupe, caraway, carrot, cauliflower, celery, cherry, cinnamon, cloves, cocoa, coffee (brewed), comfrey tea, dill, eggplant (aubergine), endive, fennel, grapefruit juice, grape, honey, honeydew melon, horseradish, kale, lettuce, mace, mango, mushroom, mustard (brown), nutmeg, orange juice, parsley, parsnip, peach, pear, pepper (black), pineapple, plum, potato, radish, raspberry, rosemary, sage, sesame seeds (heated), strawberry, tarragon, thyme, and turnip.

The naturalism heuristic means that people are less willing to pay money to combat harm caused by events perceived as natural, as compared to when the source of harm is human. For instance, 68 per cent of respondents were willing to contribute to save endangered dolphins from pollution, but only 44 per cent were willing to contribute when the danger was described as a new virus. This translated into an average contribution of $18.85 for the pollution danger and $6.35 for the virus (Kahneman & Ritov, 1994; see also Kahneman *et al.*, 1993). Kahneman *et al.* actually proposed a similar, but rather more general, heuristic to explain their results: they suggested that people's willingness to contribute to alleviating harm is determined by an *outrage heuristic*, whereby their feelings are related to the cause of the harm.

Eliminating versus reducing risk Studies of consumers have shown that people are more willing to pay a premium for the elimination of a risk compared to its reduction. This tendency is known as the *certainty effect* (Samuelson & Zeckhauser, 1988; see also Chapter 7). Such reactions can result in a *pseudo-certainty effect*, as demonstrated by Slovic *et al.* (1982). They found that a vaccine against a disease affecting 20 per cent of the population was considered less attractive when described as effective in half of all cases than when described as providing full protection against one of two exclusive and equally probable (10 per cent in each case) virus strains causing identical symptoms.

The pseudo-certainty effect might be considered rational, in the sense that the removal of one disease means that effort can then be concentrated on ameliorating the threats posed by the alternative disease. By contrast, tackling two distinct diseases might, all other things being equal, pose more of a challenge. However, for certain types of risk it is not clear that the elimination of risk is a desirable aim. In the United States, the 1980 Superfund law concerns the clean-up of hazardous waste that has been left in the ground. The law mandates the complete removal of such waste. However, it has been argued that the greatest expense is incurred during the removal of the last 10 per cent of such waste (Breyer, 1993, cited in Baron, 2000). Thus, the money that is spent on completely removing the final remains of waste from one site could be better spent on removing waste from other areas.

'Do no harm' Ritov and Baron (1992) have suggested that an omission bias occurs with some decisions (see Chapter 8). This is a greater reluctance to risk negative outcomes by one's actions, compared to risking negative outcomes by not taking action. The omission bias can be considered as reflecting a 'do no harm' heuristic (Baron, 1998), a heuristic that may also be behind calls to apply the precautionary principle that we encountered earlier. Baron (1998) has suggested that the reluctance of some people to vaccinate their children may be an instance of omission bias. He gave the example of polio vaccination. The Salk vaccine uses a killed virus whereas the Sabin vaccine uses a live virus (Sabin has actually replaced the Salk vaccine). Neither virus is 100 per cent effective, but whereas Salk occasionally fails to *prevent* polio occurring the Sabin vaccine occasionally *causes* polio to occur. However, Sabin is more effective overall. Nonetheless, Baron noted that 'Nobody ever sued the makers of the Salk vaccine for failing to prevent polio, but many people have sued the makers of the Sabin vaccine for causing polio' (1998, p.112).

The 'do no harm' principle may also lie behind another perplexing finding. Consider an automobile company that uses a cost-benefit analysis, trading off dollars against lives saved, in order to decide whether to implement a safety precaution. On the basis of the analysis, even though a high value was placed on human life, the company decides against the safety precaution. Viscusi (2000) reports that people view such a company more unfavourably than a similar company that imposes the same risk on motorists without conducting a cost-benefit analysis. Sunstein (2005) has suggested that a 'cold heart' heuristic may be operating.

Betrayals Koehler and Gershoff (2003) noted that people are especially averse to risks of death that come from products (such as airbags) designed to promote safety. In one study, people heard that there was a 2 per cent chance that drivers of Car A, with Air Bag A, will be killed in serious accidents. For drivers of Car B, with Air Bag B, there was a 1 per cent chance of death, but an additional chance of one in 10,000 (0.01 per cent) of dying as a result of the air bag deploying. When asked to choose between these two equally priced cars, most people chose Car A – the riskier car. In other words, people seem to be choosing a higher-risk option in order to avoid the possibility of betrayal. Whether or not this example illustrates the use of a moral heuristic gone awry (Sunstein, 2005) as opposed to simply showing that people will incur *some* cost (but not necessarily any cost) to avoid betrayal (Koehler & Gershoff, 2005) is a matter of debate.

AFFECTIVE INFLUENCES ON RISK PERCEPTION

The observation that people's assessments of risk are influenced by an underlying dimension of *dread*, and its associated factors, suggests that perception of risk is influenced by emotion as well as cognition. However, prior to the 1990s there was little discussion of emotion in relation to decision making. It was often assumed that feelings arose as a consequence of cognitive evaluation, but without having a direct input into decisions or behaviour (although the anticipation of emotion was sometimes recognised as a possible input into cognitions).

On the basis of more recent work, there is now reason to believe that the relationship between cognition and emotion is much more interactive. Figure 12.2 shows the *risk-as-feelings* model proposed by Loewenstein *et al.* (2001). This suggests that cognitions and emotions can act upon each other, but also that they can both act directly on behaviour without the mediation of the other (the relationship between cognition, emotion, and decision making will be explored further in Chapter 15).

In Chapter 9 we saw that different emotions have different effects on people's risk judgments and their optimism. Induced anger and happiness produced equal optimism about events that were ambiguous in terms of their certainty and controllability, whereas induced fear led to pessimism. For unambiguous events, only the 'happy' participants were optimistic, whereas the fearful and angry participants were about equally pessimistic (Lerner & Keltner, 2001, Study 3). Lerner and Keltner interpreted their results in terms of *appraisal-tendency theory*. This states that emotions elicit cognitive appraisals that interpret the situation that gave rise to the emotions, and thereby help respond to the situation. However, emotions can persist beyond the situation that elicited them, such that they may affect the interpretation of other situations (Figure 12.3).

Shortly after the attacks on the World Trade Center on 11 September 2001, Jennifer Lerner and colleagues asked people to rate their emotional responses. Then, six to 10 weeks later, the same people were asked to assess the risk to themselves and other Americans from a diverse range of events. People who showed greater anger in the wake of 9/11 tended to give lower ratings of risk. By contrast, people who showed greater fear tended to give higher ratings of risk. These emotional responses also related to

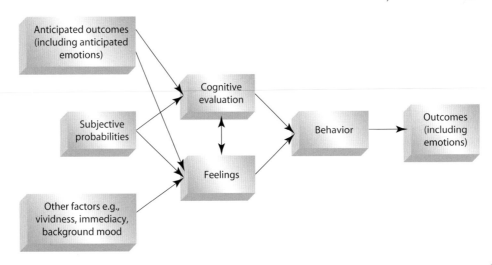

Figure 12.2. *The risk-as-feelings perspective*
Source: Loewenstein *et al.*, 2001.

© Scott Adams, Inc./Dist. by UFS Inc.

Figure 12.3. *Emotions tend to persist beyond the situation that elicited them*

different views about policy: Anger was associated with the wish to deport foreigners who did not possess a valid visa, whereas fear was associated with the desire to build stronger contacts with the Muslim world (Lerner *et al.*, 2003). This study also found that experimentally induced fear led to higher risk estimates than did anger. Women rated the risks as higher than did men, though this did not interact with the experimental manipulations.

Other researchers have proposed that people use an *affect heuristic* to make judgments of risks and benefits. Alhakami and Slovic (1994) found that, if people liked an activity, they tended to rate its risks as low and its benefits as high. On the other hand, if they disliked an activity then they rated its risks as high and its benefits as low. They suggested that people were using their affective feelings to make these judgments. This interpretation of their findings was supported by a further study in which half the participants made risk and benefit judgments under time pressure (Finucane *et al.*, 2000, Study 1). Time pressure reduces the cognitive resources available for analytical deliberation and may increase arousal, making affective processes more salient (Maule & Svenson, 1993). For most items on a list of 23 hazardous facilities

or activities, the risk–benefit correlations were more strongly negative for the judgments made under time pressure. In a follow-up study, enhancing the awareness of benefits through the provision of information not only tended to increase the ratings of benefits, but also decreased the ratings of risks. Conversely, enhancing the awareness of risks increased the ratings of risks, but decreased the ratings of benefits (Finucane *et al.*, 2000, Study 2).

THE SOCIAL AMPLIFICATION OF RISK

How are perceptions of risk influenced by social and cultural factors? The psychometric approach to risk has shown that many factors do influence risk perceptions, but only recently have researchers tried to incorporate the wider social and cultural factors into a theory (or, perhaps more accurately, a framework). The basic idea behind the social amplification of risk framework (SARF) is that:

> risk events interact with psychological, social, and cultural processes in a way that can heighten or attenuate public perception of risk and related risk behavior. Behavioral patterns, in turn, generate secondary social or economic consequences but may act also to increase or decrease the physical risk itself. Secondary effects trigger demands for additional institutional responses and protective actions, or, conversely (in the case of risk attenuation), impede needed protective actions. (Kasperson et al., 1988, p.234)

In short, social amplification involves two stages. The first stage is the transfer of information about the risk or risk event. For risks that are not directly experienced, risk amplification may be influenced by the volume of information, the degree to which information is disputed, the extent of dramatisation, and the symbolic connotations of the information. For example, a risk message about a chemical may be interpreted differently, depending on whether it comes from a pharmaceutical company or a consumer organisation. Both have symbolic value, depending on a person's prior views. A pharmaceutical company message may be regarded as less credible if it arouses the mental image of uncaring big business. The consumer organisation may lead to a more positive image of a body that is on the side of the ordinary person, therefore more attention is paid to the content of the message.

The second stage involves the response mechanisms of society. Response mechanisms may involve the use of heuristics and values, social group relationships, signal value, and stigmatisation. Kasperson et al. (1988) refer to risk events having a 'ripple effect'. For example, the Three Mile Island nuclear incident was followed by nuclear plants around the world being shut down and restarted more often for safety checks, despite the fact that these phases of operation are by far the riskiest.

In reviewing 15 years of research into the social amplification of risk, Kasperson et al. (2003) noted the importance of *trust* as a response mechanism. Distrust increases the perception of risk, intensifies the public's reaction to risk signals, contributes to the perceived unacceptability of risk, and stimulates political activism (p.32).

PERSONALITY, SEX, RACE, AND EXPERTISE

Personality

Is risk-taking domain-specific or domain-general? One constant finding from several studies is that the intercorrelations between risk taking in different domains tend to be weak. On the face of it, this would appear to indicate that there are not really any risk-seeking or risk-avoiding personalities (e.g. Salminen & Heiskanen, 1997; Weinstein & Martin, 1969). However, a complicating factor here is that people's *perceptions* of risk can vary depending on the characteristics of the situation; in fact, for many people, attitudes to the risks that they *perceive* tend to be quite stable across situations (Weber & Millman, 1997). In other words, when variations in risk perception are controlled for, people who tend to take risks in one domain are more likely to take risks in other domains. In the remainder of this section I shall look at how other aspects of a person's personality may affect their propensity to take risks.

The evolution of personality variations MacDonald (1995) proposed that variations in personality could be viewed as representing alternative strategies for maximising evolutionary fitness. This idea has been explored in more detail by Nettle (2005, 2006), who makes explicit the notion that any given personality trait involves a tradeoff between the benefits and costs incurred by that trait. For example, extraversion is associated with greater mating success, more social support, more physical activity, and more exploration of one's environment. However, extraverts tend to expose themselves to higher levels of risk. People who are hospitalised due to accident or illness tend to be higher in extraversion than those who are not (Nettle, 2005). Furthermore, people who suffer traumatic injury tend to be high in sensation seeking (Field & O'Keefe, 2004), which is one of the underlying facets of extraversion.

In addition, extraverts are more likely to migrate, be involved in criminal or antisocial behaviour, or get arrested. As Nettle (2006, p.625) notes, all of these are sources of risk, 'that in the ancestral environment might have meant ostracism or death'. Because extraverts tend to have more sexual partners, they are more likely to expose offspring to step-parenting, itself a risk factor for child well-being.

The other aspects of personality have similar costs and benefits, though these may not always be as apparent in our contemporary environment as they would have been in our ancestral environment. For instance, neuroticism may have a protective effect by making people vigilant with regard to dangers. However, high levels of neuroticism are associated with negative health issues, such as stress and depression. Nettle (2006, p.626) notes that certain groups of risk takers, such as alpinists and mountaineers, are frequently found to be low in neuroticism (e.g. Egan & Stelmack, 2003; Goma-i-Freixanet, 1991).

There is not a stable optimum level of any personality trait. The costs and benefits of different traits vary across time depending on the nature of the environment, and may also be different for males and females. For example, an important trait in animal species is exploratory behaviour, which has a substantial heritable component. In the great tit species (*Parus major*), bolder females are more likely to survive poor years when food is less abundant, because they engage in greater exploratory behaviour and competition for what resources there are (Dingemanse et al., 2004). However, when food is abundant, bolder females do less well, possibly because they become involved in dangerous and aggressive encounters that have no benefit. Males, who are the dominant sex, show the opposite pattern. Much of their effort is devoted to defending territory. Thus, when food is scarce, competition for territory is relaxed due to the higher levels of mortality, and so the less bold males do well. However, when food is abundant it is the bolder males that thrive.

The five-factor model of personality and its relation to risk taking A model of personality that has received wide attention is the five-factor model proposed by Costa and McCrae (1985, 1992). It proposes that a considerable amount of the variation in personality can be explained in terms of extraversion, neuroticism, openness, conscientiousness, and agreeableness. Nicholson *et al.* (2005) investigated the relationship between the 'Big 5' personality factors and risk propensity in a variety of domains, using a sample of MBA students and company executives. The risk domains investigated were recreation, health, career, finance, safety (for example fast driving), and social (for example standing for election). Participants were asked to rate themselves in terms of both past and present behaviour.

Higher levels of extraversion were associated with greater risk propensity in all domains, apart from career risk. Similarly, greater openness was associated with greater risk propensity in all domains, apart from safety. By contrast, higher levels of neuroticism, agreeableness, and conscientiousness were associated with lower levels of risk propensity in almost all domains. One exception was a small positive association between neuroticism and health. Nicholson *et al.* also found that sensation-seeking was the primary predictor of risk taking in four domains, and for risk taking overall.

As expected, men showed higher levels of risk propensity than women, but this declined significantly with age. Age-related reductions in risk taking were greatest for the domains of recreation, health, and safety – domains where risky behaviours are most strongly associated with youth.

Sensation seeking As has been noted above, sensation seeking is one of the facets of extraversion in the 'Big 5' model of personality. However, it is worth noting that sensation seeking has been a major topic of investigation in its own right (e.g. Zuckerman, 1979; Zuckerman *et al.*, 1964). The trait of sensation seeking appears to have quite a strong heritable component (Zuckerman, 2005). Risky behaviour in various domains has been linked to sensation seeking, for example: recreational sport (Zuckerman, 1983), driving (Burns & Wilde, 1995), drug use (Franques *et al.*, 2003; Pedersen, 1991), alcohol use and sex (Kalichman *et al.*, 2003). Interestingly, given the contention that personality variations represent cost-benefit tradeoffs, there is research linking low levels of sensation seeking to Parkinson's disease (e.g. Evans *et al.*, 2006).

The most recent version of Zuckerman's Sensation Seeking Scale is Form V (SSSV) (Zuckerman *et al.*, 1978). This contains four subscales:

1. Thrill and Adventure Seeking (TAS). This scale measures the desire to engage in activities that provide unusual sensations of speed or gravity, and which may be a little frightening.

2. Experience Seeking (ES). This measures the desire for stimulation via the mind and senses, through music, art, travel, and psychedelic drugs.

3. Disinhibition (Dis). This measures sensation seeking via social activities such as drinking, parties, varied sexual partners, and so on.

4. Boredom Susceptibility (BS). This represents an intolerance for repetitive experience of any kind.

There have been many studies examining the sensation-seeking profiles of those involved in sports. For instance, two studies have reported that climbers, including alpinists and mountaineers, score higher than controls on ES and TAS (Cronin, 1991; Goma-i-Freixanet, 1991). A recent survey of people involved in sports found that those involved in high-risk sports (e.g. mountaineering) scored higher on all subscales than those involved in low risk sports (e.g. swimming). However, although it has been hypothesised that sensation seeking is often associated with impulsiveness (e.g. Zuckerman, 1994), the high-risk sportspeople were no more impulsive than the low-risk sportspeople. Evidence suggests that sensation-seeking tendencies in sportsmen are often mediated by the skill and knowledge required to cope with the risks involved (Kerr, 1997).

Sex and race[3]

A wide range of studies have shown that men tend to judge risks as smaller than women (Slovic, 2000). Furthermore, these sex differences have been observed among certain groups of experts. Female physical scientists have been found to judge the risks from nuclear technologies as higher than their male counterparts (Barke *et al.*, 1997). Likewise, female members of the British Toxicological Society judged societal risks as higher than did the male members (Slovic *et al.*, 1997).

Although it is tempting to look towards biological explanations Slovic (2000) pointed to other factors that may be involved. Reviewing data reported by Flynn *et al.* (1994), he noted that white males tended to perceive less risk than non-white males and both white and non-white women (the latter three groups all shared fairly similar perceptions). In fact, the white males with the lowest risk-perception scores (about 30 per cent of white males) were better educated than most of the rest of the sample, had higher household incomes, and were politically more conservative. They also tended to hold different attitudes, characterised by 'trust in institutions and authorities and by anti-egalitarian attitudes, including a disinclination toward giving decision-making power to citizens in areas of risk management' (2000, p.401).

In short, Slovic (2000) suggested the possibility that people's risk perceptions may be related to the extent to which they 'create, manage, control, and benefit from' major technologies and activities. Consistent with this notion, experimental research has shown that manipulating a person's feelings of power changes their level of risk taking. Anderson and Galinsky (2006) found that increasing a person's feelings of power (either consciously, or unconsciously via a priming manipulation) led them to perceive risks more optimistically. They also behaved in a more risky fashion in a business scenario, a sexual scenario, and a negotiation scenario.

Nonetheless, it is likely that biological factors do play a part. Indeed, from an evolutionary psychology viewpoint behavioural differences associated with status are entirely compatible with a biological viewpoint. Consider testosterone, a hormone that contributes to the development and maintenance of masculine features, and is implicated in risk-taking and dominance behaviours (Buss, 1999). In one study, researchers measured the testosterone levels of MBA students, some of whom had been involved in a new business venture start-up prior to their studies (White et al., 2006). Those with entrepreneurial experience showed higher levels of testosterone,[4] as well as a greater propensity for risk taking (as measured by a questionnaire). Another study found that, among male fans of both soccer and basketball, a victory led to an increase in testosterone whereas a defeat led to a decrease (Bernhardt et al., 1998).

In most, but not all, domains men take greater risks than women (see for example the meta-analysis by Byrnes et al., 1999). This can have both anti-social and pro-social outcomes. Consider violence as a case in point. On average, men are more violently aggressive than women; in particular, the majority of murders are committed by men, and other men are usually the victims (e.g. Daly & Wilson, 1990). When examined by age, the number of male murder victims shoots up during the adolescent years, peaks in the mid-twenties, and slowly declines thereafter. Female victims increase slightly in the adolescent years, but are nowhere near as numerous as male victims.

Women's aggression, when it occurs, is more likely to be verbal than physical, so carries less risk. These patterns can be explained by an evolutionary model of intrasexual competition (see Buss, 1999). In brief:

> Males are more often the perpetrators of violence because they are the products of a long history of mild but sustained effective polygyny characterized by risky strategies of intrasexual competition for access to the high-investing sex. The fact that men die on average seven years earlier than women is but one of the many markers of this aggressive intrasexual strategy. (Buss, 1999, p.287)

For women, physical risk taking entails greater potential costs in relation to benefits, except when they are called upon to protect their children (Campbell, 1999). However, their verbal aggression often focuses on the physical attractiveness of the other person, or involves the use of unfavourable names relating to sexual behaviour (for example 'whore'), or involves the spread of rumours designed to damage their reputation.

There are also sex differences in certain pro-social forms of risk taking. For instance, Johnson (1996) analysed data for the 676 recipients of Carnegie heroism awards up to 1995. About one in five of all rescue attempts ended in the rescuer's death. Johnson found that about 92 per cent of the acts were performed by males, and about 60 per cent of the objects of rescue attempts were also male. Of rescue attempts by women, 20 per cent were to assist relatives, as compared to just 6 per cent of attempts by men. Of rescue attempts by men, 68 per cent were to assist strangers, as compared to 47 per cent of attempts by women. These contrasts were even stronger in cases where the rescuer died.

Why do people take risks to help others (and animals too; see Box 12.1)? Hamilton's (1964) *theory of kin selection* proposed that organisms are more likely to make sacrifices for another organism if that other carries copies of their own genes. In particular, sacrifices are more likely to be made for close relatives such as siblings and offspring, as compared to cousins and to strangers. This behaviour is predicted to occur when the costs for the helper are lower than the benefits for the recipient multiplied by the degree of relatedness between the two individuals. Hamilton summed this up in the following formula:

(12.1) $rB > C$

where r represents the degree of relatedness, B is the benefit to the recipient, and C is the cost to the helper.

Scenario studies support this model of altruism (e.g. Burnstein et al., 1994; Neyer & Lang, 2003). What is slightly more puzzling is why people should take risks for people who are not related to them. One possibility is based on the fact that, throughout most of human history, people have lived in small, kin-based groups. Perhaps we have not evolved a perfect mechanism for distinguishing among kin and non-kin, because this has not been necessary (van Vugt & van Lange, 2006). In support of this notion is evidence that people are more willing to help unrelated children who share their facial features (DeBruine, 2004), and are more willing to help people who share their name or speak the same dialect (Barrett et al., 2002), or who hold similar attitudes (Park & Schaller, 2005).

Also, taking risks can result in enhanced status and reputation, especially for men. Indeed, Bassett and Moss (2004) found that women prefer risk-taking men as both short- and long-term partners. Farthing (2005) reported that women found heroic risk takers more attractive than did men, but were not attracted by non-heroic risk takers (for example, those involved in risky sports). However, his methodology was criticised by Wilke et al. (2006), who reported the results of their own study involving both German and American participants. They found that women gave higher attractiveness ratings to men involved in recreational risk taking and social risk taking. However, risk taking in the domains of health, ethics, and gambling was regarded as unattractive. Wilke et al. also found that male participants' ratings of female attractiveness was influenced in the same way, i.e. higher ratings for those involved in social and recreational risk taking. These authors also found that males and females tended to prefer partners who shared their own risk profiles.

Expert versus lay perceptions of risk

Are experts better than laypeople at assessing risk? The answer would appear to be 'Yes'. Slovic et al. (1979) report asking people to rank order a list of 30 risks. Three different samples of laypeople ranked nuclear power near to the top of all risks (with two of the groups ranking it as *the* riskiest item), whereas professional risk assessors ranked it twentieth. The risk judgments of all groups correlated with actual frequencies of death, but the relationship was much stronger for the experts. Furthermore, when laypeople gave their own fatality estimates these were no more closely related to their risk judgments than the actual frequencies of death.[5]

It would be a mistake, however, to assume that experts themselves view risk purely in terms of the objective characteristics of

BOX 12.1.   RISK TAKING IN ANIMALS

Like humans, animals also take risks. For example, when birds spot a predator they often engage in a 'distraction display' that is designed to attract the predator's attention away from some object, typically the bird's eggs or young. One frequently used display is the feigning of injury, such as performing normal actions but with interruptions. Although some have suggested that such risks are taken for the benefit of the social group (Wilson, 1975), most evolutionary researchers now consider that such actions are taken in the interest of perpetuating one's own genes. This is the basis of kin selection theory (see main text; see also Dawkins, 1976).

Animals have also been known to take risks to assist humans. This story is from de Waal (2005, pp.171–172):

> In 2004, Jet, a black Labrador in Roseville, California, jumped in front of his best friend, a boy, who was about to be bitten by a rattlesnake, and took the serpent's venom. Jet was rightly considered a hero. He wasn't thinking of himself; he was a genuine altruist . . . This shows the risks animals are prepared to take. The boy's grateful family spent four thousand dollars on blood transfusions and veterinary bills to save their pet.

De Waal says that Jet probably considered the boy to be a member of his pack. This example, like human examples of assistance to strangers, most likely originates from mutuality and the assistance of kin (see main text).

The examples above involve animals taking risks in order to help others. There is also evidence that, like people, animals take risks just for the thrills involved. Perhaps (as with people) there are reputational, and hence mating, benefits to be obtained, though I am not aware of any evidence for this. Here are three examples quoted from the animal researcher Jonathan Balcombe (2006, pp.86–88):

1. Orang-utans in Tanjung Putting, Borneo, play a sport that human observers call 'snag riding', which involves hanging onto a falling dead tree, then grabbing a vine or other vegetation to escape before the tree hits the ground.

2. Ravens are inclined to goad dozing wolves, which suggests the exhilaration of danger given the risk of being caught and killed. Wolf authority David Mech and others have seen ravens dive at wolves resting on lake ice, walk up and peck sleepy wolves on their tails, and even alight on their backs. Wolves will lunge at and stalk ravens, who may evade them often at the last minute, as in a game.

3. I have watched bold squirrels repeatedly approach to within an inch of the screen door at the rear of my home, behind which a cat sits riveted and ready to pounce. The squirrels seem fully aware that the cat is there, but are equally confident in their untouchability. The cat actually did pounce on one occasion, causing the squirrel to leap back and vanish in a flash. The saucy rodent returned within two minutes, as if to call on another adrenaline rush.

the entities they are assessing. Carlo *et al.* (1992) conducted a study where a large sample of epidemiologists, toxicologists, physicians, and general scientists received information about three substances. Each subject was read a brief vignette written to reflect the mainstream scientific thinking about one substance. For half of the respondents this substance was referred to only as substance X, Y, or Z. The other respondents were told that the substance was either dioxin, radon, or environmental tobacco smoke (ETS). Revealing the name of dioxin didn't have any significant effect on health risk assessments but the experts were significantly more likely to rate radon and ETS as a serious environmental health hazard when they were told the name of the substance. Carlo *et al.* concluded that experts' evaluations of scientific data may be influenced by values and experiences which might in turn bias estimates of risk.

It would also be misleading to conceive of experts as a homogenous group with a shared consensus about the risks in their domain. The Kraus *et al.* (1992) study, briefly mentioned earlier, showed differences between toxicologists and the lay public, but also substantial disagreement among the experts themselves. The toxicologists were particularly divided about the ability of animal

tests to predict a chemical's effect on humans. Toxicologists working in industry saw chemicals as more benign and were somewhat more confident than their counterparts in academia and government in the general validity of animal tests – except when those tests provided evidence for carcinogenicity, when many of the industrial experts changed their minds. Based on these findings, Kraus *et al.* suggested that controversies over chemical risks may be fuelled as much by limitations of risk assessment and disagreement among experts as by public misconceptions.

RISK COMPENSATION

Earlier, we saw that – once variations in risk *perception* are controlled for – risk taking is fairly stable across different domains. Along similar lines, Adams (1995) has described a theory of *risk compensation* in which individuals vary in their propensity to take risks. Risk-taking propensity is influenced by the rewards of risk taking, and 'individual risk-taking decisions represent a balancing act in which perceptions of risk are weighed against propensity to take risk' (1995, p.15). The more risks that a person takes, the greater the number of rewards and losses he or she incurs (on average). People's perceptions of risks and their propensity to take risks are also influenced by 'cultural filters' in the form of various belief systems. Adams likens the balancing act performed by people to a thermostatically controlled system, in which some people have their thermostat set higher than others.

One of the implications of this model is that when people's perceptions of risks are reduced, they respond by taking greater risks. An example of this risk compensation is the Davy lamp. This device

> which most histories of science and safety credit with saving thousands of lives, is usually described as one of the most significant safety improvements in the history of mining. But it appears to have been a classic example of a potential safety benefit consumed as a performance benefit. Because the lamp operated at a temperature below the ignition point of methane, it permitted the extension of mining into methane-rich atmospheres; the introduction of 'the safety lamp' was followed by an *increase* in explosions and fatalities. (Albury & Schwarz, 1982, cited in Adams, 1995, p.211)

Of course, when people's perceptions of risk are *increased* then the opposite effect is predicted: they should take less risks. In Sweden in September 1987, all motorists were required to switch from driving on the left side of the road to driving on the right. Consequently, pedestrians had to remember to look left rather than right when crossing a road. Considerable publicity was devoted to the dangers involved in this change. In the event, however, Sweden had the safest September on the roads in many years. Eventually, people got used to the new system and 'by November they were back to their normal (acceptable?) rate of killing each other' (Adams, 1995, p.143).

Adams's own test case for the risk compensation model is the impact of motor vehicle seat belt legislation. His review of road death statistics from around the world showed that seat belt legislation has had no appreciable effect on the level of driver fatalities. The only country to show a decrease in driver fatalities following legislation appears to have been the UK, but this reduction seems to have actually been due to a drink-driving campaign rather than to the effect of seat belt use. On the other hand, deaths of rear-seat passengers (who were originally exempt from legislation) increased, as did the deaths of pedestrians and cyclists. In other words, once compelled to wear seat belts drivers felt more safe and drove faster, displacing the risk onto other road users.

A similar lack of positive evidence can be found in relation to the use of safety helmets for cyclists. Indeed, there is evidence that wearing safety equipment actually puts cyclists at greater risk. Walker (2007) fitted a camera to his own bicycle so that he could measure the proximity of overtaking vehicles. He found that vehicles passed closer to his bicycle when he was wearing a safety helmet than when he was not. Walker suggested that motorists expect cyclists without helmets to be less reliable. He also found that vehicles gave him a wider berth when he donned a long-haired wig that made him look like a female in the eyes of approaching drivers.

RISK COMMUNICATION AND MENTAL MODELS

Given the numerous factors described in this chapter that influence risk judgments, it is little surprise that the communication of risk continues to pose a major challenge for governments, companies, and public bodies. Morgan (1993, p.29) described a traditional method for communicating risk, in this case the risk to US householders from radon:

> The EPA prepared this brochure according to traditional methods: ask scientific experts what they think people should be told and then package the result in an attractive form. In fact, people are rarely completely ignorant about a risk, and so they filter any message through their existing knowledge. A message that does not take this filtering process into account can be ignored or misinterpreted.

Aside from the background knowledge that people may bring to bear on a risk communication, there are other issues too, some of which we have encountered in previous chapters. For instance, given the difficulty that people sometimes have in thinking about probabilities, would it be better to use natural frequencies instead – for example, '10 people out of every 1000' instead of '1 per cent' (see Chapter 3)? What about low-probability risks? Zeckhauser and Viscusi (1990) pointed out that with an estimated 10^{-7} annual risk it would take many years of widespread observation even to learn whether the risk is of an order of magnitude that is higher or lower. As carcinogenic risks are often coupled with long time lags and a complex (multiple factor) causality, precise inferences may not be possible.

A widely held view in current risk research is that public risk perceptions should not be regarded as an annoyance that needs correcting but as informative regarding people's concerns, and something that needs to be taken into account when devising risk communications (e.g. Pidgeon *et al.*, 1992). A fruitful recent approach has been to investigate people's mental models (see Chapter 6):

> We have concluded that the only way to communicate risks reliably is to start by learning what people already know and what they need to know, then develop messages, test them and refine them until surveys demonstrate that the messages have conveyed the intended information. (Morgan, 1993, p.29)

Morgan and colleagues have described how they developed a brochure to communicate information about radon gas in private homes (Bostrom *et al.*, 1992; Morgan, 1993). This involved the use of open-ended interviews beginning with the request, 'Tell me about radon.' As the interviews proceeded the questions got more specific. After about a couple of dozen people had been interviewed no further new ideas emerged, so the researchers used the responses to devise a closed-form questionnaire that was then administered to a much larger sample.

Responses to the questionnaire revealed that people sometimes held incorrect beliefs that could undermine the effectiveness of the EPA's messages. For instance, many people believed that radon contamination was permanent, a belief that presumably was inferred from knowledge about chemical contaminants or radio-active isotopes. This was an issue that was not even covered in the EPA's first brochure 'Citizen's Guide to Radon'. Morgan (1993) reports devising two new brochures that were then compared with the EPA's guide. People did equally well in recalling facts from each of the three brochures, but when faced with a task requiring an inference – such as advising a neighbour with a high radon reading – people who had read one of the new brochures did far better than those who had read the EPA brochure.

As we have discussed in previous chapters, people's mental models are particularly likely to be in error when thinking about complex dynamic systems with delayed feedback. A very important example of this is global warming. Carbon dioxide (CO_2) emissions have been increasing since the industrial revolution. Likewise, CO_2 in the atmosphere has been increasing, as has the earth's surface temperature. If anthropogenic CO_2 emissions were to suddenly stop altogether what would happen to atmospheric CO_2 and global mean temperature over the next 50 years?

Sterman and Sweeney (2002) found a widespread misunderstanding of the relationship between carbon dioxide (CO_2) emissions on the one hand, and atmospheric CO_2 and the earth's surface temperature on the other.[6] When given this question in 1999, just 22 per cent of MIT students and 36 per cent of MBA students at Chicago knew that CO_2 would peak at or shortly after 2000, then decline at a diminishing rate. Likewise, just 36 per cent of MIT students and 21 per cent of Chicago students were aware that the earth's temperature would continue to rise for about 20–30 years and then fall slowly. It seemed to make little difference whether or not participants received graphical presentations of global warming and emissions data with their task information (though MIT students actually did slightly *worse* with graphical information).

Participants also showed high levels of erroneous responding when the task was made somewhat more realistic by describing either a mild decline in atmospheric CO_2 or a further increase prior to stabilisation in 2100. For example, in a scenario where CO_2 levels fell from 370 parts per million (ppm) to 340 ppm in year 2100, just 44 per cent of participants recognised that this could only be achieved if CO_2 emissions immediately fell by over 8 per cent before stabilising. By contrast, 45 per cent of erroneous responses indicated a *gradual* drop in emissions. In this and other questions, people seemed to apply a pattern-matching heuristic, whereby output trajectories were matched to input trajectories. Some subjects indicated as much in their written explanations.

Sterman and Sweeney (2000) have found similar misunderstandings about much simpler tasks, such as filling a bathtub, when – for example – the latter is described in terms of rate of inflow and volume of water. However, whereas one can visually inspect a filling bathtub and turn off the tap when the water has reached the desired level, the same is not true for global warming. The notion – described elsewhere in this book – that people behave rationally in familiar naturalistic settings is of little comfort with an issue like global warming. When discussing this, and other complex contemporary issues, people

typically present information in the form of spreadsheets, graphs, or text – the same type of data presentation in our experiments. Managers are called on to evaluate spreadsheets and graphs projecting revenue and expenditure, bookings and shipments, hiring and attrition . . .

For global warming, and many of the most pressing issues in business and public policy, the mode of data presentation in our tasks *is* the naturalistic context. (2000, p.232)

Failure to understand the dynamics at work in global warming may be a serious barrier to addressing it with effective action. Sweeney and Sterman suggest that an education in system dynamics may be essential for a proper understanding of the modern world.

SUMMARY

Modern research into risk perception and risk taking was spurred by Starr's (1969) landmark publication that used cost-benefit analyses (the revealed preference method) to quantify the levels of risk that people were willing to take. However, the psychometric approach (based on expressed preferences) has shown that people's assessments of risks are not based on a straightforward comparison of risks and benefits.

Also, the psychometric approach failed to support Starr's finding that the relationship between risks and benefits differs for voluntary and involuntary risks. However, the voluntary/involuntary factor did relate to people's acceptable levels of risk. Nonetheless, this factor also correlates with other factors, such as the potential for catastrophic consequences, so it is not clear to what extent this factor is crucial in determining what is acceptable.

The many factors that relate to risk perceptions are highly intercorrelated, and factor analysis has found that two basic dimension of risk can be identified. Different studies have sometimes used different labels for the dimensions, but a common labelling is *unknown risk* and *dread risk*.

The various factors underlying risk judgments can be considered as intuitions, and some intuitions have been identified outside of the psychometric approach. The existence of various intuitions suggests that people's *feelings* play a large role in their judgments, and this view is supported by research. Indeed, the *risk-as-feelings* model states that cognitions and emotions not only influence each other, but each can also act independently on behaviour.

The recognition that many processes are involved in risk judgments has given rise to a unifying framework, called the *social amplification of risk*. This concerns the way in which psychological, social, and cultural processes interact so as to amplify or attenuate perceptions of risk.

Although various studies have appeared to show that risk taking tends to be domain-specific, these studies have not taken into account variations in *risk perception* across different situations. Once this is taken into account, risk taking turns out to be more stable: people who take risks in one domain are more likely to take risks in other domains.

Variation in risk taking is related to personality factors (for example the Big 5: extraversion, neuroticism, openness, agreeableness, and conscientiousness). In particular, sensation seeking is strongly associated with risk taking. Sex and race are also associated with different levels of risk taking. The possibility that power relations underlie these effects is an explanation that has some experimental support. Nonetheless, it is likely that all these findings can be related within an evolutionary psychology framework.

In general, judgments of risk made by experts tend to be closer to objective figures than do those of lay people. However, there is variation even among experts, and – as with the lay public – there are sex differences among experts. Experts, too, can be biased according to prior knowledge.

The theory of risk compensation likens people to a thermostatic system in which people attempt to balance their perceptions of risk against their propensity to take risks. The theory has important implications for attempts to manage risks, because there is evidence to suggest that safety benefits are sometimes consumed as performance benefits; that is, when people feel safer they take more risks.

Contemporary approaches to risk communication have abandoned the assumption that experts decide what the risks are and then simply communicate these to people. Instead, the complexity of people's understanding of risk needs to be taken into account. The mental models approach seeks to elicit people's beliefs and knowledge about risks, using open-ended interviews followed by specific questions. Once a picture has been obtained of people's understandings and misunderstandings, then risk communications are devised. These then undergo empirical evaluation as to their effectiveness before they are eventually used for real.

QUESTIONS

1. Design an experiment to investigate risk compensation.

2. Collect some recent media articles concerning risk and comment on these from a psychological point of view.

3. Discuss sex differences in risk perception and risk taking.

4. Do you agree with the precautionary principle? Give your reasons.

5. What role do personality differences play in risk taking?

6. What is betrayal aversion?

7. Summarise the psychometric approach to risk perception.

CHAPTER 12. RISK

1. http://www.unep.org/Documents.multilingual/ Default.asp?DocumentID=78&ArticleID=1163 (accessed 18 Dec, 2006).

2. http://en.wikipedia.org/wikiΩPrecautionary_principle (accessed 18 Dec. 2006).

3. I use the term 'race' here because it is the term used in the literature that I review in this section. However, I do not mean to imply that 'race' has a biological basis and tend to prefer the term 'ethnicity' to refer to attributes of skin colour and culture that 'race' is normally used to describe.

4. It is unlikely that the entrepreneurial activity was the cause of the higher testosterone. Although exogenous events can raise testosterone levels, these effects dissipate within hours or days (Mazur & Booth, 1998).

5. Lichtenstein *et al.* (1978) found that people overestimated the frequency of infrequent types of fatality, and underestimated the frequency of frequent types of fatality. They provided evidence that people used the availability heuristic when making these judgments. More recently, Hertwig *et al.* (2005) investigated the availability account in more detail. They found that people's frequency judgments were influenced by the number of instances they could recall from their social circle (availability-by-recall) but not by how easily instances came to mind (availability-as-fluency). They also found that people tended to regress their judgments towards the mean.

6. For a description of the mechanisms underlying the correct responses, the reader is referred to Sterman and Sweeney (2000).

RECOMMENDED READING

Adams, J. (1995). *Risk*. London: UCL Press. Adams presents thought-provoking evidence of risk compensation.

Fenton-O'Creevy, M., Nicholson, N., Soane, E. & Willman, P. (2005). *Traders: Risks, decisions, and management in financial markets*. Oxford: Oxford University Press. This is an interesting account of risk perception, risk taking, optimistic bias, illusion of control, and personality profiles of financial traders.

Slovic, P. (Ed.) (2000), *The perception of risk*. London and Sterling, VA: Earthscan. This book is a collection of Paul Slovic's influential papers on risk perception.

13 | Decision Making in Groups and Teams

INTRODUCTION

Many of the decisions that people make are not taken in isolation but as part of a group. A group is defined as 'Two or more people who share a common definition and evaluation of themselves and behave in accordance with such a definition' (Hogg & Vaughan, 2005, p.276).

Much recent literature has also concerned a specific kind of group, the *team*, which has been defined as:

> (a) two or more individuals who (b) socially interact (face-to-face or, increasingly, virtually); (c) possess one or more common goals; (d) are brought together to perform organizationally relevant tasks; (e) exhibit interdependencies with respect to workflow, goals, and outcomes; (f) have different roles and responsibilities; and (g) are together embedded in an encompassing organizational system, with boundaries and linkages to the broader system context and task environment. (Kozlowski & Ilgen, 2006, p.79)

For the sake of simplicity, I shall largely use the term 'group' in this chapter,[1] except where citing literature that has specifically talked about teams.

Group decision making is particularly common within the work environment. There is a kind of folk intuition that the interactions between people in a group will lead to more creative ideas and better decisions than those same people would be capable of individually. This optimism is reflected in the saying that *Two heads are better than one* (and, presumably, more than two heads is even better). However, the actual experience of working in a group can sometimes lead to disillusionment, as expressed in the saying that *A camel is a horse designed by committee*.

So, are groups more or less effective than individuals at generating ideas and making decisions? Evidence suggests that groups *can* be effective decision-making units but often fail to be. In the first part of this chapter I shall review the factors that work against and for the effectiveness of groups. Then I shall look at specific procedures that have been recommended in order to improve the decision making in groups and teams. I shall also look at leadership, and, finally, at the use of advice in decision making.

STRUCTURE AND PROCESS IN GROUPS AND TEAMS

Information sharing and team diversity

Although we might expect groups and teams to call upon a greater stock of knowledge and experience during decision making, several studies have shown that discussion tends to focus on information that was already known and shared by the group prior to any interaction (e.g. Stasser et al., 1989; Stasser & Stewart, 1992). Poor decisions might arise as a result of important information remaining uncovered (referred to as *hidden profiles*). The problem may be worse in teams composed of strangers as opposed to socially connected individuals (Gruenfeld et al., 1996). Perhaps an advantage of socially cohesive teams is that people feel there is less risk involved in sharing their unique information. However, teams that are socially tied tend to be composed of people who are more similar to each other, and therefore they may have less unique information in the first place.

It is not clear to what extent this *group discussion bias* is a problem in real-life decision-making groups. People often know about the kind of expertise, experience, or knowledge that other team members have ('meta-knowledge'). Even in ad hoc groups people may form expectations about other people's knowledge, based on their professions, ages, sexes, and so on. Nonetheless, where meta-knowledge is lacking there is a high probability that hidden profiles will remain hidden.

One might expect team diversity to help (diversity has been defined as 'variation based on any attribute people use to tell themselves that another person is different': Mannix & Neale, 2005, p.33). Although some studies support the effectiveness of diverse teams, others have not (Mannix & Neale, 2005). In short, it appears that diversity *can* bring benefits when different knowledge and perspectives are brought to bear on a problem. However, diversity can also bring conflict. Among the reasons for this (discussed by Mannix & Neale, 2005) are that (a) people are more attracted to people who are similar to themselves and find it easier to communicate with them, and (b) heterogeneous groups are more likely to activate self-concepts and stereotypes about people perceived as belonging to an out-group – in essence, an 'us and them' feeling becomes salient. To the extent that diversity is increasingly a fact of life, these results suggest that an important challenge is to find ways of facilitating integration between team members such that they view themselves as members of the same in-group, thus facilitating communication.

Conformity

Early research into group processes focused on conformity. Some classic experiments by Asch in the 1950s required participants in a seven-person group to make a series of very easy line judgments (e.g. Asch, 1956). However, only one of the seven was a genuine participant, and this person was unaware that the other six were confederates of the experimenter. After hearing five members of the group give the same wrong answer, about a third of participants repeated the same wrong answer. Across all trials about three quarters of people gave at least one incorrect conforming response. However, when the confederates were not unanimous then conforming behaviour was greatly reduced.

Conforming behaviour has also been observed under conditions where there is no overt or covert pressure to conform (Coultas, 2004), where other group members are not physically present (Crutchfield, 1955), and has also been observed in chimpanzees (Whiten et al., 2005).

Most of the human research into conformity involves instances where the majority is incorrect. Hence, conformity has come to be seen as a bad thing. However, in evolutionary terms it is unlikely that humans would have evolved a trait for conformity if majorities were normally incorrect. It is more likely that throughout human history the majority position has been well suited to the environment, in which case the tendency towards conformity can be regarded as a useful heuristic (for a further discussion, see Kameda & Tindale, 2006).

Obedience to authority

In many groups and work teams, some people are under the authority of another person or people. However, sometimes people are reluctant to challenge or question authority figures, which can cause serious problems in some situations. In a famous series of studies Stanley Milgram (1963, 1974) asked ordinary men and women to deliver electric shocks to a 'learner' every time he made an error (no shocks were really delivered, though the people did not know this). Although people's willingness to deliver the shocks varied according to certain situational factors – and people did often express their concern for the learner – people were surprisingly obedient in the face of the experimenter's insistence. In one condition, 65 per cent of participants continued to deliver shocks up until the maximum 450 volts, even though the learner – unseen in another room – had gone completely quiet.

Even physically and mentally strong people may subordinate themselves to authority, as the example in Box 13.1 shows.

Minority influence

We have just seen evidence for conformity to the majority, but we also saw that many people resist pressure towards conformity. Indeed, experience teaches us that well-organised minorities can influence majorities and bring about great social change. Minorities can be particularly influential when speed is emphasised above accuracy, as has been observed in animal populations (Conradt & Roper, 2005). In particular, minorities who are perceived to possess expertise are more likely to change the views of majority members (e.g. Thomas-Hunt et al., 2004). Perceptions of one's own ability also influence the extent to which a person resists majority influence:

BOX 13.1.   TRAGEDY ON EVEREST

Failure to challenge authority appears to have played a part in the tragedy on Mount Everest in 1996, in which nine people from two expeditions lost their lives. The two expeditions, led by Rob Hall and Scott Fischer, consisted of experienced guides leading paying clients who were often very inexperienced and many of whom had never climbed together before. Both leaders had a golden rule that if their climbers were not within 'spitting distance' of the summit by 2 p.m. they would be turned back for their own safety. In the event, the leaders, guides, and most clients ignored this golden rule, with both leaders and most other climbers summiting well after 2 p.m. Consequently, as darkness fell and a blizzard blew across the mountain, there were climbers stranded on the mountain or struggling down it during the middle of the night.

As the two o'clock mark was drawing near, why did no one draw attention to the need to turn back? In both teams, it was clear that authority rested with the leaders and, to a lesser extent, their guides. One leader, Rob Hall, had said

> I will tolerate no dissension up there ... My word will be absolute law, beyond appeal. If you don't like a particular decision I make, I'd be happy to discuss it with you afterward, but not while we're on the hill. (Krakauer, 1998, p.166)

When one of Hall's guides showed signs of irrational judgment due to hypoxia (oxygen deprivation), climber Jon Krakauer was slow to spot this because

[Andy Harris] had been cast in the role of invincible guide, there to look after me and the other clients; we had been specifically indoctrinated not to question our guides' judgment. The thought never entered my crippled mind that Andy might in fact be in terrible straits – that a guide might urgently need help from me. (Krakauer, 1998, p.188)

On Scott Fischer's expedition, the guides themselves were conscious of *their* lack of status. The Russian guide Anatoli Boukreev explained why he had held back from voicing his concerns about the conditions on the mountain:

> My voice was not as authoritative as I would have liked, so I tried not to be argumentative, choosing instead to downplay my intuitions. (Boukreev and DeWalt, 2001, p.121)

The other guide on Fischer's expedition, Neil Beidleman, said that

> I was definitely considered the third guide ... so I tried not to be too pushy. As a consequence, I didn't always speak up for myself when maybe I should have, and now I kick myself for it. (Krakauer, 1998, p.200)

As the third guide, Beidleman, had told Fischer, he didn't want the responsibility of turning clients away from the summit given that they had paid $65,000 to be on the expedition. Therefore Fischer had agreed that would be his responsibility but then did not enforce his own golden rule.

Hochbaum (1954) found that people who were led to believe that they were good at making certain judgments consistently resisted social influence and group pressure. Most people conformed to group pressure when they were led to believe that they were poor at making such judgments. Generally, though, experimental research has shown that minorities are much more likely to exert influence on the majority if they take a consistent position over time (Wood *et al.*, 1994). The weakest position to be in is a minority of one: the views of a person in this situation can more easily be dismissed as idiosyncratic (Mugny & Papastamou, 1980).

Group polarisation

Stoner (1961) asked people to consider some imaginary choice dilemmas that involved choosing between a risky option with greater potential reward and a safer option with a lesser potential reward. They had to imagine they were giving advice to other people who were faced with these dilemmas. One such dilemma involved choosing to work on a difficult long-term scientific problem that would bring great rewards if successful but few rewards otherwise, or a series of short-term problems that would be easier

to solve but were less important. Participants indicated the minimum probability of success that would make it worth working on the long-term problem, as well as the actual estimated probability of success. The study had two stages. Firstly, people read the problems and made private recommendations. Next, they discussed the problems in small groups and made unanimous group recommendations.

Stoner identified a *risky shift* in the group responses: the groups recommended the risky option more than they had as individuals (see also Wallach *et al.*, 1962). However, subsequent research has found that groups sometimes recommend options that are more cautious than those initially recommended by their individual members (Moscovici & Zavalloni, 1969). The tendency for groups to make more extreme recommendations than the mean of members' pre-discussion opinions, in the direction favoured by the mean, is referred to as *group polarisation*.

Three explanations of group polarisation are reviewed by Hogg and Vaughan (2005). One view is that group members who share a majority view not only get to hear familiar arguments again, but may also hear some new arguments that support their opinion. A second view is that group discussion reveals which ideas are socially desirable or culturally valued, and so members shift their stated views in the majority direction in order to gain the group's approval and avoid disapproval. Both explanations have support from some studies but not others, though it is possible that both mechanisms can contribute to group polarisation under particular circumstances (Isenberg, 1986).

A third view treats group polarisation as another instance of conformity. This says that discussion reveals the positions held by group members in relation to the positions assumed to be held by people not in the group or in an explicit out-group. These in-group positions are used by members to construct an in-group norm. Categorising oneself as a member of the in-group produces conformity to the norm and, if the norm is polarised, group polarisation in order to construct a representation of the group norm. This account has support from various strands of research, including the observation that polarisation does not occur if the initial group tendency is seen merely as an aggregate of initial opinions as opposed to a norm (e.g. Turner *et al.*, 1989).

Groupthink

In 1972 Irving Janis published an analysis of several US foreign policy decisions, some of which resulted in successful outcomes and some of which led to 'fiascos' (updated in 1982 to include the Watergate scandal). His thesis was that these fiascos resulted from a failure in group decision making that he referred to as *groupthink*. The term 'groupthink' was described as

> a quick and easy way to refer to a mode of thinking that people engage in when they are deeply involved in a cohesive ingroup, when the members' strivings for unanimity override their motivation to realistically appraise alternative courses of action. (Janis, 1982, p.9)

Notably, groupthink does not occur as a result of *deliberate* manipulation of the group:

> During the group's deliberations, the leader does not deliberately try to get the group to tell him what he wants to hear but is quite sincere in asking for honest opinions. The group members are not transformed into sycophants. They are not afraid to speak their minds. Nevertheless, subtle constraints, which the leader may reinforce inadvertently, prevent a member from fully exercising his critical powers and from openly expressing doubts when most others in the group appear to have reached a consensus. (1982, p.3)

Janis argued that groupthink occurred as the result of a combination of high group cohesiveness, structural faults in the organisation (for example, the lack of a tradition of impartial leadership), and a provocative situational context. His model is laid out in Figure 13.1. This shows that a tendency for concurrence seeking (groupthink) arises from a combination of three antecedent conditions: (1) the decision makers constitute a cohesive group, (2) there are structural faults within the organisation, and (3) there is a provocative situational context. The resulting groupthink is manifested in three main symptoms: (1) overestimation of the

group, (2) closed-mindedness, and (3) pressures towards uniformity. These factors reduce the quality of information processing. For example, less information seeking takes place and fewer alternative courses of action are considered.

The groupthink theory has had a considerable impact on the way people think about decision making. In business, social psychology, and organisational psychology, textbooks often give considerable space to the topic. There are several likely reasons for the success of the theory, including the efforts made by Janis himself to promote the theory (Paulus, 1998). However, there have been relatively few empirical studies of groupthink, and most of these have only reported partial support for hypotheses derived from the theory (Esser, 1998; Park, 1990). In reviewing a collection of papers on groupthink for a special issue of *Organizational Behavior and Human Decision Processes* (Vol. 73, issues 2/3), Paulus (1998) noted that there was little consensus among the authors.

Esser (1998) reviewed historical case studies and experimental studies of groupthink. Two of the historical analyses reanalysed Janis's original case studies (McCauley, 1989; Tetlock *et al.*, 1992). Both concluded that structural faults of the organisation (for example insulation, promotional leadership, group homogeneity) were the main antecedent conditions for groupthink, as opposed to group cohesion and a provocative situational context. Similarly, Esser's review of laboratory research found no strong support for a causal role of cohesiveness in producing groupthink (despite a few supportive findings, group cohesion sometimes produced *fewer* groupthink symptoms).

One structural factor which has received support in several laboratory studies is *lack of impartial leadership*. There is evidence that groups with directive leaders suggest fewer solutions (Flowers, 1977; Leana, 1985; though for an inconsistent result, see Moorhead & Montanari, 1986), use less available information, rate their leader as more influential in the decision process (Flowers, 1977), report more self-censorship and mindguarding, produce higher total scores on an index of groupthink symptoms, and mention fewer facts during the decision process (Richardson, 1994, cited in Esser, 1998). Leana (1985) also reported that groups with directive leaders who stated their preferred solution early in the discussion tended to acquiesce to their leader's preferred solution. Groups with leaders who show a high need for power tend to share less information and consider fewer solutions than groups whose leaders are low in need for power (Fodor & Smith, 1982). Finally, groups whose leaders promote a preferred solution tend to discourage dissent and adopt an illusion of morality (Moorhead & Montanari, 1986).

Given the relative paucity of strong evidence for groupthink, it is perhaps ironic that it has come to occupy such a prominent cultural position. Janis himself warned that a little knowledge of groupthink might be a dangerous thing if:

- naive leaders concluded that decisions would be better made by just one person (notably themselves);
- safeguards were implemented without regard to their hidden costs (see next section);
- 'faddists' in management wasted precious time in meetings by trying to conduct some kind of group therapy.

ANTECEDENT CONDITIONS

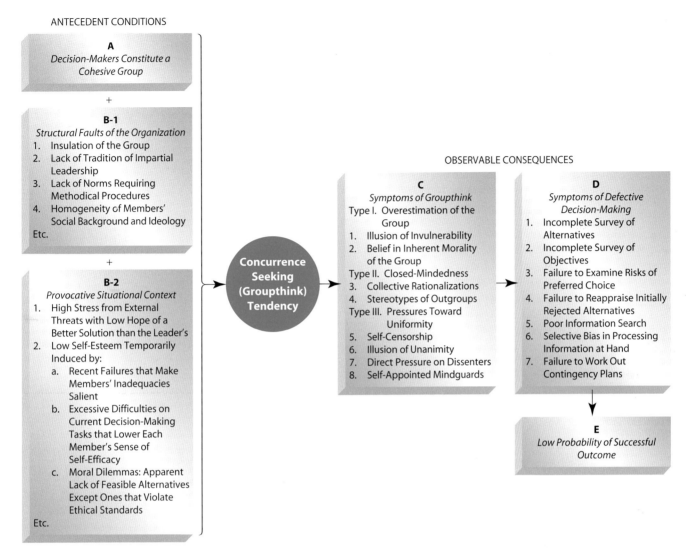

Figure 13.1. *Theoretical analysis of groupthink*
Source: Janis, 1982 (adapted from Janis & Mann, 1977).

Vigilant decision making

One of the decision-making disasters that Janis attributed to groupthink was the decision of President Kennedy's administration (originally formulated by the previous administration) to attempt to overthrow Castro's regime in Cuba by supporting an invasion at the Bay of Pigs. It appears that Kennedy may have learned an important lesson from this episode, because the style of decision making during the subsequent Cuban missile crisis was apparently much more open.[2] Janis referred to this as vigilant decision making. In his analyses of foreign policy decisions he found that successful outcomes occurred when this kind of decision process was adopted.

Vigilance was said to be associated with:

- acknowledgment of grave dangers even after arriving at a decision;

- explicit discussion of moral issues;

- reversals of judgment;

- nonstereotyped views of the enemy.

All these behaviours were recommended by Janis as important ways to avoid groupthink.

Empirical studies using small groups have shown that devil's advocacy does facilitate the quality of group decisions (e.g. Schweiger *et al.*, 1986; Schweiger *et al.*, 1989). Also, where group members share the same position prior to discussion, they tend to seek information that confirms that position (Schulz-Hardt *et al.*, 2000), but the use of devil's advocacy facilitates the search for conflicting information (Schultz-Hardt *et al.*, 2002).

Nonetheless, the use of devil's advocacy is not entirely uncontroversial. For example, Robert Kennedy was such a forceful devil's advocate during the Cuban missile crisis that he made himself unpopular with many people, and his position might have become untenable if he had not been the President's brother. Conversely, people who are appointed as devil's advocates risk becoming 'domesticated', and therefore not very challenging, if they do the task for too long. Their objections become tokenistic and may be discounted before they are even voiced. Nonetheless, they may allow a leader to claim that an issue has been fully aired prior to decision. Both side-effects suggest that it might be sensible to rotate the role of devil's advocate among different members.

In some empirical investigations of devil's advocacy, improved decision quality has been accompanied by lower satisfaction with both process and outcome (Schweiger et al., 1986; Schwenk & Cosier, 1993), less acceptance of the decision (Schweiger et al., 1986), and less desire to work together in the future (Schweiger et al., 1986; Valacich & Schwenk, 1995). Nonetheless, it may be that increasing familiarity with the technique counteracts such effects (e.g. Schweiger et al., 1989).

Janis himself noted that there were potential disadvantages, as well as advantages, associated with vigilant decision making. Where confidentiality and security are important, bringing more people into the discussion increases the chances of a security leak. If too many subgroups are formed, there is a risk that people will feel less responsible for carefully addressing a particular issue ('Let someone else do it'). The more that disagreements are aired within a group ('cognitive conflict'), the greater the risk that people's feelings will be hurt or that anger will be aroused ('affective conflict'). This may have undesirable effects. For example, emotional arousal may negatively affect a person's ability to focus on the arguments in a rational way, unhappy members may leave the group, and the group may find it harder to work together on future problems.

Nonetheless, one of the advantages of cohesive groups may be that affective conflict is less of a problem. Peterson and Behfar (2003) reported a longitudinal study of MBA students working on two team tasks separated by several weeks. They found evidence that negative feedback on the first task caused task conflict on the second task, but that this effect was much weaker when there was a high level of trust between team members. High trust also served to prevent relationship conflict occurring on the second task following negative feedback.

Vigilant decision processes may also be more time-consuming. In some contexts, it may be that simpler decision procedures are a better use of time. For example, Frederickson and Iaquinto (1989) found that analytical decision processes worked less well in turbulent and complex business environments.

Peterson et al. (1998) reported an analysis of organisational case studies by independent observers. This found that measures of organisational processes did distinguish between successful and unsuccessful organisations, although the successful ones did not always conform to the ideal of vigilant decision making. For example, successful organisations often had stronger leaders and were more centralised than might be expected. However, as the authors themselves point out it is possible that outcome knowledge may have influenced the assessments of the organisations. They appear not to really believe this, but other research suggests this could be a serious problem: previous studies have found that group members' own retrospective assessments of group processes were coloured by *randomly determined* outcome feedback that was provided by the experimenter. Negative feedback led to much less positive evaluations of group processes (Downey et al., 1979; Staw, 1975; see also Rosenzweig, 2007).

In short, more research is needed to determine the effectiveness of different decision procedures in real environments.

TECHNIQUES FOR IMPROVING GROUP DECISION PROCESSES

Brainstorming

Brainstorming is a technique for facilitating the generation of creative ideas. It was originally popularised by Osborn (1957), who was concerned with the need to separate the phases of idea generation and decision making during group interaction. The brainstorming technique asks people to mention whatever ideas come to mind, as many as possible regardless of quality, and to build on the ideas of others. In order that people are not inhibited from doing this, group members are told not to criticise the ideas of others.

Brainstorming is especially popular in the advertising industry and in other business organisations. However, the research evidence suggests that this popularity is unwarranted. Although brainstorming groups do produce more ideas than groups without brainstorming instructions, they are *less* creative than nominal groups in which the members generate ideas without interacting with their colleagues (Diehl & Stroebe, 1987; Mullen et al., 1991).

What might be the reasons for this counterintuitive result? Paulus et al. (1993) suggested four possible reasons. One reason is *evaluation apprehension*: despite the nature of the brainstorming instructions, people are still concerned with impression management. Therefore, they hold back from suggesting any ideas that they think might lead others to view them in a poorer light (Camacho & Paulus, 1995). A second reason is *social loafing*, whereby individuals reduce the effort they make when working as part of a group. For example, Latané et al. (1979) found that individual members of a tug-of-war team reduced their effort by 10 per cent for every member that was added to the team. A third reason is *production matching*: people observe the productivity of others and use this to construct a performance norm that guides their own behaviour. This produces regression to the mean. The fourth – and possibly most important – reason is *production blocking*: in a group only one person can express their ideas at any one time. Early research suggested that the impact of production blocking was that it led people to forget their ideas while waiting to present them or that they were distracted by hearing the ideas of others (Diehl & Stroebe, 1987). However, more recent evidence suggests that a more important problem is that group discussion can prevent people from getting a productive train of thought started or disrupt an ongoing train of thought (Nijstad, 2000, cited in Kerr & Tindale, 2004).

Members of brainstorming groups tend to believe they have performed very well (Paulus et al., 1995). This may partly be because people find it more enjoyable than working alone. Also, compared to individuals in nominal groups individuals in brainstorming groups report having ideas that were actually voiced by others. It appears that people in brainstorming groups may inaccurately recall other people's ideas as their own, and so overestimate their own contribution (Stroebe *et al.*, 1992). Another factor contributing to this overestimation is lack of awareness of other people's unvoiced contributions; being aware of their *own* unvoiced contributions, people may rate themselves as highly productive.

Despite the negative findings, there may be ways to improve idea generation in groups. Osborn (1963) proposed that trained facilitators should be used to assist in group deliberations, and that there should be alternation between private and group idea-generating sessions. Stroebe and Diehl (1994) suggested that production blocking is the main reason for the ineffectiveness of brainstorming groups, and proposed two ways to overcome the problem. First, they suggested that a greater diversity of knowledge in brainstorming groups would create the kind of stimulating environment that would help alleviate production blocking. Second, they noted that blocking factors such as listening or waiting for one's turn are reduced in *electronic brainstorming*. Evidence indicates that electronic brainstorming groups are more productive than nominal electronic groups (Dennis & Valacich, 1993) and non-electronic groups (Gallupe *et al.*, 1994).

Decision rules

There are a number of ways to actually make a decision (for a list of decision 'rules' see Hastie & Kameda, 2005). The most common method, in both contemporary committees and hunter-gather groups, is to let each person cast one vote for their favoured alternative, and the alternative that attracts the most votes is chosen (Figure 13.2). This is called the *majority/plurality rule*. The second most common method is an autocratic 'leader decides' rule (Hastie & Kameda, 2005). These methods involve little effort on the part of those involved.

Another version of majority voting is the *Condorcet majority rule*. This is also based on the idea that the candidate favoured by the majority wins, but when there are more than two candidates then a series of votes is held in which each candidate is paired against the other candidates. The winner is any candidate that wins all the pairwise elections by a simple majority (it is possible that there is no outright winner). This method is obviously more effortful, and

Table 13.1. *Condorcet's paradox: Intransitivity resulting from pairwise voting*

Pairwise votes	Committee members' voting preferences			Majority preferences
	Jill	Mary	Steve	
A vs. B	A	A	B	A > B
B vs. C	C	B	B	B > C
A vs. C	C	A	C	C > A
Overall individual preferences	C > A > B	A > B > C	B > C > A	

it is not clear whether it is ever used in practice (Hastie & Kameda, 2005), although it has received a lot of attention from social choice theorists.

The Condorcet rule can also lead to intransitivities in choice. For example, suppose three committee members (Jill, Mary, and Steve) are choosing between plans A, B, and C. Table 13.1 shows which plan each member votes for in each of three pairwise votes. As the bottom row of the table shows, Jill, Mary, and Steve each have a different pattern of transitive preferences. However, when we look at the majority voting patterns in the right-hand column, we can see that the resulting preferences are intransitive: A is preferred to B, B is preferred to C, but C is preferred to A.

A more common situation (Goodwin & Wright, 2004, p.316) is where a committee does not make each pairwise comparison, but discards from consideration any candidate as soon as that candidate loses a vote. This, too, is problematical. Suppose our committee members begin by comparing A and B. The majority prefer A, so B is eliminated. In the remaining comparison, C is preferred, so C wins overall. However, if the committee begins by comparing B and C, then C is eliminated; and in the next comparison A is preferred to B, so A wins overall. Thus, the order in which comparisons are made can affect the eventual winner.

This type of procedure is also vulnerable to manipulation. Suppose the initial comparison is between A and B. Also, it so happens that Mary would prefer A to win the competition overall, but definitely does not want C to win. As is often the case, she already knows or suspects the preferences of her colleagues. Despite preferring A to B, she realises that if she votes this way then C will win out in the final round. Therefore, she dishonestly states her first round preference as B, because this will defeat C in the final round.

Another decision rule is *averaging*. This is appropriate when the output of the process is a number. This would be the case where members assign each candidate a numerical value, or where the group is tasked with producing some kind of estimate or forecast (for example monthly sales of a product).

One interesting question is whether rules based on majorities or averaging will outperform reliance on the 'best' member in the group (for example an expert in a particular domain). As it happens,

Figure 13.2. *Majority rule.* © cartoonbank.com

there is substantial evidence that judgments and decisions based on majorities and averaging are more effective than other rules, such as reliance on the best member. Surowiecki (2004) has recounted the impromptu study conducted by Sir Francis Galton at a country fair in 1906 (originally reported in Galton, 1907). Galton looked at the estimates of 787 people, including farmers and non-expert people from a range of occupations, who had taken part in a competition to judge the weight of an ox. Galton had very little faith in the intelligence of the average person, so was presumably very surprised that the average of all 787 estimates was just one pound short of the correct weight (1198 pounds).

Many subsequent studies show that averaging individual judgments leads to more accurate estimates than those of the average individual judge (e.g. Bruce, 1935; Smith, 1931). The reason is quite simple: the aggregation of imperfect estimates reduces error. Larrick and Soll (2006) gave a simple example of how this works. Suppose two people forecast tomorrow's temperature as $60°$ and $80°$, respectively. The actual temperature turns out to be $73°$, meaning that the respective errors are $13°$ and $7°$, which is $10°$ on average. However, the average of the two guesses is $70°$, which misses the correct temperature by only $3°$. Thus, averaging is more accurate than the average individual. In this example, the two estimates 'bracketed' the correct answer, in the sense that they fell either side of it. This is not always the case with people's estimates, but: 'An important implication of the averaging principle is that, over multiple judgments, the mean absolute deviation (MAD) of averaging is less than the MAD of the average individual if there is at least one instance of bracketing' (Larrick & Soll, p.112). In a reanalysis of 30 forecasting studies, Armstrong (2001) found that averaging improved accuracy by a mean of 12.5 per cent relative to the mean performance of the forecasts being averaged.

In this kind of procedure, should we give more weight to the judgments of people who are regarded as more expert? This, of course, is not without its problems as it requires a method for judging just how expert people are (Goodwin & Wright, 2004). In any case, evidence indicates that simple averages are as good as, or only slightly inferior to, weighted averages (e.g. Ashton & Ashton, 1985).

The averaging technique appears to be counterintuitive for many people. Across a series of studies, Larrick and Soll (2006) asked participants to estimate the MAD that would occur if averaging and other strategies were used (based on data provided from two judges). They found that a large proportion of participants failed to recognise the usefulness of averaging (for example, in Experiment 1, 57 per cent thought that averaging would perform no better than the average judge). Participants were sensitive to conditions that made averaging more effective, such as a high frequency of bracketing, but they underestimated the extent of its benefit. Unfortunately, in everyday life it is rare that people will simultaneously receive judges' estimates together with the correct outcome, which makes it harder to perceive the benefits of averaging.

Hastie and Kameda (2005) used computer simulations to test the performance of various decision rules. In particular, detailed tests were made of the following rules: averaging, Condorcet, majority/plurality, best member (accept the judgment of the most accurate individual), and random member (accept the judgment of a randomly chosen individual). The simulations involved groups of foragers whose fitness depended on accurate predictions of the rewards to be obtained at various locations. Predictions were based upon three imperfect cues. Some simulations assumed that each individual forager only knew about a subset of all locations. Also, the simulations varied the degree of discrepancy between the best and the worst cues.

The only scenarios where the best member rule appeared advantageous were where a large discrepancy existed between the best and worst cues, especially with complete information about locations. In general, the averaging, majority/plurality, and Condorcet rules performed in a similar fashion, and outperformed the best member and random member rules. Notably, the best member rule seemed to suffer when there was incomplete information about locations. The averaging rule seemed to have an advantage under the highest degree of incomplete information.

A follow-up study asked Japanese students to individually make a series of similar judgments (predicting the most profitable of ten companies, based on three cues). The experimenters then created 1000 nominal groups and, based on the students' data, evaluated the performance of three rules: the majority/plurality rule, the best member rule, and the random member rule (because the judgment was not quantitative in this case the averaging rule could not be examined). They found that the majority plurality rule outperformed the other rules. This advantage was diminished when there was a large discrepancy between the cues, but the majority plurality rule still performed about as well as the best member rule. This suggests that the majority plurality rule may be even more robust in actual decision making than in Hastie and Kameda's computer simulations.

Given the apparent superiority of judgments and decisions based on averaging or majorities *in the absence of discussion*, not to mention the superiority of electronic brainstorming groups over traditional brainstorming groups, some authors have wondered whether there is any point in having face-to-face discussions (Armstrong, 2006, and subsequent commentaries) or, indeed, whether there is any point in having discussions at all (Larrick & Soll, 2006, p.125). This is an interesting point. However, in practical terms one serious concern must be that people may fail to properly implement a decision if they do not feel that they were properly involved in the decision process (Roberto, 2005). Furthermore, research on social dilemmas shows group discussion in a more positive light. Social dilemmas are situations where the exercise of individual rationality by two or more interacting people leads to a worse collective outcome than if each person had acted in the collective interest. Many studies have shown that group discussion tends to result in an improved collective outcome. This topic will be explored in more detail in the next chapter.

In the next section I review some systematic decision procedures that attempt to involve people fully in the decision process while minimising the problems that can arise in unstructured discussions.

Systematic decision procedures

The Delphi technique The Delphi technique is used for making quantitative judgments. The process starts with a panel of people submitting judgments anonymously. These could be sales forecasts, or judgments of the likelihood of particular future events occurring, for example. Next, the panellists are provided with statistical feedback about the group's responses. This might involve, say, information about the group range or median. At this point, anonymous discussion may occur, giving people a chance to express their viewpoint. After discussion has taken place, people submit a second judgment. The panel may or may not cycle through more such rounds until, eventually, a quantitative consensus is produced, normally in the form of the group's median judgment.

Rowe and Wright (1999) reviewed 27 evaluations of the Delphi technique that had been published in English-language journals. This review found strong evidence that the variability in responding did diminish across rounds of the Delphi process. However, this result in itself does not distinguish increasing accuracy from conformity behaviour. Indeed, among the studies reviewed there was evidence that:

- the reduction in disagreement during Delphi (based on post-group individual responses) is less than that achieved in an alternative structured group technique (Rohrbaugh, 1979); there was also little increase in agreement in the Delphi groups;

- compared to other structured techniques, post-group individual responses did not correlate any more with group responses as a result of Delphi; indeed, one other technique showed a higher such rate of 'acceptance' of the outcome (Erffmeyer & Lane, 1984);

- respondents with extreme views are more likely to drop out of a Delphi procedure, indicating that consensus may be due, in part, to a process of attrition (Bardecki, 1984).

Does the Delphi technique increase group accuracy? Rowe and Wright described the results as 'equivocal'. They found that five studies reported a statistically significant increase in accuracy over rounds, another five found an increase in accuracy that was not statistically significant, and two studies where accuracy was greater under certain conditions but not under others. With regard to the specific conditions that might affect performance, Parenté *et al.* (1984) found increased accuracy for predicting *when* an event might occur, but not *if* it would occur, and Jolson and Rossow (1971) found that accuracy increased for panels of 'experts' but not for 'non-experts'. Two other studies found no difference between Delphi and staticised groups, and two more studies found that Delphi groups were less accurate than both their first-round aggregates and staticised groups.

Rowe and Wright also compared Delphi with other structured group techniques, such as the nominal group technique, in which people give estimates, then engage in face-to-face discussion, and then give new estimates. On the whole, there appeared to be little appreciable difference in accuracy between Delphi and other techniques.

In their discussion, Rowe and Wright noted that there is not just variation between the procedures used in the evaluation studies, but there is also often a difference between evaluative studies and the way in which Delphi is normally conducted in the real world. For instance, evaluative studies often use student participants rather than panels of experts. Even when experts are used, they tend to be from the same domain, which reduces the possibilities for sharing hidden information.

Often, the panellists themselves are not instrumental in determining the topic of the procedure, and the topic is rarely a serious long-term issue; rather, panellists might be asked to give estimates for some topic of general knowledge. This might preclude panellists from constructing some coherent task scenario.

Finally, in evaluative studies the feedback to participants is often simply the group's medians or means, or a list of the individual estimates. In applications of Delphi, however, panellists also receive arguments from panellists who gave extreme estimates (outside the upper and lower quartiles).

In short, it is possible that Delphi, as it is normally applied, is more effective than might be suggested by the modest findings from experimental studies. However, more research is needed before such a conclusion could be accepted.

Decision conferencing Decision conferencing is used for major decisions and typically lasts over a period of days. Attendees often sit around a large, round table, and they discuss the issue at hand with the aid of a decision analyst who facilitates the proceedings, encouraging everybody to share information and express their views. Using interactive decision-aiding technology, a second analyst models individual and group views. Attendees are asked to consider the initial output of the modelling process in relation to their unaided holistic judgments. Almost certainly, there will be discrepancies between the two. This leads on to further discussion, in order to explore the reasons for the discrepancy, perhaps identifying new ideas or information. When no new intuitions emerge, the final representation is considered to be a 'requisite decision model' (Phillips, 1984).

Thus, the point is not to impose a solution on people, but to allow team members to develop a shared understanding of the problem at hand. By adjusting the parameters of the model, panellists are able to see whether disagreements made any difference to the final preferred alternative. Because panellists have been involved in a thorough process before arriving at a consensus, they are more likely to feel committed to implementing the final decision.

As with the Delphi technique, there appear to be few evaluations of decision conferencing. Goodwin and Wright (2004) note that clear evidence may be difficult to obtain because real-world applications do not provide enough baselines of comparison. Phillips (2007) also points out that decision conference facilitators may be too engaged in their work to write it up for publication. Nonetheless, these authors do report review studies indicating that participants found decision conferences to be more effective than regular meetings. This perceived effectiveness appears to be greater at senior executive level than at lower levels in organisations, and more effective for smaller groups (four to eight participants) than for medium-sized groups (nine to 11 participants) or large groups (15 to 18 participants) (Chun, 1992, cited in Phillips, 2007).

It seems that small, interacting, facilitated groups can perform better than their best member, contrary to much of the research discussed earlier (Regan-Cirincione, 1994). However, decision conferences can be ineffective when the executive teams feel little pressure to reach consensus or construct a plan of action (McCartt & Rohrbough 1989, cited in Goodwin & Wright, 2004, p.325).

LEADERSHIP

In this chapter we have seen that decision making in groups and teams frequently falls short of our expectations. A variety of factors seem to lead to the stifling of creativity, failure to share knowledge and ideas, and failure to engage in critical evaluation. Nonetheless, there are successful groups. Perhaps one important factor in overriding the barriers to effectiveness is the quality of leadership.

The literature on leadership is generally negative about the autocratic style of leadership. Autocratic leaders take control of most of the decision making in a group or organisation and are more likely to be disliked by subordinates. Peterson *et al.* (1998) found that this style was associated with business failures.

One of the classic studies of leadership (Lippitt & White, 1943) engaged the 11-year-old members of boys' clubs in the task of making Halloween masks. Each club had a leader who was trained in three different leadership styles by the experimenter. The leaders were swapped around every few weeks, so that each club was exposed to each leader but only one style of leadership. *Autocratic leaders* decided what would be done, when, how, and by whom. They were aloof and focused exclusively on the task at hand. *Democratic leaders* elicited suggestions from the boys about what to do, and a plan was arrived at through group discussion. *Laissez-faire* leaders provided materials and information, but otherwise left the boys to their own devices.

Autocratic leaders were the least liked. They created an unpleasant atmosphere and productivity slacked off when the leader was absent. Laissez-faire leaders created a pleasant, playful, atmosphere but productivity was low (though it rose in the absence of the leader). The most effective type of leader was the democratic one. He created a friendly group atmosphere, but one that focused on the task. Consequently, productivity was high in both the presence and absence of the leader. This type of leader was also best liked out of the three.

There are various different theories of leadership (see e.g. Furnham, 2005; Kozlowski & Ilgen, 2006). Some of these emphasise the need for the right fit between a particular style of leadership and a particular context. For example, Fiedler's (1965) contingency theory suggests that leadership styles develop from a person's personality traits, such that a leader tends to be oriented towards either the *task in hand* (more authoritarian) or *interpersonal relationships*. The degree to which either style is effective depends upon the leader's level of situational control. This in turn depends on the quality of leader–member relations, the extent to which the task is well or poorly structured, and the extent to which the leader has the power to enforce the compliance of group members via rewards and punishments. Fiedler (1965) reported that the task-oriented style was associated with poorer group performance under intermediate levels of situational control, but with better group performance under high and low levels of situational control.

In recent years there has been considerable interest in the concepts of *transformational* and *transactional* leadership (Bass, 1985; Burns, 1978). Transformational leadership is based on the leader's charisma and his or her ability to inspire and stimulate employees, as well as to attend to their individual needs and concerns. Transactional leadership is concerned with the setting of clear expectations and rewards for meeting those expectations, and distinguishes between leaders who are proactive in anticipating problems and those who are reactive in dealing with problems. Sometimes also included is laissez-faire leadership, which is associated with the avoidance of decision making, hesitation before taking action, and being absent when needed.

One meta-analysis of 87 studies (Judge & Piccolo, 2004; see also Stewart, 2006) concluded that contingent-reward leadership was more effective in business settings, but transformational leadership was more effective in college settings, the military, and the public sector. The level of the leader within the organisation was not associated with type of leadership. However, as has previously been noted, one difficulty with such studies is that they rely on ratings from employees and performance indicators such as financial results, although the former may well be influenced by knowledge of the latter.

TAKING ADVICE

Decision-making groups (and individuals) may sometimes wish to take advice from people who they think may be able to provide useful information, opinions, or insight. Most of the research into advice taking appears to have focused on the use of advice by individuals rather than groups, but the findings may be relevant. A typical study involves participants being assigned to the role of judge or adviser. They read a scenario and the judge makes an initial decision, possibly also giving a confidence rating. The adviser, who is normally unaware of the judge's initial decision, is asked to make a recommendation, possibly also accompanied by a confidence rating, and this is conveyed to the judge. The judge then considers the recommendation and makes a final decision (possibly with a confidence rating).

A review of such studies by Bonaccio and Dalal (2006) reported that one of the most robust findings is that of *egocentric advice discounting*. Although the provision of advice generally improves the judges' accuracy, judges tend to overweight their own opinion relative to that of the adviser and only shift a token amount towards the adviser's recommendation. This is so even when making judgments about novel situations, indicating an *egocentric bias* (Krueger, 2003).

Nonetheless, judges are more responsive to advice that is perceived to have come from an expert, from an older person, or from someone perceived to have greater life experience and wisdom. People also weigh advice more heavily when they have paid for it (Gino, 2005), consistent with the sunk cost effect (see Chapter 8).

As we saw earlier, where two or more advisers provide different forecasts the best strategy is to average these, because this reduces the effects of random error and converges towards the correct value. However, we also saw that people frequently fail to appreciate the benefits of such averaging. Indeed, judges appear to rely on a *confidence heuristic*, whereby an adviser's confidence is used to infer their ability, expertise, task-related knowledge, or accuracy (Price & Stone, 2004). Consequently, people more often follow the advice of a more confident adviser than that of a less confident one. Nonetheless, higher levels of disagreement between advisers result in judges' reduced confidence, especially if the advisers had access to the same information (Budescu & Rantilla, 2000).

SUMMARY

It might be expected that decision making in groups and teams should be more effective than individual decision making, due to the sharing of knowledge, ideas, and insights. This should particularly be the case when there is greater diversity among group members. In fact, group discussion in experiments tends to focus on information that all members already know rather than on non-shared information. It is not clear to what extent this is a problem in real-life groups and teams. However, studies of real work teams have failed to find any overall benefit of greater diversity.

Individuals within groups may also be affected by pressure to conform or to demonstrate obedience to authority. Nonetheless, minorities of more than one may be able to exert influence if they demonstrate consistency of behaviour. Other evidence shows that groups often polarise towards the position that was held by most members prior to discussion.

The theory of groupthink has had considerable influence on the way people think about group decision making. It suggests that a combination of high group cohesion, structural faults in the organisation, and a provocative situational conflict leads members to strive for unity above a realistic appraisal of alternative courses of action. However, there has been relatively little research into groupthink and what there has been is only partially supportive. There is a lack of support for the role of cohesiveness, though rather more support for the idea that a lack of impartial leadership is associated with groupthink symptoms.

Janis (1982[1972]) proposed vigilant decision making as a way to avoid groupthink, but noted that this also had potential costs so should not be implemented unthinkingly. There is evidence that successful teams are based on achieving a balance between flexibility and control, rather than on being vigilant.

Brainstorming is a popular technique for generating creative ideas. However, research has shown that brainstorming groups are actually less creative than a collection of non-interacting individuals. Electronic brainstorming groups, on the other hand, *are* effective at facilitating ideas. For actually making a decision, the greatest accuracy seems to be obtained by accepting a majority rule or (where a quantitative judgment is required) by taking an average of all values. Some authors have argued that such results even indicate that discussion may not be needed in order to reach accurate decisions.

Two systematic decision procedures are the Delphi technique and decision conferencing. Delphi provides group members with statistical feedback from a round of anonymous polling, elicits anonymous discussion, and then a second round of polling takes place. Decision conferencing aims to develop a shared understanding of an important issue through facilitated discussion and decision modelling.

Leadership appears to play an important role in the performance of groups and teams. Evidence suggests that autocratic leadership has a negative effect on group performance except, perhaps, in extreme situations. Transformational leadership is associated with charismatic individuals who inspire subordinates to work towards an appealing vision of the future. Studies show that this is associated with positive team performance. In business settings, there appears to be an advantage for contingent-reward leadership, whereby clear expectations are set out and subordinates are rewarded for meeting them.

Studies of advice use show that advice does tend to improve a judge's accuracy, but that judges place too much emphasis on their own views. However, this is moderated by factors such as the adviser's perceived expertise, age, life experience, and wisdom. People also weight advice more heavily if they have paid for it. Where two advisers give different forecasts, people tend to rely on the person who appears more confident.

QUESTIONS

1. Why is averaging an effective strategy for numerical estimation?

2. Discuss the role of leadership in group/team decision making.

3. In what ways is group decision making in non-human animals like that of humans? (I have only briefly touched upon animal decision making in this chapter; for a longer answer here a literature search could be undertaken.)

4. Summarise the current scientific standing of the theory of groupthink.

5. Discuss the potential and possible pitfalls of group decision making.

6. Are different types of leader better suited to different types of situation (e.g. crisis versus routine decision making)? Design an experiment to investigate this question.

NOTES

1. Research on group decision making has not always distinguished between groups and teams, despite the fact that some studies have involved teams. It is likely that many of the findings from groups also apply to teams, but it would be

premature to assume as much except where there is compelling reason to believe that is the case.

2. Although the resolution of the Cuban missile crisis is often cited as the outcome of good decision making, it is worth bearing in mind that things could easily have gone wrong.

RECOMMENDED READING

Janis, I.L. (1982). *Groupthink: Psychological studies of policy decisions and fiascos* (2nd edn). Boston: Houghton Mifflin. The original classic study of groupthink.

Kozlowski, S.W.J. & Ilgen, D.R. (2006). Enhancing the effectiveness of work groups and teams. *Psychological Science in the Public Interest*, 7(3), 77–124. An academic review article examining work groups and teams.

Roberto, M.A. (2005). *Why great leaders don't take yes for an answer: Managing for conflict and consensus.* New Jersey: Wharton. Roberto provides well-written advice about decision making in an organisational setting.

Surowiecki, J. (2004). *The wisdom of crowds: Why the many are smarter than the few.* London: Little, Brown. A best-selling book that explores the benefits of judgments made by many people rather than by individuals. I'm not sure that Surowiecki quite proves his thesis, but there is much fascinating research in here and it is very well written.

14 Cooperation and Coordination

INTRODUCTION

Human interactions can be characterised as involving cooperation, coordination, and competition, sometimes in combination. This chapter looks at the first two of these, although we will also see some instances of competitive behaviour. I shall begin by briefly considering game theory, which is a mathematical discipline devised to analyse how rational people would behave in interactive situations (behavioural game theory is concerned with how people actually behave). We will return to some of the game-theoretic ideas throughout the chapter, but without getting into any deep mathematical waters.

In the second main part of the chapter, I shall look at cooperation: how it has been studied, why it exists at all, and the factors that influence whether or not people will behave cooperatively in a given situation. In the third part of the chapter, I shall look at situations where people need to coordinate their behaviour. This is distinguished from mere cooperation in the sense that the situations concerned allow for more than one 'best'[1] combination of behaviours by the individuals concerned, hence they must coordinate on a single combination.

GAME THEORY AND BEHAVIOURAL GAME THEORY

In a task known as the *ultimatum game* two participants bargain over an amount of money, such as $10. A Proposer has to offer some proportion of the $10 to a Responder. If the Responder accepts the offer, then she gets to keep that sum and the Proposer keeps whatever he has left.[2] If the Responder rejects the offer then neither party gets to keep any money. In the experimental situation there is no communication between Proposer and Responder, so there is no discussion or negotiation about the offer made. In fact, there are normally very tight experimental controls such that Proposers and Responders are anonymous to each other. Take a moment to think about the sum that you would offer if you were in the Proposer's position, and what you would accept if you were the Responder.

From the point of view of analytical *game theory*, described below, both participants should act in a way that maximises their self-interest. The Responder should accept any amount that is offered, because however small this is she will still go away with more than she had before. The Proposer should anticipate this and offer the smallest amount possible ($0.01, unless the study stipulates some other 'smallest unit of exchange').

You may not be surprised to learn that people actually behave in a rather different way than that suggested by this analysis. Camerer (2003, pp.50–55) has reported the results of many 'one-shot' studies from around the world, involving monetary stakes of different sizes. The results are highly consistent: the modal and median offers are usually 40–50 per cent and the means are 30–40 per cent. Offers of 40–50 per cent are normally accepted, whereas offers below 20 per cent are rejected about half the time.

Game theory is the analysis of interactions between rational agents. The term 'game' does not literally mean a game as in football or hockey; rather, it simply refers to a situation involving two or more agents, each of whom has two or more *strategies* (courses of action) available to them, where strategies are associated with payoffs, and the payoffs also depend on the action that the other person(s) takes. In reality, people may not demonstrate perfect rationality, but game theorists expect that people will converge towards rational solutions as they gain experience with a game.

Game theory assumes that players in a game share common knowledge of the rules. Where this is not the case then game theory cannot be applied. Game theory also assumes *common knowledge of rationality*, meaning that players assume the rationality of other players.

As with the ultimatum game, studies of other games have often found that people do not behave in accordance with the predictions of game theory, though as mentioned above this may change with experience. *Behavioral game theory*, sometimes also called *psychological game theory*, is the study of how people actually behave in interactive situations.

COOPERATION

Extending our cooperation to other people always involves some sacrifice on our part. We give up time that we could be devoting to other purposes, we invest cognitive or physical effort, and we may also contribute financially. Cooperation in everyday life takes many forms, from helping a friend to move house, to paying taxes, belonging to a union (and possibly engaging in industrial action), to recycling one's household waste, and so on. Of course, not everyone cooperates in such behaviours. Understanding why anyone should cooperate at all, and how we can encourage greater cooperation, has been widely investigated.

The prisoner's dilemma and public goods games

One of the tasks that has been used to investigate cooperation is the *prisoner's dilemma*. This is a very influential problem that mirrors many real-life situations, but was first studied by Merrill Flood of the RAND corporation (Flood, 1952, cited in Poundstone, 1992). Here is an example of a prisoner's dilemma.

Suppose Dan and Joe have been arrested by the police for their part in a serious crime. They have been put in separate cells and cannot communicate. The police don't have enough evidence to convict them of the most serious charge unless at least one of the men confesses. If neither confesses, then they can each expect a year in prison on a lesser charge. Each man gets a visit from a police officer who tells them that they can escape prison by implicating their partner, who will be sent to prison for 10 years. The catch is that if both men implicate each other then they will each get five years in prison. These outcomes are shown in Table 14.1.

The strategies open to Dan and Joe are usually referred to as cooperation or defection, where cooperation means not telling the police anything, hence not implicating your partner. Defection means implicating your partner. Suppose, for argument's sake, that you were in Dan's position. What would you do?

Game theory makes a very specific prediction about what Dan and Joe both do if they are rational people. Suppose Dan believes that Joe will stay quiet. If Dan also stays quiet then he will get a year in prison. However, he can improve on this outcome by implicating Joe, thereby not going to prison at all. But what if Dan thinks that Joe will defect? If Dan stays quiet, he will get 10 years

Table 14.1. *The prisoners' dilemma. Each cell shows the prison sentence (years) for Dan and Joe, respectively, if that combination of strategies is chosen*

		Joe	
		Implicate Dan	*Stay quiet*
Dan	Implicate Joe	5, 5	0, 10
	Stay quiet	10, 0	1, 1

in prison. But he can improve on this outcome by implicating Joe. In other words, implicating Joe is the best strategy for Dan. As you can see from Table 14.1, by the same process of reasoning on Joe's part his best strategy is also to implicate his partner.

Many games, though not all, have a *Nash equilibrium* (or more than one in some games). This is a combination of strategies that cannot be improved upon, as long as the other player sticks with their chosen strategy. In the prisoner's dilemma, joint defection is the Nash equilibrium, and because there is only one equilibrium point mutual defection is regarded as the dominant strategy. Sure, the outcome is less than ideal for both Dan and Joe, but it is the best they can get *if they are both rational actors pursuing their self-interest*. In reality, people cooperate more than game theory predicts – about a third of the time, and more so on repeated plays of the game. Nonetheless, they do not do as well as they might do because there is always the temptation to defect at some point, which leads to retaliation by the other player.

A similar task to the prisoner's dilemma is the *public goods game* or resource allocation task. In a typical task, individuals are provided with an endowment and then given the option to contribute some, all, or none of that endowment to a pool of resources. After a round during which contributions may have been made, whatever is in the pool of resources is increased by some proportion. Then the resources are divided up among all participants. As with the prisoner's dilemma, the collectively rational action is to contribute to the pool whereas individually rational action is to withhold contribution. This has parallels with many real-life situations, such as (in the UK) the temptation not to buy a television licence while taking advantage of the public broadcasting service – the BBC – that has been funded by the people who did pay their licence fee.

Alternatively, a task may give people the opportunity to withdraw resources from a limited pool, thus risking the depletion of a public good. This also has parallels with many contemporary problems, such as concerns over energy consumption and over-fishing by competing trawlers (see Hardin, 1968). In these situations, the collectively rational solutions are to use less energy and to catch less fish, but in each case the individually rational solution is the opposite.

The evolution of cooperation

Why should cooperative behaviour exist at all? To understand how cooperation might evolve in a population, Axelrod (1984) pitted various strategies against each other in a series of repeated-play prisoner's dilemma computer tournaments. Most of these strategies had been submitted by game theorists, psychologists, economists, and other academics. In his discussion of the strategies, Axelrod distinguished between 'nice' rules, which always begin by cooperating, and 'nasty' rules, which always begin by defecting. In two of the tournaments, the strategies were played for points. In a third round, the reward for successful strategies was 'offspring', such that some strategies thrived and others became 'extinct'.[3]

Axelrod found that the sophistication of the strategies was not an indicator of their success. For example, one of the most

sophisticated strategies was called the *Downing* strategy. This began by assuming that the other program would be unresponsive to its own cooperation or defection, but then amending this assumption on the basis of how the other program actually did respond to cooperation and defection. If the other program tended to punish defection but reward cooperation, then Downing would settle for cooperation. Otherwise, it tended to defect. Unfortunately, the opening assumption of unresponsiveness led Downing to get punished for its own early defection. By contrast, the most successful strategy was also the simplest: *tit for tat* (TFT), submitted by Anon Rapoport. TFT begins by cooperating and every subsequent action copies the action of the other player. In other words, TFT punishes defection but rewards cooperation.

In the 'evolutionary' competition, overly nice strategies were preyed upon by nasty strategies, to the point of extinction. However, when the nasty strategies had no prey left they too died out, paving the way for TFT. Thus, Axelrod's computer tournaments showed how the capacity for cooperation can evolve within a population.

The astute reader will by now have noticed that I have shifted from talking about one-shot games to talking about repeated games. Many real-life interactions may be more like repeated games, because we often engage repeatedly in similar interactions, often with the same person or organisation. In fact, because we often do not know when we will cease to interact with someone our interactions may be considered indefinitely repeated games. Importantly, the notion of finite equilibria that applies in one-shot games does not apply in indefinitely repeated games. In fact, for players who are patient any individually rational payoffs can be supported by an equilibrium; this result – not explored further here – is known as the Folk theorem.

In the next part of this chapter I shall examine the factors that influence the extent to which people cooperate.

Consideration of others

About a third of participants cooperate on a single-shot prisoner's dilemma. This is more than would be expected if people were rational actors behaving according to self-interest (as in the game-theoretic analysis). Can this cooperation be attributed to a kind of moral imperative on the part of the participants? Shafir and Tversky (1992) thought not. They asked participants to play a series of one-shot games, each against a different person. Participants were told that they had been allocated to a bonus group that would occasionally be told their opponent's strategy prior to making their own choice. If the third of participants who normally cooperate in a one-shot game are behaving according to a moral imperative, then we might expect the highest rate of cooperative responses to occur when it is *known* that the other person has cooperated.

Shafir and Tversky found that 37 per cent of games resulted in cooperation when the other person's strategy was *not* known, which – as we have seen – is about the usual rate of cooperation. However, contrary to the expectation based on moral imperative, only 16 per cent of responses were cooperative when it was known that the opponent had cooperated (3 per cent of responses were cooperative when it was known that the opponent had defected). Shafir and Tversky argued that people fail to think through the standard prisoner's dilemma. Specifically, they do not consider all the hypothetical outcomes, so do not know how they would behave if they knew their opponent's strategy. The cooperative responses that do occur may involve a degree of wishful thinking.

Is cooperation facilitated by taking the perspective of the other person? Epley *et al.* (2006) reported a series of studies involving simulated and actual resource-allocation negotiations (for example, one study involved role playing the representative of a fishing organisation in negotiations with other such groups regarding the reduction of harvesting levels). All participants began by stating what they thought was a fair allocation. Half of the participants were then asked to consider what resource allocation other groups might consider fair for themselves and then asked again what they thought a fair allocation would be for all groups. Taking the other groups' perspective into account in this way led people to reduce what they thought a fair allocation was. However, when asked to state how much they would actually take for themselves (or when given the opportunity to actually take some resources), these participants took a larger allocation for their group than did those who had not considered the other groups' perspectives. It appears that taking others' perspectives led people to generate egoistic theories of their likely behaviour, thus leading them to behave more egoistically themselves.

Similar results have been reported by Caruso *et al.* (2006), including one study using the prisoner's dilemma task (Experiment 3). This task included a control group, as well as participants who were asked to take the cognitive perspective of the other person, and participants who were asked to empathise with the other person. The rate of defection was the same for empathisers and control participants (40 per cent vs. 41 per cent, respectively), whereas there was a 68 per cent defection rate among those who had taken the cognitive perspective of the other person.

Another study found that reducing people's capacity for thinking made them behave more fairly in a resource problem (Roch *et al.*, 2000). In this study, participants were given the opportunity to withdraw resources from a common pool, and asked to verbalise their thoughts as they did so. However, people in a high cognitive load condition were asked to hold in mind an eight-digit number while they did the task. These participants were less likely to verbalise task-relevant thoughts, and were more likely to draw an equal share from the pool, whereas those without the extra cognitive load referred to the task more often and tended to take more than their 'fair share'.

In short, these studies lead to the slightly disturbing conclusion that greater cooperation is not more likely to occur when people think harder about a task, at least not in laboratory studies. The following section reviews evidence that different levels of cooperation are actually related to the motives and different values that people possess.

Fear, greed, and punishment

Several studies have examined the effect that *fear* and *greed* might have on rates of cooperation in social dilemmas. Fear, of course,

could mean two things in this context. It could mean fear of being taken for a sucker, for example if one behaves in an environmentally friendly fashion when no one else does. Alternatively, it could mean fear of being punished for acting in a self-interested manner, for example being fined for behaving in an environmentally unfriendly manner.

Fear appears to partly explain the generosity of most Proposers in the anonymous ultimatum game. If this generosity is related to the fear that Responders will reject small offers, then we can gauge the extent of this fear by seeing what happens if we take away the Responder's power of rejection. This is the basis of the *dictator game*. It turns out that Proposers do offer less when there is no possibility of rejection, but they still offer more than they would if they were behaving out of pure self-interest (for example, about 20 per cent in studies by Forsythe *et al.*, 1994). However, there is also evidence that dictators are even less generous when great pains are taken to convince them that their responses are anonymous and that their identity is hidden from both the recipient and the experimenter (e.g. Hoffman *et al.*, 1994). Thus, greed may be the flip side of fear: people often behave in a greedy fashion once the fear is removed.

Along similar lines, Ahn *et al.* (2001; see also Dawes *et al.*, 1986; Yamagishi & Sato, 1986) found effects of fear and greed in a repeated-play prisoner's dilemma, but only when participants were randomly paired in each game, and not when the same people played each other in each game. These authors linked greed and fear to particular payoff relationships in the task, as shown in Table 14.2. The four possible outcomes are temptation (T), reward (R), punishment (P), and sucker (S), where $T > R > P > S$. Greed is based on the payoff that can be obtained if you defect when the other player cooperates ($T - R$). Fear is based on the cost to you of cooperating when the other player defects ($P - S$). Ahn *et al.* asked participants to play a series of prisoner's dilemma games in which the size of the $T - R$ and $P - S$ relationships was manipulated. Initially, fear and greed appeared to have little effect. However, when these relationships were normalised, by dividing each by $T - S$, then both fear and greed were related to the degree of cooperation. In fact, greed had a stronger effect on behaviour than did fear.

Fear is also an important factor in a situation where there is a possibility of punishment. Fehr and Gächter (2002) found that above-average contributors to an anonymous public goods game were willing to punish below-average contributors, even though this entailed a cost to themselves. The effect of this was to substantially increase the level of contributions above what was observed in non-punishment periods of the game. Fehr and Gächter considered

Table 14.2. *A generalised view of the payoffs in prisoner's dilemma tasks (P: punishment; R: reward; S: sucker; T: temptation)*

		Player 2	
		Defect	Cooperate
Player 1	Defect	P, P	T, S
	Cooperate	S, T	R, R

the punishment to be altruistic because it benefited the group at a cost to the punisher. However, they also found that punishment was motivated by anger, which might suggest that the benefit to the group was merely an incidental effect of revenge.

Evidence of a revenge motive has been seen in a neuroimaging study by Singer et al. (2006). They found different types of brain activation when people observed pain being experienced by a partner who had previously behaved fairly and one who had behaved unfairly in an economic game. Seeing a fair partner experience pain led to activation in pain-related brain areas (the fronto-insular and anterior cingulate cortices). When seeing an unfair partner experience pain this elevated activity was slightly reduced for women, whereas men no longer showed significant activity in these areas. This decreased activity for men was accompanied by increased activity in the nucleus accumbens, an area associated with reward processing. Furthermore, the degree of activity in this area correlated with men's rated desire for revenge.

Differences in values

Other research indicates that people's values may affect behaviour on social dilemma problems. Along similar lines to the concepts of fear and greed discussed earlier, Van Lange (1999) proposed that people can be categorised according to their *social value orientation*. *Prosocial* people wish to maximise joint gain and equality in outcomes, *individualists* are interested only in maximising their own gains, and *competitors* wish to maximise relative gain (meaning the difference between one's own and the other's outcome). In one investigation, participants were interrupted halfway through a repeated prisoner's dilemma game and asked to think about the choices they had made and outcomes they had received, and to list some alternatives that were better or worse than what had actually happened. Higher numbers of upward counterfactuals ('It could have been better') were associated with an increased level of cooperation in the second half of the game. By contrast, downward counterfactual thinking ('It could have been worse') was associated with a decrease in cooperation in the second half of the task (Parks et al., 2003).

Furthermore, Parks et al. found that prosocials generated the most upward counterfactuals and fewest downward counterfactuals, competitors showed the reverse pattern, and individualists generated the same number of each type. Social value orientation was thus linked to the post-thoughtlisting rate of cooperation, but this relationship was entirely due to the nature of the thoughts that the different types of people had generated. In short, inducing competitive individuals to think about how things might have worked out differently is likely to make them less, not more, cooperative.

Where do our social value orientations come from? Studies reported by Van Lange et al. (1997) found that prosocial individuals exhibited a more secure attachment style; that is, they found it easier to get closer to others and to allow others to get closer to them, and did not worry about being abandoned. Furthermore, they found evidence that prosociality may develop as a result of one's family background, because prosocial people reported having more siblings, especially sisters. It is likely that people in large families are exposed to more situations in which resources need to be shared, although perhaps prosociality has a heritable component and prosocial people have more children. In any case, Van Lange et al. reported a study of different age groups that found higher proportions of prosocial individuals as age increased. They suggested that younger adults more often find themselves in competitive situations, whereas older adults more frequently experience situations requiring them to give help to others or to receive help from others. This certainly indicates that experience can lead people to become more prosocial.

However, despite the evidence for greater cooperation by prosocials in laboratory tasks, it is not yet clear how far this extends to real life. A survey carried out at US gas stations and connecting points for buses found that social value orientation did not predict people's perception of the environmental impact of cars, nor their preference for public or private transportation. By contrast, people who engaged in more thought about future consequences tended to perceive a greater public impact of cars and to prefer public transport (Joireman et al., 2004). This result would appear to contradict the conclusion of the section before last, but perhaps what matters is not how much one thinks, but what one thinks about (in this instance the future, as opposed to considering what someone else might be thinking or what we might have done differently in the past).

On the other hand, there is some slightly startling evidence that economics majors behave more in accordance with self-interest than do non-economics majors both in real life and in the laboratory. They are more likely to free-ride in public goods tasks (Marwell & Ames, 1981), to offer less and be willing to accept less in the ultimatum game (Carter & Irons, 1991), to give less to private charities (Frank et al., 1993), and to defect more often on the prisoner's dilemma (Frank et al., 1993). In the last study, although both economics majors and non-economics majors defected less as they proceeded from their freshman to their senior year, the trend towards cooperation was less among the economics majors.

Other evidence suggested that this might be at least partly due to the training that economics students receive, as opposed to more selfish students opting to study economics. Frank et al. gave the same questionnaire to three different groups of students at the start of the semester and again at the end of the semester. The questionnaire assessed whether students would behave honestly or dishonestly in certain scenarios (for example by reporting or not reporting a billing error) and whether they expected that other people would behave honestly in the same scenario. One group of students was studying introductory astronomy and the other two were taking different introductory microeconomics classes. However, one of the microeconomics professors emphasised game theory in his course, whereas the other didn't.

The astronomy class showed a tendency towards greater honesty by the end of the semester. However, the microeconomics students who were taught game-theoretic concepts showed less honesty and more cynicism about others at the end of semester. The other microeconomics class showed no clear change, with slightly less honesty on one item, greater honesty on two items, and no change on another.

In short, as with the research by Van Lange and colleagues, it looks as though certain values can be learned.

Culture, cooperation, and economic success

Some of the clearest differences in ultimatum game behaviour have been identified in relation to culture. Henrich *et al.* (2005) conducted games in 15 small-scale societies around the world, including peoples living in mountainous tropical forests, high-latitude deserts, and savanna woodlands. Each society was based around one of the following: family groups, family groups plus extended ties, villages, bands, clans, clan chiefdoms, or multiclan chiefdoms. In the ultimatum game, the mean offer between these small-scale societies showed more variation than it did between different industrialised societies. The smallest mean offer was 26 per cent (the Machiguenga of Peru), whereas the highest mean offer was 57 per cent (the Lamelara of Indonesia). The variation in rejection rates was much less, and rejection rates were strikingly low. Four societies had no rejections at all, including the Quichua of Ecuador, where the mean offer was just 25 per cent.

Henrich *et al.* identified two factors that were associated with much of the between-group variation. The first factor was *payoff to cooperation*: cooperation was stronger in societies where there was more cooperation with non-immediate kin (for example in hunting for whales). The second factor was *market integration*: there was more cooperation in societies where there was greater trading via markets.

It is interesting that societies with higher payoffs to cooperation and greater market integration should show higher levels of cooperation in the ultimatum game, levels that are more like those observed in industrialised societies. Although we often think of business as a competitive, and even ruthless, human activity, it actually could not survive unless there were cooperation and trust between the people involved (this theme is explored in more detail by Surowiecki, 2004). When one person pays another for some good or service, he trusts that person to provide what he has paid for. Should that good or service not be provided, then the person defaulting on the arrangement risks damage to his reputation and the loss of future customers. The link between cooperation and economic success is explored further in Box 14.1.

One unusual aspect of the data reported by Henrich *et al.* concerned the Au and Gnau of New Guinea. In these societies, Proposers occasionally made offers above 50 per cent, yet these offers were often rejected. The authors drew a parallel between this behaviour and the culture of gift-giving that is prevalent in these villages and throughout Melanesia. In these societies, the acceptance of gifts, even unsolicited ones, creates an obligation on the recipient to return the favour. When the favour is asked for it may be of a different kind, such as support in a political alliance, and it may be at a time inconvenient to the recipient. For this reason, large gifts may be refused.

Trust, generosity, and communication

Trust Earlier we saw that fear of rejection influenced offers in the ultimatum game, fear of partner's defection motivated some defections in the prisoner's dilemma, and fear of other free-riders led some people to also free-ride in the public goods task. We also saw that fear was not a factor in the public goods task when people were interacting with their friends, rather than strangers, and the level of contribution increased so long as payoffs were based on the lowest contributing member or the average level of contribution. This suggests that cooperation might be increased where trust in one's partner or other members is increased.

Trust has been defined as *the willingness to accept vulnerability based upon positive expectations about another's behaviour* (Dunn & Schweitzer, 2005). Berg *et al.* (1995) devised a game specifically to measure trust. In this game, an Investor was given $10 and told she could either keep this or invest as much as she liked. If she wished to invest some money, then the investment would be placed in the hands of an anonymous Trustee in a separate room. The invested money would earn interest. However, it was entirely up to the Trustee as to how much of the invested money would be passed back to the Investor. Berg *et al.* found that Investors invested about 50 per cent of their endowment on average. When the investment tripled in value, the average repayment by Trustees was about 95 per cent of the initial investment (about a third of the resulting amount after interest). However, there was considerable variation in the amount returned, with about half the Trustees returning nothing or just $1. The amount returned can be considered a measure of trustworthiness.

Trust and trustworthiness appear to vary considerably by country. Camerer (2003, citing Ensminger, 2000) has noted that the Orma herders of Kenya invested about 40 per cent on average but returned only 55 per cent:

> Kenya is considered one of the more corrupt countries in the world, measured by indices of 'transparency', which guess the extent of bribery, bureaucratic corruption, and black market trade, so it is encouragingly consistent that this simple game shows low levels of trust also. (2003, p.87)

People are more likely to trust people who have developed a good reputation. In the prisoner's dilemma study reported by Ahn *et al.* (2001), discussed earlier, people who played against the same person on each game cooperated more often than those who played a different person each time (42 per cent vs. 32 per cent, respectively). Cooperating on all four games was twice as frequent among those who were paired on all four games compared to those who were randomly matched (31 per cent vs. 15 per cent).

In another study (Delgado *et al.*, 2005), participants in a trust game were provided with positive, negative, or neutral information hinting at their (fictional) partner's moral character. These three biographies, respectively, referred to the partner as having rescued a friend from a fire, having tried to sell tiles from the ill-fated space shuttle Columbia, and having missed a doomed airplane flight. Although participants were told that their partner's responses (share or keep) might or might not be consistent with their description, those who were partnered with the 'good' partner rated them as more trustworthy prior to the game and shared more money with them during both early and late stages of the game, although after the game the good partners were no longer rated as any more trustworthy than the bad or neutral partners.

BOX 14.1.   COOPERATION AND ECONOMIC SUCCESS

A study by Paciotti *et al.* (2005) has linked more closely the extent of cooperation within a society and its economic success. They compared the Sukumu ethnic group in Tanzania with the Pimbwe. The Pimbwe are the indigenous ethnic group and live in Rukwa, in the south-west of Tanzania, near Lake Tanganyika and the border with Zambia. The Sukuma originate from the north of Tanzania, but in the 1960s and 1970s they migrated to all areas of the country, including Rukwa, where they live outside the villages of the Pimbwe. The Sukuma are farmer-herders, whereas the Pimbwe are small-scale farmers who also fish and eat wild game.

The Sukuma have a successful justice system, the Sungusungu. This originated in Sukuma villages in the north of Tanzania during the 1980s as a group devoted to fighting back against cattle raiders from Uganda. The Sungusungu system has since been replicated in Sukuma villages throughout Tanzania, and has expanded to deal with property crime, debt disputes, adultery, and witchcraft. The Sungusungu are quite sophisticated, having various procedural rules and keeping extensive documentation (although by Western standards their processes are not always fair and can be quite brutal).

Why are the Sukuma so successful, whereas the Pimbwe have many social and economic problems and find it harder to meet their daily needs? Paciotti *et al.* suggest that the Sukuma's success is due to their high propensity for cooperation:

Sukuma families have a reputation across Tanzania for exceptional hospitality and generosity. Visitors from their own and other ethnic groups are welcomed with lavish spreads of food. In contrast to the Sukuma, Pimbwe families are quite suspicious of others, living and eating in tightly bounded family groups and rarely opening their homes to people outside their family or clan. (2005, p.59)

Although the Pimbwe do have social institutions, these only promote social interaction and cooperation within clans and villages. As a result, the Sukuma are competing successfully with other ethnic groups and possibly Sukuma culture is beginning to replace Pimbwe culture, especially with intermarriage between Pimbwe and Sukuma and the learning of the latter's cultural traditions.

Paciotti *et al.* presented the ultimatum game to individuals from the Sukuma and the Pimbwe. Half of the participants were paired with a person from their own village and half were paired with someone from a different village. The mean offers are shown in Figure 14.1. The within-village offers by the Sukuma are the highest yet recorded (61 per cent on average) and even offers to someone of a different village are above 50 per cent. By contrast, the Pimbwe offered considerably less, especially to people from a different village.

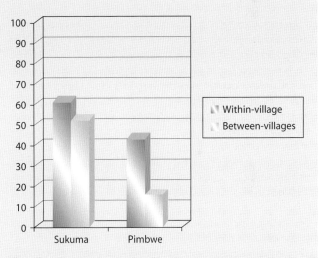

Figure 14.1. *Mean (%) amount offered by the Sukuma and Pimbwe in the ultimatum game*

This study also used functional magnetic resonance imaging (fMRI) to record brain activity during the decision and outcome phases on each trial. A brain region associated with learning (the caudate[4]) showed activity in response to partners' choices but not while the participants themselves were deciding. For neutral partners, caudate activity differed depending on whether their decision was to share or keep. For the non-neutral partners, especially the good partner, there was little difference in activity as a result of outcome decisions. Thus, it appears that prior moral perceptions reduced the extent to which learning occurred as a result of feedback.

When the participants themselves decided not to pass money to a good partner, or to share with a bad partner, there was increased activity in the cingulate cortex, an area associated with conflict monitoring. Decision making also activated the ventral striatum – associated with making predictions and anticipating outcomes – but there was only a weak indication that activity differed according to the type of partner and type of decision.

Generosity We saw earlier that the TFT strategy is highly successful for maximising outcomes in the prisoner's dilemma. However, one drawback to TFT is *noise*. Noise refers to an erroneous response. For example, in real life we are sometimes let down by other people, or we ourselves let other people down, through circumstances beyond our control rather than intentionally (for example the car breaks down on the way to a meeting).

The danger is that noise causes two interacting TFT players to enter into a cycle of never-ending retaliation.[5] Computer simulations have shown that cycles of recrimination can be avoided by adding an element of generosity or forgiveness to TFT (Bendor *et al.*, 1991; Kollock, 1993). TFT + 1 is a strategy that behaves slightly more cooperatively than the interaction partner did on the previous trial. Using real participants, Van Lange *et al.* (2002) found that TFT + 1 led to even higher levels of cooperation than TFT. Furthermore, the intentions of a partner using TFT were judged as less benign under conditions of noise, whereas partners using TFT + 1 were judged equally benign under conditions of noise and no noise.

However, in some situations people may not be able to act in a generous way (for example if generosity requires resources that one cannot afford to provide). In such circumstances communication can overcome the problem of noise, particularly for people who show low levels of dispositional trust who otherwise tend to respond more negatively to noise.

Communication Tazelaar *et al.* (2004) examined how communication would affect people's responses to a social dilemma where noise was introduced. Participants played a game that involved passing some coins (out of an endowment of 10) to a partner, to whom the coins were worth more in value. Unknown to participants, their 'partner' was a computer program playing TFT or TFT + 1. In this game TFT + 1 involved passing back one more coin than the participant had previously passed across. On a few trials, noise was introduced by giving the participant fewer coins than the computer had 'intended'. However, some participants also received an occasional communication from their bogus partner. For example: 'I wanted to give you six coins, but the computer changed my decision. I think you only received three coins.' Tazelaar *et al.* (2004, Experiment 1) found that communication eliminated the otherwise detrimental effects of noise on co-operation, and led people to view their partner as just as benign as in a no-noise condition.

A second experiment examined whether communication had a bigger effect on people who scored low on dispositional trust, as compared to those scoring high. The results are shown in Figure 14.2. The introduction of noise reduced cooperation among those low in trust when there were no accompanying messages, but people with high levels of trust were unaffected. However, when the noise was accompanied by communications from the 'partner', then there was just as much cooperation from low trusters as from high trusters. Accordingly, participants low in trust rated their partner's intentions as less benign when there was noise and no communication. However, noise accompanied by communication led these participants to rate their partner as just as benign as under the no-noise condition, and as just as benign as the high-trust participants rated their partners.

Dunn and Schweitzer (2005) have reported several studies that explore the influence emotions can have on trust. This is important because decisions about trust are often made in affect-rich contexts. Their results showed that emotions can influence trust in an individual, even though that individual was not the cause of the emotion being experienced. In particular, emotions that can be strongly aroused by other people (for example anger and

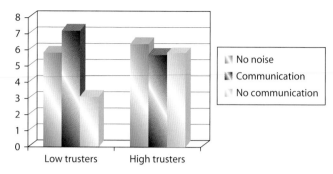

Figure 14.2a. *Mean level of cooperation (coins given), according to dispositional trust and communication condition*
Source: Tazelaar *et al.*, 2004, Experiment 2.

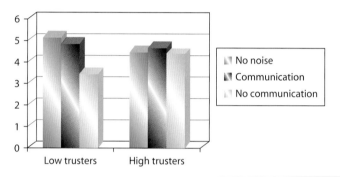

Figure 14.2b. *Mean ratings of benign intent, according to dispositional trust and communication condition*
Source: Tazelaar *et al.*, 2004, Experiment 2.

gratitude) have a bigger effect on trust than emotions that are characterised by personal control (pride and guilt) or situational control (sadness).

Some of Dunn and Schweitzer's studies elicited emotions in participants by asking them to write in detail about (a) things that might make them feel a particular emotion, and (b) a previous situation that had aroused that feeling. In another study, film clips were used to arouse emotions. After the emotion-induction procedure, participants made trust judgments about an unfamiliar co-worker or acquaintance. Across the studies, anger led to the lowest levels of trust whereas happiness and gratitude caused the highest levels of trust. However, pride and guilt (personal control emotions) appeared to have little effect on trust judgments. In these studies, the effect of emotions on trust appeared to be specific to individuals that the participants were not familiar with. When participants rated their trust in a person familiar to them they were unaffected by emotion (see Figure 14.3).

We have seen that communication can help overcome the problems caused by noise in social dilemmas. Other studies have found that cooperation is increased when group members are allowed to communicate (for a review see Sally, 1995). Various reasons have been proposed as to why communication increases cooperation, though Kerr and Kaufman-Gilliland (1994) concluded that only two explanations are supported. One explanation says

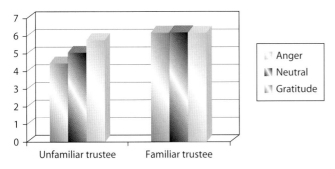

Figure 14.3. *Mean trust ratings for an unfamiliar or familiar student*

Source: Dunn & Schweitzer, 2005.

that communication promotes group solidarity, and the second explanation is that communication allows group members to express their commitment to mutually cooperate.

However, Wilson and Sell (1997) have pointed out that misleading communications could potentially decrease cooperation, if people do not live up to their promises. They conducted a public goods study which varied the ability of participants to announce how much they were going to contribute and the ability to see the past contributions of group members, thus giving rise to four conditions: (a) information about past investments only, (b) information about announcements only, (c) information about past investments and announcements, and (d) information about neither past investments nor announcements.

Wilson and Sell found that average group contributions were highest when there was no information at all and lowest when there was only one type of information available. Information about announcements and past behaviour did increase contributions, but not to the level of the no-information condition. At the start of the experiment, contributions were very high when both types of information were available, but this condition showed the strongest decline in contributions over the course of the experiment (declines also occurred in all other conditions).

More than half of the announcements (53.4 per cent) made by participants were 'lies'; that is, they did not contribute as much as they said they would. Participants contributed exactly what they had said they would in just 27.8 per cent of instances. However, in these latter cases, just over half the time (51.1 per cent) participants were signalling that they would contribute nothing. As Wilson and Sell pointed out, this is hardly the basis on which participants could build a set of cooperative strategies.[6]

Many tasks that have allowed communication between group members have nonetheless tried to keep them physically separate, with each person seated in front of a computer monitor and not easily able to see other people. We might expect that greater cooperation would occur if people were allowed to talk face to face, because nonverbal cues may be used to communicate cooperative intent. Indeed, this is what research indicates (Kurzban, 2001; Roth, 1995). One study has even reported that university staff contributed more money to an honesty box in their coffee room when a pair of eyes, rather than a control image, was displayed on a cupboard door above the box (Bateson *et al.*, 2006).

Scharlemann *et al.* (2001) found that greater cooperation was produced in a one-shot trust game involving strangers after participants saw a photograph of their partner smiling, as opposed to not smiling. Furthermore, whilst male participants were more cooperative towards female images, females were the least cooperative towards other females. Even more strongly predictive of cooperation than smiling was a rating of cooperativeness that a separate group of people had assigned to the images. In other words, people are more inclined to cooperate with people who others agree *look* cooperative.

COORDINATION

People are continually coordinating their behaviour. They manage to avoid bumping into each other (usually) on busy pavements, they behave in a fairly orderly way on underground trains, they arrange to meet friends, and so on. Airplanes take people from one place to another with very few collisions, companies provide the goods that meet customer demand, and so on. How do we manage to do these things so effectively?

'Chicken'

Game theorists have represented these kinds of problems in various games. A very well known game is called *chicken*. The game of chicken was made famous in the 1955 movie *Rebel Without a Cause*. In this film two teenage boys drive their cars towards the edge of a cliff, leaving it until the last moment before jumping out. The first person to jump out is considered 'chicken'. Subsequent movies involving tearaway teenagers showed the game of chicken as it is more often thought about; two teenagers drive cars towards each other (Poundstone, 1992). The first one to swerve away from the other is 'chicken'. Of course, you do not even need to get in a car to play chicken. Merely by turning down an invitation to play the game, you have *de facto* played the game and lost.

The game of chicken is shown in Table 14.3, where the payoffs are represented as points. The worst outcome for both is if both players drive straight, shown in the table as (−2, −2). This is considered to be mutual defection. There are two Nash equilibria in chicken, and these are shown in the top right-hand cell and bottom left-hand cell. Both involve one player driving straight and the other swerving. For example, if Player 1 drives straight then Player 2's payoff from swerving is −1. Player 2 can't improve on this by driving straight because that has a payoff of −2. Likewise, if Player 2 swerves, then Player 1 cannot improve on driving straight. Thus, this combination is an equilibrium point. The players' problem arises because there are two equilibria: how do they coordinate which of the two to settle for?

One way to play chicken is to convince your opponent that you are not going to swerve. You could do this through macho boasting, physical acts of machismo, or plain irrationality. Kahn (1965) suggested throwing bottles of whisky out of the car, wearing dark glasses to make it plain that you cannot see much, or

Table 14.3. *The game of chicken*

		Player 2	
		Swerve	*Drive straight*
Player 1	Swerve	0, 0	–1, 1
	Drive straight	1, –1	–2, –2

Table 14.4. *The free-rider problem as a chicken game*

		Player 2	
		Work hard	*Slack*
Player 1	Work hard	2, 2	1, 3
	Slack	3, 1	0, 0

throwing the steering wheel out of the car as you reach a high speed. Of course, if your opponent doesn't notice this, then you have a problem! Not for nothing has chicken been referred to as the 'prototypic dangerous game' (Colman & Wilson, 1997). Indeed, Colman and Wilson used chicken to show how evolutionary processes could give rise to antisocial personality disorder (APD). Briefly, his model showed that the payoff for a 'dangerous' strategy exceeded that for a 'cautious' strategy when the population contained a middling to high proportion of cautious players. However, whereas evolution appears to have equipped people to be both cooperative and non-cooperative in various degrees, depending on personality and circumstances, only about 2 per cent of the population exhibit APD.

By now, you may have realised that chicken is not just about driving cars. There are many situations where different parties confront each other and need to decide whether either of them is going to back down. One widely studied real-life situation is the Cuban missile crisis, briefly mentioned in the previous chapter. To recap: when it was discovered that the Soviet Union was in the process of installing nuclear missiles in Cuba, President Kennedy's military advisers wanted the USA to launch a preemptive military attack on Cuba. Kennedy's administration decided that this was too risky; however, in opting to seek a peaceful solution to the crisis they themselves risked looking weak. Therefore, the enforcement of a naval blockade around Cuba made the Soviet Union realise the need to agree a negotiated settlement, because suddenly the Kennedy administration looked tough, thereby raising the possibility that it *might* be willing to engage in military action.

This kind of brinkmanship occurs often in world affairs. Some leaders even make a public show of irrational behaviour. Of course, the danger is that neither side gives way, and escalation leads to the outcome that is worst for everybody. Few people realise just how close the Cuban missile crisis came to nuclear war. In 2002 it was revealed that a Soviet submarine had considered firing a nuclear-tipped torpedo, but one of the three officers involved in the decision prevented them from reaching the unanimity that was required to fire the missile (Dixit & Skeath, 2004, p.484).

Helping behaviour

Suppose the farmers on two neighbouring farms are putting up a fence between their properties, in order to prevent their livestock from wandering onto their neighbour's land. It is hard work, and each farmer is tempted to slack off a bit and let the other person do

the bulk of the work. This situation is shown in Table 14.4. It is actually a chicken game (I have simply added two points to each payoff in Table 14.3). The temptation for one person to slack off in a task like this is known as the *free-rider problem* or *social loafing*. Actually, when there are only two people involved one person is quite likely to notice if the other is slacking off. However, the chicken game, like other kinds of game, can involve multiple players.[7] When that is the case, it is harder to spot that any one individual is slacking off.

In some situations it is probably better to use the term *diffusion of responsibility* rather than 'free-riding', because the latter implies a slightly more malign intent, whereas that is not always the case with people who fail to act. Diffusion of responsibility occurs when there is ambiguity about who should provide help to someone in need of assistance. Experimental studies have found that help is less likely to be given as the number of potential helpers increases. In one study, people were less likely to assist someone who appeared to be having an epileptic seizure when there were other people present (Darley & Latané, 1968).

It should be noted that people often do go to the help of others and normally do give assistance to someone who is screaming. There are many factors that influence helping. These include noticing that something is wrong (which can depend on the nature of the event and how much of it was seen), the social norms that apply within the context, as well as the potential costs and rewards associated with helping (see Schroeder *et al.*, 1995). However, the fragility of helping behaviour in the face of situational factors is well documented, such as in the 'good Samaritan' study reported by Darley and Batson (1973). In this study, theological students who were in a hurry frequently failed to provide assistance to someone who appeared to be in distress. In some cases, they literally stepped over the man, who was slumped in the entrance to a building. For some people, a kind of 'cognitive narrowing' appeared to have occurred: they simply hadn't noticed the man. Other participants did appear to be concerned about the man but were also worried about letting down the person they were on their way to see.

An emotion that has often been linked to helping behaviour is *empathy*, an emotional reaction involving compassion, concern, and tenderness. It has been suggested that empathy is actually a selfish emotion, being based on a merging of images of the self and other person (Cialdini *et al.*, 1997). Nonetheless, strong feelings of empathy are more likely to lead to helping behaviour (e.g. Batson, 1998; Dovidio *et al.*, 1990). However, other research indicates that empathy only motivates helping in-group members, whereas helping out-group members is motivated by attraction. For instance, Krebs (1975) found that people experienced stronger physiological reactions and were more altruistic towards someone highly similar, as opposed to less similar, to themselves when that person showed signs of pain or pleasure during the course of a game.

There is evidence for in-group/out-group differences in the motivations for helping other people. Stürmer *et al.* (2005, Study 1) found differences in the motivations of homosexual and heterosexual HIV/AIDS volunteers who were assigned as a 'buddy/home helper' to a male client. Homosexual volunteers were more likely to view their clients as in-group members, but did not differ from heterosexuals in their perceptions of their clients' needs. For homosexual volunteers, measures of helping and time spent with the client were both predicted by empathy, but not by measures of attraction, such as liking and respect for their client, perceived friendliness of the client, and so on. For heterosexual volunteers the reverse was true: helping and time spent with the client were predicted by attraction but not by empathy. In fact, heterosexuals reported giving a higher level of practical help, on average. Heterosexuals also reported a longer duration of service, and this was predicted by attraction, not empathy. Empathy was a marginally significant predictor of service duration among homosexuals, but attraction had no predictive value.

Similar results were found in an experimental follow-up study. Participants who believed they were taking part in an internet communication study were more likely to indicate willingness to assist a partner who seemed distressed when that partner was of the same sex (in-group) as opposed to the opposite sex (out-group). For the in-group participants, helping intentions were predicted by empathy, but not by measures of interpersonal attraction, oneness, sadness, or distress. For the out-group participants, interpersonal attraction predicted stronger helping intentions. Also, higher levels of participant distress were associated with weaker helping intentions. Sadness and oneness had no predictive value.

Solving coordination problems through the use of conventions

For many repeated forms of interaction people have developed conventions that most people understand operate for the benefit of all. By internalising such conventions people are able to coordinate their activities in an effortless fashion. Consider public transport, such as buses and underground trains. Typically, you do not need to purchase a seat-specific ticket, nor do you need to enter into negotiations with other passengers as to where you can sit. The convention that everyone observes is *first come, first served* (FCFS).

In a series of studies, Milgram and his colleagues inadvertently found how deeply ingrained the FCFS convention is. For example, one study (reported in Milgram, 1977) found that New York subway commuters were often surprisingly willing to give up their seats in response to a request (68 per cent complied in one study). However, what was much harder than getting people to agree was

actually mustering the courage to ask them in the first place. The students involved felt anxiety, tension, and embarrassment, and often were unable to go through with asking the question.

Likewise, a study of people's responses to queue-jumping (Milgram *et al.*, 1986) produced significant effects on the people asked to do the jumping, many of whom

> procrastinated at length, often pacing nervously near the target area, spending as much as a half hour working up the 'nerve' to intrude. For some, the anticipation of intruding was so unpleasant that physical symptoms, such as pallor and nausea, accompanied intrusions. (1986, p.686)

What these findings show is not merely that conventions exist, but that we internalise them. Indeed, the queue itself has been described as a 'social system' (Mann, 1969; Schmitt *et al.*, 1992). Evidence suggests that people's objections to queue-jumping are less to do with the costs to themselves, which might be a negligible loss of seconds or a couple of minutes, and more to do with moral outrage at the violation of norms and values on which the queue is based. As listed by Schmitt *et al.* (1992, p.806), these include egalitarianism, orderliness, principles of fairness, and duties of justice. If people's objections to intrusions into queues *were* based on the costs to themselves, then it should not matter whether a five-minute delay is caused by someone who pushes in front of you or by a service provider, such as a museum security guard, who delays you right by the entrance because he only allows in a certain number of people every five minutes. In a series of studies, Schmitt *et al.* showed that people are much more bothered by the former than the latter.[8]

SUMMARY

Human interaction is sometimes analysed using game theory. This predicts how rational people acting in their own interests would behave, assuming that the people they are interacting with are also rational and share common knowledge of the situation. Behavioural game theory is concerned with explaining how people actually behave, which is sometimes different from the predictions of analytical game theory.

Examples of 'games' analysed by researchers are the ultimatum game, the prisoner's dilemma, and the public goods game. In the latter two, there is a conflict between individual and collective rationality. Many real-life situations involve such tensions, as with the collective need to reduce fishing catches and the interest of the individual fishing boats in maximising their catch.

There is evidence that people do not always fully think through the possible consequences of their actions on social dilemmas. However, inducing them to think more (for example about other people's strategic options) does not seem to help. Indeed, one task found that people behaved more fairly when they thought less.

A considerable body of research shows that variation in responding is related to motivational factors, such as fear or greed, and social value orientation (prosociality, individualism, or competitiveness). Some of the largest variations in responding on the ultimatum game have been observed between cultures. There is evidence that the degree of cooperativeness within a culture is related to economic success.

Trust, generosity, and communication have been shown to be important factors influencing cooperation in laboratory dilemmas. In particular, these can prevent defections occurring when responses are disrupted by noise (i.e. erroneous responses that were not intended by the actor).

Other interactions (also represented in games) involve coordination of behaviour between people. A 'prototypic dangerous game' is *chicken*, which involves a stand-off between two or more people. Each person wishes to follow a different strategy from the other person. A person may attempt to influence another by way of various signals, such as acting tough. It has been suggested that the recurrence of real-life chicken situations

throughout history has caused the evolution of antisocial personality disorder.

Chicken can also be used to model situations of mutual helping behaviour, in which one or more parties are tempted to free-ride if their behaviour cannot easily be observed. In other situations, where a person in distress may need assistance, diffusion of responsibility may be a better term to use – where other potential helpers are involved, individuals are more likely to hold back from giving assistance where there is ambiguity as to who is responsible for doing so. Social psychology research has also identified various other factors that influence the incidence of helping behaviour.

In general, the existence of conventions helps people to solve a range of coordinations. This chapter has looked at the conventions that people hold in relation to seating and queuing, and has shown the depth of feeling that people have about threats to those conventions.

QUESTIONS

1. Think of a real-life situation – other than those mentioned in this chapter – that could be represented as a prisoner's dilemma or a resource dilemma. Show this in the form of a diagram.

2. Discuss the idea that people might be more cooperative in social dilemmas if they were to try and imagine things from the other party's point of view.

3. What is the weakness of Tit-For-Tat as a driver of cooperative behaviour and how can this be overcome?

4. Does it pay to always be nice?

5. Why does our memory for other people matter in relation to social dilemmas? What would it be like if we were unable to create new memories of our social interactions?

6. Design an experiment to examine the impact of in-group/out-group identification on helping behaviour.

7. What is the chicken game?

NOTES

1. 'Best' is not quite the right word, but I will address this concept more accurately when we get to it.

2. Some studies pay all participants, whereas other studies pay two or more randomly chosen Proposer–Responder pairs.

3. For more on the evolutionary implications see also Dawkins, 1976[2006], Chapter 12.

4. This will be discussed further in Chapter 15.

5. Of course, in real life we can usually just withdraw from contact with a person who 'defects'.

6. An interesting variation on the public goods game, involving competition both within and between groups, has been reported by Goren and Bornstein (2000).

7. To keep things simple I am not showing the game representations of multi-person situations, but I refer the interested reader to Dixit and Skeath (2004).

8. For a fascinating study of behaviour in very long queues, see Brady (2002).

RECOMMENDED READING

Poundstone, W. (1992). *Prisoner's dilemma*. Oxford: Oxford University Press. William Poundstone describes the development of game theory, and its application to the Cold War and to public policy.

Ridley, M. (1996). *The origins of virtue*. New York: Viking Press/Penguin Books. Matt Ridley explains how our positive moral instincts arose from evolution.

Surowiecki, J. (2004). *The wisdom of crowds: Why the many are smarter than the few*. London: Little, Brown. This book, recommended in Chapter 13, also contains material relevant to this chapter.

15 Intuition, Reflective Thinking, and the Brain

CHAPTER OUTLINE

Before reading any further, try and answer the following questions (from Frederick, 2005):

1. A bat and ball cost $1.10 in total. The bat costs $1 more than the ball. How much does the ball cost? _____ cents

2. If it takes 5 machines 5 minutes to make 5 widgets, how long would it take 100 machines to make 100 widgets? _____ minutes

3. In a lake, there is a patch of lily pads. Every day, the patch doubles in size. If it takes 48 days for the patch to cover the entire lake, how long would it take for the patch to cover half of the lake? _____ days

INTRODUCTION

Throughout the various chapters of this book we have reviewed evidence that people do not always follow normative principles in their judgments and decisions. In this chapter I explore the idea that the heuristics that people use in order to arrive at their judgments are the outcome of intuitive processes inaccessible to introspection. In doing so, I shall look at individual differences in intelligence and tendency to reflect on problems. This leads on to an exploration of the idea that there are two systems for thinking, one intuitive and one reflective. I shall then look at the evidence that indicates that people lack insight into their own underlying cognitive processes, including their tendency to rationalise their judgments.

In the final section, I shall look at the neuroscience perspective on rationality. This includes looking at hemispheric differences in relation to intuition and reflection, as well as looking at the brain areas involved in implicit learning and monitoring conflicting items of information. I also look at the role of emotion in decision making.

INTELLIGENCE AND THE INTUITIVE–REFLECTIVE DISTINCTION

The fundamental computation bias

Stanovich (1999) has proposed that people have a *fundamental computational bias*, whereby they automatically tend to perceive the full context of a problem. However, the contextual details sometimes lead people to underappreciate the most relevant parts of a problem. Higher levels of intelligence are associated with the ability to decontextualise problems, that is, to abstract structural form from the content and context within which they are embedded, thus enabling the identification of relevant rules and principles. Accordingly, Stanovich and West (2000) proposed that the examination of cognitive ability differences on judgment and decision problems could help inform the discussion of what is normative on a given task.

For example, some authors (e.g. Hilton, 1995) have argued that the participants in experiments often interpret problems in ways unintended by the experimenters. The experimental materials may contain *conversational implicatures*, whereby readers are invited to draw inferences beyond the information that is stated. Thus, participants' responses can be seen as rational in the context of their interpretations. However, on many judgment tasks, as well as reasoning and decision-making tasks, individuals of higher cognitive ability tend to behave more in accordance with normative rules, which may be taken to cast doubt on the conversational account (Stanovich & West, 2000). Stanovich and West arrived at this conclusion on the basis of a series of studies in which the task performance of American university students was examined in relation to their SAT (Scholastic Aptitude Test) scores (SATs correlate highly with measures of general intelligence (*g*)).

An example of a judgment task where individual differences are found is the Linda problem, discussed in Chapter 3. There we saw that people who had read a description of 'Linda' as a socially concerned individual subsequently indicated that she was more likely to be a *feminist and a bank teller* than she was to be *a bank teller*, thus violating the conjunction rule of probability theory. Stanovich and West (1998) found that the 29/150 (19 per cent) people who did *not* violate the conjunction rule had an SAT score 82 points higher on average than the 121/150 (81 per cent) people who did violate the rule.

Cognitive reflection

Reflection leading to more normative outcomes It could be argued that more intelligent individuals perform better on judgment tasks without engaging in more reflection; maybe they create a different initial representation of problems or have a greater store of knowledge to call upon. One way to determine whether better task performance is due to greater reflection is by comparing the response times for correct and incorrect responders. On the Linda problem and the 'Bill' problem (a similar conjunction task), De Neys (2006) found that correct responses were indeed associated with longer response times than conjunction errors. Another way to examine the role of reflection is to make it harder for people to engage in thinking. De Neys also found that requiring participants to carry out a secondary task while reasoning, such as tapping their fingers in a particular sequence or holding a pattern of dots in the memory, led to more conjunction errors being made.

In another study Selart *et al.* (2006) found that people who make more normative responses on judgment tasks tend to engage in more information searching on multiattribute choice tasks.

Also, on resource allocation tasks and prisoner's dilemma tasks people appear to behave more in accordance with game theory predictions – i.e. self-interestedly – when they are prompted to take the other side's perspective (Caruso *et al.*, 2006; Epley *et al.*, 2006), whereas they behave less in accordance with game theory predictions – i.e. cooperatively – when their capacity for thinking is reduced (Roch *et al.*, 2000; see Chapter 14 for more on these studies). Reducing people's capacity for thought also leads them to rely more on their feelings when making judgments about risks (Finucane *et al.*, 2000).

Other evidence has been produced by Frederick (2005), who developed the *cognitive reflection test* (CRT). The CRT is intended to identify individual differences in the extent to which people engage in reflective, rather than intuitive, thinking. It consists of the three questions that are listed at the start of this chapter:[1] each of these problems tends to elicit a particular intuitive response that accounts for the majority of errors (the intuitive responses are 10 cents, 100 minutes, and 24 days). The correct responses are 5 cents, 5 minutes, and 47 days. Frederick obtained responses to the CRT from several student samples at different American universities, as well as from members of the general public in Boston, and from respondents in two online studies. He noted that correct answers were sometimes given after the intuitive answer had been crossed out, but never vice versa, supporting the notion that the task measures reflective thinking. People who scored high on the CRT were also more likely to select the delayed response in hypothetical choices between immediate or delayed rewards, but this finding was strongest where the delayed reward was next month or next year. Differences were smaller or non-existent where the delayed reward was in 10 years' time, or where the delayed reward was to be paid in instalments over a period of years. The relationship between CRT score and time preference was more pronounced for women than for men (Figure 15.1 shows the results from one of Frederick's problems).

The least reflective people also believed themselves to be more impulsive than the average person, whereas the most reflective believed themselves to be slightly less impulsive. Consistent with this, the least reflective were willing to pay more on average for the overnight shipping of a chosen book ($4.54) than were the most reflective ($2.18).

Frederick also found that high CRT scores were associated with more selections of the risky (gain) option over sure things of lower expected value. However, other results suggested that the high-

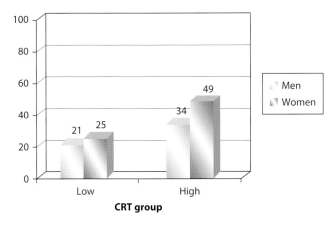

Figure 15.1a. *Cognitive reflection and decision making: percentage of participants choosing $140 next year rather than $100 this year*

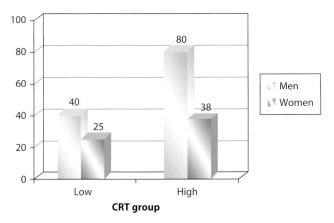

Figure 15.1b. *Cognitive reflection and decision making: percentage of participants choosing a 15% chance of $1,000,000 rather than $500 for sure*

CRT respondents were not computing expected value when they made these choices: when the risky option had a *lower* expected value this was less often chosen by all participants, but nonetheless the high-CRT respondents were still more likely to choose this than were the low-CRT group. For problems involving losses, the high-CRT respondents were more likely to select the sure loss than were the low-CRT respondents.

In contrast to the time preference problems, for the risky choice tasks the relationship between CRT and type of response was stronger for men than for women (one example is shown in Figure 15.1b). That is, men were more likely to choose the risky option, but especially so in the high-CRT group.

Frederick found that CRT correlated with various other measures of motivation and ability. However, CRT was the only test that showed a relationship with all four domains of choice (intertemporal choice, gain-domain gambles where the expected value favoured the gamble, gain domain gambles where the

expected value favoured the sure gain, and gambles where the expected value favoured the sure loss). Nonetheless, the sex differences that were observed with CRT were also observed with the other cognitive measures.

Reflection leading to non-normative outcomes We have seen evidence that people often behave more in accordance with normative theories when they engage in reflective thinking. However, on other types of task this is not always the case. A number of studies have been reported in which people made worse choices when they were asked to give reasons for their choices. For example, one study asked people to rate the taste of five brands of strawberry jam (Wilson & Schooler, 1991). Prior to giving their ratings, some participants were also asked to write down reasons for their liking or disliking each jam, ostensibly to help organise their thoughts, and with the understanding that they would not need to hand in their reasons to the experimenter (hence any effects could not be attributed to concerns about accountability).

People who gave reasons for their judgments gave different overall ratings from the no-reasons control group. In addition, the preference orderings of the reasons group were more discrepant from those of experts as published in the journal *Consumer Reports*.

Another study asked female students to rate their liking for two art posters and three humorous posters (Wilson *et al.*, 1993), and to then choose one to take home. Analysing reasons led to a reduction in liking for the art posters and an increase in liking for the humorous posters (Figure 15.2a). At the end of the semester the students were phoned at home and asked a series of questions to determine overall post-choice satisfaction with their poster. Questions included whether they had hung the poster on the wall and whether they planned to keep it when they left college for the summer. Students who had analysed reasons in the earlier part of the study were now less satisfied with their posters, but particularly those who had chosen a humorous poster. The most satisfied students were control-group participants who had chosen an art poster (Figure 15.2b).

In other studies, Wilson *et al.* (1989) had found that analysing reasons did not reduce people's confidence in their preferences, so this would not appear to explain their results. Rather, Wilson and his colleagues assume that people's likes and dislikes are often quite intuitive and hard to articulate. This may particularly be the case with something like art. It is easy to say why one likes a humorous poster. Thus, when asked to give reasons for one's liking of posters, it is easier to do so for the humorous posters and this affects one's overall judgment of liking. However, the feature of a humorous poster that is easy to articulate may have little bearing on how much one likes it over a longer period. In short, introspecting on reasons may disrupt the intuitive processes that underlie certain choices.

The disruptive effects of introspection have even been observed on a prediction task. Halberstadt and Levine (1999) asked self-described basketball experts to make predictions about the outcomes of games: some gave reasons for their predictions and some did not. Over 16 predictions, reasoners picked the winning team 65 per cent of the time, compared to 70 per cent for non-reasoners, a small but statistically significant difference. Reasoners' estimated

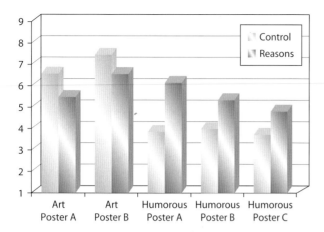

Figure 15.2a. *The effect of reasons on pre-choice liking and post-choice satisfaction: reported pre-choice liking of the posters. 1 = dislike very much; 9 = like very much*

Source: Wilson *et al.*, 1993.

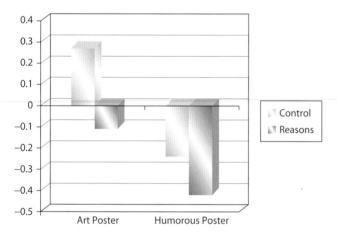

Figure 15.2b. *The effect of reasons on pre-choice liking and post-choice satisfaction: post-choice satisfaction with the posters (adjusted for pre-choice liking)*
The scores are the mean of five measures and have been standardised.

Source: Wilson *et al.*, 1993.

margins of victory were also more discrepant from the actual point spreads and further from the Las Vegas point spreads.

Other studies have shown that preferences and choice behaviour can become more accurate when people are *prevented* from even consciously thinking. Betsch *et al.* (2001, Experiment 1) asked participants to view a series of pictorial adverts on a computer screen while being distracted by information about five different shares. Participants were told that the study concerned the ability to memorise adverts while being distracted, hence they were to concentrate on the adverts. In fact, it was the participants' implicit processing of the share information that was of interest. During the course of displaying this distracting information,

15 returns were reported for each share, such that the sum of their returns was, respectively, 300, 400, 500, 600, and 700 Deutschmarks (DM).[2]

Following the presentation of the adverts and distracting share information, participants completed 30 multiple-choice questions about the adverts in order to maintain the credibility of the cover story and to extinguish any concrete memories about individual share returns. Finally, participants were asked to estimate the sum and the average of the share returns, and also to indicate their attitude to the shares on a rating scale running from −5 (very bad) to +5 (very good). Estimates of the total and average share returns bore no relationship to the true values. However, the average attitude scores for the 300, 400, 500, 600, and 700 DM shares were, respectively, 0.05, 0.44, 0.77, 1.25, and 2.20. In other words, participants' implicitly formed attitudes accurately tracked the values of the shares, whereas their attempts to explicitly estimate their values were wholly inaccurate.

How can value information be processed accurately, apparently at an unconscious level, but not consciously? In Chapter 1, I noted that this possibility was foreseen by Herbert Simon's paper on the limitations of human decision making: 'we cannot, of course, rule out the possibility that the unconscious is a better decision-maker than the conscious' (1955, p.104). Nørretranders (1998) has estimated the capacity for conscious processing as 40–60 bits per second, but the capacity of the entire cognitive system as about 11,200,000 bits. Although one should probably be a little cautious about accepting these particular figures, nonetheless they indicate that the unconscious has massive processing capacity.

On the basis that the capacity for conscious information processing appears to be quite limited relative to the capacity of the unconscious, Dijksterhuis *et al.* (2006) predicted that conscious thought should lead to better choices being made on simple tasks but worse choices on complex tasks. Results supported this prediction. For instance, in Study 1 participants were asked to read information about four hypothetical cars, one of which was superior by virtue of its balance of positive and negative attributes. Some people were presented with four attributes of each car (simple condition) and others with 12 attributes (complex condition). In a conscious thought condition the participants were asked to think about the cars for four minutes before making their choice. In an unconscious thought condition participants completed a distracter task (anagrams). As predicted, the superior car was chosen more frequently in the simple condition by conscious thinkers, whereas it was chosen more frequently in the complex condition by unconscious thinkers.

TWO SYSTEMS FOR THINKING?

The rational soul, as it were presiding, beholds the images and impressions presented by the sensitive soul, as in a looking-glass, and according to the conceptions and notions drawn from these, exercises the acts of reason, judgment, and will. (Thomas Willis, 17th-century scientist and philosopher, cited in Zimmer, 2005)

Table 15.1. *Dual processes of thinking*

Intuitive	Reflective
Processes and properties	
Associative	Rule-based
Holistic, heuristic	Analytic
Automatic	Controlled
Rapid, parallel	Slow, serial
Requires little cognitive capacity	Demanding of cognitive capacity
Acquisition by biology, exposure, and personal experience	Acquisition by cultural and formal tuition
Content on which processes act	
Affective	Neutral
Causal propensities	Statistics
Concrete, specific	Abstract
Prototypes	Sets

Source: Based on Kahneman & Frederick, 2002; Stanovich & West, 2000.

System 1 and System 2

Many psychologists argue that intuitive and reflective thinking are carried out by distinct psychological systems (a list of various proposals is given in Stanovich & West, 2000, p.659). Theorists often refer to these, respectively, as System 1 and System 2. System 1 is said to be fast and effortless, and most likely involving parallel processes,[3] whereas System 2 is slow, effortful, and involves serial processing (Table 15.1). A version of dual-process theory proposed by Evans (1989; see also Wason & Evans, 1975) suggested that the reflective system essentially constructed rationalisations for conclusions that had been reached by the intuitive system.[4] Other versions of dual-process theory (including subsequent proposals by Evans; see Evans, 2006; Evans & Over, 1996) allow the reflective system greater scope to check and overrule the output from the intuitive system.

Note that the kinds of thoughts that we call intuitions may be based on experience or may be part of our genetic inheritance (or a combination of both). Thus, an experienced firefighter in a burning building may develop an intuition that leads him to evacuate his team, although he may find himself unable to immediately articulate exactly what the danger is.[5] This kind of intuition is the result of exposure to similar instances in training or in other real-life situations. However, there is evidence that evolution has prepared people and other organisms to more easily acquire some intuitions than others. For instance, the most predominant types of phobias are those where the object of fear would have posed some danger to the earliest humans. Cage-reared monkeys develop a fear of snakes after a single exposure to a film in which a monkey responds fearfully to a snake. However, they do not develop a similar fear of flowers after viewing a film in which a monkey responds fearfully to a flower (Cook & Mineka, 1990; Mineka & Cook, 1993).

According to Haidt (e.g. 2001) moral judgments are also largely based on intuition, with analytical thinking frequently relegated to the role of post hoc justification. This can lead to *moral dumbfounding*, whereby people continue to feel that something is morally wrong even though their objections have been refuted. Reasoning is more likely to occur in fairly impersonal situations, where the consequences of one's actions feel more distant, or when a person experiences conflicting intuitions. Consider the following scenario:

> A runaway trolley is headed for five people who will be killed if it proceeds on its present course. You are standing next to a large stranger on a footbridge that spans the tracks, in between the oncoming trolley and the five people. The only way to save the five people is to push this stranger off the bridge, onto the tracks below. Ought you to save the five others by pushing this stranger to his death?

This is a problem where utility maximisation (saving five people from death) conflicts with personal morality (killing a person). On this and similar *personal* moral dilemmas, Greene *et al.* (2001) found that people took longer to respond when judging the personal moral violation to be appropriate.

The same study also presented people with some *impersonal* dilemmas in which the available course of action was not 'up close and personal', as in the previous dilemma. The dilemmas included a version of the trolley problem in which the five people can be saved by throwing a switch that will divert the trolley onto a different track. However, the trolley will still kill one person who happens to be wandering on this other track. On these types of dilemma people are much more willing to take the utilitarian action (throwing the switch, in the case of the trolley problem), and response times do not differ according to the action taken.

In this study and a subsequent replication (Greene *et al.*, 2004), fMRI scanning showed that the impersonal dilemmas mainly engaged brain areas associated with working memory and other cognitive processes. Personal dilemmas, on the other hand, engaged brain regions associated with both cognitive and emotional processing. In particular, the personal dilemmas activated the anterior cingulate cortex (ACC), a region known to be involved in the monitoring of conflict and recruitment of control processes (see the section *Neuroscience perspective*, below). Furthermore, within the personal dilemmas ACC activity was higher on the more difficult problems, as defined by the longer response time on these. On these harder problems, Greene *et al.* also observed greater activity in the dorsolateral prefrontal cortex, a region involved in abstract reasoning and cognitive control.

It may be that cognitive processes actually lie on a continuum between the intuitive and reflective, as proposed in Hammond's (1996) *cognitive continuum theory*. In this theory, the nature of the cognitive process depends on the nature of the task at hand. When people feel that it would be irresponsible to rely on their intuition to solve a task they shift towards a more analytical mode of thought. However, they may also shift in the opposite direction if the results of analytical thinking conflict with their intuitions.

The theory of intuitive confidence

Simmons and Nelson (2006) proposed that the very ease with which intuitions spring to mind leads people to hold them with high confidence. Such an account explains why even highly motivated and able decision makers may rely on their intuitions, a fact that cannot be explained by the social psychological dual-process models (the heuristic-systematic model and the elaboration likelihood model – see Chapter 5). Based on the notion of intuitive confidence Simmons and Nelson developed a series of hypotheses (2006, p.411):

1. *Intuitive bias hypothesis.* Because intuitions are often held with high confidence, people will choose intuitive options more frequently than equally valid nonintuitive options.

2. *Constraint magnitude hypothesis.* People will choose intuitive options less frequently when constraint information seems to more strongly favour a nonintuitive option.

3. *Intuitive confidence hypothesis.* People will choose intuitive options more frequently when they are more confident in their intuitions.

4. *Intuitive betrayal hypothesis.* People who betray their intuitions will feel less confident in their choices than people who choose in line with their intuitions.

Simmons and Nelson realised that spread-betting markets would provide a good test of these hypotheses. They gave the following example. Suppose the perenially dominant Baltimore Ravens are to play the comically weaker Washington Redskins in a National Football League game. A bookmaker offers a point spread of 14 points in favour of the Ravens. This means that if you bet on the Ravens, you will only win if they win by a margin of more than 14 points, although your reward will increase with each extra point scored above the spread. Alternatively, if you bet on the Redskins then you will be rewarded if the Ravens win by less than 14 points or if the Redskins win. The key point to note is that the bookmaker's spread essentially places both teams on an equal footing in betting terms. Even though the Ravens are the better team, there is no advantage to betting on them rather than the Redskins, because the 14-point spread eliminates the effect of the Ravens' superiority to the bettor.

However, in studies of real-life online betting markets, as well as experimental betting markets played for real money, Simmons and Nelson found that people more frequently bet on the favourite, thus supporting the intuitive bias hypothesis. Secondly, people's tendency to bet on the favourite declined as the size of the spread increased, consistent with the constraint magnitude hypothesis. Thirdly, as intuitive confidence increased people became more likely to bet on the favourite and to place more money on the favourite. In the studies of online betting, intuitive confidence was estimated from the proportion of people simply betting on the favourite rather than betting against the spread. In the experimental betting studies, participants were asked to rate their confidence in their predictions. Fourth, when people bet on the underdog they tended to bet less money, consistent with the intuitive betrayal hypothesis.

Simmons and Nelson also conducted betting studies in which participants were invited to set their own spreads. Having set their own spreads, people still preferred to bet on favourites than underdogs. Again, the number of people betting on favourites was correlated with intuitive confidence. However, introducing uncertainty into the situation, even irrelevant uncertainty (such as not knowing what time the game would start or presenting the task details in a poor-quality font), reduced the preference for the favourite. For example, 78 per cent of participants predicted the favourite to win when they knew what time the game would begin, as compared to just 54 per cent when the game's start time was not known.

SELF-INSIGHT IN JUDGMENT AND DECISION MAKING

The confabulation of reasons in normal people

Nisbett and Wilson (1977) argued that people's retrospective verbal accounts of their behaviour are actually theories about their behaviour, constructed after the event. These theories may be correct, but sometimes they are not.

Nisbett and Wilson described an earlier study by Nisbett and Schacter (1966) in which participants were asked to take a series of electric shocks of steadily increasing intensity. Prior to taking these shocks, some participants were administered a placebo pill. They were told that this pill would 'produce heart palpitations, breathing irregularities, hand tremors, and butterflies in the stomach. These are the physical symptoms most often reported by subjects as accompanying the experience of electric shock' (Nisbett & Wilson, 1977, p.237).

It was expected that these participants would be willing to take more shock on the basis that they believed the pill, not the shock, was the cause of their symptoms. And indeed they did accept more shock than people who were not administered the pill (and accompanying instructions). However, during a thorough debriefing procedure only three of 12 participants attributed their symptoms of arousal to the pill. When questioned as to why they thought they had taken more shock than average, participants gave reasons such as 'Gee, I don't really know . . . Well, I used to build radios and stuff when I was 13 or 14, and maybe I got used to electric shock' (1977, p.237)

When participants were told of the experimental hypothesis regarding the attribution of symptoms, the participants typically said that they thought this was a very interesting idea and that many people would probably go through the process described, but that they themselves had not.

Nisbett and Wilson identified a similar lack of insight in several other studies, and in their own experiments that – unlike the earlier studies – had been specifically designed to investigate this issue. The study which the authors themselves regarded as the most 'remarkable' involved participants viewing a teacher being interviewed about teaching practices and the philosophy of education: 'Half the subjects saw the teacher answering the questions in a pleasant, agreeable, and enthusiastic way (warm condition). The other half saw an autocratic martinet, rigid, intolerant, and distrustful of his students (cold condition)' (1977, p.244).

When asked to rate the likeability of the teacher, the participants unsurprisingly rated the warm teacher as more likeable than the cold teacher. The participants were also asked to rate the attributes of appearance, speech, and mannerisms. *These attributes did not actually vary between conditions.* However, the participants rated each attribute as attractive in the warm condition but irritating in the cold condition. Some participants were also asked if their liking or disliking of the teacher had affected their judgments of the teacher's appearance, speech, and mannerisms, whereas other participants were asked about the reverse causal direction; that is, whether these attributes had affected their liking or disliking of the teacher.

Participants in both the warm and cold conditions denied that their liking or disliking of the teacher had affected their attribute ratings. In the warm condition, participants also did not believe that their liking of the attributes had affected their overall liking. However, in the cold condition participants claimed that their disliking of the teacher's appearance, speech, and mannerisms *had* caused them to dislike the teacher more overall. In short, these participants inverted the true causal relationship. Their ratings of the teacher's attributes had been affected by their overall liking of the teacher, but they themselves claimed that it was their assessment of the teacher's attributes that had affected their overall liking.

Nisbett and Wilson proposed that people's verbal accounts of their behaviour are increasingly likely to be erroneous when:

- the verbal report becomes increasingly distant from the event in question (because relevant factors are forgotten or become less available, and an individual may inadvertently invent plausible causes of behaviour);
- judgments are affected by certain 'mechanical' factors, such as anchoring effects, serial order effects, contrast effects, and position effects (for example one study found that shoppers preferred items at the right-hand end of an array, but were unaware of this fact);
- a questioner draws attention to contextual factors that an individual might otherwise not have considered;
- the non-occurrence of an event is the influential factor (because occurrences are more salient and available to memory);
- nonverbal behaviours affect our judgments of others people (because explanations will tend to draw upon verbal memory, which will more strongly encode verbal behaviours);
- there is a mismatch between the size of a cause and the size of an effect.

In essence, Nisbett and Wilson argued that what people are aware of are the products of their thought processes, not the processes themselves.

More recently, Wilson (2002) has modified his earlier view, proposing that people may have insight into the causes of their behaviours where those behaviours were consciously willed.

However, Wegner (2002) has argued that our experience of conscious will is essentially an illusion. When we perform some action our experience is that we made this happen by an act of conscious will. However, Wegner argues that both the action and the experience of willing it had separate causes at an unconscious level. It is possible that there is also an unconscious path between the unconscious cause of the experience of will and the unconscious cause of action. However, what we experience is an *apparent* causal path between experienced will and action, which may or may not bear a relationship to some possible pathway between the two unconscious causes.

Wegner reviews a wealth of historical phenomena and fascinating research studies that are consistent with this model. In one study (Wegner & Wheatley, 1999) two people sat opposite each other, wearing headphones, with their fingertips placed on a 12cm-square board that was mounted on a computer mouse. One of these two people was, in fact, a confederate of the experimenter; the other was a genuine participant. For about 30 seconds or so, the two individuals moved the mouse around, thus moving the cursor on the screen among about 50 small objects. After they had moved the cursor around for this time, the genuine participant would hear a ten-second clip of music through the headphones, which acted as a cue that he or she should shortly stop moving the cursor. During this period the participant would also hear a word spoken (e.g. *swan*). On the basis of some practice trials, during which the participant and confederate were asked to say what word they had heard, the participant believed that the confederate was hearing a different word. In fact, the confederate either heard no word at all or heard an explicit instruction to stop the cursor on a particular object (e.g. the *swan*). In the latter case, the participant heard the relevant word either 30 seconds before, 5 seconds before, 1 second before, or 1 second after the confederate stopped the cursor on the object.

After each stop, the participant and confederate would rate how much they had intended to make that stop. Of course, on some trials the participants had not caused the stop at all. Nonetheless, when they heard the key word 30 seconds before the stop, they rated their intention to cause it at nearly 45 per cent. This rose to just over 60 per cent when they heard the word 5 seconds or 1 second before the stop, and dropped to just over 45 per cent when they heard the word 1 second after the stop. Wegner reports that in post-experimental interviews the participants often reported having searched the screen for the item that they had heard through the headphones. Possibly this may have contributed to the feeling that they had intended, to some extent, to cause the stop. In other situations, the reverse of this phenomenon can occur; that is, people may attribute the cause of an action to another person, whereas in fact they have caused it themselves (see Wegner, 2002).

The confabulation of reasons in surgical or brain-damaged patients

Before looking at some evidence for such processes of rationalisation in normal individuals, let us first look at how this occurs in certain particular types of patients. Split-brain patients are people who have had the brain's two hemispheres disconnected by cutting through the corpus callosum, the bundle of nerve fibres that connect the hemispheres. This operation is sometimes performed on people who suffer badly from epilepsy, in order to prevent a seizure that begins in one hemisphere from spreading to the other hemisphere. Researchers have been particularly interested in how such patients perceive visual stimuli when they are prevented from moving their head or eyes. This is because the structure of the visual system is such that stimuli in the left visual field impinge on the right side of each retina and are processed in the right hemisphere, whereas stimuli in the right visual field impinge on the left side of each retina and are processed in the left hemisphere. What happens when the two hemispheres cannot communicate with each other?

In experimental studies, split-brain patients are unable to repeat back words that are flashed to the right hemisphere only (in such studies, the participant stares at a fixation point on a screen and the word is flashed to the left or the right side of this point). However, if the word is the name of an object sitting in front of them on the table, then the participant is able to point to that object with their left hand (which is controlled by the right side of the brain). Although the extent of hemispheric specialisation can be overemphasised, in general the right hemisphere seems to be more visually 'intelligent' whereas the left seems to be more involved in linguistic processing and in higher-level cognitive processes (Corballis, 2003).

In relation to the way we attach meaning to the world we perceive, Gazzaniga (2000) has suggested that the left hemisphere behaves as an 'interpreter'. In another set of studies, split-brain patients were shown different pictures to the left and right side of the fixation point. In front of them, on the left side of the table was a set of pictures and the participants had to use their left hand to point to the picture that bore some relationship to the picture on the left of the screen. Likewise, on the right-hand side of the table they had to point to a picture that related to the picture on the right side of the screen. When asked why they had chosen these two pictures, the left hemisphere invented reasons. For instance, Patient P.S. picked out a picture of a shovel on the left of the table that matched a snowy scene on the left of the fixation point. He also picked a picture of a chicken's head on the right of the table that matched a chicken's claw shown to the right of the fixation point. When asked why he had chosen these two pictures he said: 'Oh, that's simple. The chicken claw goes with the chicken, and you need a shovel to clean out the chicken shed.'

Another example concerns the phenomenon of *probability matching*. Suppose you are asked to predict, across a long series of trials, whether a blue card or a red card is about to appear. If blue actually occurs 70 per cent of the time and red 30 per cent of the time, then the best thing to do – once you have realised that blue is much more frequent – is to predict blue on every trial. In fact, people engage in probability matching; that is, they predict blue on 70 per cent of the trials and red on 30 per cent of the trials. However, with split-brain patients, *when the stimuli are flashed to their right hemisphere* their performance on the task begins to approach the optimal level. By contrast, when the stimuli are flashed to the left hemisphere the patients probability match. In this latter

case, just like normal participants they appear to be attempting to develop complicated hypotheses about the task (Wolford *et al.*, 2000).

Similar evidence has been reported for stroke patients. When patients have a stroke in one hemisphere of the brain, they sometimes experience paralysis in the opposite side of their body. However, when the stroke is in the right hemisphere, such patients occasionally deny that there is any problem or, alternatively, they may confabulate reasons as to why they cannot perform certain actions. For instance, Ramachandran asked patients to perform certain actions, such as clapping their hands or touching their nose with their left hand. When asked why they had not complied, these patients would say that they *had* performed the action, or would invent a reason why they had not, such as the fact that they had already helped out the experimenter with other tasks and were getting tired or bored (Ramachandran & Blakeslee, 1998).

A NEUROSCIENCE PERSPECTIVE ON RATIONALITY

Intuitive versus reflective judgment

There are, of course, many brain structures involved in judgment, decision making, and other cognitive activities, and this section will not attempt to document all that has been discovered in this rapidly developing area of research.[6] However, I shall briefly discuss some areas of the brain that have a bearing on the distinction between intuitive and reflective thinking.

Hemispheric differences Earlier, we saw that the brain's left hemisphere acts as an 'interpreter'. In fact, it has also been proposed that the left hemisphere is responsible for maintaining a stable representation of one's body image, whereas the right hemisphere is responsible for detecting anomalies in one's self-image and updating this image as appropriate (Ramachandran, 1995; Ramachandran & Blakeslee, 1998). Other evidence indicates that the role of the two hemispheres in creating representations goes beyond merely that of self-image. For instance, Drake (1991) found that spoken arguments presented to the left ear (thus giving a right-hemisphere advantage) were better recalled if the participants disagreed with the argument, whereas arguments presented to the right ear (left-hemisphere advantage) were better recalled if the participants agreed with the argument. Likewise, Rausch (1977) found that patients with right temporal lobectomies were resistant to information that disconfirmed a hypothesis that they held to be true – that is, they continued to believe in the incorrect hypothesis. However, patients with left temporal lobectomies often changed their hypotheses in the light of new information, even when their original hypotheses were correct. Such studies support the idea that the right hemisphere is involved in the updating of events, but may do so too readily if there is no balancing contribution from the left hemisphere.

Other evidence for such hemispheric processing differences has been reviewed by Jasper and Christman (2005), who proposed that handedness may be an index of individual differences in thinking. Specifically, evidence indicates that the degree of inter-hemispheric interaction relates to functional asymmetry: that is, decreased communication via the corpus callosum is associated with greater hemispheric specialisation (Aboitiz *et al.*, 2003). Right-handed people show greater functional asymmetry than non-right-handers (e.g. Hellige, 1993) and also have a smaller corpus callosum (Witelson & Goldsmith, 1991).[7]

The link between handedness and degree of interhemispheric interaction predicts that mixed-handers should more readily update their beliefs and change their attitudes. Early evidence supports this view. For instance, as a result of biological education mixed-handers were more likely to shift from holding creationist beliefs to holding evolutionary beliefs. Mixed-handers also appear better equipped to hold contradictory representations. Niebauer and Garvey (2004) found that mixed-handers – compared to strong right-handers – reported greater understanding of Gödel's Incompleteness Theorem[8] and showed greater appreciation of Escher prints containing visual paradoxes. Jasper and Christman (2005) found some – rather weaker – evidence that mixed-handers made larger adjustments away from initial anchors than did strong-handers.

The basal ganglia and the anterior cingulate cortex

Lieberman (2000) has linked intuition to the phenomenon of implicit learning. In implicit learning studies participants engage in a task over a large number of trials, during the course of which their performance improves but the participants themselves are unable to articulate the underlying rule that they have learned. There is clear evidence that different memory systems are involved in explicit and implicit learning. Notably, anterograde amnesics (associated with damage to the hippocampus) are unable to learn new semantic information but are able to learn new skills. In a typical task, amnesics improved their performance across trials at reading and recognising mirror-reversed words, but were unable to explicitly recognise the words as ones they had seen previously (Cohen & Squire, 1980).

In one example of implicit learning, Lewicki *et al.* (1987) had people view a screen in which targets appeared successively in one of four quadrants. The participants had to indicate as quickly as possible which quadrant the target had appeared in. Unknown to the participants, the trials were divided into groups of seven. The location of the target in the seventh trial was determined by the sequence of locations in Trials 1, 3, 4, and 6 (and was not predicted by any one trial alone). After several hours of practice on the task, participants showed a faster response time on Trial 7 compared to other trials. In the twelfth hour of practice the relationship between the predictor sequence and the target location in Trial 7 was changed. Now, participants' responses on this trial were substantially slowed.

The learning of sequences and probabilistic relationships that are not accessible to consciousness appears to be associated with a brain structure known as the basal ganglia. The basal ganglia are a group of components (striatum, substantia nigra, and globus pallidus) that are centrally located below the cortex, and receive input from most areas of the cortex and limbic system. Lieberman (2000) reviewed evidence that the basal ganglia are heavily involved in intuition and implicit learning. Much of this evidence comes from the task performance of patients with Parkinson's disease (PD) or Huntingdon's disease (HD), both of which involve damage to the basal ganglia.

For example, in one task participants had to learn to predict the weather using four predictor clues, each of which was present or absent on a given trial (Knowlton & Squire, 1996; Knowlton *et al.*, 1996). This task did not require any motor movements, yet both PD and HD patients showed impaired performance relative to normal controls, whereas amnesics and frontal lobe patients were unimpaired.

Lieberman's review examined intuition in the form of nonverbal communication, the experience of emotion, and linguistic automation, finding evidence for a central role of the basal ganglia in each of these. For example:

- When viewing pictures of faces HD patients have been found to be impaired at recognising five out of the six basic emotions (surprise, fear, sadness, disgust, and anger, but not happiness). Patients were almost entirely unable to recognise expressions of disgust (Sprengelmayer *et al.*, 1996).

- Several neuroimaging studies have found that positive, but not negative, stimuli activate a part of the striatum known as the caudate (e.g. Canli *et al.*, 1998; Lane, Reiman, Ahern, *et al.*, 1997; Lane, Reiman, Bradley, *et al.*, 1997; Phillips *et al.*, 1997). Negative stimuli appear to activate a different brain structure, the amygdala.

- Damage to the basal ganglia can impair a person's ability to use automatic speech, linguistic sequences that are formulated without conscious planning. One case study concerned a 75-year-old Jewish man with basal ganglia damage who was no longer able to produce greetings, clichés, swear words, or songs. He was also unable to recite a Jewish prayer that he had recited before every meal since the age of 5 (Speedie *et al.*, 1993).

In summary, there is now good reason to believe that the basal ganglia play a key role in intuitive thinking. However, people do not always behave in accordance with their intuitions, so what area of the brain is involved in determining whether or not reflective thinking takes place?

Earlier, I described the Simmons and Nelson (2006) theory of intuitive confidence. This proposed that people often fail to recognise faulty intuitions because the ease with which they spring to mind leads people to hold them in high confidence. However, information that appears to conflict with one's intuition – even if actually irrelevant – leads to a reduction in confidence and increases the likelihood that people will act against that intuition. Much evidence now indicates that the brain's anterior cingulate cortex (ACC) is responsible for monitoring conflicting sources of information. Carter *et al.* (1998) gave participants variants of the *continuous performance test*, in which the letter A or B is briefly flashed, followed 9.5 seconds later by an X or Y. The participant is required to make a response if she sees an A followed by an X. However, in the Carter *et al.* study some of the trials involved degraded stimuli that were much harder to read. fMRI scanning revealed that the ACC and three other cortical areas were activated when people made errors. Only the ACC, though, showed significant activation in relation to degraded stimuli. Furthermore, although degraded stimuli led to an increase in erroneous responding, accuracy remained well above chance levels. Thus, the ACC appears not to be involved in error monitoring per se, but rather it detects the conditions under which errors are likely to occur.

Botvinick *et al.* (2001) have provided a review of ACC's role in conflict monitoring on tasks such as the Stroop task.[9] In essence, when the ACC is activated by a particular task it then engages control mechanisms in other brain regions. These control mechanisms may regulate both cognitive and emotional processes in judgment and decision tasks, as we have seen in this and other chapters. Specifically, the ACC was activated in the following circumstances:

- During causal judgment tasks when data were inconsistent with a focal causal theory (i.e. strong data for an implausible theory or weak data for a plausible theory; see Fugelsang & Thompson, 2003; described in Chapter 6).

- Among those people who acted against their behavioural tendency during a framing effects task; that is, they behaved in an anti-framing direction (De Martino *et al.*, 2006; described in Chapter 7).

- When participants viewed the administration of pain (mild electric shock) to a partner who had behaved fairly in an economic game. Women, but not men, also showed ACC activity when an 'unfair' partner experienced pain (Singer *et al.*, 2006; described in Chapter 14). ACC activity was not associated with an overt behaviour or judgment in this study, as participants were merely asked to view the administration of pain. However, as we saw, empathy is often a precursor to some kind of helping activity.

- When declining to share money with a person of good perceived moral character during a trust game, and when sharing money with a person of perceived bad moral character (Delgado *et al.*, 2005; described in Chapter 14).

- When considering personal moral dilemmas. The more difficult the dilemma, the greater the activity (Greene *et al.*, 2004; this chapter).

Emotion and rationality

Emotion prepares us for action. It establishes the context in which action is experienced. It creates a world that resolves conflicts, a possible world, acceptable to our brain, its desires, its constraints, its hopes. Fundamentally, emotions are like colours: they help to categorize the world and simplify neurocomputation. In the infinite complexity of the physical world, they aid the brain in sorting things out. (Berthoz, 2006, p.226)

We have seen that moral dilemmas activate brain regions associated with emotional processing and with conflict monitoring. In this section I am going to take a closer look at the relationship between emotion, judgment and decision making, as this is an area that has received considerable attention since the mid-1990s. Historically, emotions have been viewed as something that can impair rationality. It is now clear that the true picture is more complicated.

Much of the relevant research on emotion concerns people with frontal lobe brain damage. Such individuals are often unaffected in their intellectual abilities, memory, use of language, and motor skills, yet they also show an emotional 'flatness' in the sense that they do not respond to reward or punishment and show no signs of emotions such as embarrassment or sadness. Despite this general emotional flatness, fairly minor frustrations or provocations can induce a sudden burst of anger or abusiveness in these patients. What has most interested decision researchers is the fact that frontal lobe patients are poor decision makers: They often prevaricate about decisions that other people would find straightforward and, generally, appear unable to regularly choose the options that would be in their best interests (Damasio, 1994).

It appears that this emotional flatness and poor decision making are not independent. Two similar hypotheses have tried to describe the role that emotions play in decision making. The *risk-as-feelings* hypothesis (Loewenstein *et al.*, 2001; see Chapter 14) proposes a two-way relationship between cognitions and emotions, such that they may influence each other. Also, both cognitions and emotions may sometimes act directly on behaviour unmediated by the other.

The *somatic marker hypothesis* proposes that body-related responses (emotions) influence decisions (Bechara & Damasio, 2005; Damasio, 1994). These responses are referred to as *somatic states*. Somatic states may arise in response to *primary inducers*, which are 'innate or learned stimuli that cause pleasurable or aversive states' (Bechara & Damasio, 2005, p.340), or *secondary inducers*, which are thoughts and memories of the primary inducer. Somatic states may operate within or outside of consciousness, but help direct attention towards certain stimuli and away from others. In this way they influence decision making, though do not determine it because an individual may still apply reasoning processes to the contents of working memory.

These two proposals are highly alike, although the somatic marker hypothesis has perhaps been formulated in more detail. One difference is that the somatic marker hypothesis proposes that emotions are always involved in the decision-making processes of normal people. The evidence supporting this proposal comes from the study of people who, due to brain damage, are unable to process emotion in the same way as undamaged individuals.

Several studies of decision making in frontal lobe patients have adopted the *Iowa gambling task* (IGT), first reported in Bechara *et al.* (1994). The target participants in this study had damage to the ventromedial prefrontal region of the cortex (VMPC)[10] and had a documented record of abnormal decision making. Normal participants also took part, as well as a group of people with damage to other brain regions. The task begins with participants being given a $2000 loan of play money, and then drawing cards, one at a time, from four decks. Each card from decks A and B carries a reward value of $100, whereas each card in decks C and D is worth $50. However, some cards in each deck also contain a punishment. The punishments in decks A and B are larger than in C and D, such that the first 10 cards in A and B lead to a net loss of $250, whereas the first 10 cards in C and D lead to a net gain of $250. In other words, participants need to learn to draw from the two decks, C and D, that provide the smaller individual rewards but greater overall benefit.

In Bechara *et al.* (1994) all participants sampled cards from each deck, but only the frontal lobe patients failed to learn to draw mainly from decks C and D. In sum, most of their draws came from decks A and B, whereas the other participants drew mostly from C and D. Participants were also presented with a version of the task in which they received immediate punishment and the reward was delayed. Patients' card choices were influenced more by immediate punishment than by delayed rewards.[11] These results discount the possibility that patients were insensitive to punishment and highly sensitive to reward, but instead suggests that they were insensitive to future consequences.

A subsequent study (Bechara *et al.*, 1997) measured participants' skin conductance responses (SCR) during the task, and also questioned the participants after every 10 cards as to whether they knew what was going on and what they felt about the task. All normal participants eventually developed a hunch about the task and, subsequently, 75 per cent of them reported a correct understanding of the task. During the hunch period, these participants began to select the good decks more frequently than the bad decks. However, people arrived at their hunch only *after* they had already shown an elevated SCR. During the periods in which the hunch was reported and full understanding developed, SCRs in response to the good decks began to decline, but SCRs in response to the bad decks remained elevated.

By contrast, although 50 per cent of prefrontal patients eventually reported a correct understanding of the task, nobody developed a hunch at any point. Furthermore, the patients did not show elevated SCRs and the bad decks were chosen more often throughout all stages of the study, although for patients who finally developed a full understanding the bad decks were only chosen very slightly more in this final stage.

There has been considerable discussion and controversy regarding the interpretation of IGT results (for critical reviews see Dunn *et al.*, 2006; Krawczyk, 2002). One criticism is that VMPC patients show impaired IGT performance because they are unable to engage in *reversal learning*; that is, having learned a particular contingency they are unable to inhibit their initial responses when circumstances change (Maia & McClelland, 2004). Thus, on the IGT having learned to select the cards with the biggest rewards, VMPC patients may be unable to inhibit their response to these once they receive punishments. Bechara *et al.* (2005) noted that although some VMPC patients do have difficulties with reversal learning, this is not incompatible with the somatic marker hypothesis. In order for reversals to occur, an emotional signal is necessary, and as it happens the brain regions associated with reversal learning are the same as those associated with emotional processing (Rolls, 1999).

However, it is not clear that a failure of reversal learning can explain all IGT results, given that patients often *do* actually switch decks after encountering a large loss; the difference is that they switch back to the bad decks sooner (e.g. Busemeyer & Stout, 2002). This explanation also does not explain why patients who develop a correct understanding of the task nonetheless fail to play advantageously.

Other evidence also indicates that emotions are crucial for decision making. In Chapter 7, we saw that patients with damage to various emotion processing regions actually made more rational decisions across a series of 50/50 gambles, where the outcome was either a gain of $2.50 or the loss of the $1 that it cost to play the gamble. These target patients invested more often than normal controls or patients with damage to different brain regions. By contrast, normal controls and other brain-damaged patients showed myopic loss aversion. Likewise, VMPC patients have been found to behave like normal patients on impersonal moral dilemmas, but to behave in a utilitarian fashion on personal moral dilemmas (Koenigs *et al.*, 2007). For example, VMPC patients are more likely than most people to endorse pushing a stranger to his death from a railway bridge in order to prevent a runaway trolley from killing five people.

Nonetheless, it is also the case that frontal lobe patients, while mostly emotionally flat, can show sudden bursts of anger in response to fairly minor provocations. In line with this observation, VMPC patients are more likely to reject poor offers in the ultimatum game (Koenigs & Tranel, 2007).

In summary, it is now clear that emotions play a prominent role in decision making. In this section I have focused on what we have learned about decision making from those with emotional processing deficits. There is, of course, far more that could be said about other brain regions (and the connections between them) that underlie the processing of emotion and cognition in the service of decision making. Lack of space precludes that here, but more detail can be found in Frank and Claus (2006) and Berthoz (2006).

SUMMARY

Stanovich (1999) has proposed that people have a fundamental computation bias whereby they perceive problems within their full context. This can lead people to focus on details that are irrelevant to a normative solution. On various judgment tasks, people of a higher cognitive ability are better able to abstract the most relevant features in order to apply normative processes to them.

On some tasks, such as resource allocation and prisoner's dilemma tasks, greater reflection is associated with more normative responding. An individual differences measure, the cognitive reflection test (CRT), differentiates people on risky choices and time preference problems. However, the relationship between CRT score and decision performance is mediated by sex differences. Furthermore, although high-CRT scorers are more likely to choose the risky option on decision tasks, they do not appear to be computing expected value, so it is not clear that reflection always leads to more normative behaviour.

Reflective thinking can also lead to less normative responding on some tasks. Notably, asking people to give reasons for their preferences can lead them to make poorer choices. In this situation, people tend to focus on easily articulated attributes, but these may not in fact be the main determinants of quality or long-term satisfaction. Other evidence shows that *preventing* people from engaging in conscious thinking can lead them to make better judgments and choices, particularly when the options are complex.

Two interacting systems of thinking have been proposed to explain intuitive and reflective thinking. The theory of intuitive confidence says that people are confident about their intuitions precisely because they come to mind so easily. However, this confidence can be reduced – and reflection engaged – if there is information available that appears to favour a nonintuitive option. Moral judgment can also be interpreted within the two-system framework. Indeed, the social intuitionist approach suggests that moral judgments are driven by our intuitions but are then justified or explained through post hoc rationalisations.

A considerable body of evidence indicates that people have little, if any, insight into the processes underlying their judgments and decisions. A classic paper by Nisbett and Wilson (1977) showed that people's reports on their own behaviour are essentially rationalisations. Research with split-brain patients indicates that the left hemisphere acts as an 'interpreter'. The right hemisphere, on the other hand, is more specialised for detecting anomalies and creating new mental representations on the basis of these anomalies.

Mixed-handedness appears to be an index of the extent to which the brain's two hemispheres communicate with each other. Mixed-handers are better at holding two contradictory representations in mind and show a greater appreciation of visual paradoxes.

Two important brain regions (at least) are important for understanding intuition and reflection. Firstly, the basal ganglia are associated with the learning of sequences and probabilistic relationships. However, people are frequently unable to report explicit knowledge of such relationships. Secondly, the anterior cingulate cortex is responsible for monitoring conflicting items of information and recruiting control mechanisms.

Emotion is now widely recognised to play a central role in decision making, as proposed in the risk-as-feelings hypothesis and the somatic marker hypothesis. Both hypotheses propose that cognitions and emotions may influence each other, as well as act on behaviour. Much support for this central role of emotion in decision making has come from patients with lesions to their ventromedial prefrontal cortex. On the Iowa gambling task patients fail to learn about rewards and punishments and so make disadvantageous choices. However, on personal moral dilemmas they make utilitarian choices, unlike normal people, and on repeated gambles of positive expected value they are less susceptible to myopic loss aversion.

QUESTIONS

1. What are the costs and benefits of cognitive reflection?

2. What is reversal learning?

3. If it is true that conscious will is an illusion, should people be held legally responsible for their actions?

4. Suppose you are asked to write a film review for a magazine. How might the act of reviewing affect your enjoyment of the movie?

5. Discuss the roles of the anterior cingulate cortex and basal ganglia in judgment and decision making.

6. What have we learned about decision making from studies using the Iowa Gambling Task?

NOTES

1. Frederick reports that the three questions were embedded within several other questions.
2. This study was run at the University of Heidelberg in Germany.

3. As Wilson (2002) has pointed out, the unconscious system that constitutes System 1 is actually a collection of different modules.
4. The actual terminology used by Evans referred to a heuristic–analytic distinction.
5. See for example the discussion of recognition-primed decision making in Chapter 13.
6. For detailed reviews see Berthoz (2006), Krawczyk (2002), Lieberman (2000), Frank and Claus (2006), Bechara and Damasio (2005) and Dunn *et al.* (2006).
7. Jasper and Christman (2005) point out that the important difference is not specifically between right-handers and the rest, but between *strong-handedness* (whether right or left) and mixed-handedness. In practice, however, there are so few strong left-handers (about 2 per cent of the population) that these are rarely used in research studies.
8. Gödel's Incompleteness Theorem shows that, for any consistent formal, computably enumerable theory that proves basic arithmetical truths, it will always be possible to construct an arithmetical statement that is true but not provable within the theory.
9. The classic Stroop task involves a colour-naming conflict. Words such as *red* are written in a colour different from the one that the word itself is referring to. The participant is required to name the colour of the font rather than to read the word. People typically make few errors, but only because their responses are considerably slowed down as they attempt to overcome their initial tendency to say the word.
10. Patients with lesions to the dorsolateral prefrontal cortex also show impaired IGT performance. However, these

patients also have impairments in working memory and other cognitive processes that can account for the problems on the IGT (Bechara *et al.*, 1998; Manes *et al.*, 2002).

11. Bechara *et al.* (1994) does not report these results in detail. See pp.13–14 of that paper.

RECOMMENDED READING

....

Berthoz, A. (2006). *Emotion and Reason: The cognitive neuroscience of decision making*. Oxford: Oxford University Press. This book gives a neuroscience view on various aspects of decision making, from decisions about bodily movements to the processing of rewards and punishments.

Damasio, A.R. (1994). *Descartes' error: Emotion, reason and the human brain*. New York: Grosset/Putnam. Damasio sets out the somatic marker hypothesis and describes the way in which frontal lobe damage affects the ability to make decisions.

Gladwell, M. (2005). *Blink: The power of thinking without thinking*. London: Allen Lane. Another best-selling popular science book in which Malcolm Gladwell describes the power (and some pitfalls) of intuitive thinking.

Stanovich, K.E. (1999). *Who is rational? Studies of individual differences in reasoning*. Mahwah, NJ: Erlbaum. This is a review of a major programme of research examining cognitive ability differences in relation to performance on reasoning tasks.

Wegner, D.M. (2002). *The illusion of conscious will*. Cambridge, MA: Bradford Books, MIT Press. A self-explanatory title, for which Daniel Wegner presents some fascinating evidence.

Wilson, T.D. (2002). *Strangers to ourselves: Discovering the adaptive unconscious*. Cambridge, MA: Belknap, Harvard University Press. Another fine book presenting evidence of our lack of self-insight.

Zeki, S. & Goodenough, O. (Eds.) (2004). *Law and the brain*. Oxford: Oxford University Press. This is an edited collection of chapters discussing the legal implications of neuroscience research.

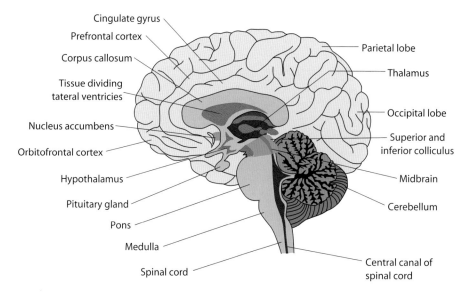

Cingulate gyrus

Prefrontal cortex

Corpus callosum

Tissue dividing
tateral ventricies

Nucleus accumbens

Orbitofrontal cortex

Hypothalamus

Pituitary gland

Pons

Medulla

Spinal cord

Parietal lobe

Thalamus

Occipital lobe

Superior and
inferior colliculus

Midbrain

Cerebellum

Central canal of
spinal cord

A sagittal section through the human brain

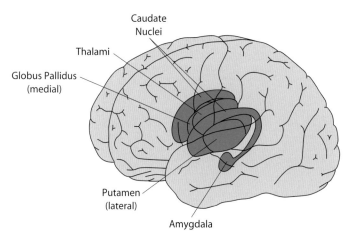

Caudate
Nuclei

Thalami

Globus Pallidus
(medial)

Putamen
(lateral)

Amygdala

The basel ganglia

References

CHAPTER 1. INTRODUCTION AND OVERVIEW

Ayton, P. (2000). Do the birds and bees need cognitive reform? *Behavioral and Brain Sciences*, 23(5), 666–667.

De La Rochefoucauld, F. (1678/2007). *Collected maxims and other reflections.* Oxford: Oxford University Press.

Dijksterhuis, A. (2004). Think different: The merits of unconscious thought in preference development and decision making. *Journal of Personality and Social Psychology*, 87(5), 586–598.

Dijksterhuis, A. & Nordgren, L.F. (2006). A theory of unconscious thought. *Perspectives on Psychological Science*, 1(2), 95–109.

Freud, D. (2006). *Freud in the city.* UK: Bene Factum.

Gigerenzer, G., Todd, P.M. & the ABC Group (1999). *Simple heuristics that make us smart.* Cambridge: Cambridge University Press.

Gintis, H. (2006). The foundations of behaviour: The beliefs, preferences, and constraints model. *Biological Theory*, 1(2), 123–127.

Haigh, M.S. & List, J.A. (2005). Do professional traders exhibit myopic loss aversion? An experimental analysis. *The Journal of Finance*, 40(1), 523–534.

Jensen, A.R. (1998). *The g factor: The science of mental ability.* Westport, CT: Praeger.

Kahneman, D., Slovic, P. & Tversky, A. (1982). *Judgment under uncertainty: Heuristics and biases.* Cambridge: Cambridge University Press.

Laming, D. (2004). *Human judgment: The eye of the beholder.* London: Thomson.

Payne, J.W., Bettman, J.R. & Johnson, E.J. (1993). *The adaptive decision maker.* Cambridge, England: Cambridge University Press.

Shafir, S. (1994). Intransitivity of preferences in honey bees: support for 'comparative' evaluation of foraging options. *Animal Behaviour*, 48, 55–67.

Simon, H. (1955). A behavioral model of rational choice. *The Quarterly Journal of Economics*, LXIX, 99–118.

Simon, H. (1956). Rational choice and the structure of environments. *Psychological Review*, 63, 129–138.

Stanovich, K.E. & West, R.F. (2000). Individual differences in reasoning: Implications for the rationality debate? *Behavioral and Brain Sciences*, 23, 645–726.

CHAPTER 2. THE NATURE AND ANALYSIS OF JUDGMENT

Blattberg, R.C. & Hoch, S.J. (1990). Database models and managerial intuition: 50% model + 50% manager. *Management Science*, 36, 887–899.

Bröder, A. (2000). Assessing the empirical validity of the 'take-the-best' heuristic as a model of human probabilistic inference. *Journal of Experimental Psychology: Learning, Memory, and Cognition*, 26, 1332–1346.

Bröder, A. (2003). Decision making with the 'adaptive toolbox': Influence of environmental structure, intelligence, and working memory load. *Journal of Experimental Psychology: Learning, Memory, and Cognition*, 29(4), 611–625.

Bröder, A. & Eichler, A. (2006). The use of recognition information and additional cues in inferences from memory. *Acta Psychologica*, 121, 275–284.

Brunswik, E. (1955). Representative design and probabilistic theory in a functional psychology. *Psychological Review*, 62, 193–217.

Dawes, R.M. (1979). The robust beauty of improper linear models in decision making. *American Psychologist*, 34, 571–582.

Dawes, R.M. & Corrigan, B. (1974). Linear models in decision making. *Psychological Bulletin*, 81, 95–106.

Dawes, R.M., Faust, D. & Meehl, P.E. (1989). Clinical versus actuarial judgment. *Science*, 243, 1668–1673.

De Vaul, R.A., Jervey, F., Chappell, J.A., Caver, P., Short, B. & O'Keefe, S. (1987). Medical school performance of initially rejected students. *Journal of the American Medical Association*, 257(1), 47–51.

Dhami, M.K., Hertwig, R. & Hoffrage, U. (2004). The role of representative design in an ecological approach to cognition. *Psychological Bulletin*, 130(6), 959–988.

Einhorn, H.J. (1972). Expert measurement and mechanical combination. *Organizational Behavior and Human Performance*, 7, 86–106.

Gigerenzer, G. & Goldstein, D.G. (1996). Reasoning the fast and frugal way: Models of bounded rationality. *Psychological Review*, 103, 592–596.

Gigerenzer, G., Hoffrage, U. & Klëinbolting, H. (1991). Probabilistic mental models: A Brunswikian theory of confidence. *Psychological Review*, 98, 506–528.

Gigerenzer, G., Czerlinski, J. & Martignon, L. (2002). How good are fast and frugal heuristics? In T. Gilovich, D. Griffin, D. Kahneman (Eds.), *Heuristics and biases: The psychology of intuitive judgment*. Cambridge: Cambridge University Press.

Goldberg, L.R. (1965). Diagnosticians vs. diagnostic signs: The diagnosis of psychosis vs. neurosis from the MMPI. *Psychological Monographs*, 79(9) (whole no. 602).

Goldberg, L.R. (1968). Simple models or simple processes? Some research on clinical judgments. *American Psychologist*, 23, 483–496.

Goldberg, L.R. (1970). Man versus model of man: a rationale, plus some evidence, for a method of improving on clinical inferences. *Psychological Bulletin*, 73, 422–432.

Goldberg, L.R. (1976). Man vs. model of man: Just how conflicting is that evidence? *Organizational Behavior and Human Performance*, 16, 13–22.

Goldstein, D. & Gigerenzer, G. (2002). Models of ecological rationality: The recognition heuristic. *Psychological Review*, 109(1), 75–90.

Grove, W.M., Zald, D.H., Lebow, B.S., Snitz, B.E. & Nelson, C. (2000). Clinical vs. mechanical prediction: A meta-analysis. *Psychological Assessment*, 12, 19–30.

Guilmette, T.J., Faust, D., Hart, K. & Arkes, H.R. (1990). A national survey of psychologists who offer neuropsychological services. *Archives of Clinical Neuropsychology*, 5, 373–392.

Hammond, K.R. (1955). Probabilistic functioning and the clinical method. *Psychological Review*, 62, 255–262.

Libby, R. (1976). Man versus model of man: Some conflicting evidence. *Organizational Behavior and Human Performance*, 16, 1–12.

Meehl, P. (1954). *Clinical versus statistical prediction.* Minneapolis: University of Minnesota Press.

Meehl, P. (1957). When shall we use our heads instead of the formula? *Journal of Counseling Psychology*, 4, 268–273.

Meehl, P. (1965). Seer over sign: The first good example. *Journal of Experimental Research in Personality*, 1, 27–32.

Meehl, P. (1986). Causes and effects of my disturbing little book. *Journal of Personality Assessment*, 50(3), 370–375.

Newell, B.R. & Fernandez, D.R. (2006). On the binary quality of recognition and the inconsequentiality of further knowledge: Two critical tests of the recognition heuristic. *Journal of Behavioral Decision Making, 19*, 333–346.

Newell, B.R. & Shanks, D.R. (2003). Take the best or look at the rest? Factors influencing 'one-reason' decision making. *Journal of Experimental Psychology: Learning, Memory, and Cognition, 29*(1), 53–65.

Newell, B.R., Rakow, T., Weston, N.J. & Shanks, D.R. (2004). Search strategies in decision making: The success of 'success'. *Journal of Behavioral Decision Making, 17*, 117–137.

Oppenheimer, D.M. (2003). Not so fast! (and not so frugal): Rethinking the recognition heuristic. *Cognition, 90*, B1–B9.

Oskamp, S. (1965). Overconfidence in case-study judgments. *The Journal of Consulting Psychology, 29*, 261–265.

Richter, T. & Späth, P. (2006). Recognition is used as one cue among others in judgment and decision making. *Journal of Experimental Psychology: Learning, Memory, and Cognition, 31*(1), 150–162.

Rieskamp, J. & Otto, P.E. (2006). SSL: A theory of how people learn to select strategies. *Journal of Experimental Psychology: General, 135*(2), 207–236.

Sawyer, J. (1966). Measurement and prediction, clinical and statistical. *Psychological Bulletin, 66*, 178–200.

Wiggins, J.S. (1981). Clinical and statistical prediction: Where are we and where do we go from here? *Clinical Psychology Review, 1*, 3–18.

CHAPTER 3. JUDGING PROBABILITY AND FREQUENCY

Ayton, P. & Wright, G. (1994). Subjective probability: What should we believe? In G. Wright & P. Ayton (Eds.), *Subjective probability.* Chichester: Wiley.

Betsch, T. & Pohl, D. (2002). Tversky and Kahneman's availability approach to frequency judgment: A critical analysis. In P. Sedlmeier & T. Betsch (Eds.), *Etc.: Frequency processing and cognition.* Oxford: Oxford University Press.

Biller, B., Bless, H. & Schwarz, N. (1992, April). *Die Leichtigkeit der Erinnerung als Information in der Urteilsbildung: der Einflunmβder Fragenreihenfolge* [Ease of recall as information: The impact of question order]. Tagung experimentell arbeitender Psychologen, Osnabrück, FRG.

Brase, G.L., Fiddick, G.L. & Harries, C. (2006). Participant recruitment methods and statistical reasoning performance. *The Quarterly Journal of Experimental Psychology, 59*(5), 965–976.

Brown, N.R. (2002). Encoding, representing, and estimating event frequencies: a multiple strategy perspective. In P. Sedlmeier & T. Betsch (Eds.), *Etc.: Frequency processing and cognition.* Oxford: Oxford University Press.

Clotfelter, C.T. & Cook, P.J. (1993). The gambler's fallacy in lottery play. *Management Science, 39*(12), 1521–1525.

Cosmides, L. & Tooby, J. (1996). Are humans good intuitive statisticians after all? Rethinking some conclusions from the literature on judgment under uncertainty. *Cognition, 58*, 1–73.

Desvouges, W.H., Johnson, F., Dunford, R., Hudson, S., Wilson, K. & Boyle, K. (1993). Measuring resource damages with contingent valuation: Tests of validity and reliability. In J.A. Hausman (Ed.), *Contingent valuation: A critical assessment.* Amsterdam.

Dougherty, M.R.P., Gettys, C.F. & Ogden, E. (1999). Minerva DM: A memory process model for judgements of likelihood. *Psychological Review, 106*, 180–209.

Dougherty, M.R.P. & Franco-Watkins, A.M. (2002). A memory models approach to frequency and probability judgment: applications of Minerva 2 and Minerva DM. In P. Sedlmeier & T. Betsch (Eds.), *Etc.: Frequency processing and cognition.* Oxford: Oxford University Press.

DuCharme, W.M. & Peterson, C.R. (1968). Intuitive inference about normally distributed populations. *Journal of Experimental Psychology, 78*, 269–275.

Eddy, D.M. (1982). Probabilistic reasoning in clinical medicine: Problems and opportunities. In D. Kahneman, P. Slovic & A. Tversky (Eds.), *Judgment under uncertainty: Heuristics and biases.* Cambridge: Cambridge University Press.

Edwards, W. (1968). Conservatism in human information processing. In B. Kleinmuntz (Ed.), *Formal representation of human judgment.* New York: Wiley.

Feller, W. (1950). *An introduction to probability theory and its applications: Vol. 1.* Wiley.

Frederickson, B.L. & Kahneman, D. (1993). Duration neglect in retrospective evaluations of affective episodes. *Journal of Personality and Social Psychology, 65*, 45–55.

Gigerenzer, G. (2003). *Reckoning with risk: Learning to live with uncertainty.* London: Penguin.

Gigerenzer, G. & Hoffrage, U. (1995). How to improve Bayesian reasoning without instruction: Frequency formats. *Psychological Review, 102*(4), 684–704.

Gigerenzer, G., Hoffrage, U. & Ebert, A. (1998). AIDS counseling for low-risk clients. *AIDS Care, 10*, 197–211.

Gilovich, T., Vallone, R. & Tversky, A. (1985). The hot hand in basketball: On the misperception of random sequences. *Cognitive Psychology, 17*, 295–314.

Haigh, J. (2003). *Taking chances: Winning with probability* (2nd edn). Oxford: Oxford University Press.

Hoffrage, U., Lindsey, S., Hertwig, R. & Gigerenzer, G. (2000). Communicating statistical information. *Science, 290*, 2261–2262.

Johnson-Laird, P.N., Legrenzi, P., Girotto, V., Legrenzi, M.S. & Caverni, J.P. (1999). Naive probability: A mental model theory of extensional reasoning. *Psychological Review, 106*(1), 62–88.

Kahneman, D. & Frederick, S. (2002). Representativeness revisited: Attribute substitution in intuitive judgment. In T. Gilovich, D. Griffin & D. Kahneman (Eds.), *Heuristics and biases: The psychology of intuitive judgment.* Cambridge: Cambridge University Press.

Kahneman, D. & Tversky, A. (1972). Subjective probability: A judgment of representativeness. *Cognitive Psychology, 3*, 430–454.

Kahneman, D. & Tversky, A. (1973). On the psychology of prediction. *Psychological Review, 80*, 237–251.

Kahneman, D., Slovic, P. & Tversky, A. (1982). *Judgment under uncertainty: Heuristics and biases.* Cambridge: Cambridge University Press.

Koehler, J.J. (1996). The base rate fallacy reconsidered: Descriptive, normative and methodological challenges. *Behavioral and Brain Sciences, 19*(1), 1–53.

Levy, S. (2006a). *The perfect thing: How the iPod shuffles commerce, culture, and coolness.* New York: Simon & Schuster.

Levy, S. (2006b; 31 January). Does your iPod play favorites? *Newsweek online.* Downloaded on 2 August 2007, from http://www.msnbc.msn.com/id/6854309/site/newsweek/.

Macchi, L. (1995). Pragmatic aspects of the base rate fallacy. *Quarterly Journal of Experimental Psychology, 48A*, 188–207.

Macchi, L. (2003). The partitive conditional probability. In D. Hardman & L. Macchi (Eds.), *Thinking: Psychological perspectives on reasoning, judgment, and decision making.* Chichester: Wiley.

Malkiel, B.G. (2003[1973]) *A random walk down Wall Street: The time-tested strategy for successful investing* (revised edn). New York: Norton. Burton Malkiel explains how an understanding of randomness can help you negotiate the stock market.

Nisbett, R.E., Krantz, D.H., Jepson, C. & Kunda, Z. (1983). The use of statistical heuristics in everyday inductive reasoning. *Psychological Review, 90*, 339–363.

Paulos, J.A. (2003). *A mathematician plays the market.* London: Allen Lane. Another book about randomness and the stock market, by one of its victims.

Pinker, S. (1998). *How the mind works.* London: Penguin.

Redelmeier, D. & Kahneman, D. (1996). Patients' memories of painful medical treatments: Real-time and retrospective evaluations of two minimally invasive procedures. *Pain, 66*, 3–8.

Ross, M. & Sicoly, F. (1979). Egocentric biases in availability and attribution. *Journal of Personality and Social Psychology, 37*, 322–336.

Schwarz, N. & Vaughn, L.A. (2002). The availability heuristic revisited: Ease of recall and content of recall as distinct sources of information. In T. Gilovich, D. Griffin & D. Kahneman (Eds.), *Heuristics and biases: The psychology of intuitive judgment*. Cambridge: Cambridge University Press.

Schwarz, N., Bless, H., Strack, F., Klumpp, G., Rittenauer-Schatka, H. & Simons, A. (1991). Ease of retrieval as information: Another look at the availability heuristic. *Journal of Personality and Social Psychology, 45*, 513–23.

Sloman, S.A., Over, D., Slovak, L. & Stibel, J.M. (2003). Frequency illusions and other fallacies. *Organizational Behavior and Human Decision Processes, 92*, 296–309.

Terrell, D. (1994). A test of the gambler's fallacy: Evidence from para-mutuel games. *Journal of Risk and Uncertainty, 8*(3), 309–317.

Tversky, A. & Kahneman, D. (1973). Availability: A heuristic for judging frequency and probability. *Cognitive Psychology, 5*, 207–232.

Tversky, A. & Kahneman, D. (1983). Extensional versus intuitive reasoning: The conjunction fallacy in probability judgment. *Psychological Review, 90*, 293–315.

Tversky, A. & Koehler, D.J. (1994). Support theory: A nonextensional representation of subjective probability. *Psychological Review, 101*, 547–67.

Winkler, R.L. & Murphy, A.H. (1973). Experiments in the laboratory and the real world. *Organizational Behavior and Human Performance, 20*, 252–270.

Yates, J.F. & Carlson, B.W. (1986). Conjunction errors: Evidence for multiple judgment procedures, including 'signed summation'. *Organizational Behavior and Human Decision Processes, 37*, 230–253.

CHAPTER 4. JUDGMENTAL DISTORTIONS

Arkes, H.R., Faust, D., Guilmette, T.J. & Hart, K. (1988). Eliminating the hindsight bias. *Journal of Applied Psychology, 73*(2), 305–307.

Campbell, J.D. & Tesser, A. (1983). Motivational interpretations of hindsight bias: An individual difference analysis. *Journal of Personality, 51*, 605–620.

Carli, L.L. (1999). Cognitive reconstruction, hindsight, and reactions to victims and perpetrators. *Personality and Social Psychology Bulletin, 25*(8), 966–979.

Chapman, G.B. & Bornstein, B.H. (1996). The more you ask for, the more you get: Anchoring in personal injury verdicts. *Applied Cognitive Psychology, 10*, 519–540.

Chapman, G.B. & Johnson, E.J. (1994). The limits of anchoring. *Journal of Behavioral Decision Making, 7*, 223–242.

Chapman, G.B. & Johnson, E.J. (1999). Anchoring, activation, and the construction of value. *Organizational Behavior and Human Decision Processes, 79*, 115–153.

Chapman, G.B. & Johnson, E.J. (2002). Incorporating the irrelevant: Anchors in judgments of belief and value. In T. Gilovich, D. Griffin & D. Kahneman (Eds.), *Heuristics and biases: The psychology of intuitive judgment*. Cambridge: Cambridge University Press.

Choi, L. & Nisbett, R.E. (2000). The cultural psychology of surprise: Holistic theories and recognition of contradiction. *Journal of Personality and Social Psychology, 79*, 890–905.

Davies, M.F. (1987). Reduction of hindsight bias by restoration of foresight perspective: Effectiveness of foresight-encoding and hindsight-retrieval strategies. *Organizational Behavior and Human Decision Processes, 40*, 50–68.

Davies, M.F. (1992). Field-dependence and hindsight bias: Cognitive restructuring and the generation of reasons. *Journal of Research in Personality, 26*, 58–74.

Englich, B. & Mussweiler, T. (2001). Sentencing under uncertainty: Anchoring effects in the courtroom. *Journal of Applied Social Psychology, 31*, 1535–1551.

Epley, N. (2004). A tale of tuned decks? Anchoring as accessibility and anchoring as adjustment. In D.J. Koehler and N. Harvey (Eds.), *Blackwell handbook of judgment and decision making* (pp.240–257). Oxford: Blackwell.

Epley, N. & Gilovich, T. (2001). Putting adjustment back in the anchoring and adjustment heuristic: Differential processing of self-generated and experimenter-provided anchors. *Psychological Science, 12*(5), 391–396.

Epley, N. & Gilovich, T. (2004). Are adjustments insufficient? *Personality and Social Psychology Bulletin, 30*, 447–460.

Epley, N. & Gilovich, T. (2006). The anchoring and adjustment heuristic: Why the adjustments are insufficient. *Psychological Science, 17*, 311–318.

Fischhoff, B. (1975). Hindsight ≠ foresight: The effect of outcome knowledge on judgment under uncertainty. *Journal of Experimental Psychology: Human Perception and Performance, 1*, 288–299.

Fischhoff, B. (1977). Perceived informativeness of facts. *Journal of Experimental Psychology: Human Perception and Performance, 3*, 349–358.

Fischhoff, B. & Beyth, R. (1975). 'I knew it would happen'. Remembered probabilities of once-future things. *Organizational Behavior and Human Performance, 13*, 1–16.

Galinsky, A.D. & Mussweiler, T. (2001). First offers as anchors: The role of perspective-taking and negotiator focus. *Journal of Personality and Social Psychology, 81*, 657–669.

Hastie, R. (1984). Causes and effects of causal attribution. *Journal of Personality and Social Psychology, 46*, 44–56.

Hawkins, S.A. & Hastie, R. (1990). Hindsight: Biased judgments of past events after the outcomes are known. *Psychological Bulletin, 107*, 311–327.

Hertwig, R., Gigerenzer, G. & Hoffrage, U. (1997). The reiteration effect in hindsight bias. *Psychological Review, 104*(1), 194–202.

Jacowitz, K.E. & Kahneman, D. (1995). Measures of anchoring in estimation tasks. *Personality and Social Psychology Bulletin, 21*, 1161–1166.

Ji, L.-J., Peng, K., & Nisbett, R.E. (2000). Culture, control, and perception of relationships in the environment. *Journal of Personality and Social Psychology, 78*(5), 943–955.

Kahneman, D. & Frederick, S. (2002). Representativeness revisited: Attribute substitution in intuitive judgment. In T. Gilovich, D. Griffin & D. Kahneman (Eds.), *Heuristics and biases: The psychology of intuitive judgment*. Cambridge: Cambridge University Press.

Keren, G. & Teigen, K.H. (2004). Yet another look at the heuristics and biases approach. In D.J. Koehler and N. Harvey (Eds.), *Blackwell handbook of judgment and decision making* (pp.89–109). Oxford: Blackwell.

Musch, J. (2003). Personality differences in hindsight bias. *Memory, 11*(4/5), 473–489.

Mussweiler, T. & Strack, F. (1999). Hypothesis-consistent testing and semantic priming in the anchoring paradigm: A selective accessibility model. *Journal of Experimental Social Psychology, 35*, 136–164.

Mussweiler, T. & Strack, F. (2000). The use of category and exemplar knowledge in the solution of anchoring tasks. *Journal of Personality and Social Psychology, 78*, 1038–1052.

Mussweiler, T., Strack, F. & Pfeiffer, T. (2000). Overcoming the inevitable anchoring effect: Considering the opposite compensates for selective accessibility. *Personality and Social Psychology Bulletin, 26*, 1142–1150.

Nelson, T.O. & Narens, L. (1990). Metamemory: A theoretical framework and some new findings. In G.H. Bower (Ed.), *The psychology of learning and motivation: Vol. 26* (pp.125–173). San Diego, CA: Academic Press.

Nisbett, R.E. (2003). The geography of thought: How Asians and Westerners think differently . . . and why. New York: Free Press.

Northcraft, G.B. & Neale, M.A. (1987). Experts, amateurs, and real estate: An anchoring-and-adjustment perspective on property pricing decisions. *Organizational Behavior and Organizational Decision Processes, 39*, 84–97.

Ofir, C. & Mazursky, D. (1997). Does a surprising outcome reinforce or reverse the hindsight bias? *Organizational Behavior and Organizational Decision Processes, 69*, 51–57.

Pezzo, M.V. (2003). Surprise, defence, or making sense: What removes hindsight bias? *Memory, 11*(4/5), 421–441.

Sanna, L.J. & Turley, K.J. (1996). Antecedents to spontaneous counterfactual thinking: Effects of expectancy violation and outcome valence. *Journal of Personality and Social Psychology, 22*, 906–919.

Sanna, L.J., Schwarz, N. & Stocker, S.L. (2002). When debiasing backfires: Accessible content and accessibility experiences in debiasing hindsight. *Journal of Experimental Psychology, 28*(3), 497–502.

Schwarz, N., Bless, H., Strack, F., Klump, G., Rittenauer-Schatka, H. & Simons, A. (1991). Ease of retrieval as information: Another look at the availability heuristic. *Journal of Personality and Social Psychology, 61*, 195–202.

Schwarz, S. & Stahlberg, D. (2003). Strength of hindsight bias as a consequence of metacognitions. *Memory, 11*(4/5), 395–410.

Slovic, P. & Fischhoff, B. (1977). On the psychology of experimental surprises. *Journal of Experimental Psychology: Human Perception and Performance, 3*, 544–551.

Strack, F. & Mussweiler, T. (1997). Explaining the enigmatic anchoring effect: Mechanisms of selective accessibility. *Journal of Personality and Social Psychology, 73*, 437–446.

Tversky, A. & Kahneman, D. (1974). Judgment under uncertainty: Heuristics and biases. *Science, 185*, 1124–1131.

Weiner, B. (1985). 'Spontaneous' causal thinking. *Psychological Bulletin, 97*, 74–84.

Wells, G.L. & Petty, R.E. (1980). The effects of overt head movements on persuasion: compatibility and incompatibility of responses. *Basic and Applied Social Psychology, 1*, 219–230.

Werth, L. & Strack, F. (2003). An inferential approach to the knew-it-all-along phenomenon. *Memory, 11*(4/5), 411–419.

Wilson, T.D., Houston, C., Etling, K.M. & Brekke, N. (1996). A new look at anchoring effects: Basic anchoring and its antecedents. *Journal of Experimental Psychology: General, 4*, 387–402.

Wood, G. (1978). The knew-it-all-along effect. *Journal of Experimental Psychology: Human Perception and Performance, 4*, 345–353.

CHAPTER 5. ASSESSING EVIDENCE AND EVALUATING ARGUMENTS

Baron, J. (1991). Beliefs about thinking. In J.F. Voss, D.N. Perkins & J.W. Segal (Eds.), *Developmental perspectives on teaching and learning thinking skills* (pp.169–186). Basel: Karger.

Baron, J. (1995). Myside bias in thinking about abortion. *Thinking and Reasoning, 1*(3), 201–288.

Beckman, L. (1973). Teachers' and observers' perceptions of causality for a child's performance. *Journal of Educational Psychology, 65*, 198–204.

Bless, H., Mackie, D.M. & Schwarz, N. (1992). Mood effects on attitude judgments: Independent effects of mood before and after message elaboration. *Journal of Personality and Social Psychology, 63*(4), 585–595.

Brem, S.K. & Rips, L.J. (2000). Explanation and evidence in informal argument. *Cognitive Science, 24*(4), 573–604.

Chaiken, S., Lieberman, A. & Eagly, A.H. (1989). Heuristic and systematic processing within and beyond persuasion context. In J.S. Uleman & J.A. Bargh (Eds.), *Unintended thought*. New York: Guilford.

Curley, S.P. & Benson, P.G. (1994). Applying a cognitive perspective to probability construction. In G. Wright and P. Ayton (Eds.), *Subjective probability* (pp.105–209). Chichester: Wiley.

Ditto, P.H. & Lopez, D.F. (1992). Motivated scepticism: Use of differential decision criteria for preferred and nonpreferred conclusions. *Journal of Personality and Social Psychology, 63*(4), 568–584.

Ditto, P.H., Jemmot III, J.B. & Darley, J.M. (1988). Appraising the threat of illness: A mental representation approach. *Health Psychology, 7*, 183–200.

Edwards, K. and Smith, E.E. (1996). A disconfirmation bias in the evaluation of arguments. *Journal of Personality and Social Psychology, 71*(1), 5–24.

Evans, J. St B.T., Newstead, S.E. & Byrne, R.M.J. (1993). *Human reasoning: The psychology of deduction*. Hove: Erlbaum.

George, C. (1995). The endorsement of the premises: Assumption-based or belief-based reasoning. *British Journal of Psychology, 86*, 93–111.

Glassner, A., Weinstock, M. & Neuman, Y. (2005). Pupils' evaluation and generation of evidence and explanation in argument. *British Journal of Educational Psychology, 75*, 105–118.

Handley, S.J., Capon, A., Beveridge, M., Dennis, I. & Evans, J. St B.T. (2004). Working memory, inhibitory control and the development of children's reasoning. *Thinking and Reasoning, 10*, 175–195.

Hastie, R. & Pennington, N. (2000). Explanation-based decision making. In T. Connolly, H.R. Arkes & K.R. Hammond (Eds.), *Judgment and decision making: An interdisciplinary reader* (2nd edn, pp.212–228). Cambridge: Cambridge University Press.

Hastorf, A.H. & Cantril, H. (1954). They saw a game: A case study. *Journal of Abnormal and Social Psychology, 49*, 129–134.

Hovland, C.I., Lumsdaine, A.A. & Sheffield, F.D. (1949). *Experiments on mass communication. Studies in social psychology in World War II: Vol. 3.* Princeton, NJ: Princeton University Press.

Klaczynski, P.A. (1997). Bias in adolescents' everyday reasoning and its relationship with intellectual ability, personal theories, and self-serving motivation. *Developmental Psychology, 33*, 273–283.

Klaczynski, P.A. & Robinson, B. (2000). Personal theories, intellectual ability, and epistemological beliefs: Adult age differences in everyday reasoning tasks. *Psychology and Aging, 15*, 400–416.

Kleindorfer, P.R., Kunreuther, H.C. & Schoemaker, P.J.H. (1993). *Decision sciences: An integrative perspective*. Cambridge: Cambridge University Press.

Koehler, J.J. (1993). The influence of prior beliefs on scientific judgments of evidence quality. *Organizational Behavior and Human Decision Processes, 56*, 28–55.

Kuhn, D. (1991). *The skills of argument*. Cambridge: Cambridge University Press.

Kuhn, D. (2004). Developing reason. *Thinking and Reasoning, 10*(2), 197–219.

Lord, C.G., Ross, L. & Lepper, M.R. (1979). Biased assimilation and attitude polarization: The effects of prior theories on subsequently considered evidence. *Journal of Personality and Social Psychology, 37*, 2098–2109.

MacCoun, R.J. (1998). Biases in the interpretation and use of research results. *Annual Review of Psychology, 49*, 259–287.

Mackie, D.M. & Worth, L.T. (1989). Cognitive deficits and the mediation of positive affect in persuasion. *Journal of Personality and Social Psychology, 57*, 27–40.

Manktelow, K.I. (1999). *Reasoning and Thinking*. Hove: Psychology Press.

McHoskey, J.W. (1995). Case closed? On the John F. Kennedy assassination: Biased assimilation of evidence and attitude polarization. *Basic Applied Social Psychology, 17*, 395–409.

Mulligan, E.J. & Hastie, R. (2005). Explanations determine the impact of information on financial investment judgments. *Journal of Behavioral Decision Making, 18*, 145–156.

Myers, D.G. (2005). *Social psychology* (8th edn). New York: McGraw-Hill.

Neuman, Y. (2003). Go ahead, prove that God does not exist! On high school students' ability to deal with fallacious arguments. *Learning and Instruction, 13*, 367–380.

Neuman, Y. & Weizman, E. (2003). The role of text representation in students' ability to identify fallacious arguments. *The Quarterly Journal of Experimental Psychology, 56A*(5), 849–864.

Pennington, N. & Hastie, R. (1986). Evidence evaluation in complex decision making. *Journal of Personality and Social Psychology, 51*, 242–258.

Pennington, N. & Hastie, R. (1988). Explanation-based decision making: The effects on memory structure on judgment. *Journal of Experimental Psychology: Learning, Memory, and Cognition, 14*, 521–533.

Pennington, N. & Hastie, R. (1992). Explaining the evidence: Tests of the story model for juror decision making. *Journal of Personality and Social Psychology, 62*(2), 189–206.

Pennington, N. & Hastie, R. (1993). Reasoning in explanation-based decision making. *Cognition, 49*, 123–163.

Perkins, D.N. (1985). Postprimary education has little impact on informal reasoning. *Journal of Educational Psychology, 77*, 562–571.

Petty, R.E. & Cacioppo, J.T. (1986). The elaboration likelihood model of persuasion. In L. Berkowitz (Ed.), *Advances in experimental social psychology: Vol. 19*. New York: Academic Press.

Petty, R.E., Schumann, D.W., Richman, S.A. & Strathman, A.J. (1993). Positive mood and persuasion: Different roles for affect under high and low elaboration conditions. *Journal of Personality and Social Psychology, 64*, 5–20.

Pyszczynski, T., Greenberg, J. & Holt, K. (1985). Maintaining consistency between self-serving beliefs and available data: A bias in information evaluation following success and failure. *Personality and Social Psychology Bulletin, 21*, 195–211.

Sá, W.C., Kelley, C.N., Ho, C. & Stanovich, K.E. (2005). Thinking about personal theories: individual differences in the coordination of theory and evidence. *Personality and Individual Differences, 38*, 1149–1161.

Sá, W.C., West, R.F. & Stanovich, K.E. (1999). The domain specificity and generality of belief bias: searching for a generalizable critical thinking skill. *Journal of Educational Psychology, 91*(3), 497–510.

Shaw, V.F. (1996). The cognitive processes in informal reasoning. *Thinking and Reasoning, 2*(1), 51–80.

Stanovich, K.E. & West, R.F. (1997). Reasoning independently of prior belief and individual differences in actively open-minded thinking. *Journal of Educational Psychology, 89*, 342–357.

Stanovich, K.E. & West, R.F. (1998). Individual differences in rational thought. *Journal of Experimental Psychology: General, 127*, 161–188.

Stanovich, K.E. & West, R.F. (2007). Natural myside bias is independent of cognitive ability. *Thinking and Reasoning, 13*(3), 225–247.

Toulmin, S. (1958). *The uses of argument*. Cambridge: Cambridge University Press.

Vallone, R.P., Ross, L. & Lepper, M.R. (1985). The hostile media phenomenon: Biased perception and perceptions of media bias in coverage of the Beirut massacre. *Journal of Personality and Social Psychology, 49*, 577–585.

Walton, D.N. (1989). *Informal logic: A handbook for critical argumentation*. Cambridge: Cambridge University Press.

Walton, D.N. (1996). *Argumentation schemes for presumptive reasoning*. Mahwah, NJ: Erlbaum.

Williams, D.K., Bourgeois, M.J. & Croyle, R.T. (1993). The effects of stealing thunder in criminal and civil trials. *Law and Human Behavior, 17*, 597–609.

Wyer, R.S. & Frey, D. (1983). The effects of feedback about self and others on the recall and judgments of feedback-relevant information. *Journal of Experimental Social Psychology, 19*, 540–559.

CHAPTER 6. COVARIATION, CAUSATION, AND COUNTERFACTUAL THINKING

Ahn, W., Kalish, C.W., Medin, D.L. & Gelman, S.A. (1995). The role of covariation versus mechanism information in causal attribution. *Cognition, 54*, 299–352.

Anderson, J.R. (1990). *The adaptive character of thought*. Hillsdale, NJ: Erlbaum.

Anderson, J.R. (2000). *Learning and memory: An integrated approach* (2nd edn). New Jersey: Wiley.

Anderson, J.R. & Sheu, C.-F. (1995). Causal inferences as perceptual judgments. *Memory and Cognition, 23*(4), 510–524.

Carroll, J.S. (1978). The effect of imagining an event on expectations for the event: An interpretation in terms of the availability heuristic. *Journal of Experimental Social Psychology, 14*(1), 88–96.

Chapman, L.J. (1967). Illusory correlation in observational report. *Journal of Verbal Learning and Behavior, 6*, 151–155.

Chapman, L.J. & Chapman, J.P. (1967). Genesis of popular but erroneous psychodiagnostic observations. *Journal of Abnormal Psychology, 72*, 193–204.

Chapman, L.J. & Chapman, J.P. (1969). Illusory correlation as an obstacle to the use of valid psychodiagnostic signs. *Journal of Abnormal Psychology, 74*, 271–280.

Chapman, L.J. & Chapman, J.P. (1971). Test results are what you think they are. *Psychology Today, November*, 18–22, 106–110.

Cheng, P.W. (1997). From covariation to causation: A causal power theory. *Psychological Review, 104*(2), 367–405.

Craik, K.J.W. (1943). *The nature of explanation*. Cambridge: Cambridge University Press.

Davis, C.G., Lehman, D.R., Wortman, C.B., Silver, R.C. & Thompson, S.C. (1995). The undoing of traumatic life events. *Personality and Social Psychology Bulletin, 21*, 109–124.

Dougherty, M.R.P., Gettys, C.F. & Thomas, R.P. (1997). The role of mental simulation in judgments of likelihood. *Organizational Behavior and Human Decision Processes, 70*(2), 135–148.

Feynman, R.P. (1986). *Surely you're joking Mr. Feynman*. London: Unwin.

Fugelsang, J.A. & Dunbar, K.N. (2005). Brain-based mechanisms underlying complex causal thinking. *Neuropsychologia, 43*, 1204–1213.

Fugelsang, J.A. & Thompson, V.A. (2003). A dual-process model of belief and evidence interactions in causal reasoning. *Memory and Cognition, 31*(5), 800–815.

Glines, C.V. (1991, January). The cargo cults. *Air Force Magazine Online, 74*(1). Retrieved 12 February 2007 from http://www.afa.org/magazine/1991/0191cargo.asp.

Gregory, W.L., Cialdini, R.B. & Carpenter, K.M. (1982). Self-relevant scenarios as mediators of likelihood estimates and compliance: Does imagining make it so? *Journal of Personality and Social Psychology, 43*, 89–99.

Kahneman, D. & Miller, D.T. (1986). Norm theory: Comparing reality to its alternatives. *Psychological Review, 93*(2), 136–153.

Kahneman, A. & Tversky, A. (1982). The simulation heuristic. In D. Kahneman, P. Slovic & A. Tversky (Eds.), *Judgment under uncertainty: Heuristics and biases* (pp.201–208). Cambridge: Cambridge University Press.

Kao, S.-F. & Wasserman, E.A. (1993). Assessment of an information integration account of contingency judgment with examination of subjective cell importance and method of information presentation. *Journal of Experimental Psychology: Learning, Memory, and Cognition, 19*(6), 1363–1386.

Kempton, W. (1986). Two theories of home heat control. *Cognitive Science, 10*(1), 75–90.

Koehler, D.J. (1991). Explanation, imagination, and confidence in judgment. *Psychological Bulletin, 110*(3), 499–519.

Levin, I.P., Wasserman, E.A. & Kao, S-F. (1993). Multiple methods for examining biased information use in contingency judgments. *Organizational Behavior and Human Decision Processes, 55*, 228–250.

Lipe, M.G. (1990). A lens-model analysis of covariation research. *Journal of Behavioral Decision Making, 3*, 47–59.

Lober, K. & Shanks, D.R. (2000). Is causal induction based on causal power? Critique of Cheng (1997). *Psychological Review, 10*(1), 195–212.

Mackie, J.L. (1974). *The cement of the universe: A study of causation*. Oxford: Oxford University Press.

McKenzie, C.R.M. & Mikkelson, L.A. (2007). A Bayesian view of covariation assessment. *Cognitive Psychology, 54*(1), 33–61.

McKenzie, C.R.M., Ferreira, V.S., Mikkelsen, L.A., McDermott, K.J. & Skrable, R.P. (2001). Do conditional hypotheses target rare events? *Organizational Behavior and Human Decision Processes, 85*, 291–309.

Miller, D.T., Turnbull, W. & McFarland, C. (1990). Counterfactual thinking and social perception: Thinking about what might have been. In M.P. Zanna (Ed.), *Advances in Experimental Social Psychology, Vol. 23* (pp.305–331). New York: Academic Press.

N'gbala, A. & Branscombe, N.R. (1995). Mental simulation and causal attribution: When simulating an event does not affect fault assignment. *Journal of Experimental Social Psychology, 31*, 139–162.

Norman, D.A. (2002). *The design of everyday things.* (Originally published in 1988 as *The psychology of everyday things.*) New York: Basic Books.

Perales, J.C. & Shanks, D.R. (2003). Normative and descriptive accounts of the influence of power and contingency on causal judgment. *Quarterly Journal of Experimental Psychology, 56*(6), 977–1007

Rescorla, R.A. & Wagner, A.R. (1972). A theory of Pavlovian conditioning: Variations on the effectiveness of reinforcement and nonreinforcement. In A.H. Black & W.F. Prokasy (Eds.), *Classical conditioning II: Current research and theory* (pp.64–99). New York: Appleton-Century-Crofts.

Roese, N.J. (1994). The functional basis of counterfactual thinking. *Journal of Personality and Social Psychology, 66*(5), 805–818.

Roese, N.J. (1997). Counterfactual thinking. *Psychological Bulletin, 121*(1), 133–148.

Schustack, M.W. & Sternberg, R.J. (1981). Evaluation of evidence in causal inference. *Journal of Experimental Psychology: General, 110*, 101–120.

Shanks, D.R. (2004). Judging covariation and causation. In D.J. Koehler and N. Harvey (Eds.), *Blackwell handbook of judgment and decision making.* Oxford: Blackwell.

Smedslund, J. (1963). The concept of correlation in adults. *Scandinavian Journal of Psychology, 4*, 165–173.

Vallée-Tourangeau, F., Hollingsworth, L. & Murphy, R.A. (1998). 'Attentional bias' in correlation judgments? Smedslund (1963) revisited. *Scandinavian Journal of Psychology, 39*, 221–233.

Ward, W.C. & Jenkins, H.M. (1965). The display of information and the judgment of contingency. *Canadian Journal of Psychology, 19*, 231–241.

Wasserman, E.A., Dorner, W.W. & Kao, S.-F. (1990). Contributions of specific cell information to judgments of interevent contingency. *Journal of Experimental Psychology: Learning, Memory, and Cognition, 16*, 509–521.

Wasserman, E.A., Elek, S.M., Chatlosh, D.L. & Baker, A.G. (1993). Rating causal relations: The role of probability in judgments of response-outcome contingency. *Journal of Experimental Psychology: Learning, Memory, and Cognition, 19*, 174–188.

White, P. A. (1989). A theory of causal processing. *British Journal of Psychology, 80*, 431–454.

CHAPTER 7. DECISION MAKING UNDER RISK AND UNCERTAINITY

Ali, M. (1977). Probability and utility estimates for racetrack bettors. *Journal of Political Economy, 85*, 803–815.

Allais, M. (1953). Le comportement de l'homme rationnel devant le risqué, critique des posulats et axioms de l'École Americaine. *Econometrica, 21*, 503–46.

Allais, M. (1990). Criticism of the postulates and axioms of the American School. In P.K. Moser (Ed.), *Rationality in action: Contemporary approaches.* Cambridge: Cambridge University Press. Reprinted from M. Allais and O. Hagen (Eds.), *Expected utility hypotheses and the Allais paradox* (pp.67–95). Dordrecht: D. Reidel.

Battalio, R.C., Kagel, J.H. & MacDonald, D.N. (1985). Animals' choices over uncertain outcomes: Some initial experimental results. *American Economic Review, 75*, 597–613.

Bernoulli, D. (1954[1738]). *Specimen theoriae novae de mensura sortis* [Exposition of a new theory on the measurement of risk]. Translation from Latin printed in *Econometrica, 22*, 23–36.

Birnbaum, M.H. (1997). Violations of monotonicity in judgment and decision making. In A.A.J. Marley (Ed.), *Choice, decision, and measurement: Essays in honor of R. Duncan Luce* (pp.73–100). Mahwah, NJ: Erlbaum.

Birnbaum, M.H. (2006). Evidence against prospect theories in gambles with positive, negative, and mixed consequences. *Journal of Economic Psychology, 27*, 737–761.

Brandstätter, E., Gigerenzer, G. & Hertwig, R. (2006). The priority heuristic: Making choices without trade-offs. *Psychological Review, 113*(2), 409–432.

Breiter, H.C., Ahron, I., Kahneman, D., Dale, A. & Shizgal, P. (2001). Functional imaging of neural responses to expectancy and experience of monetary gains and losses. *Neuron, 30*, 619–39.

Busemeyer, J.R. & Johnson, J.G. (2004). Computational models of decision making. In D.J. Koehler & N. Harvey (Eds.), *Blackwell handbook of judgment and decision making* (pp.133–154). Oxford: Blackwell.

Camerer, C.F. (2000). Prospect theory in the wild: Evidence from the field. In D. Kahneman & A. Tversky (Eds.), *Choices, values, and frames.* Cambridge: Cambridge University Press.

Camerer, C.F., Babcock, L., Loewenstein, G. & Thaler, R.H. (2000). Labor supply of New York City cab drivers: One day at a time. In D. Kahneman & A. Tversky (Eds.), *Choices, values, and frames.* Cambridge: Cambridge University Press.

Caraco, T. (1980). On foraging time allocation in a stochastic environment. *Ecology, 61*, 119–128.

Caraco, T. (1981). Energy budgets, risk and foraging preferences in dark-eyed juncos (*Junco hyemalis*). *Behavioral Ecology and Sociobiology, 8*, 213–217.

Caraco, T. (1983). White-crowned sparrows (*Zonotrichia leucophrys*): Foraging preferences in a risky environment. *Behavioral Ecology and Sociobiology, 12*, 63–69.

Caraco, T., Martindale, S. & Whittam, T.S. (1980). An empirical demonstration of risk-sensitive foraging preferences. *Animal Behavior, 28*, 820–831.

Christensen, C., Heckerling, P., Mackesy-Amiti, M.E., Bernstein L.M. & Elstein, A.S. (1995). Pervasiveness of framing effects among physicians and medical students. *Journal of Behavioral Decision Making, 8*, 169–180.

De Martino, B., Kumaran, D., Seymour, B. & Dolan, R.J. (2006, 4 August). Frames, biases, and rational decision-making in the human brain. *Science, 313*, 684–687.

Dougherty, M.R.P. & Hunter, J.E. (2003a). Probability judgment and subadditivity: The role of working memory capacity and constraining retrieval. *Memory and Cognition, 31*(6), 968–982.

Dougherty, M.R.P. & Hunter, J.E. (2003b). Hypothesis generation, probability judgment, and individual differences in working memory capacity. *Acta Psychologica, 113*, 263–282.

Dunegan, K.J. (1993). Framing, cognitive modes, and Image Theory: Toward an understanding of a glass half full. *Journal of Applied Psychology, 78*(3), 491–503.

Ellsberg, D. (1961). Risk, ambiguity, and the Savage axioms. *Quarterly Journal of Economics, 75*, 643–669.

Erk, S., Spitzer, M., Wunderlich, A.P., Galley, L. & Walter, H. (2002). Cultural objects modulate reward circuitry. *Neuroreport, 13*, 2499–2503.

Fox, C.R. & See, K.E. (2003). Belief and preference in decision under uncertainty. In D. Hardman & L. Macchi (Eds.), *Thinking: Psychological perspectives on reasoning, judgment, and decision making* (pp.273–314). Chichester: Wiley.

Fox, C.R. & Tversky, A. (1998). A belief-based account of decision under uncertainty. *Management Science, 44*(7), 879–895.

Goldstein, E.B. (2007). *Sensation and perception* (7th edn). Belmont, CA: Thomson-Wadsworth.

Gonzalez, R. & Wu, G. (1999). On the shape of the probability weighting function. *Cognitive Psychology, 38*(1), 129–166.

Gonzalez, C., Dana, J., Koshino, H. & Just, M. (2005). The framing effect and risky decisions: Examining cognitive functions with fMRI. *Journal of Economic Psychology, 26*, 1–20.

Goodwin, P. & Wright, G. (2004). *Decision analysis for management judgment* (3rd edn.). Chichester: Wiley.

Hamm, R.M. (2003). Medical decision scripts: Combining cognitive scripts and judgment strategies to account fully for medical decision making. In D. Hardman & L. Macchi (Eds.), *Thinking: Psychological perspectives on reasoning, judgment, and decision making* (pp.315–345). Chichester: Wiley.

Harder, L. & Real, L.A. (1987). Why are bumble bees risk-averse? *Ecology, 68*, 1104–1108.

Heath, C. & Tversky, A. (1991). Preference and belief: Ambiguity and competence in choice under uncertainty. *Journal of Risk and Uncertainty*, 4, 5–28.

Kacelnik, A. & Bateson, M. (1996). Risky theories – the effects of variance on foraging decisions. *American Zoologist*, 36, 402–434.

Kagel, J.H., MacDonald, D.N. & Battalio, R.C. (1990). Test of 'fanning out' of indifference curves from animal and human experiments. *American Economic Review*, 80, 912–921.

Kahneman, D. & Tversky, A. (1979). Prospect theory: An analysis of decision making under risk. *Econometrica*, 47, 263–91.

Kahneman, D. & Tversky, A. (1984). Choices, values, and frames. *American Psychologist*, 39(4), 341–350.

Kahneman, D. & Tversky, A. (1992). Advances in prospect theory: Cumulative representation of uncertainty. *Journal of Risk and Uncertainty*, 5, 297–324.

McClure, S.M., Tomlin, J.L.D., Cypert, K.S., Montague, L.M. & Montague, P.R. (2004). Neural correlates of behavioural preference for culturally familiar drinks. *Neuron*, 44, 379–387.

McGlothlin, W.H. (1956). Stability of choices among uncertain alternatives. *American Journal of Psychology*, 69, 604–615.

McNeil, B.J., Pauker, S.G., Sox, H.C. Jr. & Tversky, A. (1982). On the elicitation of preferences for alternative therapies. *New England Journal of Medicine*, 306(21), 1259–1262.

Montague, R. (2006). *Why choose this book? How we make decisions*. London: Dutton.

Montague, P.R. & Berns, G.S. (2002). Neural economics and the biological substrates of valuation. *Neuron*, 36, 265–284.

Odean, T. (2000). Are investors reluctant to realize their losses? *Journal of Finance*, 53(5), 1775–1798.

Payne, J.W., Bettman, J.R. & Johnson, E.J. (1993). *The adaptive decision maker*. Cambridge: Cambridge University Press.

Pietras, C.J. & Hackenberg, T.D. (2001). Risk-sensitive choice in humans as a function of an earnings budget. *Journal of the Experimental Analysis of Behavior*, 76, 1–19.

Pietras, C.J., Locey, M.L. & Hackenberg, T.D. (2003). Human risky choice under temporal constraints: Tests of an energy-budget model. *Journal of the Experimental Analysis of Behavior*, 80, 59–75.

Real, L.A. (1996). Paradox, performance, and the architecture of decision-making in animals. *American Zoologist*, 36, 518–529.

Rode, C., Cosmides, L., Hell, W. & Tooby, J. (1999). When and why do people avoid unknown probabilities in decisions under uncertainty? Testing some predictions from optimal foraging theory. *Cognition*, 72, 269–304.

Romo, R. & Schultz, W. (1990). Dopamine neurons of the monkey midbrain: contingencies of responses to active touch during self-initiated arm movements. *Journal of Neurophysiology*, 63(3), 592–606.

Rottenstreich, Y. & Hsee, C.K. (2001). Money, kisses, and electric shocks: On the affective psychology of risk. *Psychological Science*, 12, 185–190.

Savage, L.J. (1954). *The foundation of statistics*. New York: Wiley.

Shafir, S. (2000). Risk-sensitive foraging: The effect of relative variability. *Oikos*, 89, 1–7.

Shafir, S., Wiegmann, D., Smith, B.H. & Real, L.A. (1999). Risk-sensitive foraging: Choice behaviour of honey bees in response to variability in volume of reward. *Animal Behavior*, 57, 1055–1061.

Shiv, B., Loewenstein, G., Bechara, A., Damasio, H. & Damasio, A.R. (2005). Investment behaviour and the negative side of emotion. *Psychological Science*, 16(6), 435–439.

Siminoff, L.A. & Fetting, J.H. (1989). Effects of outcome framing on treatment decisions in the real world: Impact of framing on adjuvant breast cancer decisions. *Medical Decision Making*, 9, 262–271.

Slovic, P. & Tversky, A. (1974). Who accepts Savage's axiom? *Behavioral Science*, 19, 368–73.

Soto, R.E., Castilla, J.C. & Bozinovic, F. (2005). The impact of physiological demands on foraging decisions under predation risk: A test with the whelk *Acanthia monodon*. *Ethology*, 111, 1044–1049.

Stanovich, K.E. & West, R.F. (1998). Individual differences in framing and conjunction effects. *Thinking and Reasoning*, 4(4), 289–317.

Stephens, D.W. (1981). The logic of risk-sensitive foraging preferences. *Animal Behavior*, 29, 626–629.

Steward, W.T., Schneider, T.R., Pizarro, J. & Salovey, P. (2003). Need for cognition moderates responses to framed smoking-cessation messages. *Journal of Applied Social Psychology*, 33(12), 2439–2464.

Stewart, N., Chater, N. & Brown, G.D.A. (2006). Decision by sampling. *Cognitive Psychology*, 53, 1–26.

Thaler, R.H. (1980). Toward a positive theory of consumer choice. *Journal of Economic Behavior and Organization*, 1, 39–60.

Tom, S.B., Fox, C.R., Trepel, C., Poldrack, R.A. (2007). The neural basis of loss aversion in decision-making under risk. *Science*, 315, 515–518.

Tversky, A. & Koehler, D. (1994). Support theory: A nonextensional representation of subjective probability. *Psychological Review*, 101, 547–567.

Weber, E.U., Shafir, S. & Blais, A.-R. (2004). Predicting risk sensitivity in humans and lower animals: Risk as variance or coefficient of variation. *Psychological Review*, 111(2), 430–445.

CHAPTER 8. PREFERENCE AND CHOICE

Arkes, H.R. (1996). The psychology of waste. *Journal of Behavioral Decision Making*, 9, 213–224.

Arkes, H.R. & Ayton, P. (1999). The sunk cost and Concorde effects: Are humans less rational than lower animals? *Psychological Bulletin*, 125(5), 591–600.

Arkes, H.R. & Blumer, C. (1985). The psychology of sunk cost. *Organizational Behavior and Human Decision Processes*, 35, 124–140.

Baron, J. (1997). Biases in the quantitative measurement of values for public decisions. *Psychological Bulletin*, 122(1), 72–88.

Bernard, J. & Giurfa, M. (2004). A test of transitive inferences in free-flying honeybees: Unsuccessful performance due to memory constraints. *Learning and Memory*, 11, 328–336.

Black, J.S., Stern, P.C. & Elworth, J.T. (1985). Personal and contextual influences on household energy adaptations. *Journal of Applied Psychology*, 70, 3–21.

Bown, N.J., Read, D. & Summers, B. (2003). The lure of choice. *Journal of Behavioral Decision Making*, 16, 297–308.

Cialdini, R.B., Reno, R.R. & Kallgren, C.A. (1990). A focus theory of normative conduct. Recycling the concept of norms to reduce littering in public places. *Journal of Personality and Social Psychology*, 58, 1015–1026.

Coursey, D.L., Hovis, J.L. & Schulze, W.D. (1987). The disparity between willingness to accept and willingness to pay measures of value. *The Quarterly Journal of Economics*, 102, 679–690.

Fetherstonhaugh, D., Slovic, P., Johnson, S.M. & Friedrich, J. (1997). Insensitivity to the value of human life: A study of psychophysical numbing. *Journal of Risk and Uncertainty*, 14(3), 282–300.

Fiske, A.P. & Tetlock, P.E. (1997). Taboo trade-offs: Reactions to transactions that transgress spheres of justice. *Political Psychology*, 18, 255–297.

Gilbert, D.T. & Ebert, J.E.J. (2002). Decisions and revisions: The affective forecasting of changeable options. *Journal of Personality and Social Psychology*, 82(4), 503–514.

Gourville, J.T. & Soman, D. (1998). Payment depreciation: The effects of temporally separating payments from consumption. *Journal of Consumer Research*, 25(2), 160–174.

Heath, C. & Soll, J.B. (1996). Mental budgeting and consumer decisions. *The Journal of Consumer Research*, 23(1), 40–52.

Hopper, J.R. & Nielsen, J.M. (1991). Recycling as altruistic behaviour: Normative and behavioural strategies to expand participation in a community recycling program. *Environment and Behavior*, 23, 195–220.

Hsee, C.K. (1996). The evaluability hypothesis: An explanation for preference reversals between joint and separate evaluations of alternatives. *Organizational Behavior and Human Decision Processes, 67*(3), 247–257.

Hsee, C.K. (1998). Less is better: When low-value options are valued more highly than high-value options. *Journal of Behavioral Decision Making, 11*, 107–121.

Huber, J., Payne, J.W. & Pluto, C. (1982). Adding asymmetrically dominated alternatives: Violations of regularity and the similarity hypothesis. *Journal of Consumer Research, 9*, 90–98.

Iyengar, S.S. & Lepper, M.R. (2000). When choice is demotivating: Can one desire too much of a good thing? *Journal of Personality and Social Psychology, 79*(6), 995–1006.

Jenni, K.E. & Loewenstein, G. (1997). Explaining the 'identifiable victim effect'. *Journal of Risk and Uncertainty, 14*, 235–257.

Johnson, E.J., Hershey, J., Meszaros, J. & Kunreuther, H. (1993). Framing, probability distortions, and insurance decisions. *Journal of Risk and Uncertainty, 7*, 35–51.

Kahneman, D. & Miller, D.T. (1986). Norm theory: Comparing reality to its alternatives. *Psychological Review, 93*(2), 136–153.

Kahneman, D. & Tversky, A. (1979). Prospect theory: An analysis of decision making under risk. *Econometrica, 47*, 263–291.

Kahneman, D. & Tversky, A. (1984). Choices, values, and frames. *American Psychologist, 39*(4), 341–350.

Kahneman, D. & Tversky, A. (1992). Advances in prospect theory: Cumulative representation of uncertainty. *Journal of Risk and Uncertainty, 5*, 297–324.

Kahneman, D., Knetsch, J.L. & Thaler, R. (1990). Experimental tests of the endowment effect and the Coase theorem. *Journal of Political Economy, 98*, 1325–1348.

Kivetz, R. & Simonson, I. (2002). Self control for the righteous: Toward a theory of precommitment to indulgence. *Journal of Consumer Research, 29*(2), 199–217.

Kogut, T. & Ritov, I. (2005a). The 'identified victim' effect: An identified group or just a single individual? *Journal of Behavioral Decision Making, 18*, 157–167.

Kogut, T. & Ritov, I. (2005b). The singularity effect of identified victims in separate and joint evaluation. *Organizational Behavior and Human Decision Processes, 97*, 106–116.

Larrick, R.P., Morgan, J.N. & Nisbett, R.E. (1990). Teaching the use of cost-benefit reasoning in everyday life. *Psychological Science, 1*, 362–370.

Lichtenstein, S. & Slovic, P. (1971). Reversals of preference between bids and choices in gambling decisions. *Journal of Experimental Psychology, 89*(1), 46–55.

Lichtenstein, S. & Slovic, P. (1973) Response-induced reversals of preference in gambling: An extended replication in Las Vegas. *Journal of Experimental Psychology, 101*(1), 16–20.

Lichtenstein, S. & Slovic, P (Eds.) (2006). *The construction of preference*. Cambridge: Cambridge University Press.

List, J.A. (2004). Neoclassical theory versus prospect theory: Evidence from the marketplace. *Econometrica, 72*(2), 615–625.

Payne, J.W., Bettman, J.R. & Johnson, E.J. (1988). Adaptive strategy selection in decision making. *Journal of Experimental Psychology: Learning, Memory, and Cognition, 14*, 534–552.

Payne, J.W., Bettman, J.R. & Johnson, E.J. (1993). *The adaptive decision maker*. Cambridge: Cambridge University Press.

Peters, E. & Slovic, P. (1996). The role of affect and worldviews as orienting dispositions in the perception and acceptance of nuclear power. *Journal of Applied Social Psychology, 26*(16), 1427–1453.

Peters, E., Slovic, P. & Gregory, R. (2003). The role of affect in the WTA/WTP disparity. *Journal of Behavioral Decision Making, 16*, 309–330.

Ritov, I. & Baron, J. (1990). Reluctance to vaccinate: Omission bias and ambiguity. *Journal of Behavioral Decision Making, 3*, 263–277.

Ritov, I. & Baron, J. (1992). Status quo and omission biases. *Journal of Risk and Uncertainty, 5*, 49–61.

Schkade, D.A. & Johnson, E.J. (1989). Cognitive processes in preference reversals. *Organizational Behavior and Human Decision Processes, 44*, 203–231.

Schwartz, B., Ward, A., Monterosso, J., Lyubomirsky, S., White, K. & Lehman, D.R. (2002). Maximizing versus satisficing: Happiness is a matter of choice. *Journal of Personality and Social Psychology, 83*(5), 1178–1197.

Shafir, E. (Ed.) (2004). *Preference, Belief, and Similarity: The Selected Writings of Amos Tversky*. Cambridge, MA.: MIT Press.

Shafir, S. (1994). Intransitivity of preferences in honey bees: support for 'comparative' evaluation of foraging options. *Animal Behaviour, 48*, 55–67.

Simonson, I. & Tversky, A. (1992). Choice in context: Tradeoff contrast and extremeness aversion. *Journal of Marketing Research, 14*, 281–295.

Slovic, P. & Lichtenstein, S. (1968). Relative importance of probabilities and payoffs in risk taking. *Journal of Experimental Psychology, 78*(3/2).

Slovic, P., Griffin, D. & Tversky, A. (1990). Compatability effects in judgment and choice. In R. Hogarth (Ed.), *Insights in decision making: A tribute to Hillel J. Einhorn* (pp.5–27). Chicago: Chicago University Press.

Slovic, P., Layman, M., Kraus, N., Flynn, J., Chalmers, J. & Gesell, G. (1991). Perceived risk, stigma, and potential economic impacts of a high-level nuclear waste repository in Nevada. *Risk Analysis, 11*, 683–696.

Slovic, P., Finucane, M., Peters, E. & MacGregor, D.G. (2002). The affect heuristic. In T. Gilovich, D. Griffin & D. Kahneman (Eds.), *Heuristics and biases: The psychology of intuitive judgment*. Cambridge: Cambridge University Press.

Small, D.A. & Loewenstein, G. (2003). Helping *the* victim or helping *a* victim: Altruism and identifiability. *Journal of Risk and Uncertainty, 26*(1), 5–16.

Small, D.A. & Loewenstein, G. (2005). The devil you know: The effects of identifiability on punishment. *Journal of Behavioral Decision Making, 18*, 311–318.

Soman, D. (2001). The mental accounting of sunk time costs: Why time is not like money. *Journal of Behavioral Decision Making, 14*(3), 169–185.

Staw, B.M. (1976). Knee-deep in the big muddy: A study of escalating commitment to a chosen course of action. *Organizational Behavior and Human Performance, 16*, 27–44.

Stern, P.C., Dietz, T. & Kalof, L. (1993). Value orientations, gender, and environmental concern. *Environment and Behavior, 25*, 322–348.

Sunstein, C.R. (2005). Moral heuristics. *Behavioral and Brain Sciences, 28*, 531–573.

Tanner, C. & Medin, D.L. (2004). Protected values: no omission bias and no framing effects. *Psychonomic Bulletin and Review, 11*(1), 185–191.

Thaler, R. (1980). Toward a positive theory of consumer choice. *Journal of Economic Behavior and Organization, 1*, 39–60.

Thaler, R. (1985). Mental accounting and consumer choice. *Marketing Science, 4*, 199–214.

Thaler, R. (1999). Mental accounting matters. *Journal of Behavioral Decision Making, 12*, 183–206.

Thaler, R.H. & Johnson, E.J. (1990). Gambling with the house money and trying to break even: The effects of prior outcomes on risky choice. *Management Science, 36*(6), 643–660.

Toffler, A. (1970). *Future Shock*. London: Bodley Head.

Tversky, A. (1969). The intransitivity of preferences. *Psychological Review, 76*, 31–48.

Tversky, A. & Shafir, E. (1992). Choice under conflict: The dynamics of deferred decision. *Psychological Science, 3*(6), 358–361.

Tversky, A., Sattath, S. & Slovic, P. (1988). Contingent weighting in judgment and choice. *Psychological Review, 95*, 371–384.

Tversky, A., Slovic, P. & Kahneman, D. (1990). The causes of preference reversal. *American Economic Review, 80*, 204–217.

Tykocinski, O.E. & Pittman, T.S. (1998). The consequences of doing nothing: Inaction inertia as avoidance of anticipated regret. *Journal of Personality and Social Psychology, 75*, 607–616.

Wilson, T.D. & Schooler, J.W. (1991). Thinking too much: Introspection can reduce the quality of preferences and decisions. *Journal of Personality and Social Psychology, 60*, 181–192.

Wilson, T.D., Lisle, D.J., Schooler, J.W., Hodges, S.D., Klaaren, K.J. & LaFleur, S.J. (1993). Introspecting about reasons can reduce post-choice satisfaction. *Personality and Social Psychology Bulletin, 19,* 331–339.

CHAPTER 9. CONFIDENCE AND OPTIMISM

Allwood, C.M. & Granhag, P.A. (1996). The effects of arguments on realism in confidence judgments. *Acta Psychologica, 91,* 99–119.

Aucote, H.M. & Gold, R.S. (2005). Non-equivalence of direct and indirect measures of unrealistic optimism. *Psychology, Health and Medicine, 10*(4), 376–383.

Barber, B.M. & Odean, T. (2001). Boys will be boys: Gender, overconfidence, and common stock investment. *The Quarterly Journal of Economics, 116,* 261–292.

Baumeister, R.F. (1989). The optimal margin of illusion. *Journal of Social and Clinical Psychology, 8,* 176–189.

Bazerman, M.H. (2001). The study of 'real' decision making. *Journal of Behavioral Decision Making, 14,* 353–384.

Beyer, S. (1990). Gender differences in the accuracy of self-evaluations of performance. *Journal of Personality and Social Psychology, 59,* 960–970.

Beyer, S. & Bowden, E.M. (1997). Gender differences in self-perceptions: Convergent evidence from three measures of accuracy and bias. *Personality and Social Psychology Bulletin, 23,* 157–172.

Bobbio, M., Detrano, R., Shandling, A.H., Ellestad, M.H., Clark, J., Brezden, O., Abecia, A. & Martinezcaro, D. (1992). Clinical assessment of the probability of coronary-artery disease – judgmental bias from personal knowledge. *Medical Decision Making, 12,* 197–203.

Burson, K.A., Larrick, R.P. & Klayman, J. (2006). Skilled or unskilled, but still unaware of it: How perceptions of difficulty drive miscalibration in relative comparisons. *Journal of Personality and Social Psychology, 90*(1), 60–77.

Camerer, C.F. & Lovallo, D. (2000). Overconfidence and excess entry: An experimental approach. In D. Kahneman & A. Tversky (Eds.), *Choices, values, and frames.* Cambridge: Cambridge University Press.

Cooper, A., Woo, C. & Dunkelberg, W. (1988). Entrepreneurs' perceived chances for success. *Journal of Business Venturing, 3,* 97–108.

Covey, J.A. & Davies, A.D.M. (2004). Are people unrealistically optimistic? It depends how you ask them. *British Journal of Health Psychology, 9*(1), 39–49.

Deaux, K. & Emswiller, T. (1974). Explanations of successful performance on sex-linked tasks: What is skill for the male is luck for the female. *Journal of Personality and Social Psychology, 29,* 80–85.

Deaux, K. & Farris, E. (1977). Attributing causes for one's own performance: the effects of sex, norms, and outcome. *Journal of Research in Personality, 11,* 59–72.

Drake, R.A. (1984). Lateral asymmetry of personal optimism. *Journal of Research in Personality, 18,* 497–507.

Dun & Bradstreet (1967). *Patterns of success in managing a business.* New York: Dun & Bradstreet.

Dunne, T., Roberts, M.J. & Samuelson, L. (1988). Patterns of firm entry and exit in US manufacturing industries. *RAND Journal of Economics, 19,* 495–515.

Dunning, D. (2005). *Self-insight: Roadblocks and detours on the path to knowing thyself.* New York and Hove: Psychology Press.

Eiser, J.R., Pahl, S. & Prins, Y.R.A. (2006). Optimism, pessimism, and the direction of self-other comparisons. *Journal of Experimental Social Psychology, 37,* 77–84.

Fenton-O'Creevy, M., Nicholson, N., Soane, E. & Willman, P. (2003) Trading on illusions: Unrealistic perceptions of control and trading performance. *Journal of Occupational and Organizational Psychology, 76,* 53–68.

Fischhoff, B. & McGregor, D. (1982). Subjective confidence in forecasts. *Journal of Forecasting, 1,* 155–172.

Fischhoff, B., Slovic, P. & Lichtenstein, S. (1977). Knowing with certainty: The appropriateness of extreme confidence. *Journal of Experimental Psychology: Human Perception and Performance, 3,* 552–564.

Gigerenzer, G., Hoffrage, U. & Kleinbolting, H. (1991). Probabilistic mental models: A Brunswikian theory of confidence. *Psychological Review, 98,* 506–528.

Griffin, D.W. & Tversky, A. (1992). The weighing of evidence and the determinants of confidence. *Cognitive Psychology, 24,* 411–435.

Harvey, N. (1994). Relations between confidence and skilled performance. In G. Wright and P. Ayton (Eds.), *Subjective probability* (pp.321–352). Chichester: Wiley.

Juslin, P. (1993). An explanation of the hard-easy effect in studies of realism of confidence in one's general knowledge. *European Journal of Cognitive Psychology, 5,* 55–71.

Juslin, P. (1994). The overconfidence phenomenon as a consequence of informal experimenter-guided selection of almanac items. *Organizational Behavior and Human Decision Processes, 57,* 226–246.

Juslin, P., Olsson, H. & Björkman, M. (1997). Brunswikian and Thurstonian origins of bias in probability assessment: On the interpretation of stochastic components of judgment. *Journal of Behavioral Decision Making, 10,* 189–209.

Juslin, P., Wennerholm, P. & Olsson, H. (1999). Format dependence in subjective probability calibration. *Journal of Experimental Psychology: Learning, Memory, and Cognition, 28,* 1038–1052.

Juslin, P., Winman, A. & Olsson, H. (2000). Naive empiricism and dogmatism in confidence research: A critical examination of the hard-easy effect. *Psychological Review, 107*(2), 384–396.

Keren, G. (1987). Facing uncertainty in the game of bridge: A calibration study. *Organizational Behavior and Human Decision Processes, 39,* 98–114.

Klayman, J., Soll, J.B., González-Vallejo, C. & Barlas, S. (1999). Overconfidence: It depends on how, what, and whom you ask. *Organizational Behavior and Human Decision Processes, 79,* 216–247.

Klein, C.T.F. & Helweg-Larsen, M. (2002). Perceived control and the optimistic bias: A meta-analytic review. *Psychology and Health, 17,* 437–446.

Koehler, D.J., Brenner, L. & Griffin, D. (2002). The calibration of expert judgment: Heuristics and biases beyond the laboratory. In T. Gilovich, D. Griffin & D. Kahneman (2002), *Heuristics and biases: The psychology of intuitive judgment.* Cambridge: Cambridge University Press.

Koriat, A., Lichtenstein, S. & Fischhoff, B. (1980). Reasons for confidence. *Journal of Experimental Psychology: Human Learning and Memory, 6,* 107–118.

Krueger, J. & Mueller, R.A. (2002). Unskilled, unaware, or both? The better-than-average heuristic and statistical regression predict errors in estimates of own performance. *Journal of Personality and Social Psychology, 82,* 180–188.

Kruger, J. & Dunning, D. (1999). Unskilled and unaware of it: How difficulties in recognizing one's own incompetence lead to inflated self-assessments. *Journal of Personality and Social Psychology, 77,* 1121–1134.

Langer, E. (1975). The illusion of control. *Journal of Personality and Social Psychology, 32,* 311–328.

Lee, J.W., Yates, J.F., Shinotsuka, H., Singh, R., Onglatco, M.L.U., Yen, N.S., Gupta, M. & Bhatnagar, D. (1995). Cross-national differences in overconfidence. *Asian Journal of Psychology, 1,* 63–69.

Lenney, E. (1977). Women's self-confidence in achievement settings. *Psychological Bulletin, 84,* 1–13.

Lerner, J.S. & Keltner, D. (2001). Fear, anger, and risk. *Journal of Personality and Social Psychology, 81,* 146–159.

Lichtenstein, S., Fischhoff, B., and Phillips, L.D. (1982). Calibration of probabilities: The state of the art to 1980. In D. Kahneman, P. Slovic & A. Tversky (Eds.), *Judgment under uncertainty: Heuristics and biases.* Cambridge: Cambridge University Press.

Lundeberg, M.A., Fox, P.W. & Punæochaà, J. (1994). Highly confident but wrong: Gender differences and similarities in confidence judgments. *Journal of Educational Psychology, 86*(1), 114–121.

McClelland, A.G.R. & Bolger, F. (1994). The calibration of subjective probabilities: Theories and models 1980–1994. In G. Wright and P. Ayton (Eds.), *Subjective probability* (pp.453–482). Chichester: Wiley.

McKenna, F.P. (1993). It won't happen to me: Unrealistic optimism or illusion of control? *British Journal of Psychology, 84*, 39–50.

Murphy, A.H. & Winkler, R.L. (1977). Can weather forecasters formulate reliable probability forecasts of precipitation and temperature? *National Weather Digest, 2*, 2–9.

Myers, D. (2002). *Intuition: Its powers and perils*. New Haven: Yale University Press.

Odean, T. (1999). Do investors trade too much? *The American Economic Review, 89*(5), 1279–1298.

Perloff, L.S. (1987). Social comparison and illusions of invulnerability to negative life events. In C.R. Snyder & C. Ford (Eds.), *Coping with negative life events: Clinical and social psychological perspectives on negative life events* (pp.217–242). New York: Plenum Press.

Perloff, L.S. & Fetzer, B.K. (1986). Self-other judgments and perceived vulnerability to victimization. *Journal of Personality and Social Psychology, 50*, 502–511.

Poses, R.M. & Anthony, M. (1991). Availability, wishful thinking, and physicians' diagnostic judgments for patients with suspected bacteremia. *Medical Decision Making, 11*, 159–168.

Rosenthal, R. & Jacobsen, L. (1968). *Pygmalion in the classroom: Teacher expectation and pupil's intellectual development*. New York: Holt, Rinehart & Winston.

Russo, J.E. & Schoemaker, P.J.H. (1989). *Decision traps: Ten barriers to brilliant decision making and how to overcome them*. New York: Simon & Schuster.

Russo, J.E. & Schoemaker, P.J.H. (1992). Managing overconfidence. *Sloan Management Review, 33*, 7–17.

Sieber, J.E. (1974). Effects of decision importance on ability to generate warranted subjective uncertainty. *Journal of Personality and Social Psychology, 30*, 688–694.

Soll, J.B. & Klayman, J. (2004). Overconfidence in interval estimates. *Journal of Experimental Psychology: Learning, Memory, and Cognition, 30*, 299–314.

Taylor, S.E. & Brown, J.D. (1988). Illusion and well-being: A social psychological perspective on mental health. *Psychological Bulletin, 103*(2), 193–210.

Teigen, K.H. & Jørgensen, M. (2005). When 90% confidence intervals are 50% certain: On the credibility of credible intervals. *Applied Cognitive Psychology, 19*, 455–475.

Tetlock, P.E. (2005). *Expert political judgment: How good is it? How can we know?* Princeton, NJ: Princeton University Press.

Tversky, A. & Koehler, D.J. (1994). Support theory: A nonextensional representation of subjective probability. *Psychological Review, 101*, 547–567.

Wason, P.C. (1966). Reasoning. In B.M. Foss (Ed.), *New horizons in psychology* (pp.135–151). Harmondsworth: Penguin.

Weinstein, N. (1980). Unrealistic optimism about future life events. *Journal of Personality and Social Psychology, 39*, 806–820.

Weinstein, N. & Klein, W.M. (1995). Resistance of personal risk perceptions to debiasing interventions. *Health Psychology, 14*, 132–140.

Windschitl, P.D., Kruger, J. & Simms, E.N. (2003). The influence of egocentrism and focalism on people's optimism in competitions: When what affects us equally affects me more. *Journal of Personality and Social Psychology, 85*(3), 389–408.

Winkler, R.L. & Poses, R.M. (1993). Evaluating and combining physicians' probabilities of survival in an intensive care unit. *Management Science, 39*, 1526–1543.

Wright, G.N. & Phillips, L.D. (1980). Cultural variation in probabilistic thinking: Alternative ways of dealing with uncertainty. *International Journal of Psychology, 15*, 239–257.

Wright, G.N., Phillips, L.D., Whalley, P.C., Choo, G.T., Ng, K.O., Tan, I. & Wisudha, A. (1978). Cultural differences in probabilistic thinking. *Journal of Cross-Cultural Psychology, 9*, 285–299.

Yates, J.F., Zhu, Y., Ronis, D.L., Wang, D.-F., Shinotsuka, H. & Toda, M. (1989). Probability judgment accuracy: China, Japan, and the United States. *Organizational Behavior and Human Decision Processes, 43*, 145–171.

Yates, J.F., Lee, J.-W., Levi, K.R. & Curley, S.P. (1990). Measuring and analyzing probability judgment accuracy in medicine. *Philippine Journal of Internal Medicine, 28*(suppl. 1), 21–32.

Yates, J.F., Lee, J.-W., & Shinotsuka, H. (1996). Beliefs about overconfidence, including its cross-national variation. *Organizational Behavior and Human Decision Processes, 65*, 138–147.

Yates, J.F., Lee, J.-W., Shinotsuka, H. & Sieck, W.R. (2000). *The argument recruitment model: Explaining general knowledge overconfidence and its cross-cultural variations*. Working paper, Department of Psychology, University of Michigan, Ann Arbor.

Yates, J.F., Lee, J.-W., Sieck, W.R., Choi, I. & Price, P.C. (2002). Probability judgment across cultures. In T. Gilovich, D. Griffin & D. Kahneman (Eds.), *Heuristics and biases: The psychology of intuitive judgment*. Cambridge: Cambridge University Press.

CHAPTER 10. JUDGMENT AND CHOICE OVER TIME

Ainslie, G. & Herrnstein, R.J. (1981). Preference reversal and delayed reinforcement. *Animal Learning and Behavior, 9*(4), 476–482.

Ajzen, I. (1985). From intentions to action: A theory of planned behaviour. In J. Kuhl & J. Beckman (Eds.), *Action control: From cognitions to behaviours*. New York: Springer.

Ajzen, I. (1988). *Attitudes, personality, and behaviour*. Milton Keynes: Open University Press.

Ariely, D. & Wertenbroch, K. (2002). Procrastination, deadlines, and performance: Self-control by precommitment. *Psychological Science, 13*(3), 219–224.

Baron, J. (2000). *Thinking and deciding* (3rd edn). Cambridge: Cambridge University Press.

Baumeister, R.F. & Vohs, K.D. (2003). Willpower, choice, and self-control. In G.F. Loewenstein, D. Read & R.F. Baumeister (Eds.), *Time and decision: Economic and psychological perspectives on intertemporal choice* (pp.201–216). New York: Russell Sage.

Böhm-Bawerk, E. von (1970[1889]). *Capital and interest*. South Holland: Libertarian Press.

Boltz, M.G., Kupperman, C. & Dunne, J. (1998). The role of learning in remembered duration. *Memory and Cognition, 26*, 903–921.

Brickman, P. & Campbell, D.T. (1971). Hedonic relativism and planning the good society. In M.H. Apley (Ed.), *Adaptation-level theory: A symposium* (pp.287–302). New York: Academic Press.

Brickman, P., Coates, D. & Janoff-Bulman, R.J. (1978). Lottery winners and accident victims: Is happiness relative? *Journal of Personality and Social Psychology, 36*, 917–927.

Buehler, R., Griffin, D. & Ross, M. (1994). Exploring the 'planning fallacy': Why people underestimate their task completion times. *Journal of Personality and Social Psychology, 67*, 366–381.

Buehler, R., Griffin, D. & MacDonald, H. (1997). The role of motivated reasoning in optimistic time predictions. *Personality and Social Psychology Bulletin, 23*, 238–247.

Buehler, R., Griffin, D. & Ross, M. (2002). Inside the planning fallacy: The causes and consequences of optimistic time predictions. In T. Gilovich, D. Griffin & D. Kahneman (Eds.), *Heuristics and biases: The psychology of intuitive judgment* (pp.250–270). Cambridge: Cambridge University Press.

Chapman, G.B. (1996). Temporal discounting and utility for health and money. *Journal of Experimental Psychology: Learning, Memory, and Cognition, 22*(3), 771–791.

Cohn, B. (1999). *The lay theory of happiness*. Unpublished undergraduate dissertation, Princeton University.

Duckworth, A.L. & Seligman, M.E.P. (2005). Self-discipline outdoes IQ in predicting academic performance of adolescents. *Psychological Science, 16*(12), 939–944.

Frederick, S. (2005). Cognitive reflection and decision making. *Journal of Economic Perspectives, 19*(4), 25–42.

Frederick, S., Loewenstein, G. & O'Donoghue, T. (2002). Time discounting and time preference: A critical review. *Journal of Economic Literature, XL,* 351–401.

Geronimus, A.T. (1992). The weathering hypothesis and the health of African-American women and infants: Evidence and speculations. *Ethnicity and Disease, 2*(3), 207–221.

Geronimus, A.T. (1996). What teen mothers know. *Human Nature, 7*(4), 323–352.

Gilbert, D.T., Morewedge, C.K., Risen, J.L. & Wilson, T.D. (2004). Looking forward to looking backward: The misprediction of regret. *Psychological Science, 15*(5), 346–350.

Green, D., Fischer, E.B. Jr., Perlow, S. & Sherman, L. (1981). Preference reversal and self-control: Choice as a function of reward amount and delay. *Behavior Analysis Letters, 1*(1), 43–51.

Griffin, D. & Buehler, R. (2005). Biases and fallacies, memories and predictions: Comment on Roy, Christenfeld & McKenzie (2005). *Psychological Bulletin, 131,* 757–760.

Griffin, D.W. & Tversky, A. (1992). The weighing of evidence and the determinants of confidence. *Cognitive Psychology, 24,* 411–435.

Hinds, P.J. (1999). The curse of expertise: The effects of expertise and debiasing methods on prediction of novice performance. *Journal of Experimental Psychology: Applied, 5,* 205–221.

Hofstadter, D.R. (1980). *Gödel, Escher, Bach: An eternal golden braid.* London: Penguin.

Hogan, R. & Weiss, D.S. (1974). Personality correlates of superior academic achievement. *Journal of Counseling Psychology, 21,* 144–149.

Hsee, C.K. & Hastie, R. (2006). Decision and experience: Why don't we choose what makes us happy? *Trends in Cognitive Sciences, 10*(1), 31–37.

Hsee, C.K., Abelson, R.P. & Salovey, P. (1991). The relative weighting of position and velocity in satisfaction. *Psychological Science, 2*(4), 263–266.

Jones, E.E. & Nisbett, R.E. (1972). The actor and the observer: Divergent perceptions of the causes of behaviour. In E.E. Jones, D.E. Kanouse, H.H. Kelley, R.E. Nisbett, S. Valins & B. Weiner (Eds.), *Attribution: Perceiving the causes of behaviour* (pp.79–94). Morristown, NJ: General Learning Press.

Kahneman, D. (1994). New challenges to the rationality assumption. *Journal of Institutional and Theoretical Economics, 150*(1), 18–36.

Kahneman, D. (2000). Evaluation by moments: Past and future. In D. Kahneman & A. Tversky (Eds.), *Choices, values, and frames* (pp.693–708). Cambridge: Cambridge University Press.

Kahneman, D. & Lovallo, D. (1993). Timid choices and bold forecasts: A cognitive perspective on risk taking. *Management Science, 39,* 17–31.

Kahneman, D. & Miller, D.T. (1986). Norm theory: Comparing reality to its alternatives. *Psychological Review, 93*(2), 136–153.

Kahneman, D. & Snell, J. (1992). Predicting a changing taste: Do people know what they will like? *Journal of Behavioral Decision Making, 5,* 187–200.

Kahneman, D. & Tversky, A. (1979). Intuitive prediction: Biases and corrective procedures. *TIMS Studies in Management Science, 12,* 313–327.

Kirby, K.N. & Herrnstein, R.J. (1995). Preference reversals due to myopic discounting of delayed reward. *Psychological Science, 6*(2), 83–89.

Kirby, K.N., Winston, G. & Santiesteban, M. (2005). Impatience and grades: Delay-discount rates correlate negatively with college GPA. *Learning and Individual Differences, 15*(3), 213–222.

Kivetz, R. & Simonson, I. (2002). Self-control for the righteous: Toward a theory of precommitment to indulgence. *Journal of Consumer Research, 29,* 199–217.

Koehler, D.J. (1991). Explanation, imagination, and confidence in judgment. *Psychological Bulletin, 110,* 499–519.

Koehler, D.J. & Poon, C.S.K. (2006). Self-predictions overweight strength of current intentions. *Journal of Experimental Social Psychology, 42*(4), 517–524.

Laibson, D. (2001). A cue-theory of consumption. *Quarterly Journal of Economics, 116,* 81–119.

Lay, C.H. (1986). At last, my research article on procrastination. *Journal of Research in Personality, 20,* 474–495.

Lee, E., Clements, S., Ingham, R. & Stone, N. (2004). *A matter of choice? Explaining national variation in teenage abortion and motherhood.* York: Joseph Rowntree Foundation.

Leventhal, H., Singer, R.P. & Jones, S.H. (1965). The effects of fear and specificity of recommendation. *Journal of Personality and Social Psychology, 2,* 20–29.

Lewin, K. (1951). *Field theory in social science.* New York: Harper & Row.

Liberman, N. & Trope, Y. (1998). The role of feasibility and desirability considerations in near and distant future decisions: A test of temporal construal theory. *Journal of Personality and Social Psychology, 75,* 5–18.

Loewenstein, G. (1987). Anticipation and the valuation of delayed consumption. *The Economic Journal, 97*(387), 666–668.

Loewenstein, G. (1988). Frames of mind in intertemporal choice. *Management Science, 34,* 200–214.

Loewenstein, G. (1996). Out of control: Visceral influences on behavior. *Organizational Behavior and Human Decision Processes, 65,* 272–292.

Loewenstein, G. & Prelec, D. (1993). Preferences for sequences of outcomes. *Psychological Review, 100*(1), 91–108.

Mischel, W., Shoda, Y. & Rodriguez, M.I. (1989). Delay of gratification in children. *Science, 244*(4907), 933–938

Mitchell, T.R., Thompson, L., Peterson, E. & Cronk, R. (1997). Temporal adjustments in the evaluation of events: The 'rosy view'. *Journal of Experimental Social Psychology, 33,* 421–448.

Prelec, D. & Loewenstein, G. (1998). The red and the black: Mental accounting of savings and debt. *Marketing Science, 17*(1), 4–28.

Rae, J. (1834). *The sociological theory of capital* (reprint of original 1834 edn). London: Macmillan.

Read, D. (2004). Intertemporal choice. In D.J. Koehler & N. Harvey (Eds.), *Blackwell handbook of judgment and decision making* (pp.424–443). Oxford: Blackwell.

Read, D. & Loewenstein, G. (1995). Diversification bias: Explaining the discrepancy in variety seeking between combined and separated choices. *Journal of Experimental Psychology: Applied, 1,* 34–49.

Redelmeier, D.A. & Heller, D.N. (1993). Time preference in medical decision making and cost-effectiveness analysis. *Medical Decision Making, 13*(3), 212–217.

Robson, A.J. (2002). Evolution and human nature. *Journal of Economic Perspectives, 16*(2), 89–106.

Rogers, A.R. (1994). Evolution of time preference by natural selection. *The American Economic Review, 84*(3), 460–481.

Roy, M.M., Christenfeld, N.J.S. & McKenzie, C.R.M. (2005a). Underestimating the duration of future events: Memory incorrectly used or memory bias? *Psychological Bulletin, 131*(5), 738–756.

Roy, M.M., Christenfeld, N.J.S. & McKenzie, C.R.M. (2005b). The broad applicability of memory bias and its coexistence with the planning fallacy: Reply to Griffin and Buehler (2005). *Psychological Bulletin, 131*(5), 761–762.

Samuelson, P. (1937). A note on measurement of utility. *Review of Economic Studies, 4,* 155–161.

Schelling, T.C. (2006). *Strategies of commitment and other essays.* Cambridge, MA: Harvard University Press.

Schkade, D. & Kahneman, D. (1998). Does living in California make people happy? A focusing illusion in judgments of life satisfaction. *Psychological Science, 9,* 340–346.

Sheeran, P. (2002). Intention-behavior relations: A conceptual and empirical review. In W. Stroebe & M. Hewstone (Eds.), *European Review of Social Psychology* (pp.1–36). Chichester: Wiley.

Shoda, Y., Mischel, W. & Peake, P.K. (1990). Predicting adolescent cognitive and social competence from preschool delay of gratification: Identifying diagnostic conditions. *Developmental Psychology, 26,* 978–986.

Simonson, I. (1990). The effect of purchase quantity and timing on variety-seeking behaviour. *Journal of Marketing Research, 27*(2), 150–162.

Solnick, J., Kannenberg, C., Eckerman, D. & Waller, M. (1980). An experimental analysis of impulsivity and impulse control in humans. *Learning and Motivation, 11,* 61–77.

Sozou, P.D. & Seymour, R.M. (2003). Augmented discounting: Interaction between ageing and time-preference behaviour. *Proceedings of the Royal Society of London B, 270*(1519), 1047–1053

Thaler, R. (1981). Some empirical evidence on dynamic inconsistency. *Economic Letters, 8,* 201–7.

Thaler, R. & Shefrin, H.M. (1981). An economic theory of self-control. *Journal of Political Economy, 89*(2), 392–410.

Trope, Y. & Liberman, N. (2003). Temporal construal. *Psychological Review, 110*(3), 403–421.

Trostel, P.A. & Taylor, G.A. (2001). A theory of time preference. *Economic Inquiry, 39*(3), 379–395.

Tykocinski, O.E. & Pittman, T.S. (1998). The consequences of doing nothing: Inaction inertia as avoidance of anticipated counterfactual regret. *Journal of Personality and Social Psychology, 75,* 607–616.

Van Boven, L. & Loewenstein, G. (2003). Social projection of transient drive states. *Personality and Social Psychology Bulletin, 29,* 1159–1168.

Wilson, M. & Daly, M. (1997). Life expectancy, economic inequality, homicide, and reproductive timing in Chicago neighbourhoods. *British Medical Journal, 314,* 1271–1274.

Wilson, T.D., Meyers, J. & Gilbert, D.T. (2001). Lessons from the past: Do people learn from experience that emotional reactions are short-lived? *Personality and Social Psychology Bulletin, 27*(12), 1648–1661.

Wolfe, R.N. & Johnson, S.D. (1995). Personality as a predictor of college performance. *Educational and Psychological Measurement, 55,* 177–185.

CHAPTER 11. DYNAMIC DECISIONS AND HIGH STAKES

Anzai, Y. (1984). Cognitive control of real-time event driven systems. *Cognitive Science, 8,* 221–254.

Bandaret, L.E., Stokes, J.W., Francesconi, R., Kowal, D.M. & Naitoh, P. (1981). Artillery teams in simulated sustained combat: Performance and other measures. In L.C. Johnson, D.I. Tepas, W.F. Colquhoun & M.J. Colligan (Eds.), *Biological rhythms, sleep and shiftwork* (pp.459–477). New York: Spectrum.

Beach, L.R. (1990). *Image theory: Decision making in personalized and organizational contexts.* New York: Wiley.

Beach, L.R. & Connolly, T. (2005). *The psychology of decision making: People in organizations* (2nd edn). London: Sage.

Beach, L.R. & Strom, E. (1989). A toadstool among the mushrooms: Screening decisions and image theory's compatibility test. *Acta Psychologica,* 1–12.

Belenky, G., Penetar, D.M., Thorne, D.R., Popp, K., Leu, J., Thomas, M., Sing, H., Balkin, T.J., Wesensten, N.J. & Redmond, D.P. (1994). The effects of sleep deprivation on performance during continuous combat operations. In B.M. Marriott (Ed.), *Food components to enhance performance* (pp.127–135). Washington, DC: National Academy Press.

Berry, D.C. & Broadbent, D.E. (1984). On the relationship between task performance and associated verbalizable knowledge. *Quarterly Journal of Experimental Psychology, 36A,* 209–231.

Besnard, D., Greathead, D. & Baxter, G. (2004). When mental models go wrong: Co-occurrences in dynamic, critical systems. *International Journal of Human-Computer Studies, 60,* 117–128.

Brehmer, B. (1992). Dynamic decision making: Human control of complex systems. *Acta Psychologica, 81*(3), 211–241.

Brehmer, B. & Allard, R. (1991). Real-time dynamic decision making: Effects of task complexity and feedback delays. In J. Rasmussen, B. Brehmer & J. Leplat (Eds.), *Distributed decision making: Cognitive models for cooperative work.* Chichester: Wiley.

Burns, K. (2005). Mental models and normal errors. In B. Brehmer, R. Lipshitz & H. Montgomery (Eds.), *How do professionals make decisions?* Mahwah, NJ: Lawrence Erlbaum.

Busemeyer, J.R. (2002). Dynamic decision making. In N.J. Smelser & P.B. Baltes (Eds.), *International Encyclopedia of the Social and Behavioral Sciences: Vol. 6* (pp.3903–3908). Oxford: Elsevier Press.

Calderwood, R., Klein, G.A. & Crandall, B.W. (1988). Time pressure, skill, and move quality in chess. *American Journal of Psychology, 101,* 481–493.

Corcoran, D.W.J. (1963). Doubling the rate of signal presentation in a vigilance task during sleep deprivation. *Journal of Applied Psychology, 47,* 412–415.

Coscarelli, W.C. (1983a). *The Decision Making Inventory technical manual.* Columbus, OH: Marathon Consulting Press.

Coscarelli, W.C. (1983b). Development of a decisionmaking inventory to assess Johnson's decision-making styles. *Measurement and Evaluation in Guidance, 16,* 149–160.

Diehl, E. & Sterman, J.D. (1995). Effects of feedback complexity on dynamic decision making. *Organizational Behavior and Human Decision Processes, 62*(2), 198–215.

Dienes, Z. & Fahey, R. (1995). Role of specific instances in controlling a dynamic system. *Journal of Experimental Psychology: Learning, Memory and Cognition, 21,* 848–862.

Duckworth, A.L. & Seligman, M.E.P. (2005). Self-discipline outdoes IQ in predicting academic performance of adolescents. *Psychological Science, 16* (12), 939–944.

Edwards, W. (1962). Dynamic decision theory and probabilistic information processing. *Human Factors, 4,* 59–73.

Endsley, M.R. (1988). Design and evaluation for situation awareness enhancement. In *Proceedings of the Human Factors Society 32nd Annual Meeting, Human Factors Society* (pp.97–101). Santa Monica, CA: Human Factors and Ergonomics Society.

Endsley, M.R. (2006). Expertise and situation awareness. In K.A. Ericsson, N. Charness, P.J. Feltovich & R.R. Hoffman (Eds.), *The Cambridge Handbook of Expertise and Expert Performance* (pp.633–651). Cambridge: Cambridge University Press.

Flin, R., Salas, E., Strub, M. & Martin, L. (Eds.) (1997). *Decision making under stress: Emerging themes and applications.* Aldershot: Ashgate.

Friedrich, J.R. (1987). Perceived control and decision making in a job hunting context. *Basic and Applied Social Psychology, 8*(1 and 2), 163–176.

Furnham, A. (2005). *The psychology of behaviour at work: The individual in the organization.* Hove: Psychology Press.

Gibson, F.P., Fichman, M. & Plaut, D.C. (1997). Learning in dynamic decision tasks: Computational model and empirical evidence. *Organizational Behavior and Human Decision Processes, 71*(1), 1–35.

Gonzalez, C. (2004). Learning to make decisions in dynamic environments: Effects of time constraints and cognitive abilities. *Human Factors, 46*(3), 449–460.

Gonzalez, C. (2005a). Decision support for real-time, dynamic decision-making tasks. *Organizational Behavior and Human Decision Processes, 96,* 142–154.

Gonzalez, C. (2005b). Task workload and cognitive abilities in dynamic decision making. *Human Factors, 47*(1), 92–101.

Gonzalez, C. & Quesada, J. (2003). Learning in dynamic decision making: The recognition process. *Computational and Mathematical Organization Theory, 9,* 287–304.

Gonzalez, C., Lerch, J.F. & Lebiere, C. (2005). Instance-based learning in dynamic decision making. *Cognitive Science, 27,* 591–635.

Gonzalez, C., Thomas, R.P. & Vanyukov, P. (2005). Impact of individual differences and cognitive abilities on dynamic decision making. *Intelligence, 33*(2), 169–186.

Gonzalez, C., Vanyukov, P. & Martin, M.K. (2005). The use of microworlds to study dynamic decision making. *Computers in Human Behavior, 21,* 273–286.

Hammond, K.R. (2000). *Judgments under stress.* Oxford: Oxford University Press.

Harrison, Y. & Horne, J.A. (1999). One night of sleep loss impairs innovative thinking and flexible decision making. *Organizational Behavior and Human Decision Processes*, 78, 128–145.

Harrison, Y. & Horne, J.A. (2000). The impact of sleep deprivation on decision making: A review. *Journal of Experimental Psychology (Applied)*, 6(3), 236–249.

Harvey, N. & Bolger, F. (2001). Collecting information: Optimizing outcomes, screening options, or facilitating discrimination? *The Quarterly Journal of Experimental Psychology*, 54A(1), 269–301.

Hedlund, J., Wilt, J.M., Nebel, K.R., Ashford, S.J., Sternberg, R.J. (2006). Assessing practical intelligence in business school admissions: A supplement to the graduate management admissions test. *Learning and Individual Differences*, 16(2), 101–127.

Horne, J.A. & Pettitt, A.N. (1985). High incentive effects on vigilance performance during 72 hours of total SD. *Acta Psychologica*, 58, 123–139.

Horswill, M.S. & McKenna, F.P. (2004). Drivers hazard perception ability: Situation awareness on the road. In S. Banbury & S. Tremblay (Eds.), *A cognitive approach to situation awareness: Theory, measurement and application*. Aldershot: Ashgate.

Hunter, J. & Hunter, R. (1984). Validity and utility of alternate predictors of job performance. *Psychological Bulletin*, 96(1), 72–98.

Jensen, R.S., Guilke, J. & Tigner, R. (1997). Understanding expert aviator judgment. In R. Flin, E. Salas, M. Strub & L. Martin (Eds.), *Decision making under stress: Emerging themes and applications* (pp.233–242). Aldershot: Ashgate.

Johnson, R.H. (1978). Individual styles of decision making: A theoretical model for counseling. *Personnel and Guidance Journal*, 56, 530–536.

Kahneman, D. & Tversky, A. (1982). The simulation heuristic. In D. Kahneman, P. Slovic & A. Tversky (Eds.), *Judgment under uncertainty: Heuristics and biases* (pp.201–208). Cambridge: Cambridge University Press.

Kerstholt, J.H. (1994). The effect of time pressure on decision making behaviour in a dynamic task environment. *Acta Psychologica*, 86, 89–104.

Kerstholt, J.H. (1996). The effects of information costs on strategy selection in dynamic tasks. *Acta Psychologica*, 94, 273–290.

Kjellberg, A. (1975). Effects of sleep deprivation on performance of a problem-solving task. *Psychological Reports*, 37, 479–485.

Kjellberg, A. (1977). Sleep deprivation and some aspects of performance. *Waking and Sleeping*, 1, 139–143.

Klein, G. (1998). *Sources of power: How people make decisions*. Cambridge, MA: MIT Press.

Klein, G. (2001). The fiction of optimization. In G. Gigerenzer & R. Selten (Eds.), *Bounded rationality: The adaptive toolbox* (pp.103–121). Cambridge, MA: MIT Press.

Klein, G.A., Wolf, S., Militello, L. & Zsambok, C. (1995). Characteristics of skilled option generation in chess. *Organizational Behavior and Human Decision Processes*, 62, 63–69.

Kleinmuntz, D. (1985). Cognitive heuristics and feedback in a dynamic decision environment. *Management Science*, 31, 680–702.

Kleinmuntz, D. & Thomas, J. (1987). The value of action and inference in dynamic decision making. *Organizational Behavior and Human Decision Processes*, 39, 341–364.

Kluger, A.N. & DeNisi, A. (1996). Effects of feedback intervention on performance: A historical review, a meta-analysis, and a preliminary feedback intervention theory. *Psychological Bulletin*, 119(2), 254–284.

Lipshitz, R., Klein, G., Orasanu, J. & Salas, E. (2001). Taking stock of naturalistic decision making. *Journal of Behavioral Decision Making*, 14, 331–352.

McCammon, I. (2001). Decision making for wilderness leaders: Strategies, traps and teaching methods. *Proceedings of Wilderness Risk Manager's Conference*. 26–28 Oct., Lake Geneva, WI, pp.16–29.

McCammon, I. (2002). Evidence of heuristic traps in recreational avalanche accidents. Presentation to the International Snow Science Workshop, Penticton, British Columbia, 30 Sept.–4 Oct. Downloaded 6 Nov. 2002 from http://www.avalanche.org/~issw2004/issw_previous/2002/flashsite/Education/mccammon per cent20oral.html.

McCammon, I. (2004). Sex, drugs and the white death: Lessons for avalanche educators from health and safety campaigns. Presentation to the International Snow Science Workshop, 19–24 Sept., Jackson, WY. Downloaded 6 Nov. 2002 from http://www.avalanche.org/~issw2004/issw_previous/2004/proceedings/pdffiles/toc.pdf.

McCammon, I. & Hägeli, P. (2004). Comparing avalanche decision frameworks using accident data from the United States. Presentation to the International Snow Science Workshop, 19–24 Sept., Jackson, WY. Downloaded 6 Nov. 2002 from http://www.avalanche.org/~issw2004/issw_previous/2004/proceedings/pdffiles/toc.pdf.

McKenna, F. & Crick, J.L. (1991). *Hazard perception in drivers: A methodology for testing and training*. Transport Research Laboratory Report No. 313. Crowthorne, UK.

Menkes, J. (2005). *Executive intelligence: What all great leaders have*. NY: Collins.

Niles, S.G., Erford, B., Hunt, B. & Watts, R. (1997). Decision-making styles and career development in college students. *Journal of College Student Development*, 38, 479–488.

Omodei, M., Wearing, A. & McLennan, J. (1997). Head-mounted video recording: A methodology for studying naturalistic decision making. In R. Flin, E. Salas, M. Strub & L. Martin (Eds.), *Decision making under stress: Emerging themes and applications* (pp.137–146). Aldershot: Ashgate.

Orasanu, J. & Fischer, U. (1997). Finding decisions in natural environments. In C.E. Zsambok & G.A. Klein (Eds.), *Naturalistic decision making* (pp.434–458). Hillsdale, NJ: Erlbaum.

Payne, J.W., Bettman, J.R. & Johnson, E.J. (1993). *The adaptive decision maker*. Cambridge: Cambridge University Press.

Prince, C. & Salas, E. (1998). Situation assessment for routine flight and decision making. *International Journal of Cognitive Ergonomics*, 1(4), 315–324.

Raven, J.C. (1976). Advanced progressive matrices, Sets I and II. Oxford: Oxford Psychologists Press.

Rigas, G. & Brehmer, B. (1999). Mental processes in intelligence tests and dynamic decision making tasks. In P. Juslin & H. Montgomery (Eds.), *Judgement and decision making: Neo-Brunswikean and process-tracing approaches*. Hillsdale, NJ: Lawrence Erlbaum.

Rigas, G., Carling, E. & Brehmer, B. (2002). Reliability and validity of performance measures in microworlds. *Intelligence*, 30, 463–480.

Ross, K.G., Shafer, J.L. & Klein, G. (2006). Professional judgments and 'naturalistic decision making'. In K.A. Ericsson, N. Charness, P.J. Feltovich & R.R. Hoffman (Eds.), *The Cambridge handbook of expertise and expert performance*. Cambridge: Cambridge University Press.

Salgado, J., Anderson, N., Moscoso, S., Bertua, C., de Fruyt, F. & Rolland, J.P. (2003). A meta-analytic study of general mental ability validity for different occupations in the European Community. *Journal of Applied Psychology*, 88, 1068–1081.

Schraagen, J.M. (2006). Task analysis. In K.A. Ericsson, N. Charness, P.J. Feltovich & R.R. Hoffman (Eds.), *The Cambridge handbook of expertise and expert performance*. Cambridge: Cambridge University Press.

Scott, S.G. & Bruce, R.A. (1995). Decision-making style: The development and assessment of a new measure. *Educational and Psychological Measurement*, 55(5), 818–831.

Sterman, J.D. (1989a). Modeling managerial behaviour: Misperceptions of feedback in a dynamic decision making experiment. *Management Science*, 35(3), 321–339.

Sterman, J.D. (1989b). Misperceptions of feedback in dynamic decision making. *Organizational Behavior and Human Decision Processes*, 43(3), 301–335.

Sternberg, R.J. (1997). *Successful intelligence*. New York: Plume Books.

Stokes, A.F. & Kite, K. (1994). *Flight stress: Stress, fatigue, and performance in aviation*. Brookfield, VT: Ashgate.

Strater, L.D., Endsley, M.R., Pleban, R.J. & Matthews, M.D. (2001). *Measures of platoon leader situation awareness in virtual decision making exercises* (Research Report 1770). Alexandria, VA: Army Research Institute.

Strater, L.D., Jones, D.G. & Endsley, M.R. (2001). *Analysis of infantry situation awareness training requirements*. (SATech 01–15). Marietta, GA: SA Technologies.

Strayer, D.L. & Johnston, W.A. (2001). Driven to distraction: Dual-task studies of simulated driving and conversing on a cellular telephone. *Psychological Science, 12,* 462–466.

Wilkinson, R.T. (1965). Sleep deprivation. In O.G. Edholm & A.L. Bacharach (Eds.), *Physiology of human survival* (pp.399–430). London: Academic Press.

Van Zee, E.H., Paluchowski, T.F. & Beach, L.R. (1992). The effects of screening and task partitioning upon evaluation of decision options. *Journal of Behavioral Decision Making, 5,* 1–23.

Zsambok, C.E. & Klein, G. (Eds.) (1997). *Naturalistic decision making.* Mahwah, NJ: Lawrence Erlbaum.

CHAPTER 12. RISK

Adams, J. (1995). *Risk.* London: UCL Press.

Albury, D. & Schwarz, J. (1982). *Partial progress.* London: Pluto Press.

Alhakami, A.S. & Slovic, P. (1994). A psychological study of the inverse relationship between perceived risk and perceived benefit. *Risk Analysis, 14*(6), 1085–1096.

Ames, B.N. & Gold, L.S. (1990). Too many rodent carcinogens: Mitogenesis increases mutagenesis. *Science, 249,* 970–971.

Anderson, C. & Galinsky, A.D. (2006). Power, optimism, and risk-taking. *European Journal of Social Psychology, 36,* 511–536.

Balcombe, J. (2006). *Pleasurable kingdom: Animals and the nature of feeling good.* London: Macmillan.

Barke, R., Jenkins-Smith, H. & Slovic, P. (1997). Risk perception of men and women scientists. *Social Science Quarterly, 78*(1), 167–176.

Baron, J. (1998). *Judgment misguided: Intuition and error in public decision making.* Oxford: Oxford University Press.

Baron, J. (2000). *Thinking and Deciding* (3rd edn). Cambridge: Cambridge University Press.

Barrett, L., Dunbar, R. & Lycett, J. (2002). *Human evolutionary psychology.* Basingstoke: Palgrave.

Bassett, J.F. & Moss, B. (2004). Men and women prefer risk takers as romantic and non-romantic partners. *Current Research in Social Psychology, 9,* 133–144.

Bernhardt, P.C., Dabbs, J.M., Fielden, J.A. & Lutter, C.D. (1998). Testosterone changes during vicarious experiences of winning and losing among fans at sporting events. *Physiology and Behavior, 65*(1), 59–62.

Bostrom, A., Morgan, M.G. & Fischhoff, B. (1992). Characterizing mental models of hazardous processes: A methodology and an application to Radon. *Journal of Social Issues, 45,* 85–100.

Brun, W. (1992). Cognitive components in risk perception: Natural versus manmade risks. *Journal of Behavioral Decision Making, 5,* 117–132.

Burns, P.C. & Wilde, G.J.S. (1995). Risk taking in male taxi drivers: relationships among personality, observational data and driver records. *Personality and Individual Differences, 18*(2), 267–278.

Burnstein, E., Crandall, C. & Kitayama, S. (1994). Some neo-Darwinian decision rules for altruism: Weighing cues for inclusive fitness as a function of the biological importance of the decision. *Journal of Personality and Social Psychology, 67,* 773–789.

Buss, D.M. (1999). *Evolutionary psychology: The new science of the mind.* London: Allyn & Bacon.

Byrnes, J.P., Miller, D.C. & Schafer, W.D. (1999). Gender differences in risk taking: A meta-analysis. *Psychological Bulletin, 125*(3), 367–383.

Campbell, A. (1999). Staying alive: Evolution, culture and women's intra-sexual aggression. *Behavioral and Brain Sciences, 22,* 203–252

Carlo, G.L., Lee, N., Sund, K.G. & Pettygrove, S.D. (1992). The interplay of science, values, and experiences among scientists asked to evaluate the hazards of dioxin, radon, and environmental tobacco smoke. *Risk Analysis, 12,* 37–43.

Costa, P.T. & McCrae, R. (1985). *Manual of the NEO-PI.* Odessa, FL: Psychological Assessment Resources.

Costa, P.T. & McCrae, R. (1992). Four ways five factors are basic. *Personality and Individual Differences, 13,* 653–665.

Cronin, C. (1991). Sensation seeking among mountain climbers. *Personality and Individual Differences, 12,* 653–654.

Daly, M. & Wilson, M. (1990). *Homicide.* Hawthorne, NY: Aldine.

Dawkins, R. (1976). *The selfish gene.* Oxford: Oxford University Press.

DeBruine, L.M. (2004). Resemblance to self increases the appeal of child faces to both men and women. *Evolution and Human Behavior, 25,* 142–154.

de Waal, F. (2005). *Our inner ape: The best and worst of human nature.* London: Granta.

Diamond, J. (1998). *Guns, germs and steel: A short history of everybody for the last 13,000 years.* London: Chatto & Windus.

Dingemanse, N.J., Both, C., Drent, P.J. & Tinbergen, J.M. (2004). Fitness consequences of avian personalities in a fluctuating environment. *Proceedings of the Royal Society of London, Series B: Biological Sciences, 271,* 847–852.

Egan, S. & Stelmack, R.M. (2003). A personality profile of Mount Everest climbers. *Personality and Individual Differences, 34,* 1491–1494.

Evans, A.H., Lawrence, A.D., Potts, J., MacGregor, L., Katzenschlager, R., Shaw, K., Ziljmans, J. & Lees, A.J. (2006). Relationship between impulsive sensation seeking traits, smoking, alcohol and caffeine intake, and Parkinson's disease. *Journal of Neurology, Neurosurgery, and Psychiatry, 77,* 317–321.

Farthing, G.W. (2005). Attitudes toward heroic and nonheroic physical risk takers as mates and friends. *Evolution and Human Behavior, 26,* 171–185.

Field, C.A. & O'Keefe, G. (2004). Behavioral and psychological risk factors for traumatic injury. *Journal of Emergency Medicine, 26,* 27–35.

Finucane, M.S., Alhakami, A., Slovic, P. & Johnson, S.M. (2000). The affect heuristic in judgments of risks and benefits. *Journal of Behavioral Decision Making, 13,* 1–17.

Fischhoff, B., Slovic, P., Lichtenstein, S., Read, S. & Combs, B. (1978). How safe is safe enough? A psychometric study of attitudes towards technological risks and benefits. *Policy Sciences, 9,* 127–52.

Flynn, J., Slovic, P. & Mertz, C.K. (1994). Gender, race, and perception of environmental health risks. *Risk Analysis, 14*(6), 1101–1108.

Franques, P., Auriacombe, M., Piquemal, E., Verger, M., Brisseau-Gimenez, S., Grabot, D. & Tiqnol, J. (2003). Sensation seeking as a common factor in opioid dependent subjects and high risk sport practicing subjects. A cross sectional study. *Drug and Alcohol Dependence, 69*(2), 121–126.

Goma-i-Freixanet, M. (1991). Personality profile of subjects engaged in high physical risk sports. *Personality and Individual Differences, 12,* 1087–1093.

Hamilton, W.D. (1964). The genetical evolution of social behaviour, I, II. *Journal of Theoretical Biology, 7,* 1–52.

Hertwig, R., Pachur, T. & Kurzenhäuser, S. (2005). Judgments of risk frequencies: Tests of possible mechanisms. *Journal of Experimental Psychology: Learning, Memory, and Cognition, 31*(4), 621–642.

Johnson, R.C. (1996). Attributes of Carnegie medalists performing acts of heroism and of the recipients of these acts. *Ethology and Sociobiology, 17*(5), 355–362.

Kahneman, D. & Ritov, I. (1994). Determinants of stated willingness to pay for public goods: A study of the headline method. *Journal of Risk and Uncertainty, 9,* 5–38.

Kahneman, D., Ritov, I., Jacowitz, K.E. & Grant, P. (1993). Stated willingness to pay for public goods: A psychological perspective. *Psychological Science, 4*(5), 310–315.

Kalichman, S.C., Cain, D., Zweben, A. & Swain, G. (2003). Sensation seeking, alcohol use and sexual risk behaviors among men receiving services at a clinic for sexually transmitted infections. *Journal of Studies on Alcohol, 64*(4), 564–569.

Kasperson, R.E., Renn, O., Slovic, P., Brown, H.S., Emel, J., Goble, R., Kasperson, J.X., & Ratick, S. (1988). The social amplification of risk: A conceptual framework. In P. Slovic (Ed.), *The perception of risk.* London: Earthscan. (First published in *Risk Analysis, 8*(2), 177–187.)

Kasperson, J.X., Kasperson, R.E., Pidgeon, N. & Slovic, P. (2003). The social amplification of risk: Assessing fifteen years of research and theory. In

N. Pidgeon, R.E. Kasperson & P. Slovic (Eds.), *The social amplification of risk* (pp.13–46). Cambridge: Cambridge University Press.

Kerr, J.H. (1997). *Motivation and emotion in sport: Reversal theory*. Hove: Psychology Press.

Koehler, J.J. & Gershoff, A.D. (2003). Betrayal aversion: When agents of protection become agents of harm. *Organizational Behavior and Human Decision Processes, 90*(2), 244–261.

Koehler, J.J. & Gershoff, A.D. (2005). Betrayal aversion is reasonable. *Behavioral and Brain Sciences, 28*, 556–557.

Kraus, N., Malmfors, T. & Slovic, P. (1992). Intuitive toxicology: Expert and lay judgments of chemical risk. *Risk Analysis, 12*, 215–232.

Lerner, J.S. & Keltner, D. (2001). Fear, anger, and risk. *Journal of Personality and Social Psychology, 81*, 146–159.

Lerner, J.S., Gonzalez, R.M., Small, D.A. & Fischhoff, B. (2003). Effects of fear and anger on perceived risks of terrorism: A national field experiment. *Psychological Science, 14*(2), 144–150.

Lichtenstein, S., Slovic, P., Fischhoff, B., Layman, M. & Combs, B. (1978). Judged frequency of lethal events. *Journal of Experimental Psychology: Human Learning and Memory, 4*, 551–578.

Loewenstein, G.F., Weber, E.U., Hsee, C.K. & Welch, N. (2001). Risk as feelings. *Psychological Bulletin, 127*(2), 267–286.

MacDonald, K. (1995). Evolution, the 5-factor model, and levels of personality. *Journal of Personality, 63*, 525–567.

Maule, A.J. & Svenson, O. (1993). Concluding remarks. In O. Svenson & A.J. Maule (Eds.), *Time pressure and stress in human decision making* (pp.323–329). New York: Plenum.

Mazur, A. & Booth, A. (1998). Testosterone and dominance in men. *Behavioral and Brain Sciences, 21*, 353–363.

Morgan, M.G. (1993). Risk analysis and management. *Scientific American* (July), 32–41.

Nettle, D. (2005). An evolutionary approach to the extraversion continuum. *Evolution and Human Behavior, 26*, 363–373.

Nettle, D. (2006). The evolution of personality variation in humans and other animals. *American Psychologist, 61*(6), 622–631.

Neyer, F.J. & Lang, F.R. (2003). Blood is thicker than water: Kinship orientation across adulthood. *Journal of Personality and Social Psychology, 84*, 310–321.

Nicholson, N., Soane, E., Fenton-O'Creevy, M. & Willman, P. (2005). Personality and domain-specific risk taking. *Journal of Risk Research, 8*(2), 157–176.

Park, J.H. & Schaller, M. (2005). Does attitude similarity serve as a heuristic cue for kinship? Evidence of an implicit cognitive association. *Evolution and Human Behavior, 26*, 158–170.

Pedersen, W. (1991). Mental health, sensation seeking and drug use patterns: a longitudinal study. *British Journal of Addiction, 86*(2), 195–204 [see also the erratum in *86*(8), 1037].

Pidgeon, N., Hood, C., Jones, D. & Turner, B. (1992). Risk perception. In *Risk Assessment*. London: The Royal Society.

Ritov, I. & Baron, J. (1992). Status quo and omission biases. *Journal of Risk and Uncertainty, 5*, 49–61.

Salminen, S. & Heisekanen, M. (1997). Correlations between traffic, occupational, sports, and home accidents. *Accident Analysis and Prevention, 29*(1), 33–36.

Samuelson, W. & Zeckhauser, R. (1988). Status-quo bias in decision making. *Journal of Risk and Uncertainty, 1*, 7–59.

Slovic, P. (2000). Trust, emotion, sex, politics and science: Surveying the risk-assessment battlefield. In P. Slovic (Ed.), *The perception of risk*. London and Sterling, VA: Earthscan.

Slovic, P. Fischhoff, B. & Lichtenstein, S. (1979). Rating the risks. *Environment, 21*(3), 14–20, 36–39.

Slovic, P. Fischhoff, B. & Lichtenstein, S. (1980). Facts and fears: Understanding perceived risk. In R.C. Schwing & W.A. Albers, Jr. (Eds.), *Societal risk assessment: How safe is safe enough?* New York: Plenum.

Slovic, P., Fischhoff, B. & Lichtenstein, S. (1982). Facts versus fears: Understanding perceived risk. In D. Kahneman, P. Slovic & A. Tversky (Eds.), *Judgment under uncertainty: Heuristics and biases*. Cambridge: Cambridge University Press.

Slovic, P., Malmfors, T., Mertz, C.K., Neil, N. & Purchase, I.F.H. (1997). Evaluating chemical risks: Results of a survey of the British Toxicological Society. *Human and Experimental Toxicology, 16*, 289–304.

Soranzo, N., Bufe, B., Sabeti, P.C., Wilson, J.F., Weale, M.E., Marguerie, R., Meyerhof, W. & Goldstein, D.B. (2005). Positive selection on a high-sensitivity allele of the human bitter-taste receptor TAS2R16. *Current Biology, 15*, 1257–1265.

Starr, C. (1969). Social benefit versus technological risk. *Science, 165*, 1232–1238.

Sterman, J.D. & Sweeney, L.B. (2000). Cloudy skies: Assessing public understanding of global warming. *System Dynamics Review, 18*(2), 207–240.

Sunstein, C.R. (2005). Moral heuristics. *Behavioral and Brain Sciences, 28*, 531–573.

Teigen, K.H., Brun, W. & Slovic, P. (1988). Societal risk as seen by a Norwegian public. *Journal of Behavioral Decision Making, 1*, 111–130.

Van Vugt, M. & Van Lange, P.A.M. (2006). The altruism puzzle: Psychological adaptations for prosocial behaviour. In M. Schaller, J.A. Simpson & D.T. Kenrick (Eds.), *Evolution and social psychology*. Hove: Psychology Press.

Viscusi, W.K. (2000). Corporate risk analysis. A reckless act? *Stanford Law Review, 52*, 547–597.

Vlek, C.J.H. & Stallen, P.J. (1981). Judging risk and benefit in the small and in the large. *Organizational Behavior and Human Performance, 28*, 235–271.

Walker, I. (2007). Drivers overtaking bicyclists: Objective data on the effects of riding position, helmet use, vehicle type and apparent gender. *Accident Analysis and Prevention, 39*, 417–425.

Weber, E.U. & Millman, R.A. (1997). Perceived risk attitudes: Relating risk perception to risky choice. *Management Science, 43*(2), 123–144.

Weinstein, E. & Martin, J. (1969). Generality of willingness to take risks. *Psychological Reports, 24*, 499–501.

White, R.E., Thornhill, S. & Hampson, E. (2006). Entrepreneurs and evolutionary biology: The relationship between testosterone and new venture creation. *Organizational Behavior and Human Decision Processes, 100*, 21–34.

Wilke, A., Hutchinson, J.M.C., Todd, P.M. & Kruger, D.J. (2006). Is risk taking used as a cue in mate choice? *Evolutionary Psychology, 4*, 367–393.

Wilson, E.O. (1975). *Sociobiology: The new synthesis*. Cambridge, MA: Belknap/Harvard.

Zeckhauser, R.J. & Viscusi, W.K. (1990). Risk within reason. *Science, 248*, 559–564.

Zuckerman, M. (1979). *Sensation seeking: Beyond the optimal level of arousal*. Hillsdale, NJ: Erlbaum.

Zuckerman, M. (1983). Sensation seeking and sports. *Journal of Personality and Individual Differences, 4*, 285–293

Zuckerman, M. (1994). *Behavioral expressions and biosocial bases of sensation seeking*. Cambridge: Cambridge University Press.

Zuckerman, M. (2005). *Psychobiology of personality* (2nd edn). Cambridge: Cambridge University Press.

Zuckerman, M., Kolin, E.A., Price, L. & Zoob, I. (1964). Development of a sensation seeking scale. *Journal of Consulting and Clinical Psychology, 28*, 477–482.

Zuckerman, M., Eysenck, S. & Eysenck, H.J. (1978). Sensation seeking in England and America: Cross-cultural, age and sex comparisons. *Journal of Consulting and Clinical Psychology, 46*(1), 139–149.

CHAPTER 13. DECISION MAKING IN GROUPS AND TEAMS

Armstrong, J.S. (2001). Combining forecasts. In J.S. Armstrong (Ed.), *Principles of forecasting: A handbook for researchers and practitioners*. Kluwer: New York.

Armstrong, J.S. (2006). How to make better forecasts and decisions: Avoid face-to-face meetings. *Foresight*, *5*, 3–15 (including commentaries and reply).

Asch, S. (1956). Studies of independence and conformity: A minority of one against a unanimous majority. *Psychological Monograph*, *70*(9); whole of issue 416.

Ashton, A.H. & Ashton, R.H. (1985). Aggregating subjective forecasts: Some empirical results. *Management Science*, *31*(12), 1499–1508.

Bardecki, M.J. (1984). Participants' response to the Delphi method: An attitudinal perspective. *Technological Forecasting and Social Change*, *25*, 281–292.

Bass, B.M. (1985). *Leadership and performance beyond expectations*. New York: Free Press.

Bonaccio, S. & Dalal, R.S. (2006). Advice taking and decision-making: An integrative literature review, and implications for the organizational sciences. *Organizational Behavior and Human Decision Processes*, *101*, 127–151.

Boukreev, A. & DeWalt, G.W. (2001). *The climb: Tragic ambitions on Everest*. London: MacMillan.

Bruce, R.S. (1935). Group judgments in the field of lifted weights and visual discrimination. *Journal of Psychology*, *1*, 117–121.

Budescu, D.V. & Rantilla, A.K. (2000). Confidence in aggregation of expert opinions. *Acta Psychologica*, *104*, 371–398.

Burns, J.M. (1978). *Leadership*. New York: Harper & Row.

Camacho, L.M. & Paulus, P.B. (1995). The role of social anxiousness in group brainstorming. *Journal of Personality and Social Psychology*, *68*, 1071–1080.

Conradt, L. & Roper, T.J. (2005). Consensus decision making in animals. *Trends in Ecology and Evolution*, *20*(8), 449–456.

Coultas, J.C. (2004). When in Rome . . . An evolutionary perspective on conformity. *Group Processes & Intergroup Relations*, *70*(4), 317–331.

Crutchfield, R. (1955). Conformity and character. *American Psychologist*, *10*, 191–198.

Dennis, A.R. & Valacich, J.S. (1993). Computer brainstorms: More heads are better than one. *Journal of Applied Psychology*, *78*, 531–537.

Diehl, M. & Stroebe, W. (1987). Productivity loss in brainstorming groups: Toward the solution of a riddle. *Journal of Personality and Social Psychology*, *53*, 497–509.

Downey, H.K., Chacko, T. & McElroy, J.C. (1975). Attributions of the 'causes' of performance: A constructive, quasi-longitudinal replication of the Staw (1975) study. *Organizational Behavior and Human Performance*, *24*, 287–299.

Erffmeyer, R.C. & Lane, I.M. (1984). Quality and acceptance of an evaluative task: the effects of four group decision-making formats. *Group and Organization Studies*, *9*(4), 509–529.

Esser, J.K. (1998). Alive and well after 25 years: A review of groupthink research. *Organizational Behavior and Human Decision Processes*, *73*(2/3), 116–141.

Fiedler, F.E. (1965). A contingency model of leadership effectiveness. In L. Berkowitz (Ed.), *Advances in experimental social psychology: Vol. 1* (pp.149–190). New York: Academic Press.

Flowers, M.L. (1977). A laboratory test of some implications of Janis's groupthink hypothesis. *Journal of Personality and Social Psychology*, *35*, 888–896.

Fodor, E.M. & Smith, T. (1982). The power motive as an influence on group decision making. *Journal of Personality and Social Psychology*, *42*, 178–185.

Frederickson, J.W., & Iaquinto, A.L. (1989). Inertia and creeping rationality in strategic decision processes. *Academy of Management Journal*, *32*, 516–542.

Furnham, A. (2005). *The psychology of behaviour at work: The individual in the organization*. Hove: Psychology Press.

Gallupe, R.B., Cooper, W.H., Grise, M.-L. & Bastianutti, L.M. (1994). Blocking electronic brainstorms. *Journal of Applied Psychology*, *79*, 77–86.

Galton, F. (1907). Vox populi. *Nature*, *75*, 450–451.

Gino, F. (2005). Do we listen to advice just because we paid for it? The impact of cost of advice on its use. Harvard Business School Working Paper Series, No. 05–017.

Goodwin P. and Wright, G. (2004). *Decision Analysis for Management Judgment* (3rd edn). Chichester: Wiley.

Gruenfeld, D.H., Mannix, E.A., Williams, K.Y. & Neale, M.A. (1996). Group composition and decision making: How member familiarity and information distribution affect process and performance. *Organizational Behavior and Human Decision Processes*, *67*, 1–15.

Hastie, R. & Kameda, T. (2005). The robust beauty of majority rules in group decisions. *Psychological Review*, *112*(2), 494–508.

Hochbaum, G.M. (1954). The relation between group members' self-confidence and their reactions to group pressures to uniformity. *American Sociological Review*, *19*, 678–688.

Hogg, M.A. & Vaughan, G.M. (2005). *Social psychology* (4th edn). London: Pearson-Prentice Hall.

Isenberg, D.J. (1986). Group polarization: A critical review. *Journal of Personality and Social Psychology*, *50*, 1141–1151.

Janis, I.L. (1982[1972]). *Groupthink: Psychological studies of policy decisions and fiascos* (2nd edn). Boston: Houghton Mifflin.

Janis, I.L. & Mann, L. (1977). *Decision making: A psychological analysis of conflict, choice, and commitment*. New York: The Free Press.

Jolson, M.A. & Rossow, G. (1971). The Delphi process in marketing decision making. *Journal of Marketing Research*, *8*, 443–448.

Judge, T.A. & Piccolo, R.F. (2004). Transformational and transactional leadership: A meta-analytic test of their relative validity. *Journal of Applied Psychology*, *89*(5), 755–768.

Kameda, T. & Tindale, R.S. (2006). Groups as adaptive devices: Human docility and group aggregation mechanisms in evolutionary context. In M. Schaller, J.A. Simpson & D.T. Kenrick (Eds.), *Evolution and social psychology*. Hove: Psychology Press.

Kerr, N.L. & Tindale, R.S. (2004). Group performance and decision making. *Annual Review of Psychology*, *55*, 623–655.

Kozlowski, S.W.J. & Ilgen, D.R. (2006). Enhancing the effectiveness of work groups and teams. *Psychological Science in the Public Interest*, *7*(3), 77–124.

Krakauer, J. (1998). *Into thin air: A personal account of the Everest disaster*. London: Pan.

Krueger, J.L. (2003). Return of the ego – self-referent information as a filter for social prediction: Comment on Karniol (2003). *Psychological Review*, *110*, 585–590.

Larrick, R.P. & Soll, J.B. (2006). Intuitions about combining options: Misappreciation of the averaging principle. *Management Science*, *52*(1), 111–127 [see also the erratum in *52*(2), 309–310].

Latané, B., Williams, K. & Harkins, S. (1979). Many hands make light work: The causes and consequences of social loafing. *Journal of Personality and Social Psychology*, *37*, 822–832.

Leana, C.R. (1985). A partial test of Janis' groupthink model: Effects of group cohesiveness and leader behaviour on defective decision making. *Journal of Management*, *11*, 5–17.

Lippitt, R. & White, R. (1943). The 'social climate' of children's groups. In R.G. Barker, J. Kounin & H. Wright (Eds.), *Child behaviour and development* (pp.485–508). New York: McGraw-Hill.

Mannix, E., & Neale, M.A. (2005). What differences make a difference? The promise and reality of diverse teams in organizations. *Psychological Science in the Public Interest*, *6*(2), 31–55.

McCartt, A. & Rohrbough, J. (1989). Evaluating group decision support system effectiveness: A performance study of decision conferencing. *Decision Support Systems*, *5*, 243–253.

McCauley, C. (1989). The nature of social influence in groupthink: Compliance and internalization. *Journal of Personality and Social Psychology*, *57*, 250–260.

Milgram, S. (1963). Behavioral study of obedience. *Journal of Abnormal and Social Psychology*, *67*, 371–378.

Milgram, S. (1974). *Obedience to authority*. London: Tavistock.

Moorhead, G. & Montanari, J.R. (1986). An empirical investigation of the groupthink phenomenon. *Human Relations*, *39*, 399–410.

Moscovici, S. & Zavalloni, M. (1969). The group as a polarizer of attitudes. *Journal of Personality and Social Psychology*, *12*, 125–135.

Mugny, G. & Papastamou, S. (1980). Minority influence and psycho-social identity. *European Journal of Social Psychology, 12,* 379–394.

Mullen, B., Johnson, C. & Salas, E. (1991). Productivity loss in brainstorming groups: A meta-analytic integration. *Basic and Applied Social Psychology, 12,* 3–23.

Nijstad, B.A. (2000). *How the group affects the mind: Effects of communication in idea generating groups.* Unpublished doctoral dissertation: Utrecht University.

Osborn, A.F. (1957). *Applied imagination* (1st edn). New York: Scribner.

Osborn, A.F. (1963). *Applied imagination* (2nd edn). New York: Scribner.

Parenté, F.J., Anderson, J.K., Myers, P. & O'Brien, T. (1984). An examination of factors contributing to Delphi accuracy. *Journal of Forecasting, 3*(2), 173–182.

Park, W. (1990). A review of research on groupthink. *Journal of Behavioral Decision Making, 3,* 229–245.

Paulus, P.B. (1998). Developing consensus about groupthink after all these years. *Organizational Behavior and Human Decision Processes, 73*(2/3), 362–374.

Paulus, P.B., Dzindolet, M.T., Poletes, G. & Camacho, L.M. (1993). Perception of performance in group brainstorming: The illusion of group productivity. *Personality and Social Psychology, 19,* 78–89.

Paulus, P.B., Larey, T.S. & Ortega, A.H. (1995). Performance and perceptions of brainstormers in an organizational setting. *Basic and Applied Social Psychology, 17,* 249–265.

Peterson, R.S. & Behfar, K.J. (2003). The dynamic relationship between performance feedback, trust, and conflict in groups: A longitudinal study. *Organizational Behavior and Human Decision Processes, 92,* 102–112.

Peterson, R.S., Owens, P.D., Tetlock, P.E., Fan, E.T. & Martorana, P. (1998). Group dynamics in top management teams: Groupthink, vigilance, and alternative models of organizational failure and success. *Organizational Behavior and Human Decision Processes, 73*(2/3), 272–305.

Phillips, L.D. (1984). A theory of requisite decision models. *Acta Psychologica, 56,* 29–48.

Phillips, L.D. (2007). Decision conferencing. In W. Edwards, R.F. Miles Jr., D. von Winterfeldt (Eds.), *Advances in decision analysis: From foundations to applications* (pp.375–399). Cambridge: Cambridge University Press.

Price, P.C. & Stone, E.R. (2004). Intuitive evaluation of likelihood judgment producers: Evidence for a confidence heuristic. *Journal of Behavioral Decision Making, 17,* 39–57.

Regan-Cirincione, P. (1994). Improving the accuracy of group judgment: A process intervention combining group facilitation, social judgment analysis, and information technology. *Organizational Behavior and Human Decision Processes, 58,* 246–270.

Roberto, M.A. (2005). *Why great leaders don't take yes for an answer: Managing for conflict and consensus.* New Jersey: Wharton.

Rohrbaugh, J. (1979). Improving the quality of group judgment: social judgment analysis and the Delphi technique. *Organizational Behavior and Human Performance, 24,* 73–92.

Rosenzweig, P. (2007). *The halo effect . . . and the eight other business delusions that deceive managers.* New York: Free Press.

Rowe, G. & Wright, G. (1999). The Delphi technique as a forecasting tool: Issues and analysis. *International Journal of Forecasting, 15,* 353–375.

Schulz-Hardt, S., Frey, D., Lüthgens, C. & Moscovici, S. (2000). Biased information search in group decision making. *Journal of Personality and Social Psychology, 78,* 655–669.

Schulz-Hardt, S., Jochims, M. & Frey, D. (2002). Productive conflict in group decision making: Genuine and contrived dissent as strategies to counteract biased information seeking. *Organizational Behavior and Human Decision Processes, 88,* 563–586.

Schweiger, D.M., Sandberg, W.R. & Ragan, J.W. (1986). Group approaches for improving strategic decision making. *Academy of Management Journal, 29,* 51–71.

Schweiger, D.M., Sandberg, W.R. & Rechner, P.L. (1989). Experiential effects of dialectical inquiry, devil's advocacy, and consensus approaches to strategic decision making. *Academy of Management Journal, 32,* 745–772.

Schwenk, C.R. & Cosier, R.A. (1993). The effects of consensus and devil's advocacy on strategic decision-making. *Journal of Applied Social Psychology, 23,* 126–139.

Smith, M. (1931). Group judgments in the field of personality traits. *Journal of Experimental Psychology, 14,* 562–565.

Stasser, G. & Stewart, D.D. (1992). Discovery of hidden profiles by decision-making groups: Solving a problem vs. making a judgment. *Journal of Personality and Social Psychology, 63,* 426–434.

Stasser, G., Taylor, L.A. & Hanna, C. (1989). Information sampling in structured and unstructured discussions of three- and six-person groups. *Journal of Personality and Social Psychology, 57,* 67–68.

Staw, B.M. (1975). Attribution of 'causes' of performance: A general alternative interpretation of cross-sectional research on organizations. *Organizational Behavior and Human Performance, 13,* 414–432.

Stewart, G.L. (2006). A meta-analytic review of relationships between team design features and team performance. *Journal of Management, 32*(1), 29–54.

Stoner, J.A.F. (1961). *A comparison of individual and group decisions including risk.* Unpublished master's thesis, Massachusetts Institute of Technology, Boston.

Stroebe, W. & Diehl, M. (1994). Why groups are less effective than their members: On productivity losses in idea-generating groups. *European Review of Social Psychology, 5,* 271–303.

Stroebe, W., Diehl, M. & Abakoumkin, G. (1992). The illusion of group effectivity. *Personality and Social Psychology Bulletin, 18,* 643–650.

Surowiecki, J. (2004). *The wisdom of crowds: Why the many are smarter than the few.* London: Little, Brown.

Tetlock, P.E., Peterson, R.S., McGuire, C., Chang, S. & Field, P. (1992). Assessing political group dynamics: A test of the groupthink model. *Journal of Personality and Social Psychology, 63,* 403–425.

Thomas-Hunt, M., Ogden, T. & Neale, M. (2003). Who's really sharing: Effects of social and expert status on knowledge exchange within groups. *Management Science, 49,* 464–477.

Turner, J.C., Wetherell, M.S. & Hogg, M.A. (1989). Referent informational influence and group polarization. *British Journal of Social Psychology, 28,* 135–147.

Valacich, J.S. & Schwenk, C.R. (1995). Devil's advocacy and dialectical inquiry effects on face-to-face and computer-mediated group decision making. *Organizational Behavior and Human Decision Processes, 63,* 158–173.

Wallach, M.A., Kogan, N. & Bem, D.J. (1962). Group influence on individual risk taking. *Journal of Abnormal and Social Psychology, 65,* 75–86.

Whiten, A., Horner, V. & de Waal, F.B.M. (2005). Conformity to cultural norms of tool use in chimpanzees. *Nature, 437*(September), 737–740.

Wood, W., Lundgren, S., Oullette, J.A., Busceme, S. & Blackstone, T. (1994). Minority influence: A meta-analytic review of social influence processes. *Psychological Bulletin, 115,* 323–345.

CHAPTER 14. COOPERATION AND COORDINATION

Ahn, T.K., Ostrom, E., Schmidt, D., Shupp, R. & Walker, J. (2001). Cooperation in PD games: Fear, greed, and history of play. *Public Choice, 106,* 137–155.

Axelrod, R. (1984). *The evolution of cooperation.* New York: Basic Books.

Bateson, M., Nettle, D. & Roberts, G. (2006). Cues of being watched enhance cooperation in a real-world setting. *Biology Letters, 2,* 412–414.

Batson, C.D. (1998). Altruism and prosocial behavior. In D.T. Gilbert, S.T. Fiske & G. Lindzey (Eds.), *Handbook of social psychology: Vol. 2* (4th edn) (pp.282–315). New York: McGraw-Hill.

Bendor, J., Kramer, R.M. & Stout, S. (1991). When in doubt: Cooperation in a noisy prisoner's dilemma. *Journal of Conflict Resolution, 35,* 691–719.

Berg, J.E., Dickhaut, J. & McCabe, K. (1995). Trust, reciprocity, and social history. *Games and Economic Behavior, 10,* 122–142.

Brady, F.N. (2002). Lining up for Star-Wars tickets: Some ruminations on ethics and economics based on an internet study of behaviour in queues. *Journal of Business Ethics, 38,* 157–165.

Camerer, C.F. (2003). *Behavioral game theory: Experiments in strategic interaction.* Princeton, NJ: Princeton University Press.

Carter, J. & Irons, M. (1991). Are economists different, and if so, why? *Journal of Economic Perspectives, 5*(2), 171–177.

Caruso, E.M., Epley, N. & Bazerman, M.H. (2006). *The trouble with thinking about the thoughts of others: Cognitive versus empathic perspective taking in strategic interaction.* Paper presented at the Society for Judgment and Decision Making 27th Annual Conference, Houston, Texas. 17–20 November.

Cialdini, R.B., Brown, S.L., Lewis, B.P., Luce, C. & Neuberg, S.L. (1997). When one into one equals oneness. *Journal of Personality and Social Psychology, 73,* 481–494.

Colman, A.M. & Wilson, J.C. (1997). Antisocial personality disorder: An evolutionary game theory analysis. *Legal and Criminological Psychology, 2,* 23–34.

Darley, J.M. & Batson, C.D. (1973). 'From Jerusalem to Jericho': A study of situational and dispositional variables in helping behavior. *Journal of Personality and Social Psychology, 27*(1), 100–108.

Darley, J.M. & Latané, B. (1968). Bystander intervention in emergencies: Diffusion of responsibility. *Journal of Personality and Social Psychology, 8,* 377–383.

Dawes, R.M., Orbell, J.M., Simmons, R.T. & van de Kragt, A.J.C. (1986). Organizing groups for collective action. *American Political Science Review, 80,* 1171–1185.

Dawkins, R. (1976[2006]). *The selfish gene (thirtieth anniversary edn).* Oxford: Oxford University Press.

Delgado, M.R., Frank, R.H. & Phelps, E.A. (2005). Perceptions of moral character modulate the neural systems of reward during the trust game. *Nature Neuroscience, 8*(11), 1611–1618.

Dixit, A. & Skeath, S. (2004). *Games of strategy* (2nd edn). New York: Norton.

Dovidio, J.F., Allen, J.L. & Schroeder, D.A. (1990). Specificity of empathy-induced helping: Evidence for altruistic motivation. *Journal of Personality and Social Psychology, 59,* 249–260.

Dunn, J.R. & Schweitzer, M.E. (2005). Feeling and believing: The influence of emotion on trust. *Journal of Personality and Social Psychology, 88*(5), 736–748.

Epley, N., Caruso, E.M. & Bazerman, M.H. (2006). When perspective taking increases taking: Reactive egoism in social interaction. *Journal of Personality and Social Psychology, 91*(5), 872–889.

Fehr, E. & Gächter, S. (2002). Altruistic punishment in humans. *Nature, 415,* 137–140.

Forsythe, R., Horowitz, J.L., Savin, N.E. & Sefton, M. (1994). Fairness in simple bargaining experiments. *Games and Economic Behavior, 6,* 347–369.

Frank, R.H., Gilovich, T. & Regan, D. (1993). Does studying economics inhibit cooperation? *Journal of Economic Perspectives, 7*(2), 159–171.

Goren, H. & Bornstein, G. (2000). The effects of intragroup communication on intergroup cooperation in the repeated intergroup prisoner's dilemma (IPD) game. *Journal of Conflict Resolution, 44*(5), 700–719.

Hardin, G. (1968). The tragedy of the commons. *Science, 162,* 1243–1248.

Henrich, J., Boyd, R., Bowles, S., Camerer, C., Fehr, E., Gintis, H., McElreath, R., Alvard, M., Barr, A., Ensminger, J., Henrich, N.S., Hill, K., Gil-White, F., Gurven, M., Marlowe, F.W., Patton, J.Q. & Tracer, D. (2005). 'Economic man' in cross-cultural perspective: Behavioral experiments in 15 small-scale societies. *Behavioral and Brain Sciences, 28,* 795–855.

Hoffman, E., McCabe, K., Shachat, K. & Smith, V.L. (1994). Preferences, property rights and anonymity in bargaining games. *Games and Economic Behaviour, 7,* 346–380.

Joireman, J.A., Van Lange, P.A.M. & Van Vugt, M. (2004). Who cares about the environmental impact of cars? *Environment and Behavior, 36*(2), 187–206.

Kahn, H. (1965). *On escalation: Metaphors and scenarios.* New York: Praeger.

Kerr, N.L. & Kaufman-Gilliland, C.M. (1994). Communication, commitment and cooperation in social dilemmas. *Journal of Personality and Social Psychology, 66,* 513–529.

Kollock, P. (1993). 'An eye for an eye leaves everyone blind': Cooperation and accounting systems. *American Sociological Review, 58,* 768–786.

Krebs, D. (1975). Empathy and altruism. *Journal of Personality and Social Psychology, 32*(6), 1134–1146.

Kurzban, R. (2001). The social psychophysics of cooperation: Nonverbal communication in a public goods game. *Journal of Nonverbal Behavior, 25*(4), 241–259.

Mann, L. (1969). Queue culture: The waiting line as a social system. *American Journal of Sociology, 75,* 340–354.

Marwell, G. & Ames, R. (1981). Economists free ride, does anyone else? *Journal of Public Economics, 15,* 295–310.

Milgram, S. (1977). *The individual in a social world: Essays and experiments.* Reading, MA: Addison-Wesley.

Milgram, S., Liberty, H.J., Toledo, R. & Wackenhut, J. (1986). Response to intrusion into waiting lines. *Journal of Personality and Social Psychology, 51*(4), 683–689.

Paciotti, B., Hadley, C., Holmes, C. & Mulder, M.B. (2005). Grass-roots justice in Tanzania. *American Scientist, 93,* 58–65.

Parks, C.D., Sanna, L.J. & Posey, D.C. (2003). Retrospection in social dilemmas: How thinking about the past affects future cooperation. *Journal of Personality and Social Psychology, 84*(5), 988–996.

Poundstone, W. (1992). *Prisoner's dilemma.* Oxford: Oxford University Press.

Roch, S.G., Lane, J.A.S., Samuelson, C.D. & Allison, S.T. (2000). Cognitive load and the equality heuristic: A two-stage model of resource overconsumption in small groups. *Organizational Behavior and Human Decision Processes, 83*(2), 185–212.

Roth, A. (1995). Bargaining experiments. In J.H. Kagel & A.E. Roth (Eds.), *The handbook of experimental economics.* Princeton, NJ: Princeton University Press.

Sally, D. (1995). Conversation and cooperation in social dilemmas: A meta-analysis of experiments from 1958 to 1992. *Rationality and Society, 7,* 58–92.

Scharlemann, J.P.W., Eckel, C.C., Kacelnik, A. & Wilson, R.K. (2001). The value of a smile: Game theory with a human face. *Journal of Economic Psychology, 22,* 617–640.

Schmitt, B.H., Dubé, L. & Leclerc, F. (1992). Intrusions into waiting lines: Does the queue constitute a social system? *Journal of Personality and Social Psychology, 63*(5), 806–815.

Schroeder, D.A., Penner, L.A., Dovidio, J.F. & Piliavin, J.A. (1995). *The psychology of helping and altruism: Problems and puzzles.* New York: McGraw-Hill.

Shafir, E. & Tversky, A. (1992). Thinking through uncertainty: Nonconsequential reasoning and choice. *Cognitive Psychology, 24*(4), 449–474.

Singer, T., Seymour, B., O'Doherty, J.P., Stephan, K.E., Dolan, R.J. & Frith, C.D. (2006). Empathic neural responses are modulated by the perceived fairness of others. *Nature, 439*(7075), 466–469.

Stürmer, S., Snyder, M. & Omoto, A.M. (2005). Prosocial emotions and helping: the moderating role of group membership. *Journal of Personality and Social Psychology, 88*(3), 532–546.

Surowiecki, J. (2004). *The wisdom of crowds: Why the many are smarter than the few.* London: Little, Brown.

Tazelaar, M.J.A., Van Lange, P.A.M. & Ouwerkerk, J.W. (2004). How to cope with 'noise' in social dilemmas: The benefits of communication. *Journal of Personality and Social Psychology, 87*(6), 845–859.

Van Lange, P.A.M. (1999). The pursuit of joint outcomes and equality in outcomes: An integrative model of social value orientation. *Journal of Personality and Social Psychology, 77,* 337–349.

Van Lange, P.A.M., Otten, W., De Bruin, E.M.N. & Joireman, J.A. (1997). Development of prosocial, individualistic, and competitive orientations:

Theory and preliminary evidence. *Journal of Personality and Social Psychology*, 73(4), 733–746.

Van Lange, P.A.M., Ouwerkerk, J.W. & Tazelaar, M.J.A. (2002). How to overcome the detrimental effects of noise in social interaction: The benefits of generosity. *Journal of Personality and Social Psychology*, 82, 768–780.

Wilson, R.K. & Sell, J. (1997). 'Liar, liar . . .': Cheap talk and reputation in repeated public goods settings. *Journal of Conflict Resolution*, 41(5), 695–717.

Yamagishi, T. & Sato, K. (1986). Motivational bases of the public goods problem. *Journal of Personality and Social Psychology*, 50(1), 67–73.

CHAPTER 15. INTUITION, REFLECTIVE THINKING, AND THE BRAIN

Aboitiz, F., Ide, A. & Olivares, R. (2003). Corpus callosum morphology in relation to cerebral asymmetries in the post-mortem human. In E. Zaidel & M. Iacoboni (Eds.), *The parallel brain: The cognitive neuroscience of the corpus callosum* (pp.34–46). Cambridge, MA: MIT Press.

Bechara, A. & Damasio, A.R. (2005). The somatic marker hypothesis: A neural theory of economic decision, *Games and Economic Behavior*, 52, 336–372.

Bechara, A., Damasio, A.R., Damasio, H. & Anderson, S.W. (1994). Insensitivity to future consequences following damage to human prefrontal cortex. *Cognition*, 50, 7–15.

Bechara, A., Damasio, H., Tranel, D. & Damasio, A.R. (1997). Deciding advantageously before knowing the advantageous strategy. *Science*, 275, 1293–1295.

Bechara, A., Damasio, H., Tranel, D. & Anderson, S.W. (1998). Dissociation of working memory from decision making within the human prefrontal cortex. *Journal of Neuroscience*, 18, 428–437.

Bechara, A., Damasio, H., Tranel, D. & Damasio, A.R. (2005). The Iowa Gambling Task and the somatic marker hypothesis: some questions and answers. *Trends in Cognitive Sciences*, 9(4), 159–162.

Berthoz, A. (2006). *Emotion and reason: The cognitive neuroscience of decision making*. Oxford: Oxford University Press.

Betsch, T., Plessner, H., Schwieren, C. & Gütig, R. (2001). I like it but I don't know why: A value-account approach to implicit attitude formation. *Personality and Social Psychology Bulletin*, 27(2), 242–253.

Botvinick, M.M., Braver, T.S., Barch, D.M., Carter, C.S. & Cohen, J.D. (2001). Conflict monitoring and cognitive control. *Psychological Review*, 108(3), 624–652.

Busemeyer, J.R. & Stout, J.C. (2002). A contribution of cognitive decision models to clinical assessment: Decomposing performance on the Bechara gambling task. *Psychological Assessment*, 14, 253–262.

Canli, T., Desmond, J.E., Zhao, Z., Glover, G. & Gabrieli, J.D.E. (1998). Hemispheric asymmetry for emotional stimuli detected with fMRI. *NeuroReport*, 9, 3233–3239.

Carter, C.S., Braver, T.S., Barch, D.M., Botvinick, M.M., Noll, D. & Cohen, J.D. (1998). Anterior cingulated cortex, error detection, and the online monitoring of performance. *Science*, 280, 747–749.

Caruso, E.M., Epley, N. & Bazerman, M.H. (2006). *The trouble with thinking about the thoughts of others: Cognitive versus empathic perspective taking in strategic interaction*. Paper presented at the Society for Judgment and Decision Making 27th Annual Conference, 17–20 November, Houston, Texas.

Cohen, N. & Squire, L.R. (1980). Preserved learning and retention of pattern analyzing skills in amnesia: Dissociation of know how and know that. *Science*, 210, 207–210.

Cook, M. & Mineka, S. (1990). Selective associations in the observational conditioning of fear in Rhesus monkeys. *Journal of Experimental Psychology: Animal Behavior Processes*, 16, 372–389.

Corballis, P.M. (2003). Visuospatial processing and the right-hemisphere interpreter. *Brain and Cognition*, 53, 171–176.

Damasio, A.R. (1994). *Descartes' error: Emotion, reason, and the human brain*. New York: Grosset/Putnam.

Delgado, M.R., Frank, R.H. & Phelps, E.A. (2005). Perceptions of moral character modulate the neural systems of reward during the trust game. *Nature Neuroscience*, 8(11), 1611–1618.

De Martino, B., Kumaran, D., Seymour, B. & Dolan, R.J. (2006). Frames, biases, and rational decision-making in the human brain. *Science*, 313, 684–687.

De Neys, W. (2006). Automatic-heuristic and executive-analytic processing during reasoning: Chronometric and dual-task considerations. *The Quarterly Journal of Experimental Psychology*, 59(6), 1070–1100.

Dijksterhuis, A., Bos, M.W., Nordgren, L.F. & van Baaren, R.B. (2006). On making the right choice: The deliberation-without-attention effect. *Science*, 311(17 Feb.), 1005–1007.

Drake, R.A. (1991). Processing persuasive arguments: Recall and recognition as a function of agreement and manipulated activation asymmetry. *Brain and Cognition*, 15, 83–94.

Dunn, B.D., Dalgleish, T. & Lawrence, A.D. (2006). The somatic marker hypothesis: A critical evaluation. *Neuroscience and Biobehavioral Reviews*, 30, 239–271.

Epley, N., Caruso, E.M. & Bazerman, M.H. (2006). When perspective taking increases taking: Reactive egoism in social interaction. *Journal of Personality and Social Psychology*, 91(5), 872–889.

Evans, J. St B.T. (1989). *Bias in human reasoning: Causes and consequences*. Hove: Erlbaum.

Evans, J. St B.T. (2006). The heuristic-analytic theory of reasoning: Extension and evaluation. *Psychonomic Bulletin and Review*, 13(3), 378–395.

Evans, J. St B.T. & Over, D. (1996). *Rationality and reasoning*. Hove: Psychology Press.

Finucane, M.S., Alhakami, A., Slovic, P. & Johnson, S.M. (2000). The affect heuristic in judgments of risks and benefits. *Journal of Behavioral Decision Making*, 13, 1–17.

Frank, M.J. & Claus, E.D. (2006). Anatomy of a decision: Striato-orbitofrontal interactions in reinforcement learning, decision making, and reversal. *Psychological Review*, 113(2), 300–326.

Frederick, S. (2005). Cognitive reflection and decision making. *Journal of Economic Perspectives*, 19(4), 25–42.

Fugelsang, J.A. & Thompson, V.A. (2003). A dual-process model of belief and evidence interactions in causal reasoning. *Memory and Cognition*, 31(5), 800–815.

Gazzaniga, M. (2000). Cerebral specialization and interhemispheric communication: Does the corpus callosum enable the human condition? *Brain*, 123, 1293–1326.

Greene, J.D., Sommerville, R.B., Nystrom, L.E., Darley, J.M. & Cohen, J.D. (2001). An fMRI investigation of emotional engagement in moral judgment. *Science*, 293, 2105–2108.

Greene, J.D., Nystrom, L.E., Engell, A.D., Darley, J.M. & Cohen, J.D. (2004). The neural bases of cognitive conflict and control in moral judgment. *Neuron*, 44, 389–400.

Haidt, J. (2001). The emotional dog and its rational tail: A social intuitionist approach to moral judgment. *Psychological Review*, 108(4), 814–834.

Halberstadt, J.M. & Levine, G.M. (1999). Effects of reasons analysis on the accuracy of predicting basketball games. *Journal of Applied Social Psychology*, 29(3), 517–530.

Hammond, K.R. (1996). *Human judgment and social policy: Irreducible uncertainty, inevitable error, unavoidable injustice*. New York: Oxford University Press.

Hellige, J.B. (1993). *Hemispheric asymmetry: What's right and what's left*. Cambridge, MA: Harvard University Press.

Hilton, D.J. (1995). The social context of reasoning: Conversational inference and rational judgment. *Psychological Bulletin*, 118, 248–271.

Jasper, J.D. & Christman, S.D. (2005). A neuropsychological dimension for anchoring effects. *Journal of Behavioral Decision Making, 18,* 343–369.

Kahneman, D. & Frederick, S. (2002). Representativeness revisited: Attribute substitution in intuitive judgment. In T. Gilovich, D. Griffin & D. Kahneman (Eds.), *Heuristics and biases: The psychology of intuitive judgment* (pp.49–81). Cambridge: Cambridge University Press.

Knowlton, B.J. & Squire, L.R. (1996). Artificial grammar depends on implicit acquisition of both abstract and exemplar-specific information. *Journal of Experimental Psychology: Learning, Memory, and Cognition, 22,* 169–181.

Knowlton, B.J., Squire, L.R., Paulsen, J.S., Swerdlow, N.R., Swenson, M. & Butters, N. (1996). Dissociations within nondeclarative memory in HD. *Neuropsychology, 10,* 538–548.

Koenigs, M. & Tranel, D. (2007). Irrational economic decision-making after ventromedial prefrontal damage: Evidence from the ultimatum game. *Journal of Neuroscience, 27*(4), 951–956.

Koenigs, M., Young, L., Adolphs, R., Tranel, D., Cushman, F., Hauser, M. & Damasio, A. (2007). Damage to the prefrontal cortex increases utilitarian moral judgements. *Nature, 446*(7138), 865–866.

Krawczyk, D.C. (2002). Contributions of the prefrontal cortex to the neural basis of human decision making. *Neuroscience and Biobehavioral Reviews, 26,* 631–664.

Lane, R.D., Reiman, E.M., Ahern, G.L., Schwartz, G.E. & Davidson, R.J. (1997). Neuroanatomical correlates of happiness, sadness, and disgust. *American Journal of Psychiatry, 154,* 926–933.

Lane, R.D., Reiman, E.M., Bradley, M.M., Lang, P.J., Ahern, G.L., Davidson, R.J. & Schwartz, G.E. (1997). Neuroanatomical correlates of pleasant and unpleasant emotion. *Neuropsychologia, 35,* 1437–1444.

Lewicki, P., Czyzewska, M. & Hoffman, H. (1987). Unconscious acquisition of complex procedural knowledge. *Journal of Experimental Psychology: Learning, Memory, and Cognition, 13,* 523–530.

Lieberman, M.D. (2000). Intuition: A social cognitive neuroscience approach. *Psychological Bulletin, 126*(1), 109–137.

Loewenstein, G.F., Weber, E.U., Hsee, C.K. & Welch, N. (2001). Risk as feelings. *Psychological Bulletin, 127*(2), 267–286.

Maia, T.V. & McClelland, J.L. (2004). A re-examination of the evidence for the somatic marker hypothesis: What participants really know in the Iowa gambling task. *Proceedings of the National Academy of Sciences of the USA, 101*(45), 16075–16080.

Manes, F., Sahakian, B., Clark, L., Rogers, R., Antoun, N., Aitken, M. & Robbins, T. (2002). Decision-making processes following damage to the prefrontal cortex. *Brain, 125,* 624–639.

Mineka, S. & Cook, M. (1993). Mechanisms involved in the observational conditioning of fear. *Journal of Experimental Psychology: General, 122,* 23–38.

Niebauer, C.L. & Garvey, K. (2004). Gödel, Escher, and degree of handedness: Differences in interhemispheric interaction predict differences in understanding self-reference. *Laterality, 9,* 19–34.

Nisbett, R.E. & Schacter, S. (1966). Cognitive manipulation of pain. *Journal of Experimental Social Psychology, 2,* 227–236.

Nisbett, R.E. & Wilson, T.D. (1977). Telling more than we can know: Verbal reports on mental processes. *Psychological Review, 84*(3), 231–259.

Nørretranders, T. (1998). *The user illusion: Cutting consciousness down to size.* New York: Viking.

Phillips, M.L., Young, A.W., Senior, C., Brammer, M., Andrews, C., Calder, A.J., Bullmore, E.T., Perrett, D.I., Rowland, D., Williams, S.C., Gray, J.A. & David, A.S. (1997). A specific neural substrate for perceiving facial expressions of disgust. *Nature, 389,* 495–498.

Ramachandran, V.S. (1995). Anosognosia in parietal lobe syndrome. *Consciousness and Cognition, 4,* 22–51.

Ramachandran, V.S. & Blakeslee, S. (1998). *Phantoms in the brain.* New York: William Morrow.

Rausch, R. (1977). Cognitive strategies in patients with unilateral temporal lobe excisions. *Neuropsychologia, 15,* 385–395.

Roch, S.G., Lane, J.A.S., Samuelson, C.D. & Allison, S.T. (2000). Cognitive load and the equality heuristic: A two-stage model of resource overconsumption in small groups. *Organizational Behavior and Human Decision Processes, 83*(2), 185–212.

Rolls, E.T. (1999). *The brain and emotion.* Oxford: Oxford University Press.

Selart, M., Kuvaas, B., Boe, O. & Takemura, K. (2006). The influence of decision heuristics and overconfidence on multiattribute choice: A process-tracing study. *European Journal of Cognitive Psychology, 18*(3), 437–453.

Simmons, J.P. & Nelson, L.D. (2006). Intuitive confidence: Choosing between intuitive and nonintuitive alternatives. *Journal of Experimental Psychology: General, 135*(3), 409–428.

Simon, H. (1955). A behavioural model of rational choice. *The Quarterly Journal of Economics, 69,* 99–118.

Singer, T., Seymour, B., O'Doherty, J.P., Stephan, K.E., Dolan, R.J. & Frith, C.D. (2006). Empathic neural responses are modulated by the perceived fairness of others. *Nature, 439*(7075), 466–9.

Speedie, L.J., Wertman, E., Ta'ir, J., & Heilman, K.M. (1993). Disruption of automatic speech following a right basal ganglia lesion. *Neurology, 43,* 1768–1774.

Sprengelmayer, R., Young, A.W., Calder, A.J., Karnat, A., Lange, H., Homberg, V., Perrett, D.I. & Rowland, D. (1996). Loss of disgust: Perception of faces and emotions in Huntingdon's disease. *Brain, 119,* 1647–1665.

Stanovich, K.E. (1999). *Who is rational? Studies of individual differences in reasoning.* Mahwah, NJ: Erlbaum.

Stanovich, K.E. & West, R.F. (2000). Individual differences in reasoning: Implications for the rationality debate? *Behavioral and Brain Sciences, 23,* 645–726.

Stanovich, K.E. & West, R.F. (1998). Individual differences in framing and conjunction effects. *Thinking and Reasoning, 4,* 289–317.

Wason, P. & Evans, J. St B.T. (1975). Dual processes in reasoning? *Cognition, 3,* 141–154.

Wegner, D.M. (2002). *The illusion of conscious will.* Cambridge, MA: Bradford Books, MIT Press.

Wegner, D.M. & Wheatley, T. (1999). Apparent mental causation: Sources of the experience of will. *American Psychologist, 54,* 480–491.

Wilson, T.D. (2002). *Strangers to ourselves: Discovering the adaptive unconscious.* Cambridge, MA: Belknap, Harvard University Press.

Wilson, T.D. & Schooler, J.W. (1991). Thinking too much: Introspection can reduce the quality of preferences and decisions. *Journal of Personality and Social Psychology, 60,* 181–192.

Wilson, T.D., Dunn, D.S., Kraft, D. & Lisle, D.J. (1989). Introspection, attitude change, and attitude-behavior consistency: The disruptive effects of explaining why we feel the way we do. *Advances in Experimental Social Psychology, 22,* 287–343.

Wilson, T.D., Lisle, D.J., Schooler, J.W., Hodges, S.D., Klaaren, K.J. & LaFleur, S.J. (1993). Introspecting about reasons can reduce post-choice satisfaction. *Journal of Personality and Social Psychology, 19,* 331–339.

Witelson, S.F. & Goldsmith, C.H. (1991). The relationship of hand preference to anatomy of the corpus callosum in men. *Brain Research, 545,* 175–182.

Wolford, G., Miller, M.B. & Gazzaniga, M.S. (2000). The left hemisphere's role in hypothesis formation. *Journal of Neuroscience, 20,* RC64.

Zimmer, C. (2005). *Soul made flesh.* London: Arrow Books.

Sources and Credits

We are grateful to the following for the permission to use copyright material.

FIGURES AND ILLUSTRATIONS

Chapter opening image: © Carlos Caetano / shutterstock.com. Reproduced with permission.

12   Figure 2.2:   Dilbert 8/24/03. © United Feature Syndicate Inc. Reprinted with permission.

23   Figure 3.2:   © <www.cartoonstock.com> Reproduced with permission.

29   Figure 3.4:   G. Gigerenzer & U. Hoffrage (1995). How to improve Bayesian reasoning without instruction: Frequency formats. *Psychological Review, 102*(4), 684–704 (Fig. 1, p. 6). © American Psychological Association. Reproduced with permission.

38   Figure 4.2:   M.V. Pezzo (2003). Surprise, defence, or making sense: What removes hindsight bias? *Memory, 11*(4/5), 421–441 (Fig. 1, p. 424). © Taylor & Francis. Reproduced with permission from <www.informaworld.com>.

48   Figure 5.4:   R.E. Petty & J.T. Cacioppo (1986). The elaboration likelihood model of persuasion. In L. Berkowitz (Ed.), *Advances in experimental social psychology, vol. 19.* New York: Academic Press (Fig. 1, p. 126). Reproduced with permission from Professor Richard Petty and Elsevier.

69   Figure 7.2:   D. Kahneman & A. Tversky (1979). Prospect theory: An analysis of decision making under risk. *Econometrica, 47,* 263–291 (Fig. 3, p. 279). © Wiley-Blackwell. Reproduced with permission.

70   Figure 7.3:   D. Kahneman & A. Tversky (1979). Prospect theory: An analysis of decision making under risk. *Econometrica, 47,* 263–291 (Fig. 4, p. 283). © Wiley-Blackwell. Reproduced with permission.

74   Figure 7.4:   C.R. Fox & K.E. See (2003). Belief and preference in decision under uncertainty. In D. Hardman & L. Macchi (Eds.), *Thinking: Psychological perspectives on reasoning, judgment, and decision making* (Fig. 14.7, p. 306). © Wiley-Blackwell. Reproduced with permission.

98   Figure 9.2:   J.B. Soll & J. Klayman (2004). Overconfidence in interval estimates. *Journal of Experimental Psychology: Learning, Memory, and Cognition, 30,* 299–314 (Fig. 1, p. 301). © American Psychological Association. Reproduced with permission.

109   Figure 10.1:   I. Ajzen (1991). The theory of planned behaviour. *Organizational Behaviour and Human Decision Processes, 50,* 179–211 (Fig. 1, p. 182). © Elsevier. Reproduced with permission.

110   Figure 10.3:   © Matt Feazell. Reproduced with permission. <http://home.comcast.net/~mattfeazell/index.htm>; email: feazell038@comcast.net.

121   Figure 11.1:   C. Gonzalez (2005). Decision support for real-time, dynamic decision making tasks. *Organizational Behavior and Human Decision Processes, 96,* 142–154 (Fig. 1, p. 146). © Elsevier. Reproduced with permission.

123   Figure 11.2:   F.P. Gibson, M. Fichman & D.C. Plaut (1997). Learning in dynamic decision tasks: Computational model and empirical evidence. *Organizational Behavior and Human Decision Processes, 71*(1), 1–35 (Fig. 1, p. 8). © Elsevier. Reproduced with permission.

128   Figure 11.3:   L.R. Beach & T.R. Mitchell (1987). Image theory: Principles, goals, and plans in decision making. *Acta Psychologica, 66*(3), 201–220 (Fig. 1, p. 209). © Elsevier. Reproduced with permission.

130   Figure 11.4:   G. Klein (1998). *Sources of power: How people make decisions.* Cambridge, MA: MIT Press (Fig. 3.2, p. 27). © 1998 Massachusetts Institute of Technology, by permission of The MIT Press.

138   Figure 12.2:   G.F. Loewenstein, E.U. Weber, C.K. Hsee, & N. Welch (2001). Risk as feelings. *Psychological Bulletin, 127*(2), 267–286 (Fig. 3, p. 270). © American Psychological Association. Reproduced with permission.

138   Figure 12.3:   Dilbert 12/18/06. © Scott Adams. Reproduced by permission of United Features Syndicate.

151   Figure 13.1:   I.L. Janis (1982). *Groupthink: Psychological studies of policy decisions and fiascoes.* Boston: Houghton Mifflin (Fig. 10.1, p. 244). The figure in Janis (1982) is adapted from Figure 5, p. 132 (based on Janis, 1972) reprinted with permission of The Free Press, a Division of Simon & Schuster, Inc., from *Decision making: A psychological analysis of conflict, choice, and commitment,* by Irving L. Janis and Leon Mann. Copyright © 1977 by The Free Press. All rights reserved.

153   Figure 13.2:   © <www.cartoonbank.com>. Reproduced with permission.

TABLES

14   Table 2.1:   G. Gigerenzer & D.G. Goldstein (1996). Reasoning the fast and frugal way: Models of bounded rationality. *Psychological Review, 103,* 592–596 (Table 1, p. 655). © American Psychological Association. Reproduced with permission.

25   Table 3.1:   A. Tversky & D. Koehler (1994). Support theory: A nonextensional representation of subjective

probability. *Psychological Review, 101,* 547–567 (Table 3.1, p. 552). © American Psychological Association. Reproduced with permission.

35   Table 4.1:   N. Epley, & T. Gilovich (2001). Putting adjustment back in the anchoring and adjustment heuristic: Differential processing of self-generated and experimenter-provided anchors. *Psychological Science, 12*(5), 391–396 (Table 1, p. 392). © Wiley-Blackwell. Reproduced with permission.

58   Table 6.3:   E.A. Wasserman, S.M. Elek, D.L. Chatlosh & A.G. Baker (1993). Rating causal relations: The role of probability in judgments of response-outcome contingency. *Journal of Experimental Psychology: Learning, Memory, and Cognition, 19,* 174–188 (Table 3, p. 180). © American Psychological Association. Reproduced with permission.

80   Table 8.1:   A. Tversky (1969). The intransitivity of preferences. *Psychological Review, 76,* 31–48. (Table 5, p. 37). © American Psychological Association. Reproduced with permission.

81   Table 8.2:   C.K. Hsee (2000). Attribute evaluability: Its implications for joint-separate evaluation reversals and beyond. In D. Kahneman and A. Tversky (Eds.), *Choices, values, and frames.* Cambridge: Cambridge University Press (Table 31.1, p. 545). © Cambridge University Press 2000, Russell Sage Foundation. Reproduced with permission.

Chapter 10 (p. 111): Book XII, 'The Cattle of the Sun', from THE ODYSSEY by Homer, translated by Robert Fagles, copyright © 1996 by Robert Fagles. Used by permission of Viking Penguin, a division of Penguin Group (USA) Inc.

Every effort has been made to trace copyright holders and to obtain their permission for the use of copyright material. The publisher apologizes for any errors or omissions in the above list and would be grateful if notified of any corrections that should be incorporated in future reprints or editions of this book.

Author Index

Subject Index